Financial Sector Development in the Pacific Rim

NBER—East Asia Seminar on Economics
Volume 18

Financial Sector Development in the Pacific Rim

Edited by **Takatoshi Ito and Andrew K. Rose**

The University of Chicago Press

Chicago and London

TAKATOSHI ITO is professor of economics at the University of Tokyo and a research associate of the National Bureau of Economic Research and the Tokyo Center for Economic Research. ANDREW K. ROSE is the Bernard T. Rocca Jr. Professor of International Trade and director of the Clausen Center for International Business and Policy at the Haas School of Business, University of California, Berkeley, and a research associate of the National Bureau of Economic Research.

The University of Chicago Press, Chicago 60637
The University of Chicago Press, Ltd., London
© 2009 by the National Bureau of Economic Research
All rights reserved. Published 2009
Printed in the United States of America

18 17 16 15 14 13 12 11 10 09   1 2 3 4 5

ISBN-13: 978-0-226-38684-3 (cloth)
ISBN-10: 0-226-38684-8 (cloth)

Library of Congress Cataloging-in-Publication Data

East Asian Seminar in Economics (18th : 1007 : Singapore
    Management University)
    Financial sector development in the Pacific Rim / edited by
Takatoshi Ito and Andrew K. Rose
    p. cm. — (NBER East Asia seminar on economics ; v. 18)
    Papers presented at the 18th Annual East Asian Seminar in
Economics, held at Singapore Management University on
June 22–24, 2007.
    Includes bibliographical references and index.
    ISBN-13: 978-0-226-38684-3 (cloth : alk. paper)
    ISBN-10: 0-226-383684-8 (cloth : alk. paper) 1. Financial
institutions—Pacific Area—Congresses. 2. Financial institutions—
East Asia—Congresses. 3. Financial crises—East Asia—Congresses.
4. Financial crises—Pacific Area—Congresses. I. Ito, Takatoshi,
1950– II. Rose, Andrew, 1959– III. Title
    HG190.A2E27 2009
    332.095—dc22
                                                    2008021666

Relation of the Directors to the
Work and Publications of the
National Bureau of Economic Research

1. The object of the NBER is to ascertain and present to the economics profession, and to the public more generally, important economic facts and their interpretation in a scientific manner without policy recommendations. The Board of Directors is charged with the responsibility of ensuring that the work of the NBER is carried on in strict conformity with this object.

2. The President shall establish an internal review process to ensure that book manuscripts proposed for publication DO NOT contain policy recommendations. This shall apply both to the proceedings of conferences and to manuscripts by a single author or by one or more co-authors but shall not apply to authors of comments at NBER conferences who are not NBER affiliates.

3. No book manuscript reporting research shall be published by the NBER until the President has sent to each member of the Board a notice that a manuscript is recommended for publication and that in the President's opinion it is suitable for publication in accordance with the above principles of the NBER. Such notification will include a table of contents and an abstract or summary of the manuscript's content, a list of contributors if applicable, and a response form for use by Directors who desire a copy of the manuscript for review. Each manuscript shall contain a summary drawing attention to the nature and treatment of the problem studied and the main conclusions reached.

4. No volume shall be published until forty-five days have elapsed from the above notification of intention to publish it. During this period a copy shall be sent to any Director requesting it, and if any Director objects to publication on the grounds that the manuscript contains policy recommendations, the objection will be presented to the author(s) or editor(s). In case of dispute, all members of the Board shall be notified, and the President shall appoint an ad hoc committee of the Board to decide the matter; thirty days additional shall be granted for this purpose.

5. The President shall present annually to the Board a report describing the internal manuscript review process, any objections made by Directors before publication or by anyone after publication, any disputes about such matters, and how they were handled.

6. Publications of the NBER issued for informational purposes concerning the work of the Bureau, or issued to inform the public of the activities at the Bureau, including but not limited to the NBER Digest and Reporter, shall be consistent with the object stated in paragraph 1. They shall contain a specific disclaimer noting that they have not passed through the review procedures required in this resolution. The Executive Committee of the Board is charged with the review of all such publications from time to time.

7. NBER working papers and manuscripts distributed on the Bureau's web site are not deemed to be publications for the purpose of this resolution, but they shall be consistent with the object stated in paragraph 1. Working papers shall contain a specific disclaimer noting that they have not passed through the review procedures required in this resolution. The NBER's web site shall contain a similar disclaimer. The President shall establish an internal review process to ensure that the working papers and the web site do not contain policy recommendations, and shall report annually to the Board on this process and any concerns raised in connection with it.

8. Unless otherwise determined by the Board or exempted by the terms of paragraphs 6 and 7, a copy of this resolution shall be printed in each NBER publication as described in paragraph 2 above.

Contents

Acknowledgments

This volume is a collection of papers that were presented at the eighteenth annual East Asia Seminar in Economics (EASE). The EASE is co-organized by the National Bureau for Economic Research (NBER) in Cambridge, MA; the Productivity Commission of Australia; the Hong Kong University of Science and Technology; the Korea Development Institute in Seoul; Singapore Management University; the Chung-Hua Institution for Economic Research in Taipei; the Tokyo Center for Economic Research; and the Chinese Center for Economic Research in Beijing. The EASE 18 was held at Singapore Management University (SMU), June 22 to 24, 2007; SMU was the local organizer.

We thank all our sponsors—the NBER, All Nippon Airways, and the University of Tokyo's Center for Advanced Research in Finance, for making EASE 18 possible. The conference department of the NBER led by Carl Beck with support by Brett Maranjian for this conference and the publication department led by Helena Fitz-Patrick, as usual, made the organization and publication process run smoothly. The local team led by Professor Roberto Mariano at SMU deserves special praise for making the conference run flawlessly and with warm hospitality.

Introduction

Takatoshi Ito and Andrew K. Rose

Introduction

This volume is a collection of papers that were presented at the eighteenth annual East Asia Seminar on Economics (EASE). The EASE 18 was held at Singapore Management University (SMU) on June 22 to 24, 2007. The conference was organized around the theme of financial sector development in the Asia-Pacific region. The recent changes in Asia's financial sectors—especially in banking and stock markets—have been remarkable, especially since the Asian currency crisis of 1997 to 1998. There are a number of different elements in recent developments, which can be roughly categorized into four strands.

First, consider the reforms enacted by the East Asian countries most affected by the financial crisis (Korea comes immediately to mind). During and in the aftermath of the crisis, a number of countries introduced reforms intended both to open markets to foreign institutions and to liberalize these markets. A number of regulations on financial products and pricing were either loosened or eliminated, and some of these policies are studied in this volume. A few of these changes were recommended by the International Monetary Fund during the actual crisis (sometimes quite forcefully), but most were introduced afterward by governments intent on improving the quality and robustness of their domestic financial institutions and markets. As a result of the changes in policy, the region as a whole

Takatoshi Ito is a professor at the Graduate School of Economics and the Graduate School of Public Policy at the University of Tokyo, and a research associate of the National Bureau of Economic Research. Andrew K. Rose is the B. T. Rocca Jr. Professor of International Trade and director of the Clausen Center for International Business and Policy at the University of California, Berkeley, and a research associate of the National Bureau of Economic Research.

has shown remarkable progress and dramatic growth over the past decade, both on the real side of the economy and (especially) in financial development. Still, there have been a number of problems along the way.

Given the size of their respective economies, Japan and China both deserve special attention. While Japan avoided a *currency* crisis in 1997, it did experience a *banking* crisis. Despite sizeable injections of capital in both 1998 and 1999, the crisis was prolonged. Conventional wisdom attributes this mostly to the fact that accounting practices remained extremely opaque through the period, and the authorities avoided attempts to address this issue. Further, regulatory forbearance seemed self-evident. The regulatory reform introduced in 2002 finally ended the banking crisis by decisively intervening to handle the remaining weak banks. A number of Japanese banks were allowed to fail, while a number of banks merged (in part to preempt other failures). It was widely suspected at the time that some mergers were not motivated solely by the desire to make banking operations more efficient. Instead, it was believed that some banks were simply too big to fail, resulting in regulatory bias. A number of different aspects of these issues are examined in the articles that follow.

A third important factor in the region remains the remarkable growth in China. China has consistently achieved high economic growth during the period since the Asian crisis, averaging over 9 percent since 1998. Further, financial markets in China have been transformed. Chinese markets were once backward with a heavy regulatory burden; now they are some of the hottest markets in the world for active trading and associated activities like initial public offerings (IPOs). During the same period, the Chinese attitude toward foreign portfolio investment has also changed swiftly, from being essentially completely closed toward a cautious opening. By now, many Chinese firms have experienced IPOs, and the remarkable rises in prices on Chinese stock exchanges have created numerous opportunities, along with some risks. Mergers and acquisitions (M&As) now abound, though it remains unclear whether value is actually created by many of the Chinese M&As. The recent popularity of M&As has not been restricted to China; they have also grown in Korea, for example, since the currency crisis as family and group ownership has weakened. Cross-border M&As have also become more popular, though they are still less common in East Asia than in either North America or Europe. Understanding the reasons for this M&A activity requires careful examination, and this volume makes progress on this dimension. A related set of questions concerns the development of financial centers in Asia, both in the historically important financial activity hub of Tokyo and also the long-standing rivalry between Shanghai and Hong Kong. Here, too, the chapters of the volume provide new insights.

A final issue of great importance is the underdeveloped state of financial technology in Asia. Asian financial and capital markets often lag behind best-practice commonly seen in New York and London. For instance, there is a notable lag in financial innovation in the area of securitization, at least compared with the United States. Why is this the case? Some consider it to be a legacy of the bank-based systems that have traditionally been prevalent in Asia. Others think that it simply takes time to lure top-notch experts in financial engineering to the region or to train them domestically.

In this volume, a number of the questions and issues discussed in the preceding will be elaborated upon and addressed. The collection of papers has been written with state-of-the-art econometric techniques and modern data sets from countries in the Asia-Pacific region. Some chapters exploit a new data set, while others frame policy-relevant questions; some chapters do both. Enjoy!

I: The Evolving Nature of Regional Stock Markets

The first pair of chapters examines the past, present, and future of Asian stock markets. McCauley and Chan look forward to the future of two key financial centers, Hong Kong and Shanghai, by looking back to the past; Hamao, Hoshi, and Okazaki reflect on the historical development of the Tokyo Stock Exchange before World War I.

McCauley and Chan predict that China will ease its remaining capital controls and make the renminbi fully convertible into foreign currencies. Shortly thereafter, they predict, Shanghai will reemerge as an international financial center. The prospect of this reemergence has sharpened speculation regarding the relationship of Shanghai and its historical Hong Kong, the established international financial center that reverted to Chinese sovereignty in 1997. McCauley and Chan argue that Hong Kong will *gain* stature as an international financial center when China is more open financially, coincident with the return of Shanghai to its traditional role as a financial center. His thesis is that the development of an *onshore* international financial center (Shanghai) can contribute to the continued development of a nearby *offshore* international financial center (Hong Kong). Thus, a country (or, more precisely, a federal state) can support more than one financial center, an issue that has been much debated in the literature. It also is interesting to note that McCauley and Chan's idea is, in some ways, the inverse of another idea in the literature, namely that financial competition from offshore can spur the development of an onshore center (as happened in, e.g., Europe). McCauley and Chan develop their thesis using a century of historical evidence, while also considering the current range and intensity of financial activity in the two centers. They also provide a more prospective analysis of the evolution of China's international balance sheet and Hong Kong's share thereof. McCauley and Chan's method is eclectic and includes data ranging from rankings based on nose counts of banks, through multidimensional measures of balance sheets and trading activity, to regression analysis for future projections.

Hamao, Hoshi, and Okazaki study the role that the Tokyo Stock Exchange (TSE) played before the First World War (WWI) to draw lessons for more recent events. Recent studies have shown that the Japanese stock market had a substantial size in the prewar period and played an important role in financing economic development. However, the initial market capitalization of the TSE was not only low but also remained that way for quite a long period early on in its existence. Though the TSE eventually grew into one of the two largest stock exchanges in prewar Japan, its growth occurred surprisingly late. Hamao, Hoshi, and Okazaki examine why the TSE's development was so slow from its establishment in 1878 through the 1910s and why it then took off in the late 1910s. The chapter argues that the TSE stayed small because low liquidity discouraged new companies from listing their stocks. In turn, the lack of growth in new listed stocks meant that liquidity remained low. This equilibrium was broken in 1918 when the TSE changed its listing policy slightly and began to start listing companies without waiting for their listing applications. The chapter provides empirical evidence that shows the size of the market did indeed matter for their listing decisions, at least before 1918. Hamao, Hoshi, and Okazaki rely on an interesting data set, the listing behavior of cotton spinning firms. Before 1918, the size of TSE affected this relationship, but afterward, this relationship disappears. That is, companies found listing their shares on the stock exchange more attractive if the stock market is more liquid (in a more liquid market, the underpricing after IPO will be smaller). That is, the low liquidity and small number of listed companies mutually reinforced each other until this inferior equilibrium was altered in 1918.

II: Consequences of Financial Development

Asia is not known as being at the leading edge of financial innovation. A number of chapters in the volume investigate the reasons for this lag and explore the consequences of policies aimed at spurring financial market development. Green, Mariano, Pavlov, and Wachter attempt to find why asset securitization is not more widespread in Asia. This has been an important recent development in many financial markets and is a good example of an area in which Asia is still far technically behind the European and American markets.[1] Often financial market development has been hampered by regulations that persist as a legacy of financial repression. Ito and Chinn investigate the relationship between financial market development and macroeconomic current account imbalances. Using data for both developed and developing countries, they conclude that increases in the size of financial markets induce a decline in the current account balance in industrial countries, but the reverse for developing countries. Finally, Park pres-

---

1. Though it must be said that this gap in Asian financial markets has recently stood it in good stead, at least from the short-run perspective of early 2008!

ents a case study of policy failure in financial markets. He studies the Korean deregulation of the mortgage and credit card businesses and the associated boom-bust cycle.

Green, Mariano, Pavlov, and Wachter present a compelling argument for the potential importance of asset securitization in Asia, arguing that it has the potential to increase Asian financial transparency dramatically. They provide a conceptual basis for price discovery potential for tradable market instruments, specifically focusing on mortgage securitization. A model is presented to explain how misaligned incentives can lead to bank-generated real estate crashes and macroeconomic instability. They then examine the performance of Asian banking sectors with respect to securitized real estate returns, thus providing evidence on the importance of misaligned incentives. They also argue that the addition of mortgage-backed securities may help to protect markets from the shocks that can arise from bank-financed mortgage lending. However, in a subtle but powerful comment on the chapter, Lamberte argues that the incentive problems faced by Asian banks may not be especially important; he argues that any issues with inappropriate lending can be more effectively dealt with by improved regulation.

Ito and Chinn are interested in understanding the evolution of global trade and financial imbalances and investigate the role of budget balances, financial development, and openness. Financial development—or the lack thereof—has received considerable attention as a possible contributing factor to the development of persistent and expanding current account imbalances that have characterized both the United States and East Asia of late. Several observers have argued that the depth and sophistication of American capital markets has caused capital to flow "uphill" from relatively underdeveloped East Asian financial markets toward the United States. In this chapter, Ito and Chinn extend their previous work by examining the effect of different types and aspects of financial development. While the theoretical reasons for these linkages are not especially clear, Ito and Chinn rely on empirics almost entirely. Their data analysis relies on a cross-country data set that encompasses a sample of nineteen industrialized countries and seventy developing countries during the period from 1986 through 2005. The large amount of variation in their comprehensive study yields a number of new results. First, they confirm a role for budget balances in industrial countries when bond markets are incorporated. Second, they find that in practice both stock market capitalization and private-sector credit appear to be important determinants of current account behavior; countries with more sophisticated financial markets tend to run current account surpluses. Third, while increases in the size of financial markets induce a decline in the current account balance in industrial countries, the *reverse* is more often the case for developing countries. Fourth, a greater degree of financial openness is typically associated with a smaller current account balance in developing countries.

The V-shaped macroeconomic recovery of Korea from the currency crisis of 1997 is, by now, a well-known story. But much less is known of a smaller Korean financial crisis that occurred in 2003 as a result of a bust in the credit card market. Park provides a fascinating case study of this failed policy reform; he includes an overview of the development of the market, the subsequent crash, and the associated policy response. Park attributes the increase in household debt to financial deregulation and a paradigm shift in the financial industry that began to place more emphasis on reallocation of resources for profits. The consequence of this shift was to introduce bullet or balloon mortgages. Before the currency crisis of 1997, banks basically lent to big corporations; afterward, banks became eager to lend to consumers, using residential property as collateral. Deregulation in 1999 removed a ceiling on cash advance services for credit card holders, despite the absence of adequate credit evaluation systems. Nonbanks—credit card companies and credit-specialized financial companies—increased their lending from 14 trillion won in 1999 to 51 trillion won just three years later. Much of this increase was in cash advances. Credit card delinquency subsequently increased sharply, followed by a hard crash with numerous defaults and bad debts. As credit card companies got intro trouble, there were bailouts by the government, with associated moral hazard. Unsurprisingly, lending declined to just 18 trillion won by 2005.

Park concludes that the Korean credit card crisis is a classic example of regulatory failure. The deregulation was inappropriately done without the requisite infrastructure (in this case, a central institution to administer credit information). The government intervention was timed poorly, and an abrupt regulatory change in 2002 resulted in a crash of credit card lending. With more timely and proper policies, many of these difficulties could have been at least alleviated if not averted altogether.

III: Financial Consolidation

Using financial markets to consolidate activity in the real economy is a topic of perennial interest, but especially so in Asia where such M&As have historically been rare. However, there has been a noticeable increase in the pace of financial consolidation of late in Asia, and it is accordingly appropriate to examine these developments. Three chapters in the volume deal with M&A activities in Asia. The first chapter by Shen and Lin provides an overview and analysis of the characteristics of financial consolidation in Asia. The remaining two chapters focus on individual countries, albeit ones of great size and importance. Wu looks at M&As in China using an event study approach, while Hosono, Sakai, and Tsuru concentrate on bank mergers in Japan.

Shen and Lin study the motives that drive Asian financial institutions to engage in financial consolation; they focus on the interesting case of cross-border M&As. They are interested in distinguishing between a number of commonly discussed motivations for M&As and have a special interest in determining whether the reasons for M&As changed with the financial crisis of 1997. Five hypotheses are examined, all from an empirical perspective. These are (1) the *gravity hypothesis,* (2) the *following the client hypothesis,* (3) the *market opportunity hypothesis,* (4) the *information cost hypothesis,* and (5) the *regulatory restriction hypothesis.* While none of the hypotheses can be directly tested, they gather data on proxies for each of the hypotheses and use these to explain the number of financial M&As in Asia from 1990. It turns out that the proxies that are statistically significant for the periods both before and after the crisis include (a) the distance between the countries, (b) the level of gross domestic product (GDP), (c) bilateral trade, and (d) net foreign direct investment. Distance has a negative impact in both periods, which tends to support both the gravity hypothesis and information cost hypotheses. Gross domestic product has a negative coefficient in both periods, which is contrary to the gravity hypothesis. On the other hand, trade is found to have a positive coefficient for both periods, which supports the following the client hypothesis. Foreign direct investment also exerts a positive effect, which supports the both information cost and the following the client hypotheses. Summing up then, the results of Shin and Lin suggest that both the following the client hypothesis and the regulatory restriction idea seem reasonable, with no great differences between the periods before and after the crisis.

Wu provides the first-ever study of Chinese financial consolidation, a notable and worthy achievement. He studies 752 mergers and acquisitions involving 587 companies traded on the Shanghai and Shenzhen stock exchanges in 2005. He uses the event-study method, using a period that stretches back to fifty days before the M&A to forty days afterward; he also pays careful attention to accounting information during this window of time. The analysis indicates that within the event period, the value of most companies involved in M&As actually increased. He estimates the cumulative abnormal return for acquiring firms and target firms at 1.68 percent and 2.03 percent, respectively. Wu then examines whether the type, industry, and ownership structure of the companies has an impact on the returns; he also checks the impact of the stock market's aggregate performance. When Wu takes exploits his accounting information within a longer observation period (four years), he finds that the financial conditions of M&A companies showed a decline in the first year after consolidation, but a subsequent improvement. This is one of the first serious studies of the newly emerging issue of financial consolidation in the world's largest manufacturer, China. The positive results indicate that there is reason to think that even though China's financial markets are quite young, they seem to be doing the job of vale creation for which they are intended.

Hosono, Sakai, and Tsuru analyze the merger wave that occurred in the

Japanese banking sector in the 1990s. Using a comprehensive data set, the chapter investigates the motives for bank consolidations in Japan between 1990 and 2004, as well as their consequences. The analysis suggests that the attempts of regulators to stabilize local financial markets through consolidation played an important role in M&As conducted by both regional banks and credit cooperatives (*shinkin*). It is interesting to note that these attempts were not very successful. By way of contrast, the M&As conducted by major banks and regional banks in the early 2000s seem to have been driven by motives of value maximization. Hosono, Sakai, and Tsuro test four motives for M&A: (1) improving bank efficiency; (2) strengthening market power; (3) exploiting a policy of too-big-to-fail; and (4) managerial empire building. Their results suggest that M&As tended to occur when overall bank health is poor and where the market is less concentrated. These results are consistent with the too-big-to-fail and market power hypotheses, respectively. However, they find no evidence that supports the managerial motive of empire building.

IV: Reform and Dynamism

The last two chapters in the volume examine the effects of reform on economic performance, as measured in the stock market. Sakuragawa and Watanabe evaluate the effects of the reforms introduced in 2002 by the Japanese minister for economic and fiscal policy, Heizo Takenaka. The results demonstrate convincingly that the credibility of economic reforms increased after weak Japanese banks were decisively handled in 2003. Fogel, Morck, and Yeung examined the impact of low turnover in top companies on a variety of measures of social justice. They show that a more dynamic corporate sector is not associated with greater inequality, pollution, injustice, or other social ills.

Sakuragawa and Watanabe study how the stock market evaluated the Japanese financial reform (the "Takenaka Plan") using a conventional event study methodology. They focus on a number of financial events that occurred in 2002 and 2003, including the announcement of the Takenaka Plan, the release of the work schedule implementing the financial reforms the package of monetary policies initiated by the new governor of Bank of Japan, and the failures of Resona Bank and Ashikaga Bank. Sakuragawa and Watanabe find that market participants came to believe only gradually in the government's intentions to reform bank governance. However, the credibility of the reforms drastically increased in 2003. Thus, at least some of the widely held skeptical attitudes toward economic reform seem unwarranted, at least so far as the financial markets are concerned. Further, the evidence from the failures of Resona and Ashikaga reveal that bank shareholders differentiated between individual banks on the basis of their financial conditions, rather than cynically lumping all banks together (as might be expected if the reforms were not serious).

In earlier work, Fogel, Morck, and Yeung developed a measure of turnover in a country's biggest businesses and examined whether this measure of corporate turnover promotes or hurts economic growth. One might imagine that a more stable business sector encourages larger research and development (R&D) and faster growth, simply because monopolist firms have both the resources to encourage R&D and the incentives to protect their market power. In fact, though, the results clearly show that greater turnover in a country's list of top businesses associated with *faster* growth in per capita gross domestic product (GDP) and productivity. A corporate sector with great turnover is a vibrant one that creates value, while a more stable business sector also tends to be more stagnant. In low-income countries, the turnovers are associated with capital accumulation. All this accords with Schumpeter's early concept of "creative destruction."

In this chapter, the authors follow up their earlier analysis and ask whether countries with more business stability pay the price of lower growth but also reap the benefits of greater social justice. That is, they ask whether greater business turnover is systematically associated with a worse social infrastructure, as manifested in less liberty, fraternity, or equality (to use the French taxonomy). They use a wide range of indicators of social well-being, including measures of environmental degradation, health, education, poverty, inequality, and fundamental rights. However, despite a wide-ranging and ambitious search, they find no evidence that business stability is associated with better social outcomes.

I

The Evolving Nature of Regional Stock Markets

Hong Kong *and* Shanghai
Yesterday, Today, and Tomorrow

Robert N. McCauley and Eric Chan

1.1 Introduction

At some point in the not distant future, China will ease its capital controls and make the yuan renminbi fully convertible into foreign currencies. Shortly after, Shanghai will reemerge as an international financial center. Amid a broader debate over the competitiveness of major international financial centers (McKinsey and Company 2006; Mainelli and Yeandle 2007), the prospect of Shanghai's reemergence has sharpened speculation regarding the relationship between Shanghai and the established international financial center that has reverted to Chinese sovereignty, Hong Kong (Wong 2007; Bradsher and Barboza 2007; Meyer 2007).

This study argues that Hong Kong will gain stature as an international financial center when China is more open financially and Shanghai returns as a competing center. This thesis is in the tradition of Kindleberger (1974), who argued that federal states can support more than one financial center. The thesis that the development of an onshore international financial center can contribute to the development of a nearby offshore international financial center is in some ways the inverse of that of Rose and Spiegel (2007), who argue that offshore competition can spur the onshore center.

This thesis is developed in relation to historical evidence of the last century, the current range and intensity of financial activity in the two centers,

Robert N. McCauley is chief representative of the Representative Office for Asia and the Pacific, Bank for International Settlements. Eric Chan is a statistical analyst at the Bank for International Settlements.

Comments of and discussions with David Cook, Hans Genberg, Takatoshi Ito, Peter Kriz, Guonan Ma, Wensheng Peng, Andrew Rose, and Y. C. Yao are gratefully acknowledged. The views expressed are those of the authors and not necessarily those of the Bank for International Settlements.

and a prospective analysis of the evolution of China's international balance sheet and Hong Kong's share therein. The method is eclectic, depending on rankings based on nosecounts of banks and their links for the historical comparison, multidimensional measures of balance sheets and trading activity for the current comparison, and regression analysis for projecting the future.

The analysis is in three parts. The next section builds on the analysis of 1900 to 1980 in Reed (1981) to demonstrate that Hong Kong ranked higher among international banking centers in the twentieth century when China was financially open, that is, before and just after the Second World War. The following section supplements and updates the careful study of Jao (2003) with data from the Bank for International Settlements (BIS; 2002, 2005) and from Ho, Ma, and McCauley (2005), to emphasise the current gap between Hong Kong and Shanghai, especially in the trading of foreign exchange and derivatives. The value of Hong Kong's legal and regulatory institutions is discussed by reference to the gap between the valuations of firms listed on the Hong Kong and Shanghai stock exchanges. The following section draws on Lane (2000) and Cheung et al. (2006) to fit a Kuznets curve relating international banking assets and liabilities to real income and openness in order to assess the potential growth of China's international banking activity. Then BIS and Hong Kong data are used to estimate the share that Hong Kong can be expected to enjoy. A final section concludes that China's financial opening and Shanghai's consequent reemergence as an international financial center promise to raise Hong Kong's standing vis-à-vis London and New York.

1.2   Hong Kong and Shanghai as International Financial Centers, 1900 to 1980

Reed (1981) based his analysis on five variables that combine the number of banks in a financial center and their links to other financial centers (see appendix A for complete definitions). The first two of these count the number of locally headquartered banks and their international links. In particular, both the number of internationally active banks that are headquartered in the center and the number of their links through affiliates to other international financial centers are counted. The other three variables focus on the presence in the center of private and foreign banks. In particular, the number of merchant or investment bank offices is counted. In addition, the number of offices in the center of large, internationally active banks that are headquartered outside the center is counted. Finally, in parallel with the count of links to other centers of locally headquartered banks, the links to international financial centers through offices of large, internationally active banks headquartered elsewhere are counted.

Rankings based on these measures may be far from ideal, but they do

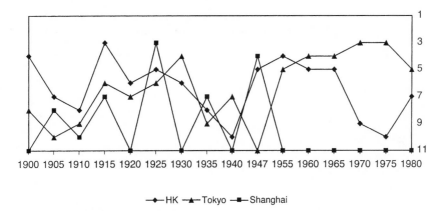

Fig. 1.1   Ranking of international financial centers
Source: Reed (1981).
Notes: 11 denotes not in the top ten. Yokohama and Tokyo are considered one center.

have the advantage of having been assembled on a consistent basis for most of a century. In particular, Reed ranked the world's international financial centers on this basis for sixteen selected years between 1900 and 1980, inclusive, at generally five-year intervals.

Reed's rankings consistently put London and New York in the top positions. Asian financial centers, including Hong Kong, Shanghai, Singapore, Tientsin, Tokyo, and Yokohama, fell into the second or third tier of centers. Focusing on the three Asian centers of Hong Kong, Shanghai, and Tokyo,[1] figure 1.1 shows that Hong Kong started the century as the preeminent Asian center, only to fall behind first Shanghai then Yokohama (aggregated with Tokyo in the graph) before World War II. Then, after 1960, Tokyo emerged as the preeminent center in Asia.

In terms of the comparison between Hong Kong and Shanghai, Reed found that internationally active banks were better represented and more connected to other centers in Hong Kong than in Shanghai. Reed put Shanghai ahead of Hong Kong in two years, 1925 and 1947. But even apart from the Second World War and the Mao years, Shanghai did not make the international top ten in 1900, 1920, and 1930, while Hong Kong always placed.

The most striking aspect of these rankings, though, is the relationship between Hong Kong's ranking and Shanghai's presence as a competitor. Shanghai was no competition for Hong Kong during the Second World War and the years after the founding of the People's Republic. During these years, Hong Kong averaged a ranking of 5.8 on Reed's measure (where London was ranked number one). In the years that Shanghai was, from an international banking perspective, out of the picture, Hong Kong was ranked

1. See Meyer (2007).

Table 1.1	Ranking of Hong Kong and Shanghai as international banking centers, 1900–1980 (top ranked center is ranked number one)		
	Hong Kong	Shanghai	Difference
Shanghai active (1900–35, 1947)	5.8	8.0[a]	2.1
Shanghai inactive (1940, 1955–80)	7.1		
Difference	–1.3		

Sources: Reed (1981) and authors' calculations.

[a]A rank of 11 is assigned to Shanghai in the years that it did not make the top ten. If only the years when Shanghai made the top ten were included, then Shanghai would show an average ranking of 6.2 in the top row while Hong Kong would show an average ranking of 6.0.

7.1 (see table 1.1). On this showing, Hong Kong did not benefit as an international banking center from the absence of Shanghai.

The result should not be surprising. Narrowly speaking, if banks headquartered in Shanghai tended to have affiliates in Hong Kong, then Hong Kong would have tended to rise on Reed's measure. More broadly, the engagement of China with the world's trading and financial system raised the weight in that system of East Asia and the ranking of those financial centers that served it.

The suggestion conveyed by this look at Hong Kong and Shanghai as international banking centers in the last century is that Hong Kong was generally more populated with international banking units and more connected to other international banking centers than Shanghai. More striking, however, is the suggestion of complementarity between the two centers. Hong Kong seemed to have done better as an international banking center when Shanghai was open for business. The next section turns to the current comparison of Hong Kong and Shanghai, in which Shanghai is handicapped by the substantial restrictions on international capital mobility between China and the rest of the world.

1.3   Hong Kong and Shanghai as International Financial Centers Today

This section extends and updates the quite comprehensive comparative profile of Hong Kong and Shanghai as financial centers provided by Jao (2003). It starts with Professor Jao's profile based on 2002 data and adds to it some data from the triennial central bank survey compiled by the BIS, mostly concerning over-the-counter derivatives. It then updates the extended profile to end-2005 (except the data from the triennial survey, which cover April 2004). Finally, the current advantage of Hong Kong's institutions and openness is measured by the price gap between the opportunity cost that the Chinese authorities pay for listings of Chinese companies in Hong Kong.

Jao's conclusion from his profile was stark: "Here, all indicators show that Shanghai was dwarfed by Hong Kong" (19). One could footnote this conclusion, for example, by noting that Hong Kong has no counterpart to Shanghai's commodity exchanges, which could eventually challenge the London-based commodity exchanges. It is hard, however, to argue against Professor Jao's assessment. Indeed, when the comparison is broadened in what follows to include derivative trading, his conclusion actually gains strength. For instance, while billions of dollars worth of interest rate swaps were traded every day in Hong Kong in April 2001 and 2004, the first renminbi swap had not yet been contracted then.[2]

But the question arises, particularly after the celebrated increase in the market capitalization of the Shanghai stock exchange in 2007, how firmly did this conclusion hold in middecade? It turns out that the updating of Professor Jao's comparison to 2005 does little damage to his conclusion.

As an international banking center, Shanghai lags Hong Kong (table 1.2). It must be admitted that broad, mostly domestic, banking aggregates, like the deposits and loans on the first and third rows of table 1.2, grew at a much faster rate in Shanghai than in Hong Kong over the years 2002 to 2005, as one would expect given the more rapid economic growth on the mainland. However, such growth tells more about Shanghai as a domestic financial center than as an international financial center.[3] Even using China-wide data on cross-border interbank positions, Shanghai engagement with the international interbank markets remained moderate in 2005, at levels only about a third of those observed in Hong Kong (see rows "Due to" and "Due from banks abroad" in table 1.2). On this showing, Shanghai has a way to go to become a major international banking center.

From the comparison of banking positions, the spotlight shifts to the trading of foreign exchange and derivatives (table 1.3). At the outset, it should be recognized that it is possible for an international financial center to operate largely on the basis of foreign currencies: consider the position of London before the abolition of exchange controls on sterling in 1979. But London was well established as an international financial center before the imposition of those controls, and policy sought to revive that role even under the capital controls. In contrast, policy drove practically all international banks out of Shanghai in the years after the founding of the People's Republic. For instance, Lu (2007) tells the story of the strained relations between the Hong Kong Shanghai Bank and the mainland authorities.

---

2. The first renminbi interest rate swap was contracted in connection with the Asian Development Bank's (ADB) sale of a so-called panda bond denominated in renminbi to Chinese investors in October 2005. The ADB reportedly exchanged its ten-year fixed coupon payments for floating rate payments based on the one-year deposit rate in China.

3. Liu and Yang (2005) argue that Shanghai's performance as a domestic financial center can be judged as unsatisfactory by the low ratio of loans to deposits in the Chinese banking system. It is certainly true that nominal lending rates well below the Chinese economy's growth rate suggest that domestic financial intermediation has serious problems. But by Liu and Yang's criterion, Hong Kong banks would be judged to have done a great job amid rising asset prices in the early to mid-1990s (with a loan-to-deposit ratio in excess of one) and a poor job since (with a low loan-to-deposit ratio).

Table 1.2   Banking assets and liabilities in Hong Kong and Shanghai (US$ billions)

	Hong Kong		Shanghai	
	2002	2005	2002	2005
Deposits	425.5	524.6	169.6	289.0
Foreign currency deposits	189.4	250.1	20.7	23.9
Loans	266.4	298.1	127.5	208.1
Foreign currency loans	66.2	83.9	14.3	30.0
Loans abroad	31.2	39.4		
Due to banks abroad	180.9	200.7	32.3[a]	76.1[a]
Due from banks abroad	257.0	325.6	79.7[a]	110.5[a]
Clearing house turnover	39.5	79.0		
Interbank market turnover	20.6	31.8	5.7	11.5
Memo: no. of depository institutions	224	199	72	130
Domestic	99	77	18	46
Foreign	125	122	54	84

Sources: Hong Kong: Hong Kong Monetary Authority (HKMA) Annual Report, Quarterly Bulletin, and Monthly Statistical Bulletin; Hong Kong Monthly Digest of Statistics; Hong Kong Annual Report; Hong Kong Stock Exchange Fact Book; Hong Kong Securities and Futures Commission Annual Report. Shanghai: Shanghai Statistical Yearbook; Shanghai Economy Yearbook; China Statistical Yearbook; China Securities and Futures Statistical Yearbook; BIS.
[a]China figures.
Note: Blank cell means not reported.

Whatever the possibilities in principle, in practice the gap between Hong Kong and Shanghai in trading foreign exchange and derivatives is wider than that in banking (table 1.3). The modal transaction in the exchange-traded Shanghai spot currency market in 2004 must have been the purchase of dollars against renminbi by the authorities. Most trading by non-residents occurred offshore in the nondeliverable forward market, with no connection to payment flows on the mainland by construction (Ma, Ho, and McCauley 2004; Ho, Ma, and McCauley 2005; Debelle, Gyntelberg, and Plumb 2006). Currency options and swaps were absent.

Moreover, the development of derivatives markets in fixed income and equity in China has been inhibited by a cautious official approach that reflects a bad experience with bond futures trading in the 1990s. Stock index futures remained to be introduced in 2005. As noted, only in commodity futures did Shanghai have an edge on Hong Kong. Indeed, because China represents the fastest growing and probably most volatile source of demand for commodities, it is not inconceivable that Shanghai traders might have some informational advantages over their commodity-trading counterparts in London and New York. For now, however, derivatives are more studied than traded in Shanghai.

Turning from foreign exchange and derivatives to capital market development, Shanghai has yet to derive the full measure of advantage over Hong

Table 1.3   **Foreign exchange and derivatives turnover in Hong Kong and Shanghai (US$ billions)**

	Hong Kong		Shanghai	
	2002	2005	2002	2005
Foreign exchange daily turnover[a,b]	68.351	105.979		0.61[c,d]
Spot	18.968	35.648	0.34	0.61[c,d]
Forward/swaps	47.855	66.514	—	
Options	1.030	2.846	—	—
Cross-currency swaps	0.498	0.971	—	—
Of which, domestic currency	24.578	27.614		0.61[c]
Spot	3.455	4.406		
Forward/swaps	21.122	22.828		
Options		0.213		
Cross-currency swaps		0.167		
Over-the-counter fixed income				
derivatives[a,b]	2.641	11.217		
Forward rate agreements	0.531	0.318		
Interest rate swaps	1.895	9.594		
Interest rate options	0.215	1.305		
Exchange traded derivatives				
Stock index futures (no. of				
contracts, daily average)	19,602[e]	40,205[e]	—	—
Commodity futures	—	—	1.98	3.24

Sources: Hong Kong Stock Exchange Fact Book; Shanghai Statistical Yearbook; BIS Triennial Survey (2002, 2005).

[a]April 2001 for 2002.

[b]April 2004 for 2005.

[c]China figures.

[d]Ho, Ma, and McCauley (2005) estimated that the daily renminbi turnover would be US$ 3.6 billions, in which US$ 2.9 billions would be spot turnover, if the unreported bank-customer transactions were taken into account.

[e]Hang Seng Index futures.

Blank cell means not reported. Dash means nil.

Kong from its very large government debt (table 1.4). Turnover of government paper other than People's Bank bills remained low, with trading awkwardly divided between the stock exchange and an over-the-counter interbank market. Fixed income mutual funds and insurers' holdings of bonds were growing very rapidly but from a low base. As noted, fixed income derivatives were absent in 2005, although the development of repo markets had allowed the possibility of short-sales. As for the international profile of the Chinese bond market, policy generally prevented foreign investment in renminbi-denominated bonds.[4]

4. A limited exception was the Pan Asia Index Fund (EMEAP 2006; Ma and Remolona 2005). Another exception to the noninternationalized nature of the Chinese bond market was the issuance of the panda bond by the Asian Development Bank in October 2005.

Table 1.4   Capital market indicators in Hong Kong and Shanghai

	Hong Kong		Shanghai	
	2002	2005	2002	2005
Debt market (US$ billion)				
Outstanding debt instruments	68.3	99.2	366.3[a]	910.9[a]
Government	16.4	17.7	215.2	610.7
Foreign	11.5	15.7	0.0	1.2
Other				
Turnover	2.9	3.5	15.5[a]	3.2[a]
Stock market (US$ billion)				
Market capitalisation	456.4	1,046.3	306.4	286.2
Daily turnover	0.83	2.35	0.84	0.99
Equity funds raised	13.0	38.5	0.67	0.37
Memo: no. of listed firms	812	934		
Domestic	802[b]	925[b]	715	834
Foreign	10[c]	9[c]		
Fund management				
Assets under management	342.1	667.6		
Memo: no. of unit trusts or				
mutual funds	1,965[d]	1,998[e]		
Domestic	91[d]	103[e]	25	26
Foreign	1,874[d]	1,895[e]	—	
Insurance				
Premium income (US$ billion)	11.4	17.7	2.9	4.1
No. of insurance companies	195	175	36	70
Domestic	96	89	21	46
Foreign	99	86	15	24

Sources: Hong Kong: Hong Kong Monetary Authority (HKMA) Annual Report, Quarterly Bulletin, and Monthly Statistical Bulletin; Hong Kong Monthly Digest of Statistics; Hong Kong Annual Report; Hong Kong Stock Exchange Fact Book; Hong Kong Commissioner of Insurance Annual Report; Hong Kong Securities and Futures Commission Annual Report. Shanghai: Shanghai Statistical Yearbook; Shanghai Economy Yearbook; China Statistical Yearbook; China Securities and Futures Statistical Yearbook; Asian Development Bank; BIS.

Notes: Blank cell means not reported. Dash means nil.

[a]China figures.

[b]All China incorporated enterprises with H shares listed in the Hong Kong Stock Exchange are included.

[c]Counted as foreign companies if incorporated overseas and have a majority of business outside Hong Kong SAR and China.

[d]March 2003.

[e]March 2006.

   Given the headlines in 2007 that the market capitalization of the Chinese stock exchanges had surpassed those of the rest of Asia, table 1.4 offers a reminder of how things were in 2005. The market capitalization of the Shanghai exchange was about a quarter of that of the Hong Kong exchange, and turnover was less than half. Fund-raising in the market through 2005 remained negligible. Again, the Chinese equity markets were very insular, with only about $10 billion of Qualified Foreign Institutional Investor inflow permitted. Table 1.4 classifies the listings of mainland firms on the Hong Kong Stock Exchange as domestic. If these are taken to be foreign listings, then the primary market offerings on the Hong Kong Stock Exchange emerge as the most international in the world (fig. 1.2).

In terms of price action, both the mainland equity and bond markets moved without reference to global markets, as represented by the Standard and Poor's 500 or U.S. Treasury bonds (fig. 1.3). In striking contrast is the high correlation of Hong Kong bond and stock markets with global movements.

Underlying Hong Kong's current advantage are not only China's capital controls but also Hong Kong's legal system; regulation, including accounting and disclosure standards; and clearing and settlement systems. The value that the mainland authorities themselves place on Hong Kong's institutions can be read from pricing differences between the Hong Kong and Shanghai stock exchanges. The willingness of the mainland authorities to pay for Hong Kong institutions is more evident in recent years owing to greater overlap between the firms traded in Hong Kong and Shanghai.

For a long time there has been evidence of pricing differences between the Hong Kong and Shanghai exchanges that suggested that the mainland authorities were paying an opportunity cost for Hong Kong listings. In particular, Chinese-based enterprises in Hong Kong have long traded at price-earnings ratios well below those of the Shanghai A shares (fig. 1.4). But drawing inferences from this pricing difference was never straightforward:

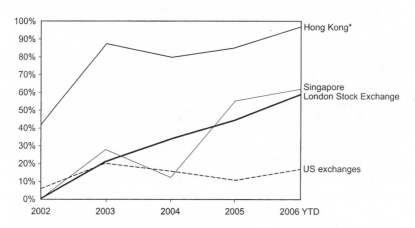

Fig. 1.2   Share of initial public offerings (IPOs) by foreign companies in major stock exchanges: Percent of total IPO value

Source: McKinsey and Company (2006, 47).

Notes: Mainland Chinese IPOs considered "foreign" for Hong Kong purposes. Year-to-date data complied as of November 2, 2006.

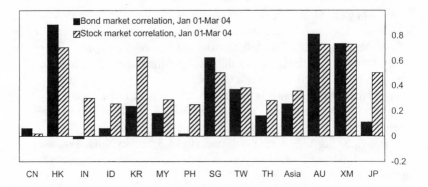

Fig. 1.3   Bond and stock market correlations with the U.S. markets

Source: McCauley and Jiang (2004).

Notes: CN denotes China; HK, Hong Kong; IN, India; ID, Indonesia; KR, Korea; MY, Malaysia; PH, the Philippines; SG, Singapore; TW, Taiwan, China; TH, Thailand; Asia, Asia local bond index of HSBC; AU, Australia; XM, the euro area; JP, Japan. Bond market correlation is based on weekly changes in benchmark yields at Thursday closing for Asia and Wednesday closing for U.S. Treasuries. Stock market correlation is based on weekly changes in stock market price indexes at Thursday closing from Asia and Wednesday closing for the S&P 500. The period is from January 2001 to March 2004.

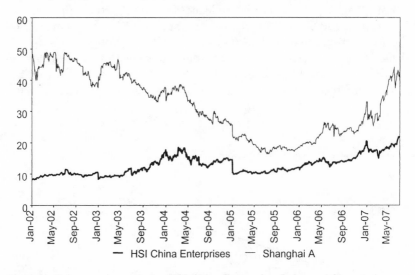

Fig. 1.4   Price-earning ratio for HSI China Enterprises Index and Shanghai A-share Index

Source: Bloomberg.

the selection of shares to be listed in one or another market was by no means random.

For some years, however, some firms listed in Hong Kong have been allowed to list in Shanghai as well, and these permit an apples-to-apples comparison. At first, these cross-listed firms were smallish ones with low turnover or large state ownership. But over time, larger firms with more liquid shares and lower state ownership have been listed. As a result, it has become sensible for the Hang Seng Index Company to compile a weighted average index of the pricing premium of Shanghai prices over Hong Kong prices for firms listed on both exchanges. The index started in January 2006, with only one firm that met the criteria of sufficient market capitalization, trading, and nonstate ownership share.[5] This capitalization-weighted index of cross-listed large firms shows the share prices in Shanghai going to a substantial premium over the prices for the same shares in Hong Kong in 2007 (fig. 1.5). The substantial gap in valuations of the identical shares in Hong Kong and Shanghai led Joseph Yam, chief executive of the Hong Kong Monetary Authority, to suggest that some arbitrage mechanism like depository receipts be allowed in order to allow the operation of the law of one price (Joseph Yam 2007; Miao and Peng 2007). In the event, the mainland authorities in 2007 increased the foreign investment quotas for qualified domestic institutional investors (banks, insurers, and mutual funds) to $42 billion and permitted investment into equities as well as fixed income, but proposals to allow a "through train" of investment by mainland retail investors into Hong Kong listed shares were sidetracked. This easing of capital controls would permit Chinese residents to invest in Hong Kong-listed shares, but the prospect of same has not brought prices in the two markets into line.

As long as the premium remains, a decision by the mainland authorities to allow a listing in Hong Kong entails a substantial opportunity cost. By revealed preference, this cost has as its compensation the legal, regulatory, and market context of Hong Kong.

This interpretation gains strength from reports that the State Administration of Foreign Exchange on the mainland is not permitting firms that have initial public offerings in Hong Kong to repatriate the proceeds. Shirley Yam (2007) reported the case of China Railway Engineering Group, a state-owned constructor of railways, which is to list simultaneously in Hong Kong and Shanghai:

> It is okay to give Hong Kong a cut in the listing pie. It is okay to let foreign investors share the profits of the effective monopoly. It is okay to put a major state-owned enterprise under the regulation of an outsider. But foreign money is not okay. (B12)

This policy, said to be applied to private Chinese enterprises that have listed in Hong Kong recently, makes it very clear why the mainland authorities are willing to "leave money on the table" in Hong Kong. It is not a mercantilist hankering for foreign exchange. We attach little weight to the

---

5. These criteria produce a sample with less divergent valuations than the universe of shares cross-listed on the two exchanges. Peng, Miao, and Chow (2007) find that, on average, over the period since July 2005, the Shanghai prices of cross-listed shares trade at a premium of 77 percent over the same shares in Hong Kong.

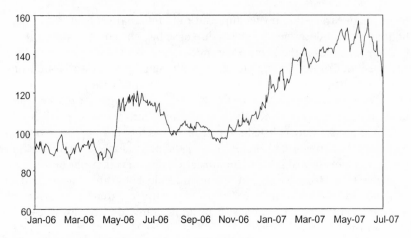

Fig. 1.5   Hang Seng China AH Index—Premium Index
Source: Hang Seng Indexes Company Limited.

desire to give Hong Kong a cut in the listing pie, that is, underwriting fees. Rather, the opportunity cost of listing a state-owned enterprise in Hong Kong is the purchase price of the Hong Kong regulation and the Hong Kong (and thereby global) equity analysis.

In sum, extension and update of Jao's comparison confirm his finding that Shanghai hardly registers as an international banking center. Still, Shanghai's role as a domestic financial center is growing rapidly, and the surge over the past couple of years of equity prices has drawn international attention, if not international funds or listings, to its stock exchange. The fact that the mainland authorities have been willing to continue to list shares of big Chinese firms in Hong Kong despite the increasingly clear evidence of the substantial cost of doing so has testified to the value that they place on the Hong Kong market's advantages, be they matters of law, regulation, or market participation. Less remarked has been the recent increase in the value of cross-border deposits and loans held by Chinese banks, especially vis-à-vis banks. The next section considers the implications for Shanghai and Hong Kong were such deposits and loans to grow in line with China's output and trade.

1.4   The Future of Shanghai and Its Implications for Hong Kong

This section investigates the near future of Shanghai as an international financial center. It focuses on only one form of international finance, namely stocks of cross-border bank claims.

At present, the international financial position of China reflects the history and the continued efficacy of capital controls (Ma and McCauley 2008). Even though cross-border bank flows, especially those between banks, have been less regulated than portfolio flows, nevertheless, the stock of international bank claims and liabilities of China is smaller than it would be without various restrictions.

How much larger? This section addresses this question by estimating the relationship between the sum of crossborder bank assets and liabilities in relation to gross domestic product (GDP), on the one hand, and the level of income and the openness of the underlying economy on the other. Following Lane (2000) and Cheung et al. (2006), the sample of economies on which this relationship is estimated is that of the Organization for Economic Cooperation and Development (OECD) economies on the ground that these economies generally have reduced or eliminated controls on the international mobility of capital. The estimated relationship is then used as a benchmark for how China's stocks of international bank assets and liabilities might be expected to evolve as capital controls are removed.

How would Hong Kong share in China's deepened financial relations with the rest of the world? Cheung et al. (2006) used a gravity model to estimate the Hong Kong stock market's attraction to portfolio outflows from the mainland. Here, a simpler approach is taken, relying on the level and trend of the Hong Kong share in the BIS, reporting bank claims and liabilities vis-à-vis China. In short, the current high share of Hong Kong in China's international banking assets and liabilities suggests that China's international opening would benefit Hong Kong to a disproportionate extent.

The following subsection reports the results of the benchmark regression of international banking positions on a small set of economic variables for the OECD countries. Then data on China's income level and openness are used to produce an estimate of the size of China's unconstrained international banking positions in 2005 and 2012. Then, data from the Hong Kong Monetary Authority and the BIS are combined to produce a projection of the Hong Kong share of China's international banking assets and liabilities. A final section considers in more general terms the relationship between Shanghai and Hong Kong over a longer horizon.

1.4.1   International Banking Positions in the OECD

How large would China's international banking position be were policy as liberal as those found in the advanced economies? This question can be approached by relating international banking positions to income and economic openness in the OECD economies.

Following Lane (2000), the dependent variable is defined as the sum of cross-border banking loans and deposits in relation to GDP. Independent variables are taken to be the log of GDP per capita, measured at market prices, economic openness, defined as the sum of imports and exports as a fraction of GDP, domestic credit as a share of GDP, and the interest differential between the relevant currency and the U.S. dollar at the three-month maturity. In addition are entered dummy variables for financial centers (Luxembourg, Switzerland, and the United Kingdom) and for the euro area. The latter dummy is to take into account the sharp rise in the cross-border banking positions that took place after the introduction of the euro as a result of the unification of the areawide short-term money market. Data for the dependent variable are obtained from the BIS and the International Monetary Fund (IMF) and for the other variables from the IMF.

In common with other such analyses, the results are much improved excluding Luxembourg from the sample (table 1.5). For the resulting sample, GDP per capita and openness, as well as the dummies for the euro area and for the financial centers, all come in as significant and show the expected signs. Neither interest rates nor the depth of domestic credit market enter significantly. Excluding the lower income countries, namely Mexico, Slovakia, and Turkey, does not materially affect the results, though it does raise the coefficient on GDP per capita noticeably. Overall, the goodness of fit is comparable to that of the more inclusive regression analysis of the total international investment position as reported by Lane (2000, 522).[6]

As a check for robustness, we repeated the exercise excluding Ireland from the sample as well (appendix B). The results were similar with regard to the sign and significance of the estimated coefficients. The somewhat lower estimated coefficient on GDP per capita implies somewhat smaller growth of China's cross-border bank deposits and loans, but leaves the broad result qualitatively similar.

At the suggestion of David Cook, we experimented with net foreign assets as an explanatory variable. However, this variable did not prove to be statistically significant. David Cook also suggested that we check the "out of sample" fit of the results on table 1.5 for Taiwan, China. In fact, the model result overstates international bank loans and deposits for this economy.[7]

1.4.2   China's Projected International Banking Position

Were China's international banking balance sheet to respond to its growing real income in line with the tendency in the OECD, it could experience very rapid growth. In particular, if the nominal GDP of China were

6. Lane's goodness of fit for the total international investment position than for direct investment or portfolio positions may suggest that his implied goodness of fit for the major nondirect investment, nonportfolio position item, namely bank flows, is as high or higher than the level reported in table 1.5.

7. According to the estimated coefficients in column (4) or (6) of table 1.5, the estimated cross-border banking loans and deposits for Taiwan would be 60.3 percent or 52.8 percent of GDP, compared to the actual number of 40.0 percent. The shortfall may reflect limitations on financial interactions with the mainland and the channeling of cross-Strait banking activity through Hong Kong.

Table 1.5   Estimated determinants of cross-border bank deposits and loans in the Organization for Economic Co-operation and Development excluding Ireland (stock of deposits plus loans in relation to GDP at end 2005)

	Full sample		Sample without Luxembourg		Sample without Luxembourg, Mexico, Slovakia, Turkey	
	(1)	(2)	(3)	(4)	(5)	(6)
Intercept	-2431.183*	-1091.584	-521.626*	-471.462**	-577.918*	-692.508**
	(0.068)	(0.272)	(0.052)	(0.019)	(0.062)	(0.013)
Openness	2.675	2.478	0.995***	0.848**	1.075***	1.028***
	(0.117)	(0.133)	(0.005)	(0.012)	(0.007)	(0.007)
GDP/Capita	233.507	89.993	46.010*	45.553**	50.793*	65.672**
	(0.088)	(0.349)	(0.091)	(0.019)	(0.102)	(0.013)
Euro area	223.546*	189.860	55.050**	46.444*	46.542	45.536*
	(0.088)	(0.137)	(0.037)	(0.068)	(0.107)	(0.079)
Financial center	899.985***	909.721***	280.171***	283.936***	273.562***	280.447***
	(0.000)	(0.000)	(0.000)	(0.000)	(0.000)	(0.000)
Interest rate	29.370		5.184		0.492	
	(0.187)		(0.232)		(0.939)	
Domestic credit/GDP	-1.314		0.261		0.283	
	(0.338)		(0.332)		(0.319)	
Adjusted R^2	0.533	0.521	0.691	0.680	0.684	0.698
No. of observations	30	30	29	29	26	26

Source: IMF, Direction of Trade, International Financial Statistics, World Economic Outlook; BIS; authors' calculations.

***Significant at the 1 percent level.

**Significant at the 5 percent level.

*Significant at the 10 percent level.

to grow by 13 percent, with 10 percent nominal growth reinforced by a trend nominal appreciation of the renminbi against the dollar of 3 percent, then dollar GDP per capita could grow at 12.5 percent. In table 1.6, this scenario (given the coefficient of less than one-half estimated in column [4] of table 1.5) would produce a 5.4 percent per annum growth in international bank positions in relation to GDP. If trade is assumed to decelerate from a rate of growth of 20 percent by 2 percent per annum, then it at first contributes to additional international bank positions and then reduces them. On these assumptions, the mainland's cross-border bank position could quintuple over seven years to half of GDP, or $2.7 trillion.

1.4.3   Hong Kong's Share of China's Projected International Banking Position

Such an outcome could represent a lot of business for banks in Hong Kong. To see this, consider what share that Hong Kong might end up with of the $2.7 trillion in China's international banking assets and liabilities projected for the end of 2012. While Cheung et al. (2006) had to estimate how investment in Hong Kong would depend on the size of the market and its distance from the investor, the present estimation is much more straightforward. Inspection of Hong Kong's share of China's external assets and liabilities suggests that Hong Kong's share, after a prolonged decline from the time of the Asian financial crisis until early 2003, has stabilized at about 40 percent (fig. 1.6).

It remains to be demonstrated how such an increase in Hong Kong's international balance sheet would affect its standing vis-à-vis New York and London.[8] At this stage, suffice it to say that China's rapid growth and further financial integration with the world economy, like rapid growth and further financial integration in East and South Asia in general, can be expected to boost the region's financial centers, including Hong Kong.

1.4.4   Looking Ahead Further

We have argued in section 1.3 that Hong Kong as a financial center benefits from its legal and regulatory institutions, not least in its attraction of stock market listings from the mainland. In the longer term, the position of Hong Kong *and* Shanghai as financial centers depends on the character of legal and institutional convergence between the Special Administrative Region and the mainland. It may be recalled that under Hong Kong's Basic Law, Hong Kong's legal system is to remain separate from that of the rest of China for the fifty years after 1997. If the law and institutions governing financial markets in Shanghai converge to those characteristic of Hong

---

8. The effect would be indirect in the case of poll-based ratings like that of Mainelli and Yeandle (2007), which puts Hong Kong third after London and New York. See Cheung and Yeung (2007) for alternative measures of international financial centers.

Table 1.6   **Projection of China's external bank positions excluding Ireland (sum of cross-border bank assets and liabilities)**

| | GDP per capita (US$) | Trade/GDP (%) | Change in cross-border bank assets and liabilities in relation to GDP due to: | | China's external bank positions | | Memo: Hong Kong's external positions vis-à-vis China (US$ billions) |
			GDP per capita growth	Trade/GDP growth	Percent of GDP[a]	Billions of US dollars	
2005	1,716	63.4			10.0	224.6	103.3
2006	1,930	67.3	5.4	3.3	18.7	474.3	189.7
2007	2,172	70.3	5.4	2.5	26.6	762.0	304.8
2008	2,443	72.2	5.4	1.6	33.5	1,086.0	434.4
2009	2,749	72.8	5.4	0.5	39.5	1,443.3	577.3
2010	3,092	72.2	5.4	-0.5	44.3	1,830.1	732.1
2011	3,479	70.3	5.4	-1.6	48.0	2,242.8	897.1
2012	3,914	67.1	5.4	-2.6	50.7	2,678.4	1,071.4

Sources: IMF; Hong Kong Monetary Authority; BIS; authors' calculations.

[a]Change is sum of two columns to the left.

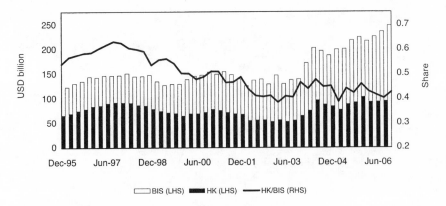

Fig. 1.6   External loans and deposits vis-à-vis China
Sources: Hong Kong Monetary Authority; BIS; authors' calculations.

Kong today, then Shanghai will join Hong Kong as a major international financial center. If, however, the eventual convergence impairs the rule of law and the predictability of the regulatory system in Hong Kong, then both may end up as more national than international financial centres.

In the former case, the maintenance of a separate monetary system in Hong Kong well into the fifty-year period after 1997 need not prove an impediment to Hong Kong's serving China as an international financial center. The relevant analogy might be the role of London vis-à-vis the euro area.[9] It must be admitted that the short-term money market benchmark for the euro area is one grounded in the euro area and not in London (as with U.S. dollar Libor; see McCauley 1999). Nevertheless, London has to a considerable extent become the financial center for the fixed income market of the euro area, notwithstanding the United Kingdom's remaining outside the euro area. The issue of the first offshore renminbi bond in Hong Kong in July 2007 points in this direction.

1.5   Conclusion

It is easy journalism to write the story of the return of Shanghai as an international financial center as a threat to Hong Kong's status as one. To be sure, Hong Kong may well enjoy some advantages that should be seen as transitory. The analogy might be the once-predominant position of the port of Hong Kong in China's external trade, which depended on political decisions rather than practical economics. Hong Kong's share of China's commodity trade is falling continuously. But finance is not the same as

9. The authors are indebted to Andy Rose for this analogy.

goods trade, and Hong Kong's share of China's external bank assets and liabilities is not falling. To write that Shanghai will displace Hong Kong is just dog-bites-man journalism.

The man-bites-dog argument of this chapter is that the return of Shanghai might boost Hong Kong as an international financial center. A certain plausibility attaches to this view when it is realized that Hong Kong ranked higher as an international banking center in the last century when Shanghai was in the running than when it was kept out of the game by international war or national politics. With regard to international banking, at least, China's financial integration into the global economy can be expected to bulk up Hong Kong's balance sheet more than that of any other center outside the mainland. There is a good prospect that Shanghai's reintegration into the global financial system will not only narrow the gap between itself and Hong Kong but also narrow the gap between Hong Kong and New York and London.

Appendix A
Reed's Measures of International Banking Preeminence

Reed depends on the following five variables:

1. *Local bank headquarters:* The number of large internationally active commercial banks headquartered in the center.

2. *Local bank direct links:* The number of foreign international financial centers with direct links to the international financial center through the large internationally active local banks headquartered in the center.

3. *Private banks:* The number of private (merchant or investment banks) with an office in the center.

4. *Foreign bank offices:* Large internationally active foreign commercial banks with an office in the center.

5. *Foreign bank direct links:* Foreign international financial centers with direct links to the international financial center through the large internationally active foreign banks with an office in the center.

Sources are adapted from Reed (1981, 10).

Appendix B
Robustness Check: Excluding Ireland from the Regression

As a robustness test, we estimate our model by excluding Ireland, which is not considered a financial center in our sample but, as a low-tax host to multinational corporate treasuries, has a sizable stock of external deposits and loans in relation to GDP. The estimated results are consistent with our previous findings, with GDP per capita, openness, as well as the dummies for the euro area and for the financial centers all being statistically significant and showing the expected signs, while interest rates and the depth of domestic credit market being insignificant. These results still hold when we leave out the lower-income countries.

Using the estimated coefficients in table 1A.1 as well as our previous assumptions on growth in GDP per capita and trade, we project that China's dollar GDP per capita would generate a 4 percent per annum growth in the country's international bank positions in relation to GDP (table 1A.2). This would boost the mainland's cross-border bank positions to 41 percent of GDP, or US$2.2 trillion, by 2012.

Table 1A.1   Estimated determinants of cross-border bank deposits and loans in the Organization for Economic Co-operation and Development (stock of deposits plus loans in relation to GDP at end 2005)

	Full sample		Sample without Ireland and Luxembourg		Sample without Ireland, Luxembourg, Mexico, Slovakia, Turkey	
	(1)	(2)	(3)	(4)	(5)	(6)
Intercept	-2431.183*	-1091.584	-376.310**	-349.185***	-399.858**	-491.194***
	(0.068)	(0.272)	(0.024)	(0.007)	(0.033)	(0.005)
Openness	2.675	2.478	0.805***	0.696***	0.886***	0.849***
	(0.117)	(0.133)	(0.001)	(0.002)	(0.001)	(0.001)
GDP/Capita (log)	233.507	89.993	33.541**	34.279***	35.289*	47.054***
	(0.088)	(0.349)	(0.046)	(0.006)	(0.060)	(0.005)
Euro area	223.546*	189.860	36.669**	30.247*	29.216*	29.293*
	(0.088)	(0.137)	(0.026)	(0.059)	(0.093)	(0.065)
Financial center	899.985***	909.721***	286.705***	290.233***	281.506***	287.585***
	(0.000)	(0.000)	(0.000)	(0.000)	(0.000)	(0.000)
Interest rate	29.370		3.495		-0.248	
	(0.187)		(0.186)		(0.948)	
Domestic credit/GDP	-1.314		0.204		0.220	
	(0.338)		(0.213)		(0.193)	
Adjusted R^2	0.533	0.521	0.855	0.842	0.860	0.861
No. of observations	30	30	28	28	25	25

Sources: IMF, Direction of Trade, International Financial Statistics, World Economic Outlook; BIS; authors' calculations.

Note: Numbers in parentheses are *p*-values of the estimated coefficients.

***Significant at the 1 percent level.

**Significant at the 5 percent level.

*Significant at the 10 percent level.

Table 1A.2   Projection of China's external bank positions (sum of cross-border bank assets and liabilities)

	GDP per capita (US$)	Trade/GDP (%)	Change in cross-border bank assets and liabilities in relation to GDP due to:		China's external bank positions		Memo: Hong Kong's external positions vis-à-vis China (US$ billions)
			GDP per capita growth	Trade/GDP growth	Percent of GDP[a]	Billions of US dollars	
2005	1,716	63.4			10.0	224.6	103.3
2006	1,930	67.3	4.0	2.7	16.8	425.5	170.2
2007	2,172	70.3	4.0	2.1	22.9	655.9	262.3
2008	2,443	72.2	4.0	1.3	28.2	913.9	365.6
2009	2,749	72.8	4.0	0.4	32.7	1,196.6	478.7
2010	3,092	72.2	4.0	-0.4	36.3	1,500.6	600.2
2011	3,479	70.3	4.0	-1.3	39.0	1,822.0	728.8
2012	3,914	67.1	4.0	-2.2	40.9	2,157.8	863.1

Sources: IMF; Hong Kong Monetary Authority; BIS; authors' calculations.
[a]Change is sum of two columns to the left.

References

Bank for International Settlements. 2002. *The Triennial Survey: Foreign exchange and derivative markets activity in 2001.* Basel, Switzerland: BIS, March.
———. 2005. *The Triennial Survey: Foreign exchange and derivative markets activity in 2004.* Basel, Switzerland: BIS, March.
Bradsher, Keith, and David Barboza. 2007. Hong Kong and Shanghai vie to be China's financial centre. *International Herald Tribune,* January 15.
Cheung, Lillian, Kevin Chow, Jian Chang, and Unias Li. 2006. Outward portfolio investment from mainland China: How much do we expect and how large a share can Hong Kong expect to capture? Hong Kong Monetary Authority Research Memorandum no. 06/13, September. http://www.info.gov.hk/hkma/eng/research/index.htm.
Cheung, Lillian, and Vincent Yeung. 2007. Measuring the position of Hong Kong as an international financial centre. *Quarterly Bulletin,* no. 53 (December):5–12.
China Securities Regulatory Commission. 2004. *China securities and futures statistical yearbook, 2003.* Beijing: CSRC.
———. 2007. *China securities and futures statistical yearbook, 2006.* Beijing: CSRC.
Debelle, Guy, Jacob Gyntelberg, and Michael Plumb. 2006. NDF markets in Asia: Lessons from the Australian experience. *BIS Quarterly Review,* (September): 53–64.
Executives' Meeting of East Asia-Pacific Central Banks (EMEAP), Working Group on Financial Markets. 2006. *Review of the Asian Bond Fund 2 initiative.* http://www.emeap.org.
Ho, Corrinne, Guonan Ma, and Robert N. McCauley. 2005. Trading Asian currencies. *BIS Quarterly Review,* (March):49–58.
Hong Kong Exchanges and Clearing Limited. 2004. *Hkex fact book, 2003.* Hong Kong: Hong Kong Exchanges and Clearing Limited.
———. 2007. *Hkex fact book, 2006.* Hong Kong: Hong Kong Exchanges and Clearing Limited.
Hong Kong Monetary Authority. 2003a. *Monthly statistical bulletin,* February. Hong Kong: HKMA.
———. 2003b. *Quarterly Bulletin,* March. Hong Kong: HKMA.
———. 2004. *Annual report, 2003.* Hong Kong: HKMA.
———. 2006a. *Monthly statistical bulletin,* February. Hong Kong: HKMA.
———. 2006b. *Quarterly Bulletin,* March. Hong Kong: HKMA.
———. 2007. *Annual report, 2006.* Hong Kong: HKMA.
Hong Kong SAR Government, Census and Statistics Department. 2003. *Hong Kong monthly digest of statistics,* February. Hong Kong: Hong Kong SAR Government.
———. 2004. *Hong Kong annual report, 2003.* Hong Kong: Hong Kong SAR Government.
———. 2006. *Hong Kong monthly digest of statistics,* February. Hong Kong: Hong Kong SAR Government.
———. 2007. *Hong Kong annual report, 2006.* Hong Kong: Hong Kong SAR Government.
Hong Kong SAR Government, Office of the Commissioner of Insurance. 2004. *Annual report, 2003.* Hong Kong: Hong Kong SAR Government.
———. 2007. *Annual report, 2006.* Hong Kong: Hong Kong SAR Government.
Hong Kong Securities and Futures Commission. 2003. *Annual report, 2002–03.* Hong Kong: Hong Kong Securities and Futures Commission.
———. 2006. *Annual report, 2005–06.* Hong Kong: Hong Kong Securities and Futures Commission.

Jao, Yu Ching. 2003. Shanghai and Hong Kong as international financial centres: Historical perspective and contemporary analysis. University of Hong Kong, Working Paper.

Kindleberger, Charles P. 1974. The formation of financial centres: A study in comparative economic history. *Princeton Studies in International Finance* no 38. Princeton University, Department of Economics, International Economics Section.

Lane, R. Philip. 2000. International investment positions: A cross-sectional analysis. *Journal of International Money and Finance* 19:513–15.

Liu, Hongzhong, and Changjiang Yang. 2005. The re-emergence of Shanghai as a financial center in China's financial system. In *A new financial market structure for East Asia,* ed. Takatoshi Ito, Yung Chul Park, and Yun Jong Wang, 353–81. Cheltenham, UK: Edward Elgar.

Lu, Quing. 2007. Government control, transaction cost and trust between the Hongkong and Shanghai Banking Corporation (HSBC) and the Chinese government. Paper presented to HKIMR/Center for Asian Studies, Hong Kong University, conference on Banking and Monetary History of Hong Kong, 17 April, Hong Kong.

Ma, Guonan, Corrinne Ho, and Robert N. McCauley. 2004. The markets for nondeliverable forwards in Asia. *BIS Quarterly Review,* (June):81–94.

Ma, Guonan, and Robert N. McCauley. 2008. Do China's capital controls still bind? In *China, Asia, and the new world economy,* ed. Barry Eichengreen, Charles Wyplosz, and Yung Chul Park, 312–40. Oxford, UK: Oxford University Press.

Ma, Guonan, and Eli M. Remolona. 2005. Opening markets through a regional bond fund: Lessons from ABF2. *BIS Quarterly Review,* (June):81–92.

Mainelli, Michael, and Mark Yeandle. 2007. *The global financial centres index.* London: City of London.

McCauley, Robert N. 1999. The euro and the liquidity of European fixed income markets. In *Market liquidity: Research findings and selected policy implications.* Report of a study group established by the Committee on the Global Financial System of the central banks of the Group of Ten countries. Basel, Switzerland: BIS.

McCauley, Robert N., and Guorong Jiang. 2004. Diversifying with Asian local currency bonds. *BIS Quarterly Review,* (September):51–66.

McKinsey and Company. 2006. *Sustaining New York's and the US's global financial services leadership.* Report commissioned by Mayor Michael Bloomberg and Senator Charles Schumer.

Meyer, David. 2007. Hong Kong's transformation as a financial center. Paper presented to HKIMR/Center for Asian Studies, Hong Kong University, conference on Banking and Monetary History of Hong Kong, 17 April, Hong Kong.

Miao, Hui, and Wensheng Peng. 2007. Why is A-share volatility so high? *China Economic Issues* no. 4/07. Hong Kong: Hong Kong Monetary Authority, June.

National Bureau of Statistics of China. 2004. *China statistical year book, 2003.* Beijing: National Bureau of Statistics of China.

———. 2007. *China statistical yearbook, 2006.* Beijing: National Bureau of Statistics of China.

Peng, Wensheng, Hui Miao, and Nathan Chow. 2007. Price convergence between dual-listed A and H shares. *China Economic Issues* no. 6/07. Hong Kong: Hong Kong Monetary Authority, July.

Reed, Howard Curtis. 1981. *The pre-eminence of international financial centres.* New York: Praeger.

Rose, Andrew, and Mark M. Spiegel. 2007. Offshore financial centres: Parasites or Symbionts? *Economic Journal* 117:1310–35.

Shanghai Municipal Statistical Bureau. 2004a. *Shanghai economy yearbook, 2003.* Shanghai: Shanghai Municipal Statistical Bureau.

———. 2004b. *Shanghai statistical yearbook, 2003.* Shanghai: Shanghai Municipal Statistical Bureau.

———. 2006. *Shanghai economy yearbook, 2005.* Shanghai: Shanghai Municipal Statistical Bureau.

———. 2007. *Shanghai statistical yearbook, 2006.* Shanghai: Shanghai Municipal Statistical Bureau.

Wong, Y. C. Richard. 2007. Shanghai: Another Hong Kong? *Harvard International Review,* 16 April.

Yam, Joseph. 2007. Linking the mainland's and Hong Kong's financial markets. I and II *Viewpoint,* Hong Kong Monetary Authority, January 25 and February 1.

Yam, Shirley. 2007. Money matters: Hong Kong nears end of the line in H-share listings. *South China Morning Post,* August 18, B12.

Comment   David Cook

Introduction

The authors have written a compelling case arguing that Hong Kong will continue to thrive as an international financial center even as the further development of the People's Republic of China could result in the growth of a rival financial center in Shanghai. Certainly, current trends are very positive. The finance, insurance, and business services (FIRE and business services less real estate) sector made up less than 10 percent of Hong Kong's economy in 1990 but had grown to more than 17.5 percent in 2005. This indicates both that integration into the mainland economy has not, in fact, dampened the financial industry in Hong Kong but also that continued performance of the sector is crucial for the overall macroeconomic performance of the Special Administrative Region (SAR).

The authors make three basic points based on past historical data, present trends, and a structural forecast of the future. First, in the prewar era, both Shanghai and Hong Kong were measured as significant international financial centers. Second, by many recent measurements, the depth and breadth of Hong Kong's financial markets continue to exceed that of Shanghai's. Third, China's international banking assets are likely to grow dramatically in the future as the economy develops. If Hong Kong's share of China's international banking continues to hold steady, rapid expansion of Hong Kong's banking will continue.

A central contribution of the chapter is a well-founded prediction of the size of China's external banking assets. The authors estimate a statistical

David Cook is an associate professor of economics at the Hong Kong University of Science and Technology model of a country's external banking assets as a function of its level of development and some other macroeconomic variables using cross-country data. Capital controls have inhibited the acquisition of nonofficial foreign assets by Chinese banks. This model can then be used to predict what will happen to China's external banking assets as it normalizes its integration with world financial markets and continues to develop economically. The authors predict dramatic growth in China's external bank lending. This seems reasonable and may even underestimate financial flows from China. China has acquired a large positive net international investment position relative to its level of development. It would be interesting if the authors could test how a history of positive net flows will increase the positive gross flow of funds by including the net international investment position or average of current account surpluses as an explanatory variable. It may also be useful to evaluate how well the model works for Taiwan, which is another economy that developed with large surpluses.

The authors conclude by noting that if Hong Kong's share of China's external banking assets stays constant, then Hong Kong's financial sector will also enjoy dramatic growth. Given the relative growth rates in the two economies, continued growth in Hong Kong's financial sector of this sort will require the further development of Hong Kong as a financial entrepôt for China as a whole or as a *Chinese* domestic financial center. The following discussion will focus on this aspect of Hong Kong and China's future development.

Financial Markets

The authors present evidence that along many dimensions, financial markets in Hong Kong are more developed than those in Shanghai. While their case is compelling, there are some caveats as to whether this implies that Hong Kong can continue to develop its role as a financial entrecôte. These caveats might be examined sector by sector.

Commercial Banking

Banks located in Hong Kong are much larger in aggregate than are the banks in Shanghai. At present, Beijing is the geographical center of commercial banking in China, not Shanghai. As reported in Bowers, Gibb, and Wong (2003), 60 percent of the domestic deposits in the Chinese banking system are held at the four top banks, all of which are majority controlled by the central government. The big four state-owned banks were spun off of the People's Bank of China at the outset of China's reform process and are still headquartered in Beijing, not in Shanghai.

The authors also note that there are large gross international financial flows that are channeled through Hong Kong's banking system. A large fraction of the assets of Hong Kong banks are categorized as Due from

Banks Abroad. The demand for foreign currency deposits in Hong Kong has been much larger than the demand for foreign currency loans leaving Hong Bank banks with an overhang of foreign currency. Prior to 2001, the Hong Kong Association of Bankers set legally enforced ceilings on interest rates on Hong Kong dollar deposits while foreign currency deposits were competitive (see Schenk 2003). As the dominant deposit taking banks in Hong Kong are part of multinational conglomerates, shipping the excess foreign currency to overseas branches is an effective way to eliminate currency mismatch. A large fraction of the assets of Hong Kong banks are, thus, Due *from* Banks Abroad. There are also a large number of foreign multinational banks operating in Hong Kong that have been prevented, in the past, from building branch networks by regulations (since repealed) referred to as the "One Building" rule. Borrowing from overseas branches can be a key source of funds for these banks. Therefore, a large fraction of Hong Kong banks' liabilities are Due to Banks Abroad.

Ironically, these gross international financial flows through the banking system have been encouraged by regulations that have limited competition in the domestic banking sector in Hong Kong. Whether international flows of this type can be a sound basis for believing that Hong Kong will act as a financial entrepôt for China is questionable. The possibility certainly exists. In 2005, about 20 percent of Hong Kong banks' liabilities to banks abroad are to mainland banks, a fact attributed to mainland banks acquiring Hong Kong dollars and lending them back in the Hong Kong money market (Hong Kong Yearbook 2005, chapter 4). In addition, about 8 percent of obligations of banks abroad to Hong Kong banks overseas assets are from mainland banks. As the mainland banking system liberalizes, Hong Kong banks are likely to have a comparative advantage and, perhaps, a regulatory advantage as well in penetrating that market.

As the authors argue, Hong Kong's well-developed commercial banking sector is likely to benefit from an expanding Chinese market. However, given the dominance of banks in China's financial system, decisions about the future geographical location of commercial banking are likely to be decided for public policy reasons. Looking at the U.S. example, we can recall that the Glass-Steagall act was passed to deliberately shape the geography of banking power in the United States. Decision making about the shape of the banking sector in China is likely to be no less political in China.

Equity Markets

Both Hong Kong and Shanghai have large equity markets. According to the World Federation of Exchanges, in May 2007, both markets had capitalizations of slightly larger than US$1 trillion. Between 1993 and 2005, mainland firms raised more than $100 billion in equity offerings in Hong Kong (Hong Kong Yearbook 2005, chapter 4). In 2005 and 2006, three of the Big Four Chinese state-owned banks had large initial public offerings

(IPOs) in Hong Kong though in 2007 initial offerings have been concentrated in Shanghai (see Kwong, Tucker, and Gangahar 2007). In the immediate term, central government policy is likely to drive the location of equity business in China.

In the longer term, thick market externalities (see Diamond 1982) may be a more dominant factor in moving China's equity markets to a single geographical location. Substantial time series evidence (see Amihud 2002; Pastor and Stambaugh 2003; and Acharya and Pedersen 2005) has shown that the degree of aggregate market liquidity has strong effects on equity prices. If market locations also benefit in the long run from being very liquid, then the increasing returns to scope and scale that would come from concentrating all listings in one market might make it more efficient to have a single major equity market in China, whether that would be in Shanghai or Hong Kong.

Bond Markets

It can definitely be said that Hong Kong is an international center for bond issuance. Compared to some other developed anglophone countries, the Hong Kong dollar international bond market is relatively large. In 2005, the outstanding stock of international Hong Kong dollar bonds was 38 percent of Hong Kong's gross domestic product (GDP) compared to the Canadian dollar international bond market being 14 percent of Canada's GDP, the Australian dollar market being 21 percent of Australian GDP, and New Zealand being 35 percent.[1] At that same point in time, the renminbi international bond market was negligible.

It is not clear, however, that this implies that Hong Kong can generate a significant fraction of its GDP by being a bond issuing center for China as a whole. Hong Kong's better standards of corporate governance would give it a comparative advantage in issuing corporate bonds rather than public-sector bonds, which might be more easily traded in Beijing. However, neither Hong Kong nor China's domestic corporate bond markets are particularly well developed. Eichengreen and Luengnaruemitchai (2004) report that in 2003, the ratio of domestic credit provided by the banking sector relative to outstanding domestic debt securities issued by the corporate sector was above 150 to 1 in China and above 45 to 1 in Hong Kong. In a market so dominated by banking, the corporate debt market may continue to be less significant.

Derivative Markets

In the 2004 data cited by the authors, forex and interest rate derivative trading was much larger in Hong Kong than in Shanghai. However, a more

1. These figures are calculated using data on the stock of bonds from the Bank for International Settlements (2007) and from data on GDP from the World Bank's World Development Indicators.

global comparison may offer some perspective. For example, the authors report that in April 2004 that the monthly average of the over-the-counter trading in interest rate derivatives in Hong Kong was approximately US$11 billion. On a good month in 2006, the trading in interest rate products at the Hong Kong Futures Exchange (see Hong Kong Exchange and Clearing 2007) was about HK$1 billion. As a comparison, on any given day in 2006, about 2 million interest rate contracts with a total notional value of US$2 trillion were traded on the Chicago Mercantile Exchange. The point is not to compare Hong Kong's market negatively with the longest existing financial derivatives markets. However, in comparison with the ultimate size of China's needs in terms of trading interest rate risk, Hong Kong's current lead may not prove decisive.

Conclusion

To help us further understand Hong Kong's future role as an international financial center, specific discussion of the SAR's role as an intermediary for the flow of funds between the mainland and foreign countries would be useful. As the authors note, both Hong Kong and Shanghai operated as symbiotic banking centers in the prewar era. Clearly, that was the product of a specific series of historical circumstances. Hong Kong's relatively sophisticated economy, well-regulated market, and liberal international policies have granted the region a very well-developed financial system with a great deal of participation by multinational financial companies. However, given the early stage of development of China's own financial markets, Hong Kong's real existing advantages are insufficient to guarantee a continued role in the future equivalent to the current day. Much will depend on policy decision made in Hong Kong and Beijing. Current developments provide grounds for optimism. Up to the current day, policy changes are being made that should make it easier and more profitable for Hong Kong's financial sector to act as a financial entrepôt.

References

Acharya, Viral V., and Lasse Heje Pedersen. 2005. Asset pricing with liquidity risk. *Journal of Financial Economics* 77 (August): 375–410.

Amihud, Yakov. 2002. Illiquidity and stock returns: Cross-section and time-series effects. *Journal of Financial Markets* 5 (January): 31–56.

Bank for International Settlements. 2007. Statistical annex. *Bank for International Settlements Quarterly Review,* (June).

Bowers, Tab, Greg Gibb, and Jeffrey Wong. 2003. *Banking in Asia: Acquiring a profit mindset.* Singapore: Wiley.

Diamond, Peter A. 1982. Aggregate demand management in search equilibrium. *Journal of Political Economy* 90 (5): 881–94.

Eichengreen, Barry, and Pipat Luengnaruemitchai. 2004. Why doesn't Asia have bigger bond markets? NBER Working Paper no. 10576. Cambridge, MA: National Bureau of Economic Research.

Hong Kong Exchanges and Clearing Limited. 2007. *Monthly statistics.* http://www.hkex.com.hk/futures/statistics/index_MR.htm.
Hong Kong SAR Government. 2005. *Hong Kong annual yearbook, 2005.* Hong Kong: Hong Kong SAR Government.
Kwong, Robin, Sundeep Tucker, and Anuj Gangahar. 2007. China on course to lead world IPO league. *Financial Times,* July 5.
Pastor, Lubos, and Robert F. Stambaugh. 2003. Liquidity risk and expected stock returns. *Journal of Political Economy* 111 (June): 642–85.
Schenk, Catherine. 2003. Banking crises and the evolution of the regulatory framework in Hong Kong 1945–70. *Australian Economic History Review* 43(2): 140–54.
World Federation of Exchanges. 2007. *Monthly statistics.* http://www.worldexchanges.org/WFE/home.asp?menu=436&document=4822.

Comment   Peter Nicholas Kriz

Introduction

In a rather provocative chapter, McCauley and Chan use a combination of descriptive statistics and counterfactual estimations to persuade readers of two facts regarding Hong Kong's fate as international financial center. One, Hong Kong possesses marked leadership over Shanghai in international banking, foreign exchange, derivatives, capital market development, and internationalization, and these current advantages are of importance for how one should consider their futures. Two, recent trends portend a growing rather than diminishing gap in favor of Hong Kong with respect to the relative financial strength of these two cities. In light of their findings, the authors conclude that rather than weaken in the face of China's renaissance, Hong Kong's position as the de facto center of international finance in China should strengthen, and its financial leadership over Shanghai be retained.

My comments on this chapter are organized into three sections. First, I ask a number of questions issues related to Hong Kong's strength relative to Shanghai. In doing so, I provide some needed context to the interpretation of current data and future projections. Second, I critically discuss the main analytical feature of the chapter, the counterfactual estimation. I approach their findings from four theoretical considerations, each of which offers a different characterization of future expectations and suggests a more holistic perspective on the counterfactuals. Finally, I conclude with a few parting thoughts on economic research on China and other emerging markets.

Peter Nicholas Kriz is an assistant professor of economics at Singapore Management University.

Hong Kong's Relative Strength: A Fait Accompli?

To gain a robust appreciation of Hong Kong versus Shanghai's financial past, present, and future, one must deconstruct the myriad of facts and figures that are currently available. I suggest a three-step approach. First, develop an understanding of the economic and political processes that explain the recent past. Next, evaluate the current state of affairs based not only on the past processes but also on current forces and expectations of the future. Finally, make projections into the future based on both an understanding of processes that drive the present and also on how those processes might change going forward. Without a thorough approach to uncover the fundamental political economy that has produced the remarkable dynamism of China this past century, it would be near impossible to provide plausible projections as to the financial future of Hong Kong versus Shanghai.

To frame this analysis, I ask three sets of questions:

- One, what explains Hong Kong's current edge over Shanghai in international finance? What are the historical processes that explain the development of finance in Hong Kong and Shanghai?
- Two, is the current nature of Hong Kong finance different from that of Shanghai? Are there obstacles preventing Shanghai from matching the services offered by Hong Kong to international capital? How would Hong Kong's leadership be threatened by the developing renaissance of Shanghai finance?
- Three, what should the monetary integration of China imply for the future of finance in Hong Kong and Shanghai in both absolute and relative terms? Will economic development in China raise all boats and raise them proportionately? Is the penetration of Hong Kong-based finance into China any different from that of Shanghai? If so, how?

What Explains Hong Kong's Current Edge
over Shanghai in International Finance?

Unfortunately, the authors do not sufficiently address the question of what explains Hong Kong's relative success. Yes, it is true that Shanghai is more domestically focused, more closely tied to government bonds, and has natural leadership in commodities, but the advantages of Hong Kong are largely the result of historical legacy. For both cities, domestic and international political economy have defined their historical evolution.

From 1937 to 1992, excepting brief periods of during the Second World War and the Chinese civil war, international finance in Shanghai was effectively shut down. As a communist victory on the mainland became apparent, domestic human capital, technical expertise, and the entire international financial community fled Shanghai, primarily for Hong Kong. Therefore, by edict, finance in Shanghai turned wholly public and domestic. Even the economic liberalization that began in Shenzhen (Guangdong) in 1979 bypassed Shanghai for more than a decade. Not until 1992 did international financial operations resume with the first significant boom in economic activity. From this tumultuous perspective of history, the phoenixlike rise of Shanghai's financial community has been truly extraordinary and without historical precedent.

In comparison, Hong Kong has been the beneficiary of four fortuitous historical blessings. One, as the seat of British Colonial Empire in East Asia, Hong Kong was endowed with the legal and institutional frameworks of the world's leading capitalist nation. It was also plugged into a global network of the largest players in international finance and had direct access to London, then the undisputed financial center of the world. Two, Hong Kong was the regional depository of human capital and technical expertise in international finance that poured out of China between 1945 and 1949. More than merely a technical boost, the immigration *sinified* Hong Kong's human capital and exposure to mainland business networks far more than it had been under the British. Three, with these networks firmly in place by 1979, Hong Kong was ideally positioned, geographically and operationally, to help finance protoprivate enterprises in the Special Economic Zones (SEZs) of nearby Cantonese-speaking Guangdong. The proximity of Hong Kong and the prohibition of international finance in Shanghai effectively gave Hong Kong a thirteen-year head start in Shenzhen and with private financial dealings with China. As a result, Hong Kong was ideally suited to handle a large proportion of international capital flows entering China during the boom that started in earnest in the early 1990s.

A comparative analysis of their recent financial histories suggests that Hong Kong was handed enormous advantages over Shanghai by history, by the accident of war and implicitly by design. Only in the past fifteen years has Shanghai had any opportunity to regain its international stature. Rather than emphasize Hong Kong's advantages over Shanghai as a clear indication of Hong Kong's inherent superiority, perhaps the authors should have given more perspective to the distinctive influences of history. It would have been interesting to examine in detail the initial years of Shanghai's renaissance and its implications for Hong Kong's future.

Is the Nature of Hong Kong Finance Different from That of Shanghai?

The authors also fail to address this question of inherent differences. Although they do acknowledge that Hong Kong's financial leadership may be temporal, they do not provide any behavioral or structural insights into how Hong Kong's approach to international finance is any different from that of Shanghai. Understanding any differences in objectives, constraints, or culture would be essential in predicting the future success of Hong Kong in Chinese financial development.

Nor do the authors suggest the existence of obstacles preventing Shanghai from eventually offering equivalent services to international capital as Hong Kong. Should they in fact exist, they would ultimately be first-order importance. Knowledge of any barriers would affect the relative speed at which Shanghai closes the gap and whether the gap will ever be closed. Understanding these obstacles would also help us determine whether the future of China will feature one or two centers of international finance. Perhaps most important, the existence of obstacles would provide observable indicators that would help evaluate health of both centers.

To promote the supposition that Hong Kong has something special that will prevent Shanghai from eventually dominating international finance in China, the authors could have provided arguments based on either economic or institutional determinants. A short list of factors might include technical efficiency; capacity and economies of scale; human capital; the commitment of and interactions with big players; better ties to real domestic activity, product innovation and customization; and legal, political, and social institutions. Without clear determination of the processes driving Hong Kong's advantage, it is difficult to rule out that Hong Kong's advantages are historical accidents with a finite lifetime.

What Should Monetary Integration Imply
for the Future of Finance in Both Cities?

Of course, with China there are two forms of monetary integration: domestic (with Hong Kong) and regional (with Asia). With both, the authors rightly point out that economic development in China thus far appears to be raising all boats. However, their analysis essentially extrapolates current advantages enjoyed by Hong Kong into the future, thereby implying that both financial centers will expand proportionately. Yet it is not likely that government policy will remain passive on such a fundamental issue as determining the center of international finance in China. It seems clear that the combination of global politics and domestic public policy more than natural economic forces has shaped the financial landscape in favor of Hong Kong. If Beijing does intervene and actively promotes one center over the other, then current trends may contain little to no predictive power going forward.

Moreover, it is not altogether obvious that Hong Kong's economic advantages will continue nor for how long. The authors understate the incredible trends in Shanghai since 1992. They leave unaddressed the question of whether the penetration of Hong Kong-based finance into China is any different from that of Shanghai. The authors do not explore the determinants of financial market penetration and expansion nor argue why Hong Kong might possess special advantages over Shanghai. As the clear financial center of Cantonese-speaking China, it remains to be seen whether Hong Kong can extend to greater China the linguistic and cultural advantages it clearly had in Shenzhen and Guangzhou.

Given the absence of any effort to explain the source of Hong Kong's advantages over Shanghai or to provide some basis for how one should predict the future development of international finance, I am left to conclude that the authors' depiction of Hong Kong's strength relative to Shanghai is somewhat of a statistical tautology, a fait accompli. That Hong Kong is clearly ahead of Shanghai in virtually every financial category and continues to leverage its advantages is not particularly interesting nor is it illuminating with respect to future expectations. To provide a more persuasive analysis, the authors should provide some accounting for how history, political economy, and market integration will shape the future fortunes of Shanghai and Hong Kong.

Counterfactual Estimation: Alternative Theoretical Perspectives

In order to estimate the size of China's international banking position and the relative share that might be expected of Hong Kong and Shanghai, the authors adopt the counterfactual estimation methodology of Lane (2000). They impose the relationship of international banking positions to income and economic openness found in Organization for Economic Cooperation and Development (OECD) countries on Chinese data. Throughout, they assume that Hong Kong's share of China's external position remains stable at 40 percent. They find that growth rates for China's cross-border banking position are expected to quintuple over seven years to half of gross domestic product (GDP). They conclude that the projections for Hong Kong suggest that Hong Kong's strength as a financial center looks stable.

While it is certainly not unreasonable to expect that Hong Kong will remain a great financial center for the foreseeable future, there are a number of theoretical and empirical shortcomings to the authors' use of counterfactual estimation. A proper projection would have addressed the deeper economic and political questions that will determine Hong Kong's fate. Rather than bother with the limitations of a quantitative model, I would have preferred the authors to have laid down a qualitative road map to better forecast the fate of Hong Kong.

In the section that follows, I critically discuss McCauley and Chan from four theoretical considerations: historical legacy, institutions and nonlinearities, political economy, and strategic interactions. From each vantage point, I examine the econometric analysis of the authors and the assumptions that underlie its construction. While no single theoretical perspective owns the market on prognostication, each can contribute to the building of an analytical framework that can better contextualize future expectations for Hong Kong and Shanghai.

Implications of Historical Legacy

As presented, Hong Kong's share in China's international banking position is tautological: imposed by the authors at the recent (albeit stable) trend of 40 percent. Yet the current state of international finance in China is conditional upon its unique historical legacy. To impose an ad hoc value to what constitutes the key dependent variable in this discussion seems to undermine the point of this analysis.

Let's assume for the time being that the recent share of 40 percent is representative of some kind of steady state. If so, it would presume a constancy of underlying institutional factors. Change these factors and the steady state itself would change in virtually any economic model. Yet it is clear that China is in the process of resolving its "liberalization trilemma," that is, the challenge that financial liberalization imposes upon the macroeconomic policy framework.[1] As such, it is fundamentally restructuring its financial, legal, and regulatory institutions and has been doing so since 1979. With institutions undergoing fundamental reconstruction, it is difficult to accept the constant 40 percent assumption assigned to Hong Kong's share of China's international finance. What we may be witnessing is simply a local trend that may bear little resemblance to Hong Kong's share once the country as a whole has reached its global steady state.

Moreover, once the potential of Shanghai's financial sector is fully unlocked, the future path of Hong Kong's share is unlikely to be predictable based on past dynamics. The relative strengths of these two financial giants will be largely determined by how well each financial center can service the needs of international investors and global demands to participate in the development of China. The population data in table 1C.1 suggests that development and urbanization remain in their early stages. Where it has taken place has been in areas where Hong Kong has had natural advantages. Whether Hong Kong can continue to lead Shanghai in more neutral areas remains to be seen, particularly as the latter builds critical mass and technical know-how and the former loses its institutional advantages.

One solution to these criticisms would be use of a structural rather than counterfactual model. To properly address the content of this discussion, one needs a model that can examine how market penetration and global positioning might unfold under varying characterizations of Hong Kong and Shanghai. Such a model would be inherently dynamic, whereby structural and institutional assumptions are nontrivial.

---

1. The financial liberalization trilemma posits that exchange rate flexibility, openness of the capital account, and the extent of domestic financial institutional development are mutually determined: once one dimension is chosen, it endogenizes the other two. See Chow and Kriz (2007) for a complete presentation.

Table 1C.1   Population of China (2005 estimate; in millions)

Overall	
Northwest	89.8
Southwest	173.1
South Central	357.1
East	369.0
Northeast	107.3
North	148.0
Total	1,244.3
Urban	
Northwest	33.6
Southwest	50.0
South Central	107.4
East	171.6
Northeast	56.4
North	55.4
Total	474.4 (38%)

Source: China Business World.

Institutions and Nonlinearity

Given the internal dynamism of China, it is would seem essential to look more closely look at the role of institutions. However, the authors implicitly ignore institutions in both their argumentation and in the way in which the counterfactual estimation is structured. Imposition of data from OECD countries imposes a stable and advanced level of capitalistic institutional development onto China. Doing so avoids the messy although important fact that China has been undergoing a process of fundamentally reconstructing its institutions from those of Maoist Communism.

One outcome of this form of exogenous imposition is that econometric fit will likely overpredict strength during early years of weak institutions and underpredict the same fit in later years of the forecast. I suggest two solutions. One, the authors should capture the effect of evolving institutions. Doing so would address the issue of nonlinearities presently in their estimations. Two, the authors can find data from emerging markets that have successfully reached an advanced level of financial development. The growth dynamics would be a better model for China than that of countries whose capital market development has always been at a relatively high and constant level.

Political Economy

The study of international finance in China *is* the study of domestic and international political economy. As we have noted, the relative financial strength of Hong Kong and Shanghai was heavily shaped by colonization, war, and Beijing's own domestic policies. If the past century is any guide, China's political economy will continue to evolve. Going forward it would seem safe to assume that Beijing will continue to heavily influence the growth and emphasis of both financial centers.

Political prudence dictates that Beijing play Shanghai off Hong Kong in order to avert an asymmetric dominance of one. Although the authors note the tension between Shanghai and Beijing, they do not offer us any insights into how differences between Beijing and Shanghai or the ambivalence in Hong Kong toward the rule of Beijing might influence political control from Beijing.

The authors also fail to address the possible implications of how Hong Kong will be treated once the Basic Law ceases to be. Most assuredly, markets will move in anticipation of signals from Beijing as to its intentions for Hong Kong. Therefore, by not addressing the question of Beijing's intentions, the counterfactual estimation implicitly assumes no change in political economy going forward. Their analysis assumes further that monetary integration with Hong Kong will not play a role in Hong Kong and Shanghai's fate as financial centers.

A solution to the issue of political economy would be a structural model that allows for an exogenous mechanism that can shift both shares and composition. Such a model would generate a wider range of forecasts and produce a more robust sense of market share given Beijing. Only then can we understand how the economic determinants of financial sector development will interplay with the domestic and international political economy.

Strategic Interactions

The authors present a straightforward discussion that assumes away any strategic interplay between these two financial giants. But presumably these two cities with their historical claims to fame as great centers of Asian finance may have something to say. One would imagine that Shanghai will be leveraging its domestic advantages for a greater share of international financial markets. It would be interesting to learn what form that plan might take. Similarly, it would be interesting to know how Hong Kong will continue to present itself as the financial center for China as Shanghai continues to scale and the competitive landscape turns to new markets in China and Asia.

As we alluded to, Beijing will probably have a direct influence on this game, as it has a major stake in the outcome. What are Beijing's plans? Beijing's preferences (not yet revealed) might include market specialization and two international financial centers. Doing so would facilitate political control and improve national security. Its intervention need not be based on purely economic reasons. Counterfactuals remove any such interaction but instead freeze economic relationships at a point in time. As such, the analysis in the chapter biases the results against Shanghai in a way not too dissimilar to a linear extrapolation.

In light of these criticisms, I am somewhat skeptical with respect to both the point of the counterfactual exercise and the interpretation given to its outcome. That China's financial market potential under capitalism would be huge and that Hong Kong will have a major stake go without saying. But as economists, I feel our efforts should be focused on understanding how the financial markets will develop and through what mechanisms. Borrowing institutional relationships from the OECD, imposing them on China, and fixing the relative share of Hong Kong removes the most interesting and important features of financial market development in China. Bringing the historical, political, institutional, and strategic features back in this discussion would provide a much deeper perspective to what is a deliciously complex topic.

Parting Comments

I offer two concluding comments on this thought-provoking chapter. One, this chapter reminds me that institutional and economic dynamism represents two of the final frontiers in macroeconomic and monetary research. The New Keynesian and new open economy macroeconomics (NOEM) revolutions have only recently begun to address what has been the living reality of policy making in emerging markets, particularly those countries undergoing postsocialist transition. The profession needs to introduce more evolutionary political and institutional mechanisms as well as evolving economic structure into mainstream research on emerging markets. In my research work with the ASEAN+3, I am repeatedly struck by the need for economics to reach back to its intellectual roots in political economy. We should always reflect upon the deep institutional and political assumptions that underlie our elegant models. If we were to take a more holistic approach in emerging markets, then perhaps our record in emerging markets to date would be more enabling than it has been in the past thirty years.

Two, I am left mesmerized by the questions of whether Hong Kong will be able to effectively compete with Shanghai once Shanghai's gloves are off and how Hong Kong will manage their *raison d'être* as a part of the People's Republic of China. I simply do not know the answer to either. However, as a market socialist economy, it is certain that China will continue to direct its development from Beijing. Time will tell how Hong Kong will fit into her plans.

References

Chow, Hwee Kwan, and Peter Nicholas Kriz. 2007. The financial liberalization trilemma and regional policy cooperation: Fresh perspectives for emerging markets in Asia. Paper prepared for presentation at the Singapore Economic Review conference, Singapore, August 2–4.
Lane, R. Philip. 2000. International investment positions: A cross-sectional analysis. *Journal of International Money and Finance* 19:513–15.

2

Listing Policy and Development of the Tokyo Stock Exchange in the Prewar Period

Yasushi Hamao, Takeo Hoshi, and Tetsuji Okazaki

2.1 Introduction

The postwar Japanese financial system has been known as a bank-centered system, in which banks played a central role in corporate finance and governance. The mainstream view in the literature on economic history argued that the bank-centered system has a long history in Japan with its origin dating all the way back to the late nineteenth century, when Japan embarked upon its modern economic development (Bank of Japan, Institute for Monetary and Economic Studies 1986, 1995; Ishii 1997, 1999). Recent empirical studies have established, however, that the prewar Japanese economic system in general was substantially different from the postwar system, and, in particular, the financial system was characterized by large and active securities market with shareholders (not bankers) playing the central role in corporate finance and governance (Fujino and Teranishi 2000; Miwa and Ramseyer 2002; Okazaki 1995, 1999a,b, 2000; Okazaki, Sawada, and Yokoyama 2005; Hoshi and Kashyap 2001; Teranishi 2003).

The empirical evidence to support the importance of the stock market in

Yasushi Hamao is an associate professor of finance and business economics at the Marshall School of Business, University of Southern California. Takeo Hoshi is the Pacific Economic Cooperation Professor in International Economic Relations at the School of International Relations and Pacific Studies at the University of California, San Diego; a research associate of the Tokyo Center of Economic Research; and a research associate of the National Bureau of Economic Research. Tetsuji Okazaki is a professor of economics at the University of Tokyo.

We thank Takatoshi Ito, Andrew Rose, Youngjae Lim, Masaya Sakuragawa, and other participants of the conference for providing valuable comments. We also thank Leslie Hannah, Anil Kashyap, Craig McIntosh, Ulrike Schaede, participants of the conference in memory of Gary Saxonhouse (December 2007 at the University of Michigan), and two anonymous referees for helpful comments and suggestions. All remaining errors are our own. Financial support from the Ministry of Education and Science is gratefully acknowledged.

prewar Japan mostly comes from the data from the 1920s and the 1930s. Although the data constraint becomes more severe as we move back time, a closer look at the earlier period reveals that the size of the Japanese stock market was relatively small during the first forty years of its existence. Then it took off to be a very active and important source of industrial funds. It is not surprising that the stock market started small, but it continued to be (relatively) small for the next forty years and then started to grow rather suddenly.

This chapter asks why the Japanese stock market developed in the way it did in the prewar period. To do this, we examine the development of the Tokyo Stock Exchange (*Tokyo Kabushiki Torihikijo*, TSE hereafter), which was established as the first stock exchange in Japan in 1878 and grew to be the largest stock exchange in prewar Japan.[1] Although the TSE was the first formal stock exchange in Japan and continued its dominance (except for a brief period in the late 1890s when many new stock exchanges were established), its absolute size was relatively small in the first forty years. Moreover, for these forty years, most of the companies listed on the TSE operated locally in Tokyo and nearby areas. We ask why the TSE stayed small and local for a substantial time after its establishment in 1878 and why it rather suddenly started to grow in the late 1910s to eventually become a sizable stock exchange with the nationwide scope in the following decade.

There has been little research on the prewar Japanese stock exchanges, especially for the period before the 1920s.[2] The main impediment has been the difficulty of obtaining data. Thus, one contribution of this chapter is the compilation of relevant data that used to be scattered around in various places. For example, we have constructed a comprehensive list of the companies listed on the TSE for each year from 1878 to 1936 from internal documents at the TSE and various other supplementary materials. The database has been augmented by adding company attributes such as industry classification, size, and the year of establishment.

We have also built another panel database, which contains basic financial information for all the cotton spinning companies that include both listed and nonlisted companies. The database contains 142 companies for the period of 1905 to 1936. This database allows us to examine the listing decision of each firm on the TSE.

The chapter is organized as follows. The next section presents an overview of financial system and stock market in prewar Japan and confirms the importance of the stock market in the prewar financial system. Section 2.3

---

1. When the exchange was reorganized and reopened under the occupation of the Allied Forces in 1949, the Japanese name was changed to *Tokyo Shōken Torihikijo* (literally meaning Tokyo Securities Exchange). The English name, however, continued to be Tokyo Stock Exchange.
2. The important exceptions that we are aware of are Shimura (1970), Noda (1980), and Kataoka (1987).

examines the development of the TSE in the prewar period. We find that the market was initially small and the listed companies were predominantly those in the Tokyo area. The TSE, however, started to grow suddenly in the late 1910s. Section 2.4 argues that the sudden spurt of growth cannot be explained by macroeconomic conditions such as the World War I boom. Section 2.5 studies the changes in the listing requirements in the TSE over time to see how the growth of the TSE was influenced by changes in its listing criteria and listing policy. Section 2.6 proposes a theoretical argument that can explain the development path of the TSE in the prewar period. The explanation focuses on an externality in a company's decision to list on a stock exchange: one company's decision to list on a stock exchange may increase the attractiveness of the stock exchange to other companies by increasing the size of the market. Section 2.7 uses the database for cotton spinning firms and analyzes their listing decisions and obtains the result that is consistent with the argument in section 2.6. Section 2.8 concludes.

2.2   Japanese Stock Market in the Prewar Financial System: An Overview

The size of the stock market in prewar Japan was substantial. Figure 2.1 shows the total market value of the stocks listed on all the stock exchanges in Japan divided by gross national product (GNP; gross domestic product [GDP] after 1955). In the prewar period, this ratio was around 1.0, which

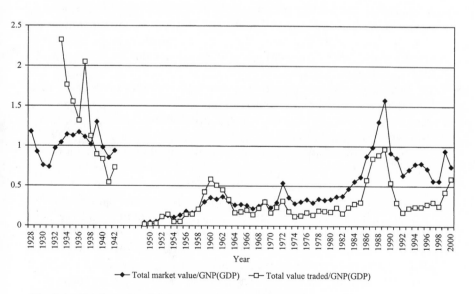

Fig. 2.1   Stock market development in Japan: 1928–2000
Sources: TSE, Tokyo Stock Exchange Annual Statistics, various issues; TSE, TSE Factbook (2004), Okawa (1974), Cabinet Office Socio-Economic Research Institute (2001).

is substantially higher than that in the postwar period, except during the stock market boom in the late 1980s. In particular, the ratio was consistently lower than 0.3 in the postwar high-growth period (1951 to 1973). The prewar stock market was large also in terms of the transaction volume. Just before the start of Sino-Japanese War in 1937, the total volume of the shares traded on all the exchanges was 2 to 2.5 times greater than GNP. On the other hand, the ratio was only 0.1 to 0.6 in the high-growth period, and it was lower than 1.0 even in the stock market boom of the late 1980s.

Table 2.1 compares the size of the prewar Japanese stock market to that of the prewar stock market in the United States and those of the stock markets in various countries (including Japan and the United States) in the early 1990s. The international data for the 1990s come from Demirguc-Kunt and Levine (2001), who report three measures of the stock market size for sixty-one countries: total market value of the listed stocks divided by GDP, the total value of the stocks traded in a year divided by GDP, and the latter divided by the former (turnover ratio). For comparison, we added data for Japan and the United States in 1936. The table shows that even though Japan was much less developed than the United States, the stock market in Japan in 1936 was much larger and more actively traded than that in the United States in 1936. Even compared with most of the countries (including Japan itself) in the 1990s, Japan's stock market in 1936 was much larger.

Another way to see the importance of the stock market in prewar Japan is to examine the sources of funds for corporations. Table 2.2, which reproduces table 2.3 in Hoshi and Kashyap (2001, 36), shows the sources of funds for the private nonfinancial corporate sector in prewar Japan. The original source of the data is Fujino and Teranishi (2000), which is considered to be the definitive work on the prewar pattern of corporate financing. The table shows the average proportion of each source of funds calculated from the levels of claims for three (overlapping) subperiods: 1902 to 1915, 1914 to 1929, and 1928 to 1940. Each subperiod uses a different primary data source for estimation.[3]

Table 2.2 shows that the shareholders contributed the majority of funds in each of the three subperiods. The proportion of paid-in capital and reserves was about 60 percent to 80 percent of the total capital and liabilities. In contrast, the proportion of the bank borrowings was small. Even if we assume all the borrowings come from banks and interpret all the bills payable as disguised bank borrowings (because some firms had their own bills discounted by banks), the amount of bank borrowings was never higher than 20 percent of the total funds in the corporate sector.

Having confirmed the importance of the use of equity and the stock market in the prewar Japanese financial system, let us now look at how it all

---

3. See the note for table 2.3 in Hoshi and Kashyap (2001, 36) for more details on the primary sources of data.

Table 2.1   **International comparison of stock market size**

	GDP per capita, 1990–1995 (US$)	Market capitalization/ GDP	Total value traded/ GDP	Turnover ratio
Japan 1936	830	1.17	1.32	1.12
United States 1936	6,727	0.72	0.25	0.34
Argentina	4,039	0.11	0.04	0.34
Australia	14,314	0.71	0.33	0.43
Austria	13,177	0.12	0.08	0.64
Bangladesh	194	0.04	0.01	0.09
Barbados	4,777	0.21	0.00	0.02
Belgium	14,482	0.36	0.05	0.15
Bolivia	755	0.02	0.00	0.01
Brazil	2,346	0.19	0.12	0.56
Canada	17,285	0.59	0.29	0.47
Chile	2,725	0.84	0.09	0.10
Colombia	1,432	0.13	0.01	0.10
Costa Rica	1,867	0.07	0.00	0.03
Cyprus	6,588	0.22	0.02	0.11
Denmark	17,023	0.34	0.16	0.45
Ecuador	1,322	0.10	0.01	0.14
Egypt	1,042	0.10	0.02	0.14
Finland	15,892	0.29	0.12	0.34
France	15,232	0.33	0.17	0.50
Germany	16,573	0.24	0.28	1.13
Ghana	533	0.15	0.00	0.03
Great Britain	11,794	1.13	0.55	0.48
Greece	6,552	0.15	0.06	0.36
Honduras	751	0.05	0.02	0.67
Hong Kong	10,538	1.96	1.08	0.52
Iceland	18,940	0.01	0.08	n.a.
India	385	0.28	0.08	0.35
Indonesia	609	0.18	0.08	0.45
Iran	2,397	0.04	0.01	0.21
Ireland	9,014	0.26	0.14	0.62
Israel	9,260	0.33	0.19	0.70
Italy	11,505	0.17	0.08	0.42
Jamaica	1,711	0.42	0.05	0.10
Japan	15,706	0.79	0.28	0.36
Jordan	1,289	0.65	0.12	0.20
Kenya	441	0.16	0.00	0.03
Korea	3,909	0.37	0.44	1.22
Malaysia	2,929	2.01	1.14	0.50
Mauritius	2,125	0.27	0.01	0.05
Mexico	2,952	0.32	0.13	0.41
Nepal	200	0.05	0.00	0.04
The Netherlands	13,955	0.69	0.43	0.56
New Zealand	9,492	0.49	0.14	0.27
Nigeria	551	0.06	0.00	0.01

(*continued*)

Table 2.1   (continued)

	GDP per capita, 1990–1995 (US$)	Market capitalization/ GDP	Total value traded/ GDP	Turnover ratio
Norway	20,135	0.26	0.14	0.53
Pakistan	436	0.16	0.06	0.34
Panama	1,950	0.09	0.00	0.04
Peru	1,292	0.11	0.04	0.30
The Philippines	734	0.52	0.15	0.26
Portugal	4,822	0.13	0.05	0.38
Singapore	11,152	1.37	0.70	0.50
South Africa	2,379	1.66	0.12	0.08
Spain	7,286	0.30	0.23	0.63
Sri Lanca	538	0.16	0.02	0.12
Sweden	18,982	0.62	0.33	0.47
Switzerland	19,530	0.98	0.76	0.74
Thailand	1,503	0.57	0.40	0.77
Trinidad and Tobago	3,685	0.01	0.10	n.a.
Tunisia	1,534	0.10	0.01	0.09
Turkey	2,259	0.14	0.16	1.04
United States	19,414	0.80	0.62	0.73
Urguay	2,514	0.01	0.00	0.03
Venezuela	3,167	0.12	0.03	0.26
Zimbabwe	804	0.23	0.01	0.07
Mean	6,547	0.39	0.17	0.35

Notes: Except for Japan 1936 and United States 1936 data, numbers are taken from De-murgüc-Kunt and Levine (2001). The data for Japan 1936 are from TSE (1937), except for the GNP data. Per capita GNP for Japan in 1936 is computed by dividing the GNP figure in Okawa (1974) by the population figure in Umemura (1988). It is the converted into U.S. dollars at the exchange rate in 1936 and translated to the 1990–1996 value by using GDP deflators in Gordon (1986) and the U.S. Council of Economic Advisors (2003). The U.S. 1936 data except for GNP figure are from the U.S. Bureau of the Census (1937). Per capita GNP for the U.S. in 1936 is computed by dividing the GNP figure in Gordon (1986) by the population figure from the U.S. Bureau of Census (1937). It is then translated into the 1990–1995 value by using GDP deflators in Gordon (1986) and the U.S. Council of Economic Advisors (2003). Means do not include Japan 1936 and United States 1936. United States 1936 data include New York Stock Exchange only. n.a. means data not available.

Table 2.2   Funding patterns of Japanese corporations: 1902–1940

Time period	Paid-in capital and reserves	Corporate bonds	Borrowings	Bills payable
1902–1915	82.3	9.5	3.2	5.1
1914–1929	74.8	14.9	4.1	6.2
1928–1940	66.4	18.5	6.7	8.4

Source: Hoshi and Kashyap (2001, 36, table 2.3).
Note: This table shows the percentage distribution of paid-in capital and debt.

started. Following the enactment of the Stock Exchange Act (*Kabushiki Torihikijo Jōrei*) in 1878 (ten years after the Meiji Restoration), the TSE was established as the first stock exchange in Japan. The Stock Exchange Act prescribed that a stock exchange must obtain a license from the government and that it must be organized as a joint-stock company with capital of 100,000 yen or larger (approximately 567 million yen in 2005 prices).[4] The Osaka Stock Exchange (*Osaka Kabushiki Torihikijo*, OSE) followed the TSE in the same year. Although the Ministry of Finance initially intended to license only the two stock exchanges, it changed the policy in 1880 and allowed new exchanges to be established, including Yokohama (1880), Kobe (1883), Kyoto (1884), and Nagoya (1886) (TSE 2002, 7).

In 1887, the Exchange Act (*Torihikijo Jōrei*, also known as the Bourse Act) was passed, which prescribed that all the exchanges, including the stock exchanges, must be membership organizations, not joint-stock companies. The existing stock exchanges were to be abolished when their current licenses expired and to restart as a new membership organization (TSE 2002, 16). The new regulation met strong resistance from the industry and was replaced by the new Exchange Act (*Torihikijo Hō*) in 1893. The new Exchange Act allowed each exchange to choose between a membership organization and a joint-stock company organization. The law continued to provide the legal basis of the exchanges throughout the rest of the prewar period.

The Exchange Act of 1893 also reduced the minimum capital of an exchange (that chose to organize as a joint-stock company) to 30,000 yen. The reduction of the minimum capital level led to the establishment of many new stock exchanges during the economic boom in the late 1890s. Some of the newly established exchanges, however, failed to generate active trading, which convinced the government to shut down small stock exchanges in rural areas (TSE 1928, 6–8; TSE 2002, 16–18; Noda 1980, 240–42).

The bar graph in figure 2.2 shows the evolution of the number of stock exchanges during this period. The number of stock exchanges began with two (Tokyo and Osaka) in 1878. While it increased to five in 1886, it decreased to three in 1891. Then a rapid increase in the number of exchanges began in 1894 as the new Exchange Act with a lower minimum capital standard took effect, and reached a peak of forty-six in 1897. After that it declined again, and has remained around ten throughout the rest of the prewar period.

Figure 2.2 also shows the total revenue of all stock exchanges (in solid line) and the percentage share of the TSE and OSE (in broken lines) revenues. As long-term data on the volume of stocks traded at all the exchanges are not available, we use the revenues (a major part of which was from trade

---

4. This is inflated by the Consumer Price Index (CPI). We linked CPI of Okawa et al. 1967 (134) with CPI by the Statistics Bureau of Ministry of Internal Affairs and Communications at 1955.

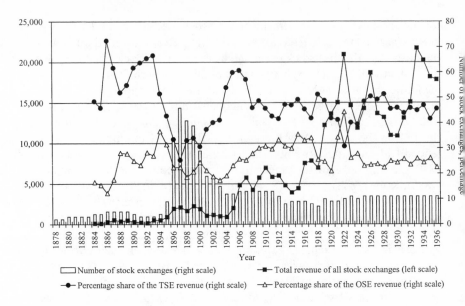

Fig. 2.2   Number of stock exchanges and the revenue share of the TSE
Sources: Toyo Keizai Shinposha (1927); Ministry of Commerce and Industry, *Handbook of Exchanges* (various issues).

commissions) as a proxy for the level of activities in the stock exchanges. The figure shows the total revenue of stock exchanges experienced two significant upward jumps: once from 1904 to 1906 and again from 1918 to 1922. The TSE continued to have the largest revenue throughout these years, except in 1922 when the OSE topped the rankings.[5] The share of the TSE started around 60 to 70 percent, but declined to 20 to 30 percent in the late 1890s, when the number of stock exchanges increased sharply, and then returned to 40 to 50 percent after that.

2.3   Development of the Tokyo Stock Exchange

This section examines the development of the Tokyo Stock Exchange in more detail. The stock market at the TSE was divided into two divisions. The Stock Exchange Act of 1878 classified stock transactions into spot transactions (*genba torihiki*) and futures transactions (*teiki torihiki*). Each spot contract required actual delivery of the traded shares.[6] *Teiki torihiki*

5. The extraordinarily large revenue of the OSE in 1922 resulted from an acquisition of another company. Thus, we can safely say that the TSE had the largest revenue from transaction commissions throughout the prewar period.
6. The Japanese name for spot transaction was changed three times during the prewar period. The Exchange Act of 1893 called it *jiki torihiki*. The organizational reform of the TSE in 1918 discussed in the following introduced the name *genbutsu torihiki*. Finally, the 1922 revision of the Exchange Act used *jitsubutsu torihiki*.

were similar to "time bargains," which were also observed in the financial centers in more advanced economies, such as London and New York.[7] In a *teiki torihiki,* a buyer (seller) could resell (repurchase) the stocks as many times as he wished, until the delivery date, and at the delivery date only the difference between the sell and the purchase was settled in cash (TSE 1928, 454). In the futures market, net cash settlement was the normal settlement method.

Before the revision of the Exchange Act in 1922, the futures market traded contracts with three different settlement days for each individual stock.[8] The shares sold had to be delivered before the settlement day, which was one day before the last trading day of the month (called *tōgiri*), one day before the last trading day of the next month (called *nakagiri*), or one day before the last trading day of the month after the next month (called *sakigiri*). Thus, the settlement period (the period between the start date of a transaction and the delivery date) never exceeded three months.

The 1922 revision of the Exchange Act ordered the exchanges to develop another type of future contracts with settlement period no longer than seven days. Following this legal change, the TSE introduced a new market for the type of transactions called the short-term futures transaction (*tanki seisan torihiki*) in 1924.[9] In the short-term futures, the deliveries of all the transactions that took place in the morning session of a day and in the afternoon session of the previous day had to happen by 2:00 P.M. of the day. The traders were allowed to postpone delivery up to a month, but they were required to pay a deferment fee in such a case.

The new Exchange Act also shortened the maximum settlement period for any futures trading from three months to two months. The old futures market of the TSE, which was now renamed the long-term futures transactions (*chōki seisan torihiki*), continued to use the system of three settlement days by changing those to the 15th of an odd month, and the 5th and the 25th of an even month.

Figure 2.3 shows the evolution of the number of stocks listed on each market of the TSE. Note that it is distinct "stocks," not companies, that are counted here. Large companies in prewar Japan often issued more than one class of shares with different proportions of paid-in parts. As a result, in 1915, for example, while the number of listed stock names was 227, the number of listed companies was 160, which meant one company issued 1.42 classes of shares, on average. As a concrete example, consider a company that had issued 20,000 shares, whose face value was 50 yen each, and

---

7. For a brief description of "time bargains" in London, see Michie (1999, 48–49). For New York, see Geisst (1997, 14).

8. Tokyo Stock Exchange (1932, 70–96) contains a detailed discussion of various transactions in the Tokyo Stock Exchange. Other sources for the discussion here include Osaka Stock Exchange (1928), Tokyo Stock Exchange (1928), and Kuwata (1940).

9. The Osaka Stock Exchange introduced the short-term futures in 1922 immediately following the enactment of the 1922 Exchange Act.

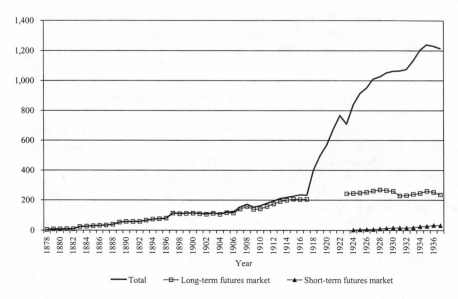

Fig. 2.3   Number of listed stocks on the TSE
Source: TSE (1938).

the capital was all paid-in. The total paid-in capital of the company is 1 million yen. Now suppose this company issues another 20,000 shares with face value of 50 yen each. Under the prewar practice of installment payment of capital, the company collects only a portion of the face value from the shareholders at the issuance. If the company collects 50 percent, the paid-in face value of the new stocks is 25 yen each, and the new total paid-in capital of the company becomes 1.5 million yen. This creates two distinct classes of stocks of the same company, which will be listed as two different stocks on an exchange.

Note also that all the stocks listed on the short-term futures market (after 1924) were also listed on the long-term futures market, and all the stocks listed on the long-term futures market were also listed on the spot market. Thus, the number of the stocks on the spot market is always larger than the number of the stocks on the long-term futures market, which in turn is larger than the number of the stocks on the short-term futures market. Finally, the number of stocks listed in the futures market is missing for the period between 1918 and 1922, presumably lost in the fire that completely destroyed the Tokyo Stock Exchange building during the Great Kanto Earthquake of 1923.

The number of the listed stocks began with four (First National Bank, Tokyo Kabutocho Rice Exchange, Tokyo Kakigaracho Rice Exchange, and the Tokyo Stock Exchange itself) in 1878. Until 1896, all of the listed stocks were listed on both the spot market and the (long-term) futures market, and after that a small number of stocks emerged that were listed only on the spot market.

Figure 2.3 shows that there was a small upward jump in the number of listed shares in 1897 followed by a slight increase in the trend growth rate of the listed shares. A larger jump and a more drastic change in the trend growth happened in 1918. The number of listed stocks increased sharply from 233 to 402 in one year and then continued to grow. In the ten years from 1918 to 1927, the number of listed stocks increased each year by seventy-eight, on average. The growth is compared to a little less than six per year during the previous forty years. The short-term futures market started in 1924, but the number of stocks listed on the short-term futures market was very small. It was just thirty-six in 1936.

Figure 2.4 shows the total amount of (the book value of) paid-in capital of the stocks listed on the TSE. Figure 2.5 plots the same series divided by the nominal GNP of each year. Both figures are qualitatively similar to figure 2.3. The only notable exception is that the series start to decline after 1932 in figure 2.5, which suggests the growth of the book value of the listed companies started to fall behind the growth of GNP in the 1930s.

In figure 2.1 and table 2.1, we saw that the Japanese stock market in the 1920s and the 1930s was very large compared to the size of the economy. Figures 2.3, 2.4, and 2.5 suggest, however, the TSE was relatively small before the 1920s. The size of the market measured in the total book value of listed firms divided by GNP increased steadily from less than 5 percent in

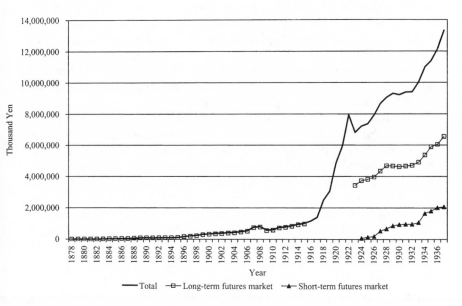

Fig. 2.4   Total book value of listed stocks on the TSE
Source: TSE (1938).

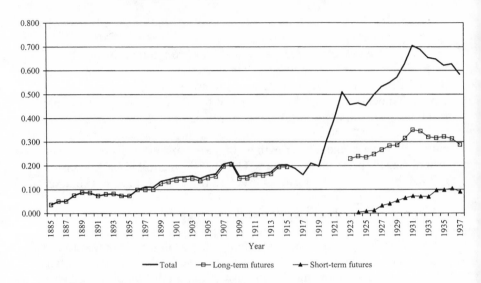

Fig. 2.5   Total face value of listed stocks on the TSE (ratio to GNP)
Sources: TSE (1938); Okawa (1974).

1885 to around 20 percent in 1920 (figure 2.5). The size during this period increased only by 0.5 percentage point every year on average. In the next three years, the size of the market jumped to 50 percent of GNP and continued to grow. In the twelve years from 1919 to 1931, the proportion of the TSE to GNP increased by 4.2 percentage point every year, on average.

Although data constraints prevent us from extending figure 2.1 back to the period before the 1920s, what happened in the TSE, the largest stock market in Japan, suggests that the size of the Japanese stock market as a whole was also relatively small before the 1920s. The growth rate of the market (measured in the book value of listed stocks) was rather small before the late 1910s, and then the market suddenly took off during the 1920s.

Before the 1920s, the TSE was also limited in its regional coverage: the listed companies were mostly from the eastern part of Japan. Over time, however, the TSE attracted companies from all over Japan and eventually became a nationwide stock market. Let us briefly trace changes in the regional distribution of the listed companies. Appendix A explains the sources of the data that we use here.

Table 2.3 shows the regional distribution of the headquarters of listed companies on the TSE. All the four listed companies in 1878 were located in Tokyo. Although the proportion of the companies in Tokyo declined to 50 percent by 1885, the share for the eastern Japan was still higher than 90 percent. The share of companies in the eastern Japan remained high (around 80 percent) in 1900 and 1915, but started to fall after that. The tim-

Table 2.3   Regional distribution of companies listed on the Tokyo Stock Exchange: 1887–1935

	1878	1885	1900	1915	1925	1935
Total	4	24	96	151	695	899
	(100.0)	(100.0)	(100.0)	(100.0)	(100.0)	(100.0)
East	4	22	77	121	536	650
	(100.0)	(91.7)	(80.2)	(80.7)	(77.1)	(72.3)
Hokkaido	0	0	4	2	7	9
	(0.0)	(0.0)	(4.2)	(1.3)	(1.0)	(1.0)
Tohoku	0	2	0	0	8	16
	(0.0)	(8.3)	(0.0)	(0.0)	(1.2)	(1.8)
Kanto	4	17	67	110	487	569
	(100.0)	(70.8)	(69.8)	(73.3)	(70.1)	(63.3)
Tokyo	4	12	54	89	440	506
	(100.0)	(50.0)	(56.3)	(59.3)	(63.3)	(56.3)
Chubu	0	3	6	9	34	56
	(0.0)	(12.5)	(6.3)	(6.0)	(4.9)	(6.2)
West	0	2	19	22	105	171
	(0.0)	(8.3)	(19.8)	(14.7)	(15.1)	(19.0)
Kinki	0	2	11	16	82	135
	(0.0)	(8.3)	(11.5)	(10.7)	(11.8)	(15.0)
Osaka	0	2	4	13	66	105
	(0.0)	(8.3)	(4.2)	(8.7)	(9.5)	(11.7)
Chugoku	0	0	3	2	11	17
	(0.0)	(0.0)	(3.1)	(1.3)	(1.6)	(1.9)
Shikoku	0	0	0	0	1	5
	(0.0)	(0.0)	(0.0)	(0.0)	(0.1)	(0.6)
Kyushu	0	0	5	5	11	14
	(0.0)	(0.0)	(5.2)	(2.7)	(1.6)	(1.6)
Colonies	0	0	0	7	32	42
	(0.0)	(0.0)	(0.0)	(4.7)	(4.6)	(4.7)
Foreign	0	0	0	0	22	36
	(0.0)	(0.0)	(0.0)	(0.0)	(3.2)	(4.0)

Notes: Numbers in parentheses are percentages.
Source: The data are from the authors' calculation based on the database discussed in appendix A.

ing coincides of the acceleration of the number of listed stocks at the TSE that we saw above. By 1935, the proportion of the listed companies in the eastern Japan declined to 72 percent, while the proportion of the listed companies in the Kinki region increased to 15 percent. Thus, over time, the TSE became the exchange with nationwide coverage.

2.4   Macroeconomic Condition and Growth of the TSE

The TSE grew to become the largest stock exchange in Japan with nationwide coverage, but the growth was rather slow, and the listed firms were skewed to eastern Japan during the first forty years of its existence. Why did the TSE originally list relatively small number of stocks but rather suddenly start to list increasing number (and capitalization) of stocks? This and the next sections consider two types of possible explanations: one focusing on macroeconomic conditions and the other focusing on TSE rules on listing new stocks.

It is important to note that the growth of the stock market after the late 1910s was not just a result of accumulation of retained earnings within the firms that had already been listed. As figure 2.5 clearly shows, the stock exchange grew by listing new stocks on the market. Thus, the explanation must include some changes in listing behavior as its key component.

The period when the TSE experienced the very rapid growth coincides with the boom during and after the World War I. Japan joined the war, but it was far from major theaters of war and did not feel disruptive effects of the war very much. Rather, the war presented opportunities for many Japanese businesses to expand their operations in Asia at the cost of Western European business interest. Thus, World War I was a boon to the Japanese economy in general and for its stock market in particular.

Figure 2.6 shows monthly series of stock price index and wholesale price index from July 1914 to December 1936. Both series are made by the Bank of Japan and taken from the Ministry of Finance (various issues). Both indexes are normalized to 100 in July 1914. We indeed find that the stock price appreciated sharply as the war prolonged and stayed high until the crash in 1920. The stock price in 1917 and again right before the crash was

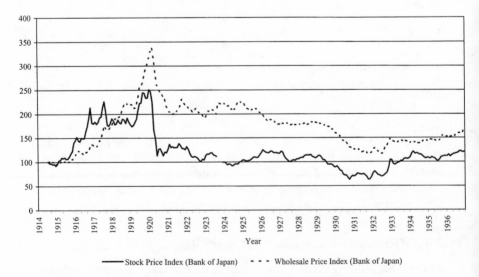

Fig. 2.6   Wholesale price index and stock price index (July 1914 = 100)

Source: Ministry of Finance, *Reference Book on Financial Issues* (various issues).

more than double the level in 1914. The WWI boom led to inflation as well. Measured in wholesale prices, the price level almost tripled between 1914 and 1920.

Thus, the macroeconomic condition in the late 1910s seemed to have been very favorable for the development of a stock market. The appreciation of stock prices, however, ended with a crash in 1920 as figure 2.6 shows. The WWI boom expanded deficit in the balance of payments, which prompted the Bank of Japan to tighten the monetary policy. The Bank of Japan discount rate, which was at 5.11 percent at the end of 1917, was raised twice each year 1918 and 1919 and reached 8.03 percent by the end of November 1919. In March 1920, the TSE experienced a crash, which spilled over to the commodities markets as well. Many stock and commodity exchanges (including the TSE and the OSE) temporarily suspended the trading. The financial crisis reached its peak in May, when the Seventy-Fourth Bank, a large bank in Yokohama that specialized in export finance, failed, which subsequently triggered failures of smaller banks and trading houses.

The high inflation, which tends to encourage investors to shift their investment from bank deposits to stock markets, also ended in 1920. Japan in the 1920s was mostly deflationary, but the listings on the TSE continued to grow well into the 1920s. This suggests it was more than just the WWI boom that caused the growth of the TSE.

Comparing the TSE with other stock markets that also benefited from the WWI boom confirms this point. Figure 2.7 shows the number of listed

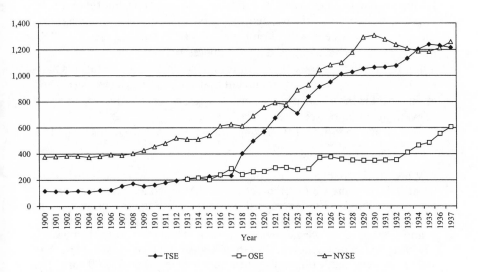

Fig. 2.7   Number of stocks listed: Tokyo, Osaka, and New York stock exchanges
Sources: TSE (1938); Osaka Stock Exchange, *Business Report* (various issues), New York Stock Exchange, *Fact Book* (www.nyse.com).

stocks on the New York Stock Exchange and the OSE, and compares those to the number of listed stocks on the TSE. The United States, like Japan, did not suffer very much from the WWI, and the economy and stock markets experienced huge boom in the 1920s. As figure 2.7 shows, the New York Stock Exchange added new listings in the late 1910s and the 1920s, but the growth rate was not very different from that of the early 1910s. We do not observe a kink in the late 1910s as we do for the TSE listings. We make similar observations for the listings on the OSE. The remarkable and sustained increase in the new listings that we see for the TSE is absent for the OSE. We conclude that the WWI boom is not sufficient to explain the sudden growth of the TSE in the 1910s.

2.5   Listing Criteria and Growth of the TSE

What can explain the sudden take off of the TSE, then? One possible explanation of the pattern of the growth of listed companies on the TSE is the relaxation of listing criteria over time. When a stock exchange starts its operation, it may want to restrict the companies that are listed to be only those that have high profitability or sizable assets to establish the reputation that the exchange deals with quality companies. As the exchange accumulates the reputation over time, it may be able to relax the tight listing regulation marginally, allowing more companies to be listed on the exchange. If we find that the TSE indeed relaxed the listing criteria around 1918, then it could explain the sudden growth of the TSE after that time.

This turns out not to be the case, however. The long-term futures market indeed had listing criteria that were relaxed over time, but there was no important change in 1918 (or nearby years). Perhaps more important, in the spot market, where most of rapid growth after 1918 took place, the TSE does not seem to have imposed any listing restrictions.

Let us first look at the changes in the listing criteria to the futures market. We are not aware of any document that summarizes the listing criteria at the TSE for the whole prewar period. Thus, we need to put together the relevant information scattered in various places.

The earliest mention of the listing restriction that we can find is in TSE (1928):

> When the Exchange Act was passed in 1893, the government instructed the TSE to increase the number of stocks traded as much as possible. Consequently, the TSE replaced the existing listing criteria (number of stocks no fewer than 4,000, total face value not less than 200,000 yen, and total paid-in face value not less than 100,000 yen) with the new criteria (number of stocks no fewer than 3,000, total face value not less than 150,000 yen, and total paid-in face value not less than 75,000 yen). The TSE decided that the stocks that do not satisfy the new criteria should be traded only on the spot market. The new criteria were used from May 1894. (33–34)

Then, following the 1914 revision of the Exchange Act, listing of securities on the futures market required an approval from the Ministry of Agriculture and Commerce (MAC). Accordingly, the MAC set the following listing criteria for the futures market.

(i) Issuing firm must have been established more than 2 years ago.

(ii) Total paid-in face value (of the newly listed class of shares) must not be less than 1,000,000 yen to be listed on the Tokyo or Osaka stock exchange.

(iii) Total paid-in face value (of the newly listed class of shares) must not be less than 500,000 yen to be listed on a stock exchange other than Tokyo and Osaka. (TSE 1963, Part on Institutions and Organizations, 3)

Compared with the 1894 TSE rule that we saw earlier (75,000 yen minimum paid-in face value), the new MAC rule tightened the listing standard by increasing the minimum paid-in face value by more than 1,300 percent, while the general price level only doubled over the twenty years.

In 1915, the MAC added the following criteria for newly listing class of shares in a company that had already listed shares on the futures market (TSE 1963, Part on Institutions and Organizations, 3).

(i) Total paid-in face value (of the newly listed class of shares) must not be less than 500,000 yen to be listed on the Tokyo or Osaka stock exchange.

(ii) Total paid-in face value (of the newly listed class of shares) must not be less than 250,000 yen to be listed on a stock exchange other than Tokyo and Osaka.

These criteria set by the MAC provided the minimum requirement that a firm that wants to list its stocks had to satisfy. The TSE seems to have evaluated some additional aspects that were not explicitly stated as well. The internal rules of the TSE enacted in 1915 prescribed as follows (Research Bureau of the Bank of Japan 1916, 93).

When a joint-stock company requests the TSE to start trading its stocks or debentures, the TSE should examine its articles of incorporation as well as its assets and business status to decide whether the request should be approved or not (Article 1).

Moreover, the revised Exchange Act of 1922 obliged the exchange to set up a council to decide on when a stock or a bond could be listed or delisted.

In May 1921, the listing criteria of the TSE were revised to be the following.

(i) Issuing firm must have been established more than 2 years ago.

(ii) Total face value (of the newly listed class of shares) must be more than 3,000,000 yen, of which more than 1,000,000 yen already paid in; the number of shares must be greater than 60,000.

(iii) For a new class shares of a company that had already listed shares in the futures market, total face value (of the newly listed class of shares) must be more than 2,000,000 yen, of which more than 500 thousand yen already paid in; the number of shares must be greater than 40,000.

These new criteria were used at least until the beginning of the Sino-Japanese War in 1937 (The Research Division of the TSE 1932; Hatano 1938).

In contrast to the futures market, the spot market of the TSE does not seem to have imposed any explicit listing criteria. In a 1932 publication, the TSE stated, "we do not impose any condition on the listing" (TSE 1932, 95) in the spot market. Although we find several documents that spell out the listing criteria for futures market as we saw above, we are not aware of any documents that specify the listing criteria for the spot market. Thus, it seems safe to conclude that the TSE did not have explicit listing criteria for the spot market.

The companies that wished to be listed on the spot market were still required to apply for it. Even this requirement to apply for the listing, however, was eliminated in 1918, and the TSE decided that they can start transaction of a stock and quoting its price without the company's application to be listed on the exchange (TSE 1928, 88).

Figures 2.3, 2.4, and 2.5 suggest that the change in 1918 had a major impact on the subsequent increase of the size of the TSE. The number and amount of shares listed on the TSE increased rapidly after 1918, especially in the spot market.

According to TSE (1928, 88; and other relevant references), the change in 1918 was motivated by the TSE's attempt to bring the spot exchange transactions that took place outside the exchange into the exchange.[10] Since the late nineteenth century, stock trading outside the exchanges was quite active (Kataoka 1987). A large number of stocks were traded over the counters of spot market brokers (*genbutsu don'ya*) and *saitori* brokers intermediated between those brokers. In 1906, these brokers outside the exchange filed an application to the local government of Tokyo to establish a new stock exchange specialized in spot trading. This attempt was not materialized mainly due to the strong opposition from the TSE.

As the outside trading increased, the TSE started to try integrating those trades inside the exchange. The spot market brokers also came to consider that it was convenient to interlink their trading with the trading inside the

---

10. This is in contrast to what happened in New York, where the curb market continued to exist and competed with the New York Stock Exchange (NYSE). In the early twentieth century, an official document by the NYSE wrote "The curb market represents, first, securities that cannot be listed; second, securities in the process of evolution from reorganization certificates to a more solid status; and third, securities of corporations which have been unwilling to submit their figures and statistics to the proper committees of the Stock Exchange" (Michie 1987, 206–7). As the New York curb market started to trade shares of large companies listed on the NYSE, competing with the NYSE, "the over-the-counter market began to emerge in New York, better known as the *unlisted market*," providing competition for the curb market. (Geisst, 1997, 165)

TSE. Thus, in 1918, the TSE invited *saitori* brokers, who intermediated spot transactions outside the TSE, to trade only inside the exchange (Association of the TSE *Saitori* Members 1975, 65, 72). The TSE also set up the Monitoring Department (*kansatsu-bu*) to ensure that spot transactions were conducted within the exchange and following the TSE rules (TSE 1928, 46; TSE 2002, 30; Association of the TSE *Saitori* Members 1975, 72). This change made it difficult for investors to trade shares outside the exchange.

The rapid increase of listed shares in the TSE after this 1918 reform may not be surprising if it was just a result of the TSE's newly listing the stocks that had been traded outside the exchange by the spot traders. If this was the only reason for the rapid expansion of the TSE, the growth would have leveled off after a while, when most of the outside trading was already brought inside the exchange. But figures 2.3, 2.4, and 2.5 show the TSE continued to grow well into the late 1920s. Furthermore, as we examine below, the integration of the outside trading took place rather quickly.

To study how the outside trading was absorbed into the TSE following the 1918 reform, we collected the advertisement that a major spot broker, Momijiya, ran in *Tokyo Asahi Shimbun,* a major newspaper in Tokyo. We obtained the first advertisement of Momijiya in the months of June and December of each year from 1916 to 1921. Then we compared the stocks on the Momijiya advertisement to the listed stocks on the TSE as of the end of March of that year published in *Kin'yū Jikō Sankōsho.* The result is summarized in table 2.4.

Because the new listing policy of the TSE was implemented in September 1918 (TSE 1928, 88), the first time we would observe that impact in table 2.4 is the June 1919 column, which compares the stocks advertised by Momijiya in June 1919 to the stocks listed on the TSE in March 1919. We find the number of stocks advertised by Momijiya but not listed on the TSE, which was around twenty before the change, fell to six by June 1919, and to zero by December 1921. Thus, we can conclude that all the major stocks in the outside market were quickly listed on the TSE following the change in 1918. The outside market was completely absorbed by the TSE by 1921.

The TSE continued to grow even after 1921. This implies that the impact of the policy change in 1918 was more than just absorbing the outside market into the TSE. In this section, we examined if the changes in listing rules on the TSE can explain the pattern of its growth. The listing criteria on the futures market went through several changes, but those are not closely related to the changes in the growth rate of the TSE that we see in figures 2.3, 2.4, and 2.5. Moreover, the growth spurt in the 1920s, which is the most prominent change, was mostly due to the expansion of the spot market. The TSE does not seem to have explicit listing restrictions on the spot market. Prior to 1918, the companies only had to apply to the TSE to be listed. This rule changed in 1918, which led to the sustained growth of the spot

Table 2.4   Stocks advertised by a spot broker (*Momijiya*) but not listed on the Tokyo Stock Exchange (TSE)

	June 1916	Dec. 1916	June 1917	Dec. 1917	June 1918	Dec. 1918	June 1919	Dec. 1919	June 1920	Dec. 1920	June 1921	Dec. 1921
No. of stocks advertised by *Momijiya* (row a)	118	114	115	116	117	115	115	111	102	95	101	97
Of which not listed on the TSE (row b)	28	27	19	28	22	22	6	5	2	1	0	0
row b / row a (%)	23.73	23.68	16.52	24.14	18.80	19.13	5.22	4.50	1.96	1.05	0.00	0.00

Source: Authors' calculation based on the data collected from *Tokyo Asahi Shimbun* (1916–1921) and *Kin'yū Jikō Sankōsho* (various years).

market. Then why did many companies fail to apply for listing before 1918? Because they did not seem to have faced any listing criteria, this suggests they did not find the benefit of being listed. Why? The next section builds an explanation for these questions based on the recent literature on initial public offerings (IPOs).

2.6 Market Liquidity and the Decision to List Stocks

There is a large and growing literature on IPOs and listing decisions of firms, but we find the results of two recent papers especially relevant for our purpose. They are Ellul and Pagano (2006) and Baruch and Saar (forthcoming).

First, Ellul and Pagano (2006) shows that the extent of IPO underpricing is high when the (expected) liquidity of the stock after the IPO is low. Thus, underpricing, which constitutes an important part of the cost of IPO, is decreasing in the expected aftermarket liquidity. Assuming there is some variation in the benefit of IPO across firms, so that only those firms whose benefits are higher than the costs decide to be listed on the stock exchange, we can argue that the number of firms that decide to be listed is a increasing function of the expected liquidity.

Second, Baruch and Saar (forthcoming) provide an example that shows (among other things) that the liquidity of an individual stock is an increasing function of the number of firms listed in the market. Using an example that is a more general case of Baruch and Saar (forthcoming), we show this is indeed the case in appendix B.

Combining these two arguments, we can now establish that the number of listed stocks is an increasing function of the market liquidity, which in turn is an increasing function of the number of listed stocks. This implies a possibility of multiple equilibria. In one equilibrium, the market liquidity is expected to be high, which encourages many firms to be listed and makes the market liquidity indeed high. In another equilibrium, the market liquidity is expected to be low, which leads to a low number of listed firms and low liquidity.

The key to the story here is externality. Market liquidity is an important factor for a company decision to list its shares on the market, but when a company makes its listing decision, it does not consider the effect of its listing on the market liquidity. In this sense, the argument here is closely related to the literature on multiple equilibria in the financial market developed by Diamond (1987) and Pagano (1989a,b), for example. Pagano (1989a) builds a model of risk-averse investors with endogenous supply of corporate equity to show two (or more) equilibria. In one equilibrium, the market for corporate equity is thin, and the price volatility is high, which reduces both demand and supply of stocks and keeps the market thin, while in the other equilibrium, the market is thick and the price volatility is low, which encourages demand and supply of stocks. Pagano (1989b) shows that the positive feedback between trading volume and liquidity can lead traders to concentrate all exchanges on a single market or create a parallel market for large trades.

Applying the dual equilibria argument to the TSE in the prewar period, we argue that the TSE before 1918 may have been in the low market liquidity equilibrium. It was in equilibrium in the sense that that the firms who were not listed did not have incentive to be listed *given* the existing level of market liquidity. From this point of view, the listing policy change in 1918 can be viewed as an exogenous shock that increased the market liquidity. This led to the listings of many companies that were previously not listed. More important, the increased market liquidity should have convinced some firms that they would be better off if their shares are listed. Thus, the 1918 policy reform may have shifted the equilibrium from the low liquidity one to the high liquidity one.

The explanation here assumes that listing on the TSE during the prewar period was very much like the IPO today. We can find evidence that suggests this characterization of listings is reasonable.

First, there are some anecdotes that show the companies decided to list their stocks to increase the capital by attracting new shareholders. For example, Noda (1980, 70–73) reports an example of Kyushu Railroad (*Kyushu Tetsudo*). The Kyushu Railroad was established in 1888 with official capital of ¥11 million, of which ¥7.5 million was planned to be funded initially. Because the financial market condition was rather tight in 1888, the shareholders were required to pay only ¥5 per share (for the par value of ¥50 per share) as the first installment to acquire shares, but collecting such a small portion was already difficult. Only 38.0 percent of the shareholders made the first installment payment by the due date. For the second installment of ¥5 per share that was due in March 1989, only 11.6 percent of the shareholders met the due date.

At this point, Seinosuke Imamura, a director of the Kyushu Railroad, advised the president to list the Kyushu Railroad stock on a stock exchange to facilitate the trades of the stock and to encourage the future installment payments.[11] Following this advice, the Kyushu Railroad listed shares on the TSE and the OSE in 1989. The strategy was successful. The stock price quickly rose above the par (paid-in) value, and the Kyushu Railroad did not have trouble collecting installment payments in time (at least until the financial panic of 1890).

Another example is Miyagi Boseki Dento, which listed its shares on the TSE in 1910. Miyagi Boseki started as a cotton spinning company in 1882

---

11. Seinosuke Imamura was also one of the founders of the Tokyo Stock Exchange and a large securities broker.

near Sendai, Miyagi Prefecture. In 1888, it succeeded in generating electricity using water mills originally designed for cotton spinning machines. In 1899, Miyagi Boseki merged an electricity company in the prefecture, Sendai Dento, and changed the name to add "Dento": Japanese for electric lamps (Kinugawa 1938, 338–46). In 1909, the company established the first hydroelectric power plant in Japan and started providing electricity for lamps in Sendai.

Figure 2.8 shows the official amount of capital, the paid-in capital, and the amount of total assets (book value) for Miyagi Boseki Dento around the listing. The figure shows that Miyagi financed the investment (including the building of the hydroelectric power plant) by collecting unpaid part of the capital first, until the existing shares were fully paid-in in 1909. The company listed its shares on the TSE next year and issued new shares. The figure suggests that the proceeds from the new share issues and subsequent collection of unpaid part of new shares were used to finance the continued expansion of Miyagi.

Figure 2.9 shows the number of shareholders and the top-ten shareholders concentration rate for Miyagi during this period. Before the listing of the shares in 1910, the number of shareholders gradually declined, and the shareholder concentration increased. This suggests that some shareholders failed to meet the required payments for the unpaid part of the shares and lost their rights. After listing the stock in 1910, the number of shareholders increased by more than 50 percent, and the shareholder con-

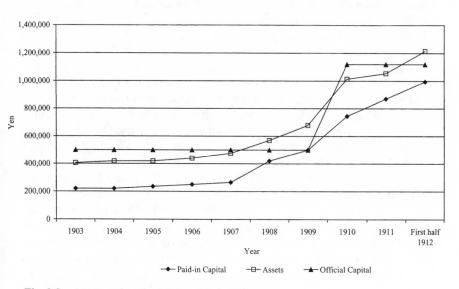

Fig. 2.8   Assets and capital, *Miyagi Boseki Dento*
Source: Miyagi Boseki Dento, Business Report (various issues).

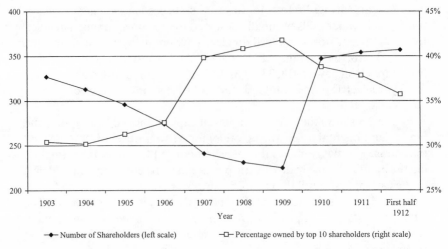

Fig. 2.9   Number of shareholders and ownership concentration of top-ten shareholders, *Miyagi Boseki Dento*
Source: Miyagi Boseki Dento, Business Report (various issues).

centration started to come down, suggesting the listing enhanced the shareholder base substantially.

The examples of Kyushu Railroad and Miyagi Boseki Dento show that the companies consciously decided to list their stock on the stock exchange to broaden the shareholder base and to increase the (paid-in) capital. The listing on the stock exchanges indeed made it easier for the companies to increase the capital.

Additional evidence that shows that listing on the stock exchange broadened the shareholder base and made it easier for the company to raise capital comes from a database of thirty-nine major joint stock companies in Tokyo during the 1890s. We divide the thirty-nine firms into three groups. The stocks of eleven companies were already listed on the TSE before 1890. Five companies are newly listed on the TSE between 1890 and 1899 (four in 1893 and one in 1894). The remaining twenty-three companies were not listed on the TSE (at least until 1900). Figures 2.10 and 2.11 respectively show the average number of shareholders and the average amount of paid-in capital for each of the three groups. To control for the size difference between these groups in 1890 so that we can focus on the difference in growth experience during the 1890s, the figure shows the index number normalizing the average for each group in 1890 to be 100. The figure clearly shows the newly listed firms increased the number of shareholders and the amount of paid-in capital during the 1890s. The already listed firms and the unlisted firms, on the other hand, did not increase the number of shareholders

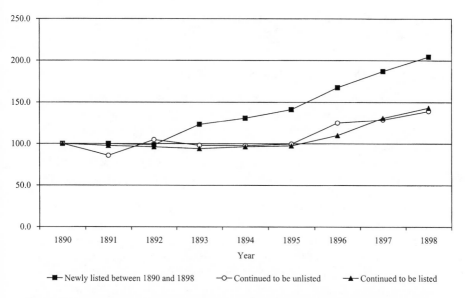

Fig. 2.10   Average number of shareholders, thirty-nine firms in Tokyo (1880 = 100)
Source: Tokyo Prefecture, *Statistical Handbook of Tokyo Prefecture* (various issues).

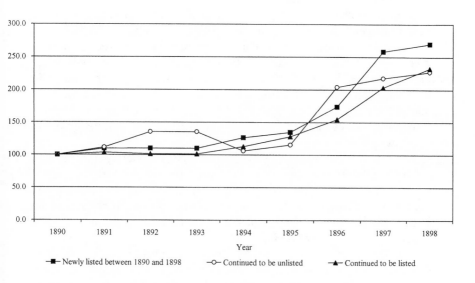

Fig. 2.11   Average amount of paid-in capital, thirty-nine firms in Tokyo (1880 = 100)
Source: Tokyo Prefecture, *Statistical Handbook of Tokyo Prefecture* (various issues).

very much. They increased the amounts of paid-in capital, but the growth rate was lower than that for the newly listed firms.

2.7   Listing Decisions of Cotton Spinning Firms

In this section, we use the data from cotton spinning industry to test a key implication of our argument that implies a listing decision depends on the size of the stock exchange. If the stock market is large and has large liquidity, the potential underpricing problem is mitigated, and the net benefit of listing increases. Thus, as a market expands, the likelihood of new listings tends to go up. This section estimates a simple probit model that explains new listing decisions of cotton spinning firms.

Cotton spinning was a leading industry in prewar Japan, and many of these companies were eventually listed on the TSE. More important, consistent data are available on both unlisted and listed companies, which allow us to analyze what factors influenced the decision to be listed. The data on cotton spinning firms are taken from the various issues of the *Menshi Bōseki Jijō Sankōsho* (*Reference Book on the Cotton Spinning Industry*) published by the Japan Cotton Spinning Association. The sample covers the period between 1905 and 1936.

We take all the companies whose financial data are available in the *Menshi Bōseki Jijō Sankōsho* and checked whether they were listed on the TSE at the end of each year by referring to the materials used in section 2.3. Figure 2.12 presents an overview of the sample. The number of firms in each year was twenty-five to thirty-five until the late 1910s and fifty and seventy after that. Of these, the number of firms listed on the TSE was five to six until the late 1910s, and it increased to more than twenty in the late 1920s and 1930s. The number of firms listed on the long-term futures market was nine at the peak (1933 to 1935). Until 1932, the only firm listed on the short-term futures market was Kanegafuchi Bōseki. Nisshin Bōseki was added in 1933.

The cotton spinning industry in Japan was geographically concentrated around Osaka (Takamura 1971). Reflecting this, the proportion of companies located in the eastern regions (Hokkaido, Tohoku, Kanto, and Chubu) was 42 percent at the peak (1936) and 14 percent at the bottom (1914). (See figure 2.13.) Companies from the eastern regions nevertheless represented a higher proportion of listed companies on the TSE. This suggests that there was home bias with respect to listing on the TSE. The magnitude of the bias substantially declined after the late 1910s.

To examine the determinants of listing on the TSE by cotton spinning firms, we estimate a regression model similar to those estimated by Pagano, Panetta, and Zingales (1998) in their study of the Italian IPOs. They analyzed the determinants of IPOs by using panel data of Italian firms in 1982

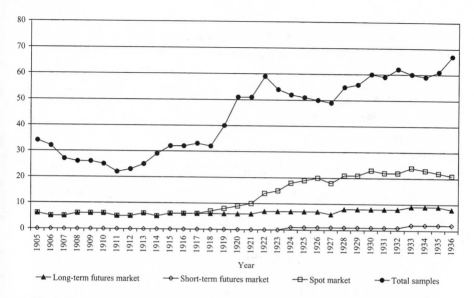

Fig. 2.12   Number of cotton spinning firms listed on the TSE: 1905–1936
Source: See next.

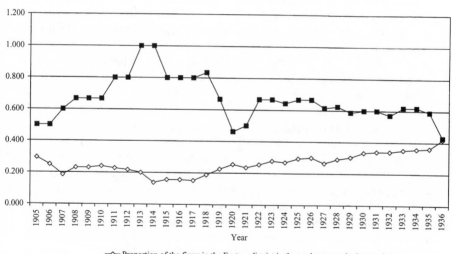

Fig. 2.13   Regional bias of cotton spinning firms listed on the TSE
Source: See text.

to 1992. Using the firms that conformed to the listing criteria for the Milan Stock Exchange but were not listed, they regressed the dummy variable denoting IPO to several explanatory variables on corporate attributes and the environment. They found that a firm is more likely to decide to go public if the amount of sales is high, the sales growth is high, it has high return on assets (ROA), and the firms in the same industry that are already listed show high market-to-book ratio.

The probit model that we estimate is the following:

$$Pr(L_{it} = 1) = \Phi[\beta_0 + \beta_1 \log(CAP_{it-1}) + \beta_2 Age_{it-1} + \beta_3 ROE_{it-1} + \beta_4 East_i + \beta_5 \log(TSE_{t-1})],$$

where L_{it} is the dummy variable that takes 0 if firm i has never listed on the TSE as of year t. It takes 1 if the firm was newly listed on the spot market of the TSE in year t. The companies that were newly listed on the TSE in year t are dropped from the sample in year $t + 1$ on. Thus, we try to estimate the factors that influence the new listings. The expression $\Phi(\cdot)$ denotes a cumulative normal distribution function. CAP is the paid-in capital normalized by the average paid-in capital of the total joint-stock companies in Japan. Age is the years from the foundation of the firm. East is the dummy variable that takes 1 if the headquarter of the firm was located in the eastern regions of Japan, and 0 otherwise. Finally, TSE_t is the total amount of capital of the stocks listed on the spot market of the TSE in year t. If the market size is the important determinant of listing decision of individual firms, we expect to find the coefficient of TSE to be positive.

We estimate the regression separately for two subperiods: the period before 1918 and the period after 1918. The listing policy change in 1918 suggests that the listings before 1918 were initiated by the firms. They had to apply to be listed. Thus, by looking at the listing events, we can study what factors influenced the firm's decision to seek listing. After 1918, the TSE was able to initiate the listing without any requests from the firms. Thus, we can consider some listing events after 1918 continued to be the firms' decision while some listing decisions were done solely by the TSE. The fact that the listing observations after 1918 include these two different types of decisions makes it difficult to interpret the regression result for this period.

Table 2.5 reports the result. The first column shows the estimation result for the period before the 1918 change. The coefficient on CAP is positive though statistically significant only at 10 percent level, suggesting that the probability of listing was higher for large firms. The coefficient on East is positive and statistically significant at 5 percent level, suggesting that there was a home bias in listing on the TSE. The coefficient on TSE is positive though it is statistically significant only at the 10 percent level.

Thus, the result from the period before 1918 suggests that large firms in the eastern part of Japan were more likely to be listed on the TSE. It also suggests larger market size of the TSE encouraged the firms to be listed on

Table 2.5   **Probit model of listing decision**

	1905–1917	1918–1935
log(paid-in capital)	3.004*	0.549***
	(1.699)	(0.205)
Age	0.050	0.013
	(0.074)	(0.013)
ROE	−6.393	0.205
	(4.029)	(1.034)
East	7.099**	−0.090
	(3.512)	(0.346)
log(TSE)	3.749*	−0.318
	(2.128)	(0.382)
No. of observations	296	644

Notes: The dependent variable is a dummy variable that takes one if the company lists its shares on the Tokyo Stock Exchange (TSE) in that year. ROE = return on equity. After the listing event, the company is dropped from the sample, so that all the observations with the dummy variable = 0 are the companies that have never been listed on the TSE. The model is estimated with probit estimation. Numbers in parentheses show the standard errors of the coefficient estimates.
***Significant at the 1 percent level.
**Significant at the 5 percent level.
*Significant at the 10 percent level.

the market, providing suggestive evidence for the key implication of our story.

The second column of table 2.5 reports the results from the period after 1918. Here the only statistically significant coefficient is CAP. This may be a result of large firms continued to be more likely to be listed. Or this may reflect the TSE's preference toward large firms when they listed the stocks without waiting for the applications. If we were able to distinguish the listings initiated by the firms from those initiated by the TSE, we could check whether the listings initiated by the companies continued to be influenced by the market size after 1918 (which is a prediction of our story). Unfortunately, we have not been able to find such information so far.

2.8   Concluding Remarks

The size of the stock market relative to the size of national economy was large in the late 1920s and 1930s Japan. During the first forty years since the establishment of the TSE in 1878, however, the market was relatively small and the listed firms were concentrated in the areas close to Tokyo. This chapter examined why the TSE stayed relatively stagnant during the first forty years and why it suddenly took off in the late 1910s.

We have found a small change in the TSE's policy toward listing in its spot market in 1918. Before 1918, the firms had to apply to the TSE to be listed. After 1918, the TSE started trading some stocks without explicit applications from those firms. We argue that this apparently small policy change allowed the TSE to escape from the low liquidity equilibrium and to take off.

The argument that we advanced to explain the existence of the low liquidity equilibrium in the prewar stock market in Japan can be generalized to consider stock market development in other parts of the world in other times. The possibility that low expected liquidity discourages firms from listing their stocks in the market and justifies the expectation may be quite general.

The self-confirming nature of the expectation about the market liquidity implies several interventions that may be necessary for stock exchanges in developing economies to develop. The TSE solved the problem by listing major companies without waiting for their applications to be listed. Alternatively, a stock exchange (or the government) may be able to subsidize new companies to be listed on the stock exchange. Finally, there may be ways to attract more traders to the stock exchange to increase the market liquidity in general. In this case, what is more important for the liquidity (in the sense that large transactions can take place without changing the market price very much) is the presence of noise traders, as is shown by the models of stock market microstructure (see, for example, Kyle 1985).

Appendix A
Compilation of Listing Data

We have compiled the list of all the listed stocks in 1878, 1885, 1900, 1915, 1925, and 1935.

The information for 1878 and 1885 was taken from the TSE (1928). The TSE (1928) reports the listing (and delisting) dates for all the stocks on the futures market. Similar information is not available for the stocks listed only on the spot market, but this is not a problem for the period before 1896, when all the stocks on the spot market were also listed in the futures market. Thus, we can use the data to create a complete list of listed stocks for 1878 and 1885.

A complete list of the listed stocks and their face values is available in the business reports of the TSE each year from 1900 to 1918. So we take the information for the years 1900 and 1915 from this source. With respect to 1925 and 1935, we take the data on the listed stocks and their face value from the unpublished version of TSE business reports, held at the TSE.

The information on the capital of each company was taken from various government reports, including *Ginkō-ka Hōkoku* (*The Report of the Bank-*

ing Section of the Ministry of Finance), *Ginkō-kyoku Nenpō* (*Annual Report of the Banking Bureau of the Ministry of Finance*), *Teikoku Tōkei Nenkan* (*The Imperial Statistical Year Book*), and *Nōshōmu Tōkei Hyō* (*The Statistics of Agriculture and Commerce*).

In addition to these government reports, we used *Zenkoku Shogaisha Yakuinroku* (*Directory of Corporate Directors*), 1900 and 1912 issues; *Ginkō Kaisha Yōroku* (*Directory of Banks and Companies*), 1925 and 1935 issues; *Teikoku Ginkō Kaisha Yōroku* (*Imperial Directory of Banks and Companies*), 1925 issue; and *Kabushiki Nenkan* (*Year Book of Corporate Stocks*), 1926 and 1936 issues, to collect the location, establishment year, and industry of each listed firm. We use the industry classification employed by the TSE (1938).

The data show interesting changes of industrial composition of listed firms over time. Of the twenty-four companies that had been listed before 1885, we see twenty of them were banks (and nineteen of them national banks). The concentration of listed companies in banking is understandable because the National Bank Act was the only law that defined joint stock companies and the limited liability of shareholders (Miyamoto 1990; Takamura 1996; Yoshida 1998, 28). Legislation for joint stock companies in other industries had to wait till the Commercial Code of 1893.

By 1890, the number of listed companies increased to ninety-six. The number of listed banks declined as the National Bank Act was phased out, but many railway companies were newly listed. Companies in other industries, including coal and petroleum, cotton spinning, and other textiles and foods, were also listed during this period.

By 1915, the number of listed companies increased further, and the industries represented became more diversified. There were 160 listed companies. We can identify the industries for 151 of them. The share of the railway companies declined to 21.2 percent. While new companies running electric railways in the urban areas emerged, large railway companies disappeared due to the nationalization of the main lines in 1906 (Noda 1980, 310–13). The electricity industry saw its share go up sharply from 1900 to 1915. The electricity companies, which were in the early stages of development and needed large-scale investment, actively raised funds from the stock market (Kikkawa 1995, chapter 1). Besides electricity, the shares of such industries as coal and petroleum, sugar, and gas also went up in this period.

By 1925, the number of listed companies reached 712, following the expansion of the spot market after 1918. The industries became even more diverse. The share of the railways, which still had the largest share, was only 8.3 percent. The shares of such industries as insurance, machinery, chemistry and metal, which developed during World War I, went up. In 1935, 919 companies were listed, and the industrial composition was similar to that in 1925.

Appendix B

This appendix shows that the market liquidity is an increasing function of the number of firms listed in the market using a standard model of stock market microstructure. Baruch and Saar (forthcoming) consider a special case of this model and obtain a similar result.

Consider k listed stocks, whose fundamental values depend on n ($\leq k$) signals:

(B1) $$V = M + FS + \Theta,$$

where V is ($k \times 1$) vector of the fundamental values, M is ($k \times 1$) vector of the mean fundamental values, S is ($n \times 1$) vector of signals, F is ($k \times n$) matrix whose (i, j) element shows how the fundamental value of stock i is influenced by the signal j, and Θ is ($k \times 1$) vector of idiosyncratic shocks. F is assumed to have rank k.

We assume the signals are distributed normally, and the covariance matrix of S is given by $\sigma^2 I$, where I is the identity matrix. The idiosyncratic shocks follow the standard normal distribution and are assumed to be independent with each other and with S.

Following Kyle (1985) and the related literature, we assume the market price of a stock is determined by the market maker so that the price is equal to the expected fundamental value of the stock given the order flows the market maker observes. Let Q be ($k \times 1$) vector of the orders by the informed traders, who observe the values of S before they submit the orders. The informed traders decide their position to maximize the expected profit from trading, given the pricing rule of the market maker. The market also has noise traders, whose orders are denoted by ($k \times 1$) vector X. We assume X follows a normal distribution with mean zero and variance $\sigma_x^2 I$. The market maker and both types of traders are assumed to be risk neutral.

Under the assumption of normal distributions, the equilibrium pricing rule and hence the optimal trading strategy for the informed traders become linear functions. Let us denote these as follows.

(B2) $$Q = BS$$

(B3) $$P = M + \Lambda(Q + X),$$

where B is ($k \times n$) matrix whose (i, j) element shows how the informed traders adjust their order of stock i responding to signal j, P is ($k \times 1$) vector of the market prices of the stocks, and Λ is ($k \times k$) matrix whose (i, j) element shows how the market maker adjust the price of stock i when the order flow for stock j changes. Note that the price cannot respond to Q and X differently because the market maker cannot distinguish which orders come from the informed traders.

The informed traders maximize their expected profits from trading:

$$E\pi = E[(\mathbf{V} - \mathbf{P})^T\mathbf{Q}] = (\mathbf{FS} - \Lambda\mathbf{Q})^T\mathbf{Q},$$

where the superscript T denotes the transpose of the matrix, and E denotes the expectation operator. The first order condition is given by:

$$\mathbf{FS} - \Lambda\mathbf{Q} - \Lambda^T\mathbf{Q} = 0.$$

Thus,

$$\mathbf{Q} = (\Lambda + \Lambda^T)^{-1}\mathbf{FS}, \text{ which implies:}$$

(B4) $$\mathbf{B} = (\Lambda + \Lambda^T)^{-1}\mathbf{F}$$

If we divide the variance-covariance matrix of the vector $(\mathbf{V}^T, \mathbf{Q}^T + \mathbf{X}^T)^T$ into submatrices as follows,

$$\text{Var}\begin{pmatrix} \mathbf{V} \\ \mathbf{Q} + \mathbf{X} \end{pmatrix} = \begin{pmatrix} \Sigma_{\mathbf{VV}} & \Sigma_{\mathbf{VQ}} \\ \Sigma_{\mathbf{QV}} & \Sigma_{\mathbf{QQ}} \end{pmatrix}.$$

Then, one can show:[12]

(B5) $$\mathbf{P} = E[\mathbf{V} \mid \mathbf{Q} + \mathbf{X}] = \mathbf{M} + \Sigma_{\mathbf{VQ}}\Sigma_{\mathbf{QQ}}^{-1}(\mathbf{Q} + \mathbf{X}).$$

From equations (B1) and (B2), we can calculate:

(B6) $$\Sigma_{\mathbf{VQ}} = \sigma^2\mathbf{FB}^T$$

$$\Sigma_{\mathbf{QQ}} = \sigma_x^2\mathbf{I} + \sigma^2\mathbf{BB}^T.$$

Substituting equation (B6) into equation (B5) and comparing the result with equation (B3), it is straightforward to see:

(B7) $$\Lambda = \sigma^2\mathbf{FB}^T[\sigma_x^2\mathbf{I} + \sigma^2\mathbf{BB}^T]^{-1} = \mathbf{FB}^T\left[\frac{1}{h^2}\mathbf{I} + \mathbf{BB}^T\right]^{-1},$$

where h denotes the square root of the signal to noise ratio ($\sqrt{\sigma_2/\sigma_x^2}$), which shows up repeatedly in the following calculation.

If Λ is symmetric (which can be confirmed), we can rewrite equation (B4) to get:[13]

(B8) $$\mathbf{B} = \frac{1}{2}\Lambda^{-1}\mathbf{F}.$$

Multiplying equation (B7) from the left by Λ^{-1} and substituting equation (B8), we get:

$$\mathbf{I} = 2\mathbf{BB}^T\left[\frac{1}{h^2}\mathbf{I} + \mathbf{BB}^T\right]^{-1}.$$

Multiplying both sides by $(1/h^2)\mathbf{I} + \mathbf{BB}^T$:

---

12. See, for example, Anderson and Moore (1979, theorem 3.1, 25–28).
13. The algebra used to get to the equation (B9) follow appendix A of Baruch and Saar (forthcoming).

$$\frac{1}{h^2}\mathbf{I} + \mathbf{BB}^T = 2\mathbf{BB}^T.$$

Thus, $\mathbf{I} = h^2\mathbf{BB}^T$.

Substituting equation (B8) into this, we get

(B9) $$\mathbf{\Lambda\Lambda}^T = \frac{h^2}{4}\mathbf{FF}^T.$$

The market liquidity is often defined as "depth" of the market, which is "the ability of the market to absorb quantities without having a large effect on price" (Kyle, 1985, 1330). Following this idea, we can argue the market liquidity is inversely related to the "magnitude" of $\mathbf{\Lambda}$ because a "large" $\mathbf{\Lambda}$ implies that the prices are very sensitive to any changes in order flows. Here we focus on the "magnitude" of $\mathbf{\Lambda\Lambda}^T$ because it moves in the same direction as the "magnitude" of $\mathbf{\Lambda}$, and use the sum of the eigenvalues of this matrix as the measure of the "magnitude."

To consider how the market liquidity changes with the number of stocks listed (k), let us partition the matrix $\mathbf{F}$ into the first $k - 1$ rows and the kth row.

(B10) $$\mathbf{F} = \begin{bmatrix} \mathbf{G} \\ \mathbf{g} \end{bmatrix}$$

Now $\mathbf{G}$ is $[(k - 1) \times n)]$ matrix, and $\mathbf{g}$ is $(1 \times n)$ vector. Similarly, partition $\mathbf{\Lambda}$ into a $[(k - 1) \times (k - 1)]$ matrix and the remaining parts.

(B11) $$\mathbf{\Lambda} = \begin{bmatrix} \mathbf{V} & \mathbf{v}^T \\ \mathbf{v} & \lambda_{kk} \end{bmatrix},$$

where $\mathbf{V}$ is $[(k - 1) \times (k - 1)]$ matrix, $\mathbf{v}$ is $[(1 \times (k - 1)]$ vector, and λ_{kk} is a scalar.

Let $\Gamma(k; j)$ denote the liquidity of the first j stocks when k stocks are listed, which we measure as the sum of the eigenvalues of the submatrix of $\mathbf{\Lambda\Lambda}^T$ that contains the upper left $j \times j$ elements. Because the sum of the eigenvalues is equal to the trace of the matrix, using equation (B9) and the partition of $\mathbf{F}$ and $\mathbf{\Lambda}$, we see:

(B12) $$\Gamma(k - 1; k - 1) = \frac{h^2}{4}\,\mathrm{tr}\,\mathbf{GG}^T,$$

where tr denotes the trace of the matrix.

To compare this to $\Gamma(k; k - 1)$, we first substitute equations (B10) and (B11) into equation (B9) to get:

$$\begin{bmatrix} \mathbf{V} & \mathbf{v}^T \\ \mathbf{v} & \lambda_{kk} \end{bmatrix}\begin{bmatrix} \mathbf{V}^T & \mathbf{v} \\ \mathbf{v}^t & \lambda_{kk} \end{bmatrix} = \frac{h^2}{4}\begin{bmatrix} \mathbf{G} \\ \mathbf{g} \end{bmatrix}[\mathbf{G}^T \quad \mathbf{g}^T].$$

Thus,

$$\begin{bmatrix} \mathbf{VV}^T + \mathbf{v}^T\mathbf{v}^T & \mathbf{Vv} + \mathbf{v}^T\lambda_{kk} \\ \mathbf{vV}^T + \lambda_{kk}\mathbf{v}^T & \mathbf{vv} + \lambda_{kk}^2 \end{bmatrix} = \frac{h^2}{4} \begin{bmatrix} \mathbf{GG}^T & \mathbf{Gg}^T \\ \mathbf{gG}^T & \mathbf{gg}^T \end{bmatrix}.$$

Therefore,

$$\mathrm{tr}\,\mathbf{VV}^T + \mathrm{tr}\,\mathbf{v}^T\mathbf{v}^T = \frac{h^2}{4}\mathrm{tr}\,\mathbf{GG}^T.$$

Because $\mathrm{tr}\,\mathbf{v}^T\mathbf{v}^T$ is the sum of square of each element of $\mathbf{v}$, it must be positive. Noting this, we establish:

$$\Gamma(k;\,k-1) = \mathrm{tr}\,\mathbf{VV}^T = \frac{h^2}{4}\mathrm{tr}\,\mathbf{GG}^T - \mathrm{tr}\,\mathbf{v}^T\mathbf{v}^T < \frac{h^2}{4}\mathrm{tr}\,\mathbf{GG}^T = \Gamma(k-1;\,k-1).$$

Thus, the price response of a set of stocks becomes smaller when an additional stock is listed on the market. In this sense, the market liquidity is an increasing function of the number of stocks listed.[14] The result has a very intuitive interpretation. As the number of listed stocks grows, the information useful in predicting the fundamental value of a stock can be found in the order flows of many stocks, as long as their fundamental values are influenced by the same factors as well. Thus, the information revealed by the order flow of any single stock becomes smaller, leading to a smaller price response to the order flow (and, hence, increased liquidity).

References

Anderson, Brian D. O., and John B. Moore. 1979. *Optima filtering.* Englewood Cliffs, NJ: Prentice-Hall.

Association of TSE Saitori Members. 1975. *Saitori Shi (History of Saitori).* Tokyo: Association of TSE Saitori Members.

Bank of Japan, Institute for Monetary and Economic Studies. 1986. *Wagakuni no Kin'yu Seido (Financial system in Japan).* Tokyo: Bank of Japan.

———. 1995. *Wagakuni no Kin'yu Seido (Financial system in Japan).* Tokyo: Bank of Japan.

Baruch, Shmuel, and Gideon Saar. Forthcoming. Asset returns and the listing choice of firms. *Review of Financial Studies.*

Cabinet Office. 2001. *Kokumin Keizai Keisan Hokoku: Choki Sokyu Suikei (Report on national accounts from 1955 to 1998).* Tokyo: Printing Office of the Ministry of Finance.

Demirgüc-Kunt, A., and R. Levine. 2001. *Financial structure and economic growth: A cross-country comparison of banks, markets and development.* Cambridge, MA: MIT Press.

Diamond, Peter. 1987. Multiple equilibria in models of credit. *American Economic Review* 77:82–86.

14. Baruch and Saar (forthcoming) also obtain this result for a special case, although this is not the main focus of their paper.

Ellul, Andrew, and Marco Pagano. 2006. IPO underpricing and after-market liquidity. *Review of Financial Studies* 19:381–421.

Fujino, Shōzaburo, and Jūrō Teranishi. 2000. *Nihon Kin'yu no Sūryō Bunseki (Quantitative analysis of Japan's finance)*. Tokyo: Toyo Keizai Shinposha.

Geisst, Charles R. 1997. *Wall Street: A history*. New York: Oxford University Press.

Gordon, Robert J. 1986. *The American business cycle*. Chicago: University of Chicago Press.

Hatano, Kanae. 1938. *Shoken Shijo Ron (On the security market)*. Tokyo: Ganshodo Shoten.

Hoshi, Takeo, and Anil Kashyap. 2001. *Corporate financing and governance in Japan: The road to the future*. Cambridge, MA: MIT Press.

Ishii, Kanji. 1997. *Nihon no Sangyo Kakumei (Industrial revolution in Japan)*. Tokyo: Asahi Sensho.

———. 1999. *Kindai Nohon Kin'yushi Josetsu (Towards the financial history of modern Japan)*. Tokyo: University of Tokyo Press.

Kataoka, Yutaka. 1987. *Meijikino Kabushiki Shijo to Kakaku Keisei*. (The stock market and price formation in Meiji Japan). *Shakai Keizai Shigaku* 53 (2): 159–81.

Kikkawa, Takeo. 1995. *Nihon Denryokugyo no Hatten to Matsunaga Yasuzaemon (Development of the electricity industry and Yasuzaemon Matsunaga)*. Nagoya, Japan: Nagoya Daigaku Shuppankai.

Kinugawa, Taichi. 1938. *Honpo Menshi Boseki Shi (History of the Japanese cotton spinning)*, vol. 3. Osaka: Nihon Mengyo Kurabu.

Kuwata, Yuzo. 1940. *Wagakuni Torihikijo no Riron to Jissai (Theory and practice of the Japanese exchange)*. Toyko: Yuhikaku.

Kyle, Albert S. 1985. Continuous auctions and insider trading. *Econometrica* 53:1315–35.

Michie, Ranald. 1987. *The London and New York stock exchanges, 1850–1914*. London: Allen and Unwin.

———. 1999. *The London Stock Exchange: A history*. Oxford, UK: Oxford University Press.

Miwa, Yoshiro, and Mark Ramseyer. 2002. Banks and economic growth: Implications from Japanese history. *Journal of Law and Economics* 18 (1): 127–64.

Miyamoto, Matao. 1990. *Sangyoka to Kaisha Seido no Hatten* (Industrialization and development of the corporate system). In *Sangoyka no Jidai (Age of industrialization)*. Vol. 1, ed. Shunsaku Nishikawa and Takeshi Abe, 352–401. Tokyo: Iwanami Shoten.

Noda, Masao. 1980. *Nihon Shōken Shijō Seiritsu-shi: Meiji-ki no Tetsudō to Kabushiki Kaisha Kin'yu (History of the formation of Japanese securities market: Railroads and joint stock company financing in Meiji)*. Tokyo: Yuhikaku.

Okawa, Kazushi. 1974. *Kokumin Shotoku (National income)*. Tokyo: Toyo Keizai Shinposha.

Okawa, Kazushi, Tsutomu Noda, Nobukiyo Takamatsu, Saaburo Yamada, Minoru Kumazaki, Yuichi Shoinoya, and Ryoshin Minami. 1967. *Bukka (Prices)*. Tokyo: Toyo Keizai Shinposha.

Okazaki, Tetsuji. 1995. *Nihon niokeru Koporeito Gabanansu no Hatten* (Evolution of corporate governance in Japan: An historical perspective). In *Shisutemu toshite no Nihon Kigyo (The Japanese firm as a system)*, ed. Masahiko Aoki and Ronald Dore, 437–84. Tokyo: NTT Shuppan.

———. 1999a. Corporate governance. In *The Japanese economic system and its origins*, ed. Tetsuji Okazaki and Masahiro Okuno-Fujiwara, 97–144. New York: Oxford University Press.

———. 1999b. *Mochikabu Gaisha no Rekishi: Zaibatsu to Kigyo Tochi (History of holding companies in Japan: Zaibastu in Perspective of Corporate Governance).* Tokyo: Chikuma Shinsho.

————. 2000. *Mochikabu Gaisha to Ginko: Koporeito Gabanansu kara Mita 1920 Nendai to Gendai* (Holding companies and banks: The 1920s and the present in perspective of corporate governance). *Hitotsubashi Business Review* 48 (3): 38–50.

Okazaki, Tetsuji, Michiru Sawada, and Kazuki Yokoyama. 2005. Measuring the extent and implications of director interlocking in the pre-war Japanese banking industry. *Journal of Economic History* 65 (4): 1082–1115.

Osaka Stock Exchange. 1928. *Daikabu 50 Nenshi (Fifty-year history of the Osaka Stock Exchange).* Osaka: Osaka Stock Exchange.

Pagano, Marco. 1989a. Endogenous market thinness and stock price volatility. *Review of Economic Studies* 56:269–88.

————. 1989b. Trading volume and asset liquidity. *Quarterly Journal of Economics* 104:256–74.

Pagano, Marco, Fabio Panetta, and Luigi Zingales. 1998. Why do companies go public? An empirical analysis. *The Journal of Finance* 53 (1): 27–64.

Research Bureau of the Bank of Japan. 1916. *Tokyo ni okeru Kabushiki Shijo no Yoko (Outline of the stock market in Tokyo).* Tokyo: Bank of Japan.

Shimura, Kaichi. 1970. *Nihon Shihonshijo Bunseki (Analysis of the Japanese capital market).* Tokyo: University of Tokyo Press.

Takamura, Naosuke. 1971. *Nihon Bosekigyo Shi Josetsu (An introduction to the history of the cotton spinning industry).* Tokyo: Hanawa Shobo.

————. 1996. *Kaisha no Tanjo (Birth of corporations).* Tokyo: Yoshikawa Kobunkan.

Teranishi, Juro. 2003. *Nihon no Keizai Shisutemu (The economic system in Japan).* Tokyo: Iwanami Shoten.

Tokyo Stock Exchange. 1928. *Tokyo Kabushiki Torihikijo Gojū-nenshi (Fifty-Year History of the Tokyo Stock Exchange).* Tokyo: Tokyo Stock Exchange.

————. 1937. *Tokyo Kabushiki Torihikijo Tokei Nenpo (The yearly statistical report of Tokyo Stock Exchange).* Tokyo: Tokyo Stock Exchange.

————. 1938. *Tokyo Kabushiki Torihikijo Shi (History of the Tokyo Stock Exchange).* Vol. 3. Tokyo: Tokyo Stock Exchange.

————. 1963. *Tokyo Shoken Torihikijo Ju-nenshi (Ten-year history of the Tokyo Stock Exchange).* Tokyo: Tokyo Stock Exchange.

————. 2002. *Tokyo Shoken Torihikijo 50 Nenshi (Fifty-Year History of the Tokyo Stock Exchange).* Tokyo: Tokyo Stock Exchange.

Tokyo Stock Exchange, Research Division. (*Chōsa-ka*). 1932. *Tokyo Kabushiki Torihikijo (Tokyo Stock Exchange).* Tokyo: Tokyo Stock Exchange.

————. 2004. *Tokyo Stock Exchange fact book.* Tokyo: Tokyo Stock Exchange.

Toyo Keizai Shinposha. 1927. *Meiji Taisho Kokusei Soran (Statistical handbook of Meiji Taisho Eras)*: Tokyo: Toyo Keizai Shinposha.

Umemura, Mataji. 1988. *Rodoryoku (Manpower).* Tokyo: Toyo Keizai Shinposha.

U.S. Bureau of the Census. 1937. *Statistical abstract of the United States.* Washington, DC: U.S. Government Printing Office.

U.S. Council of Economic Advisors. 2003. *Economic report of the president.* Washington, DC: U.S. Government Printing Office.

Yoshida, Junjo. 1998. *Nihon no Kaisha Seido Hattatsu Shi no Kenkyu (Research on the history of the corporate system in Japan).* Ryugasaki, Japan: Ryutsu Keizai Daigaku Shuppankai.

Comment   Youngjae Lim

The mainstream view in economic history is that Japan had a bank-based financial system since the late nineteenth century. The early history of postal banking system in Japan could provide a good example to support this view. Since it had been established in the late nineteenth century, the Japanese postal banking system played an important role in mobilizing national savings and channeling them into the corporate sector. On the other hand, recent empirical studies show that the prewar Japanese economic system was different from the postwar system. In particular, it is shown that the Japanese financial system before World War II was characterized by the large and active stock market. It could be implied that shareholders rather than bankers played a central role in corporate finance and governance in the prewar Japanese economic system.

With this background in mind, this chapter shows how and why the Tokyo Stock Exchange suddenly took off while it stayed stagnant during the first forty years since 1878. The authors pay a special attention to an important change in the Tokyo Stock Exchange's policy toward listing in 1918. Stocks began to be traded in the Tokyo Stock Exchange without explicit applications from the firms. It made it possible for the Tokyo Stock Exchange to integrate the trades outside the Tokyo Stock Exchange. Then the chapter empirically studies the listing decisions of cotton spinning firms during 1905 to 1936 and documents that the Tokyo Stock Exchange's policy toward listing in 1918 had an important impact on the growth of the Tokyo Stock Exchange afterward. The authors' argument is based on the idea of multiple equilibriums. The stock market has two equilibriums. An increase in the number of listed stocks leads to an increase in the market liquidity. In turn, it results in the number of listed stocks. The chapter shows that the market liquidity is, in general, an increasing function of the number of firms listed in the market using a standard model of stock market microstructure. The authors provide a theoretical basis for their empirical result.

In summary, the authors construct a plausible story of the Tokyo Stock Exchange's takeoff in the 1920s and then confirm empirically their hypothesis. Another important contribution of the chapter lies in the compilation of valuable data sets. First, the authors constructed a comprehensive list of the companies listed on the Tokyo Stock Exchange for each year from 1878 to 1936 from the raw data scattered around in various places. This data set makes it possible for the authors to compare the Tokyo Stock Exchange before and after 1918. The authors also built up another panel data set. It has basic financial information for the all the cotton spinning

Youngjae Lim is a senior fellow at the Korea Development Institute.

companies for the period of 1905 to 1936. This data set enables the authors to empirically study the listing decision of the firms in the Tokyo Stock Exchange.

The chapter discusses the funding patterns of Japanese corporations during the period of 1902 to 1940 (cited from Hoshi and Kashyap 2001). The share of the paid-in capital and reserves was about 60 to 80 percent of the total capital and liabilities. On the other hand, the share of bank borrowing was less than 20 percent of the total funds in the corporate sector. Given this information, one could ask the following questions. Who were the shareholders of the corporate sector in Japan then? Were they a large number of small individual investors? Were they a small number of wealthy families or firms? It is known that the Zaibatsu firms dominated the Japanese economy before World War II. What were the main sources of funding for the Zaibatsu firms? Were the paid-in capital and reserves also important sources of funding for the Zaibatsu firms?

Given the patterns of corporate finance in the prewar period of Japan, it would be interesting to know how the failing firms were treated in the prewar economic system. Were the failing firms allowed to be bankrupt freely in the capital market? Were they mostly liquidated? Or were there any interventions from the government? What if one of the Zaibatsu firms was to fail?

According to the authors, the share of bank borrowing in the corporate sector in the prewar Japan was at most 20 percent. What roles did the banking sector play in the prewar period of Japan? As in the case of postal banking system, did the government have influences on the banking sector? Then what roles did the private banks belonging to the Zaibatsu families play? All these interesting questions arise because the stock markets and the banking sector should have competed with each other to attract the savings in the private sector.

The authors imply that the prewar Japan was closer to a stock market based financial system rather than a bank based financial system. Then one could ask how the Japanese economy made the transition from a stock market based financial system in the prewar period to a bank based financial system in the postwar period. Here, presumably the role of the wartime economic system in Japan would be critical. Still then, the theoretical argument that the authors employed in the chapter poses a puzzle. Will only an increase in the number of listed firms in the stock exchange be sufficient for the growth of the stock market relative to the banking sector?

Reference

Hoshi, Takeo, and Anil Kashyap. 2001. *Corporate financing and governance in Japan: The road to the future.* Cambridge, MA: MIT Press.

Comment   Masaya Sakuragawa

This chapter comprises two parts. The first part provides detailed evidence on the history of development of the Tokyo Stock Exchange (hereafter, TSE), and the second part develops a theoretical and empirical analysis to explain the development of the TSE. A look at a number of figures constructed by the authors shows that the TSE took off around 1918. The authors stress that no significant institutional change happened around 1918 and try to explain the take off of the TSE by relying on the notion of expectation equilibria, the idea of which depends heavily on the search theoretic approach that began with the pioneering work by Peter Diamond (1982).

I have three comments. The first is on the theoretical explanation. The authors try to explain the take off of the TSE by relying on a model of multiple equilibria that are generated by the bilateral causations between market liquidity and the number of initial public offerings (IPOs). The "low" equilibrium is identified as the one with low liquidity and the "high" equilibrium as the one with high liquidity and the large numbers of IPOs.

Marco Pagano (1989a,b) develops sophisticated models of multiple equilibria in the development of the stock market. If the stock market is thin, prices will be volatile, and investors will exploit only small liquidity gains. Risk-averse investors anticipate to gain less from trading so that they will hesitate the entry in the market. The thin market is actually realized.

Equilibria are self-fulfilling. "Low" and "high" equilibria coexist, and a small perturbation or a change in belief of investors leads to a large change in the equilibrium from the "low" to "high" equilibrium.

The second comment is on the estimation approach. Basically, their system would be written as a two-equation system by:

(1) $\text{Number of IPO}_i = \alpha_0 + \alpha_1 \text{Liquidity}_i + \alpha_2 Z_i + u_i$

(2) $\text{Liquidity}_i = \beta_0 + \beta_1 \text{Number of IPO}_i + \beta_2 X_i + v_i,$

where Z_i is an exogenous variable to identify equation (2) with $\text{Cov}(Z_i, u_i) = 0$, X_i is an exogenous variable to identify equation (1) with $\text{Cov}(X_i, v_i) = 0$, and u_i and v_i are error terms with $Eu_i = 0$ and $Ev_i = 0$.

However, the strategy of authors is to consider only one direction from market liquidity to the number of IPOs. Why don't the authors also think the reverse causation given by equation (2)? In addition, in estimating equation (1) only, ordinary least squares (OLS) give an endogenous bias to the estimate of α_1.

Masaya Sakuragawa is a professor of economics at Keio University.

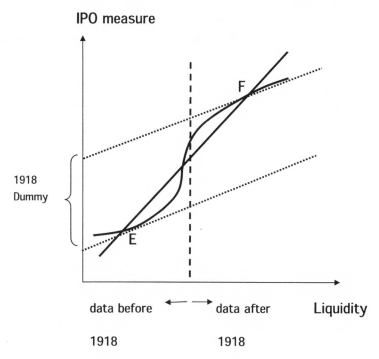

Fig. 2C.1   Multiple equilibria

Apart from the simultaneous problem, what makes thing complicated is that the pair of positive coefficients, $\alpha_1 > 0$ and $\beta_1 > 0$, does not guarantee the existence of multiple equilibria. Either $\alpha_1 > 1$ or $\beta_1 > 1$ is necessary to guarantee multiple equilibria, at least for some range of variables. This job may not be easy.

I propose an alternative approach that will be simple. As figure 2C.1 illustrates, if the authors' hypothesis is valid, samples before 1918 should roughly lie around E, while those after 1918 around F. An estimation using a time dummy may be a good idea. In doing so, the authors should make an effort to convince readers that no significant institutional change happened around 1918. Authors seem to use the market liquidity as a measure of market efficiency. The volatility of prices may become another possible measure.

The final comment is on the interpretation on the cause of the take off. Reading this chapter, readers might be tempted to imagine an alternative hypothesis for the take off. Exogenous shocks such as the economic boom during and after the WWI or the earthquake that occurred in Tokyo in 1923 may have influenced the change in the financial system.

References

Diamond, Peter. 1982. Aggregate demand management in search equilibrium. *Journal of Political Economy* 90 (5): 881–94.

Pagano, Marco. 1989a. Endogenous market thinness and stock price volatility. *Review of Economic Studies* 56 (2): 269–87.

———. 1989b. Trading volume and asset liquidity. *Quarterly Journal of Economics* 104 (2): 255–74.

II

Consequences of Financial Development

Misaligned Incentives and Mortgage Lending in Asia

Richard Green, Roberto S. Mariano,
Andrey Pavlov, and Susan Wachter

3.1 Introduction

This chapter provides a conceptual basis for the price discovery potential for tradable market instruments and specifically the development of mortgage securitization in Asia. We argue that securitization in Asia may be potentially important because it may help bring transparency to the financial sector of Asian economies. We put forth a model explaining how misaligned incentives can lead to bank-generated real estate crashes and macroeconomic instability. We provide new comparative data on the banking sector's performance in Asia compared to the performance of securitized real estate returns, to provide evidence on the potential contribution of misaligned incentives to the magnitude of the declines in the real estate sector in the past. In particular, we show both theoretically and empirically that the banking sector suffers relatively low losses following a negative demand shock compared to the losses experienced by the real estate sector. The evidence suggests that the fact that banks' shares are publicly traded does not discipline the bank lending officers who are driven by origination fees and market share and does not prevent underpriced lending.

As a remedy to the inability of public ownership of banks to prevent underpriced lending, we discuss how the addition of freely tradable and liquid market instruments backed by loans (MBS) might help to inoculate markets from the shocks arising from bank-financed mortgages, through

Richard Green is director and chair of the USC Lusk Center for Real Estate and a professor at the University of Southern California. Roberto S. Mariano is dean of the School of Economics at Singapore Management University. Andrey Pavlov is a visiting associate professor of real estate at the Wharton School, University of Pennsylvania, and an associate professor of finance at Simon Fraser University. Susan Wachter is the Richard B. Worley Professor of Financial Management at the Wharton School, University of Pennsylvania.

price signaling. Liquid securitizing mortgage loans could help to enforce greater discipline on bank underwriting and lead to improved lending evaluation standards.

The chapter proceeds as follows. Section 3.2 provides a context of bank funding of the real estate sector and its role in past real estate and financial crises. Section 3.3 presents a theoretical model of lending and development activities that demonstrates how banks can provide underpriced financing and nonetheless avoid large losses following a negative demand shock. Section 3.4 presents empirical results that indicate the impact of bank underpriced lending on real estate markets is severely negative but that the banks themselves are impacted to a far lesser extent. Section 3.5 interprets the findings and concludes.

3.2   Context

Mera and Renaud (2000) demonstrate that the phrase "Asian financial crisis" was misleading. Green's (2001) review of the book noted:[1]

[Asian Financial Crisis] suggests homogeneity: that "Asia" is one place, and that the financial crises faced by various countries there in the late 1990s were fundamentally similar. The fact that so many countries that were geographically close faced crises that were temporally close makes it easy to conclude that the crises had common roots. (216)

Ito (2007) also underscores how much Asian currency crises varied in the late 1980s. Nevertheless, many Asian countries went through serious real estate crises. In Japan, property values began falling in 1991 and continued to do so until this year.[2] Miller and Luangaram (1998) show that in Thailand and Indonesia, property values began falling in 1991, and in Thailand fell dramatically in 1997. They also show how the market capitalization of publicly traded companies specializing in real estate fell by 48 percent in Indonesia between the second quarter of 1996 and the fourth quarter of 1997 and by 88 percent in Thailand.

While property values were falling in these countries, banks actually increased their lending share to property companies (Miller and Luangaram 1998) so that a bad situation got worse. Even though values were falling and vacancies were rising, banks continued to roll over loans to property owners until they reached the point where the property owners could no longer service their debt service. According to Renaud (2001), vacancy rates in Bangkok peaked at more than 40 percent.[3] Renaud (2001) and Fis-

1. Much of the discussion of the Asian financial crisis in the following closely follows Green (2001).
2. There has been much reporting on this. See, for example, "Around the Markets: Property Investors Look Overseas for Value," *International Herald Tribune*, May 21, 2007. http://www.iht.com/articles/2007/05/21/business/sxasia.php.
3. See http://www.cushwakeasia.com/data/Bangkok/bacom0106.pdf.

cher (2001) tell vivid stories about how poorly executed underwriting and conflicts of interest made the real estate crises in these countries worse than they needed to be.

It is worth spending a little time talking about the large real estate crises in Thailand and Indonesia as well as the ability of Korea to avoid a crisis of similar magnitude. Green (2001) summarizes Renaud and Fisher as follows:

> Lenders assume rent and property value growth at some extremely high rates, which in turn produces very low capitalization rates. This in turn causes appraisers to assign high values to properties. These high values provide the support lenders need to advance loans, which typically have higher loan-to-value ratios. The high-loan-to-value ratios are justified by the fact that property values "always" rise, and that therefore the equity in the loan will quickly get sufficiently large to discourage default. At the same time, the financial institutions had reason to believe that governments (or NGOs) would prevent them from failing, meaning that the downside risk to the risky loans was attenuated. This led to a classic moral hazard problem, where risk was not appropriately priced.
>
> The problem with this, of course, is that sometimes values and rents stop rising.

Thailand did seem able to put its problems behind it fairly quickly. Renaud (2000) points to an agency Thailand created to behave as the Resolution Trust Corporation (RTC) did in response to the United States savings and loan crisis. Like the RTC, the Financial Restructuring Agency (FRA) seized the assets of failed financial institutions and sold properties at substantial discounts to replacement cost. While we are not in a position to know whether the FRA executed sales as well as possible, it did seem to restore liquidity to the market in Thailand, and Thailand returned from crisis to growth fairly quickly.

We can return to the United States savings and loan crisis to gain some historical perspective. The ignition of inflation in the late 1960s and 1970s altered the ability of depositories to fund long-term, fixed-rate mortgages (FRMs): inflation pushed up nominal interest rates and required higher returns on deposits, while asset returns were fixed at the low levels of historical fixed rates on long-term mortgages, which made up most of the thrift industry portfolios. Inadequately capitalized depository institutions (S&Ls) then advanced unsustainable commercial mortgages. Because these institutions often had no equity to protect, their managers had large incentives to make high-risk loans. If the loans failed, the institutions and their depositors were no worse off.[4] If they paid off, however, the institution would return to solvency. Because S&Ls were not required to mark

---

4. Depositors have the benefit of Federal Savings and Loan Insurance Corporation (FSLIC) Deposit Insurance.

their assets to market, they were able to hide their distress until loans began defaulting. This points to the general issue, which we will return to, of the signaling power of price discovery in capital markets.

By the late 1980s, poor real estate underwriting produced overbuilding in the U.S. commercial real estate market. This led to high vacancies (according to the U.S. Census, typical Class A Office Vacancy Rates in 1991 were in excess of 20 percent[5]) and declining rents. Buildings generated insufficient cash flow to meet debt services, and default rates rose dramatically. The poor quality of assets on savings and loan balance sheets could no longer be hidden.

Congress and the Bush administration bit the bullet by passing the Federal Institutions Reform, Recovery and Enforcement Act of 1989; this legislation liquidated insolvent savings and loans and turned their assets over to the RTC, whose function was the disposition of the assets; cash raised from the sales were used to offset the costs of the S&L failure to U.S. taxpayers. At the same time, thrift portfolios were restructured by exchanging below market mortgages for MBS that could be sold and the losses amortized rather than realized immediately. Thrifts solved their asset liability mismatch by selling FRMs into the secondary market for securitization by MBS underwritten by one of the U.S. secondary market agencies. Thompson (2006) has a good description of what happened next:

> Wall Street surveyed the mountain of defaulted S&L loans taken over by the federal Resolution Trust Corporation (RTC) and saw an opportunity to get into real estate investing in a big way. Morgan Stanley's experience is typical of other investment banks at the time. "We got into the investing side of the business primarily because the opportunity was there to buy nonperforming loan portfolios from the RTC," recalls Slaughter. From a merchant banking standpoint, Wall Street barely paid attention to commercial real estate prior to 1990. Since then, almost every major Wall Street firm has become active in real estate private equity. "Morgan Stanley alone has gone from zero dollars under management to almost $40 billion over the past fifteen years," says Slaughter.
>
> Wall Street helped the RTC solve another big problem: how to dispose of billions in S&L loans that were not in default. The agency came to Wall Street with a proposal to sell loan packages rather than one property at a time, an impractical approach given the volume of loans on the RTC books. Wall Street responded by creating commercial mortgage-backed securities (CMBS), which are similar to, but more complex than, the mortgage-backed securities long used to bundle and sell packages of residential loans. "Commercial mortgage-backed securities did not exist in 1990 and were not thought to be viable," says Slaughter. Today, CMBS represent a $550 billion market.

It's hard to overestimate the impact of this market restructuring. In fif-

---

5. See http://www.allcountries.org/uscensus/1228_office_buildings_vacancy_rates_for_major.html.

teen years, the public equity and debt markets for commercial real estate have gone from financial infancy to trillion-dollar status.

At the same time thrifts restructured their portfolios by exchanging fixed-rate mortgages for MBS to be sold to U.S. secondary market agencies. The government encouraged this through allowing the losses to be amortized rather than realized immediately (Wachter 1990). Thrifts then solved their asset liability mismatch going forward by holding in their portfolios newly available adjustable rate mortgages (ARMs). For a time in the U.S. it appeared that the short-term ARM would become common in the United States. But inflation under control by the early 1990s, relatively flat yield curves, secondary market agency (Fannie Mae, Freddie Mac, and Ginnie Mae) guarantees, and the liquidity derived from large standardized market trading of MBS resulted in competitive FRM pricing in the U.S. Elsewhere, in the absence of secondary market institutions, ARMs remained far more common (Green and Wachter 2005). While banks solve their asset liability mismatch problem by offering ARMs, these convey larger credit risks in the long run should economic shocks cause higher interest rates.

The question remains, however, why the banking sector, in the United States and elsewhere, drove itself into near bankruptcy with severe consequences for the economy. This may be because the banking sector lacks incentives to curtail or even monitor risky lending activities. In particular, if there is either deposit insurance, or if depositors assume certain institutions are too big to fail, moral hazard becomes a serious problem, unless there is adequate supervision (see Pavlov and Wachter 2006). Basel II and many commentators are newly looking to market-based monitoring of banks (Barth, Caprio, and Levine 2006) to ensure soundness and financial stability. This requires a reliance on market forces, and the threat of lost fees and profits, to align bank managers' incentives to market outcomes. In the following sections, we present a theoretical model and empirical evidence of bank lending and development activities that demonstrate how banks can provide underpriced financing and nonetheless avoid the appearance of large losses even following a negative demand shock that is, in part, induced by the banks' own behavior.

3.3   A Model of Lender and Developer Behavior

In this section, we propose a simple one-period model with zero-profit, rational developers who bid on land prices in period 1 and supply developed real estate in period 2. These developers face an upward sloping supply of land function in period 1, and a downward sloping real estate demand function in period 2. The developers know the parameters of the demand functions and choose the optimal level of development in period 1.

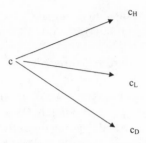

Fig. 3.1   Real estate demand function

Note: c denotes the intercept of the real estate demand function in period 2. This intercept can take one of three values, c_H, c_L, or c_D.

The uncertainty in the model is given by the intercept of the real estate demand function in period 2 (see figure 3.1). We assume it can take one of three values high (H), low (L), and disaster (D): with probability δ_H, δ_L, and δ_D, respectively.

There are two types of developers, safe and risky, who are identical in all respects except that the safe developers default only in the disaster state, D, while the risky developers (strategically choose to) default in states L as well as D.

Lenders can correctly identify the type of developer (for example, higher loan to value borrower) and price the zero-equity loans appropriately.[6] (In a later section, we also discuss the case in which lenders cannot distinguish between the two types of developers.) We show in the following that if all loans are priced correctly, then lenders have zero expected profits, and the lending activity has no impact on the underlying real estate market development or pricing.

While our model is couched in terms of developers obtaining loans from lenders directly, the more realistic interpretation is that individual homeowners obtain the loans and commit to purchase properties from the developers. Developers are then incentivized to develop and meet the demand for presales, and individual homeowners are interested in purchasing because they can obtain loans from the lenders. Therefore, this chapter can be interpreted in its entirety as a residential real estate paper.

To gain market share (and to book more short-term fees), lenders can engage in underpricing by lending to some of the risky borrowers at the safe rate. If that occurs, risky borrowers take advantage of the cheap financing, bid up land prices in period 1 above their prior levels, and overdevelop. As a result, prices are lower in period 2 in all states, lenders have negative ex-

---

6. The zero equity assumption is purely mechanical and can easily be replaced with any other fixed required LTV ratio. As will become apparent in the following, higher equity requirement does not change our results, as long as the equity is not sufficient to absorb all negative demand shocks.

pected profits, safe borrowers also have negative expected profits, and risky borrowers have zero expected profits.

We further model the profits of the lenders and their ability to hide small losses due to the overall randomness of the lender's activities in sectors other than real estate. If this is the case, lenders do extend some under-priced loans to risky borrowers, with all of the negative consequences this generates. Importantly, *reported* proportional bank losses are smaller in case of outcome (D) than the losses to real estate investors. The compensation of bank managers is rationally maximized.

3.3.1 Safe Developers and Rational Lenders

In period zero, developers will build given the following *supply* function:

$$(1) \qquad q = \frac{P - a}{b},$$

where P denotes the price of land for development in period 1, q denotes the quantity of land that is developed for period 2 and is determined in period 1, and a and b are constants specifying the supply function.

In period 1 the price of the asset is given by the following *demand* function:

$$(2) \qquad P_s = c_s - dq,$$

where c_s denotes the intercept of the demand function for each state of nature ($S = H, L,$ or D), P_s denotes the price of developed land in period 2 in each state of nature, and d is a constant specifying the slope of the demand function.

Good borrowers default only in the case of disaster (D). The price they are willing to pay is given by:

$$(3) \qquad RP = \frac{\delta_H P_H + \delta_L P_L}{\delta_H + \delta_L},$$

where R denotes $1 +$ interest rate charged on the safe loans. Solve for q:

$$(4) \qquad q = \frac{(c_H - aR)\delta_H + (c_L - aR)\delta_L}{(d + bR)(\delta_H + \delta_L)}$$

The zero-profit for a risk-neutral bank is:

$$(5) \qquad (\delta_H + \delta_L)(R - 1)P = \delta_d(P - P_D).$$

Solve for q:

$$(6) \qquad q = \frac{(a - c_D)\delta_D + a(R - 1)(\delta_H + \delta_L)}{(d + bR)(\delta_H + \delta_L)}$$

Equate q in expressions (4) and (6) to solve for R, substitute into equations (4) or (6) to find the equilibrium quantity of real estate developed, q^*:

(7)
$$q^* = \frac{c_H\delta_H + c_L\delta_L + c_D\delta_D - a}{b + d} = \frac{\bar{c} - a}{b + d},$$

where $\bar{c}$ denotes the expected intercept of the demand function in period 2. This is exactly the quantity real estate developed one would find in the absence of lending, where full equity investors take on all gains and losses, $P = \delta_H P_H + \delta_L P_L + \delta_D P_D$. Substitute q^* into equations (1) and (2) to find the equilibrium current and future price:

(8)
$$P^* = a + b\frac{\bar{c} - a}{b + d}$$

and

(9)
$$P_s^* = c_s - d\frac{\bar{c} - a}{b + d}$$

Investor expected profits are zero:

(10)
$$\frac{\delta_H P_H + \delta_L P_L}{\delta_H + \delta_L} - RP = 0$$

3.3.2 Risky Developers and Rational Lenders

Risky developers default even in moderate losses, that is, in the case of state (L) in period 2. The price they are willing to pay is given by:

(11)
$$R_B P = P_H.$$

The lender's zero-profit condition is:

(12)
$$\delta_H(R_B - 1)P = \delta_L(P_L - P) + \delta_D(P_D - P).$$

Solve for equilibrium quantity of real estate developed following the method of equations (3) to (7):

(13)
$$q^* = \frac{\bar{c} - a}{b + d}$$

This solution is identical to the optimal development quantity under no lending. Therefore, *if properly priced,* lending to risky borrowers does not in itself affect the real estate markets. In this situation, the bank takes all losses, and charges an appropriate interest rate. Therefore, for ease of exposition, in what follows, we assume the bank lends only at the safe rate. Otherwise, the bank can directly invest in real estate and not go through risky investors.

3.3.3 Risky Developers and Underpricing Lenders

Assume in this section that the lender makes a certain proportion, h, of the loans to risky borrowers at the safe rate. (In the following, we explicitly model the lender behavior and how that might occur.) Because risky developers would find the ability to borrow at the safe rate very attractive, the quantity real estate developed then becomes:

(14) $$q_u^* = (1 + h)q^*,$$

where q_u^* denotes the quantity developed in the underpricing case. The current price of real estate increases, as given by equation (1), and the future price of real estate in each of the three outcomes declines, as given by equation (2). Importantly, this new lower price of real estate affects even safe investors and reduces their expected profit:

(15) $$\frac{\partial[(\delta_H P_H + \delta_L P_L)/(\delta_H + \delta_L) - RP]}{\partial_h} < 0$$

Because current price, P, is higher under underpricing, and future price in each state, P_s, is lower under underpricing for all s, real estate markets decline more in economies that underprice. Specifically, following an outcomes L or D, the percent price decline in real estate is:

(16) $$1 - \frac{P_L}{P} = 1 - \frac{c_L(b + d) - d[E(c_s) - a](1 + h)}{a(b + d) + b[E(c_s) - a](1 + h)}$$

$$1 - \frac{P_D}{P} = 1 - \frac{c_D(b + d) - d[E(c_s) - a](1 + h)}{a(b + d) + b[E(c_s) - a](1 + h)},$$

which is increasing in h because $a \ll E(c_s)$. (Intercept of the supply function is far smaller than the intercept of the demand function.)

3.3.4   Lender Behavior

The bank can underprice by lending to the risky borrowers at the safe rate, R. Let k denote the percent of real estate loans relative to the total lending activity of the bank. Let h denote the percent of real estate loans to risky borrowers. Because the default rates on loans in other industries in which the bank participates is noisy, the bank is able to hide losses of g or less in the real estate sector. For instance, g can be two standard deviations above the average loss on the bank portfolio.

While hiding losses is unlikely to persist over the long term, it can and does happen between market crashes. Most markets accommodate this by providing higher returns to investors during normal markets and larger losses during substantial market downturns. Thus, investors receive a fare rate of return, and the hiding during up markets can persist. The added problem in real estate is that during the normal (up) markets additional development occurs, and this additional development magnifies the effects of negative demand shocks.

Even in the absence of a negative demand shock, small losses accumulate over time and eventually get discovered. This would lead to both investor and regulator response. Such a response can, in itself, tighten lending standards, reduce the availability of credit, and add to moderately weak economic fundamentals to produce a negative demand shock. That's why even in the absence of a significant economic downturn, real estate markets tend to experience substantial negative demand shocks on a regular basis.

If the bank lends only to safe borrowers, bank profits on real estate loans, π, are given by:

$$(17) \qquad \pi = \begin{cases} rP & \text{if } H \text{ or } L \\ P_D - P & \text{if } D \end{cases}.$$

If the bank lends to risky borrowers and safe borrowers at the safe rate, bank profits on real estate loans are given by:

$$(18) \qquad \pi = \begin{cases} (1 + h)rP & \text{if } H \text{ or } L \\ (P_L - P)h & \text{if } L \\ (P_D - P)(1 + h) & \text{if } D \end{cases}.$$

We assume management compensation, M, is proportional to the loans originated:

$$(19) \qquad M = (1 + h)Pkm,$$

where m denotes the origination fees the management of the bank receives as a compensation.

Therefore, managers maximize compensation by setting h:

$$(20) \qquad (P - P_L)hk = g$$

or

$$(21) \qquad h = \frac{k[c_L - E(c_S)] + \sqrt{4kg[E(c_s) - a] + k^2[E(c_s) - c_L]^2}}{2k[E(c_s) - a]},$$

which is an increasing function in g. For $g = 0$, $h = 0$, that is, if the bank cannot hide any losses, the optimal amount of loans to the risky borrowers is zero.

Following a D outcome, the *reported* unexpected bank losses on real estate loans, as a proportion of originated loans, are:

$$(22) \qquad \frac{(P - P_D)(1 + h) - g}{(1 + h)P} = 1 - \frac{P_D}{P} - \frac{g}{(1 + h)P}.$$

which is smaller than the losses to real estate investment, $1 - P_D/P$. Therefore, the reported proportional losses to the banking sector are smaller than the proportional losses to the real estate sector. If the bank cannot hide any losses, then $g = 0$, $h = 0$, and the proportional bank losses are the same as real estate losses. Under loan securitization with liquid standardized markets, the bank cannot hide any losses, and both the real estate and the banking sectors are protected.

Note that the general outcome of price inflation shown in the preceding can be obtained in an equivalent model in which lenders cannot distinguish between safe and risky borrowers or can distinguish at a cost. In that case, a proportion of the loans will be made to risky borrowers. The only difference in this alternative model is that the proportion of loans made to risky borrowers is not an outcome of maximizing management compensation but is an exogenous variable measuring the degree to which risky borrowers can borrow at the safe rate. This implicitly assumes the lenders not only cannot distinguish between safe and risky borrowers but also do not know the proportion of loans they make to risky borrowers. If this is not the case, and the lender cannot distinguish between risky and safe borrowers, then the impact on asset markets is further magnified. Mathematically, this is equivalent to setting $h = 1$ in our model, that is, the bank can hide losses of any amount. Of course, no bank can hide losses beyond a certain magnitude. This is a purely mechanical adjustment to the model that demonstrates the implications of the bank not being able to distinguish between the safe and risky borrowers.

Finally, liquid standardized securitized real estate-backed debt can be modeled by setting k in equation (19) to 1. In other words, securitized mortgage debt is like a lender whose sole operations are in a specific real estate market and property type. While liquid, standardized securitized debt investors are not more or less sophisticated than bank shareholders, because of the far more direct, uniform, and transparent link between the underlying cash flows and the investor payoffs, lenders are able to hide only far smaller losses in this model. In other words, due to the uniformity and mechanical nature of such securitized debt, even small losses get discovered quickly, and overdevelopment is stopped before it occurs.

3.4   Data Description and Empirical Results

The first data set we utilize is the Global Property Research (GPR) indexes compiled by Eichholtz et al. (1998) and refined and extended by Dr. Christopher Shun, Menang Corporation, Malaysia.[7] These data include property indexes for twenty-five countries over twenty and twelve years for developed and emerging countries, respectively. The GPR 250 Global Property Stocks index only includes property companies with a minimum of US$50 million of freely available market value and high liquidity in terms of average last-year stock trading volume. As of December 2002, the securities included in the GPR 250 index had a combined available market

---

7. For further information, see the bibliographies for Eichholtz et al. (1998) and Shun (2005).

value of US$194 billion. This data set has a number of advantages. In particular, it has the deepest history and the largest cross-sectional span across the globe of any real estate property database. Because the returns are based on publicly traded and liquid securities, the data quality is high, available at a monthly frequency, and consistent through time.

The second data set we use is the financial return data from the Global Financial Database (GBF); these data are compiled for 120 industries in more than 200 countries. The GBF has a collection of more than 200,000 entries and offers accurate and verified historical world market financial data. The financial return data refers to the return of the financial sector within each market and is provided as monthly data.

We also make use of correlation results that are derived from previous work in Pavlov and Wachter (2007). Pavlov and Wachter (2007) develop a symptom of loan underpricing in an economy. This symptom is the negative relationship between the change in lending spread and asset returns before the crash. We use the property returns data to measure the total price decline during the crash for each market as indicated in the preceding, and we calculate the correlation of the lending spread with this return to identify economies that experience lending induced real estate crashes. The lending spread for each market is calculated by the lending rate minus the deposit rate. These data are collected from the World Bank *World Development Indicators* (WDI) Web site (http://www.worldbank.org/data).

Table 3.1 provides descriptive statistics of the GPR data used. We identify twelve countries that have experienced a market decline of 20 percent or more during any period in the past. Such a large market decline corresponds to our "Disaster" outcome described in the preceding theoretical model. While market declines are a continuum, and the 20 percent cut-off is somewhat arbitrary, our empirical data really provide two types of declines—small in the order of 2 to 5 percent and large, well in excess of 20 percent. Therefore, our results are not tied to this cut-off point.

Using both the GPR and GBF databases, for each country, we compute the correlation between changes in the lending spread and asset returns *before* the market decline. This is our underpricing symptom. Figure 3.2 is replicated from Pavlov and Wachter (2007, fig. 1). The vertical axis depicts

Table 3.1   Descriptive statistics

	Correlation	Real estate % decline	Financial decline
Mean	−0.19	−0.60	−0.16
Standard error	0.14	0.06	0.13
Median	−0.15	−0.62	−0.20
Standard deviation	0.48	0.20	0.44

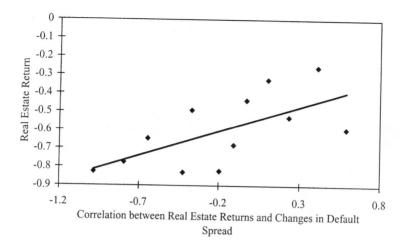

	Intercept	Slope	R^2
Estimate	0.55	0.27	0.42
t-statistic	11.30	2.72	

Fig. 3.2   Real estate return

Notes: The correlation is computed between the total index return, including dividends, and the change in the spread of lending over deposit rates. In this figure, we compute the correlation using data before the crash, that is, from the beginning of our data set to the peak of the property market. The vertical axis depicts the real estate return. This is over one or more years and is specific for each country. According to our theory, negative correlation is a symptom of underpricing and is associated with larger losses during a market downturn. Countries that do not exhibit the symptom of underpricing have zero or positive correlation, and their respective property market declines are relatively modest.

the total percent decline in the property market, from top to bottom. This is over one or more years and is specific for each country. According to Pavlov and Wachter (2007), negative correlation between price changes and changes in the lending spread is a symptom of underpricing, and, thus, we expect this negative correlation to be associated with larger losses during a market downturn, as it is. Countries that do not exhibit the symptom of underpricing have zero or positive correlation, and their respective property market declines are relatively modest, as the results indicate. We replicate this figure because it illustrates that loan underpricing can have devastating effect on the underlying real estate markets.

To test the theoretical implication of our preceding model, that the banking sector experiences smaller proportional declines than the real estate sector, we plot the same underpricing symptom against the total decline, top to bottom, of the financial services sector in the same twelve countries in figure 3.3. While the relationship is as expected, that is, lenders in countries that underprice experience larger losses following a real estate

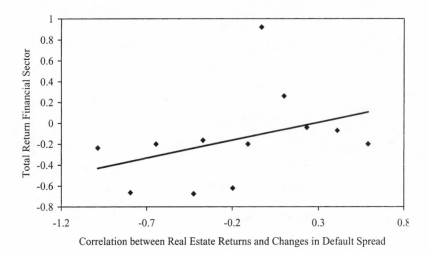

Correlation between Real Estate Returns and Changes in Default Spread

	Intercept	Slope	R^2
Estimate	-0.09	0.15	0.14
t-statistic	-0.71	1.28	

Fig. 3.3   Financial-sector return

Notes: The correlation is computed between the total real estate index return, including dividends, and the change in the spread of lending over deposit rates. The vertical axis depicts the financial-sector total return over the period of the real estate market crash. This is over one or more years and is specific for each country. According to our theory, negative correlation is a symptom of underpricing and is associated with larger losses in real estate markets during a market downturn. Countries that do not exhibit the symptom of underpricing have zero or positive correlation, and their respective property market declines are relatively modest. This figure shows that the financial-sector returns are also negatively impacted by underpricing but by a far more modest extent than real estate returns. The relationship is not statistically significant and of smaller magnitude.

negative demand shock, it is not statistically significant and very modest economically. This suggests that while underpricing hurts the financial sector following a negative demand shock, the magnitude of this effect is modest relative to the real estate sector declines.

Finally, figure 3.4 reports the relationship between real estate returns and financial-sector returns. While the relationship is positive and significant, that is, markets that experience large real estate losses also experience significant banking losses, very clearly the financial-services sector losses are far more modest. Furthermore, while we only have a few data points, it appears that real estate returns need to fall by 60 percent or more before the financial-services sector starts to experience significant losses.

There are four countries that experienced real estate market crashes but very limited banking losses or even substantially positive returns: Hong

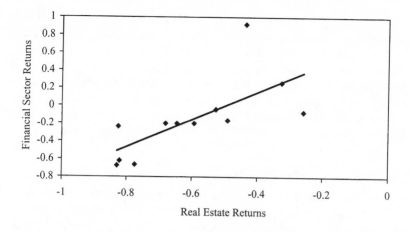

	Intercept	Slope	R^2
Estimate	0.77	1.54	0.48
t-statistic	2.43	3.06	

Fig. 3.4 Financial and real returns

Notes: This figure depicts the total real estate returns versus the total financial-sector returns following the real estate market crash. Real estate returns and financial-sector returns are positively correlated. However, financial-sector losses are generally more modest than real estate losses. Furthermore, the financial sector does not seem to experience any significant losses until real estate losses reach 60 percent or more.

Kong, New Zealand, Belgium, and Norway. First, while substantial, the real estate crashes in these countries represent the lowest four real estate market declines in our data set. Second, each one of these countries had a particularly strong banking sector that did not appear to engage in underpricing and fared the real estate losses quite well.

Hong Kong used particularly strong underwriting standards, with very low LTV ratios and close scrutiny of loan applications. New Zealand and Belgium have always had very stable and closely monitored banking systems, and while default losses did increase during the real estate market crashes in the two countries, these increases were modest and well managed. Finally, the Norwegian financial system, while exposed to real estate, was also stable and fared relatively well during the real estate downturn for two reasons. First, the Norwegian banking system experienced a major crisis during the 1988 to 1993 period, which had a cleansing effect on its loan underwriting mechanisms. Second, during the period of the Norwegian real estate market decline, 1997 to 2001, oil prices increased from about $16 to over $30 per gallon, which helped the entire Norwegian financial system.

In summary, even though the data provide for only a limited number of observations, the findings are consistent with the theoretical model. First, the banking sector of countries with strong financial systems and solid, consistent underwriting standards fare real estate market crashes well. On the other hand, countries that are likely to engage in risky, underpriced lending tend to experience larger real estate market declines, which are translated into financial-sector declines. Nonetheless, these financial declines are relatively modest, even though banks are highly levered.

3.5   Conclusions and Implications for Alternate Financial Structures

In previous work, we have demonstrated the role that bank lending plays in generating boom and bust cycles in real estate. Rational economic behavior dictates that banks charge borrowers higher interest rates, origination fees, or mortgage insurance for their imbedded put option to default. While the presence of demand deposit insurance undermines market discipline, where are the shareholders? Why can't they monitor lending officials' behavior?

In this chapter, we develop a model to explain why underpricing of risk is not detected or curtailed by bank shareholders. As a result, underpricing persists undeterred and results in compression in the spread between lending and deposit rates, lending booms, inflated asset prices, excess building, and real estate crashes.

The link between bank lending and real estate crashes is enabled by the absence of short selling in real estate, which allows optimistic investors to drive prices up (Carey 1990; and Herring and Wachter 2003). But this is an insufficient explanation for sustained underpricing episodes because optimists still need financing to buy real estate if they are not to be constrained by their own limited assets, which will eventually go to zero due to their misjudgments. This optimist-led pricing is enabled and heightened by banks that supply funds to the optimists at rates that underprice risk. The model that we put forth here is based on the very nature of banks, their diversification that makes the identification of the signals of the underpricing of risk difficult except with considerable delay.

Such underpricing behavior forces a race to the bottom across lending institutions, with marketwide consequences. The longer the underlying real estate cycle, the greater the value of the put option, the inelasticity of the supply of real estate, and the elasticity of demand for bank loans, the greater the probability that the market will enter into an equilibrium in which all banks underprice risk with marketwide consequences that will be discovered (Pavlov and Wachter 2006). Even then with forbearance of regulatory authorities and the intervention of governments, banks may be bailed out, mitigating the consequences for shareholders. Nonetheless, the fundamental factor that explains why episodes of bank underpricing of risk are likely to occur is the inability of banking shareholders to identify these episodes promptly and incentivize correct pricing.

References

Barth, J. R., G. Caprio, and R. Levine. 2006. *Rethinking bank regulation—Till angels govern.* Cambridge, UK: Cambridge University Press.

Carey, M. 1990. Feeding the fed: The federal lend banks, land market efficiency, and the farm credit crisis. PhD diss., University of California, Berkeley.

Eichholtz, P., N. deGraaf, W. Kastrop, and H. Veld. 1998. Introducing the GRP 250 property share index. *Real Estate Finance* 15 (1): 51–61.

Fischer, D. Indonesia's real estate disturbance, an ineluctable outcome. In *Asia's financial crisis and the role of real estate,* ed. K. Mera and B. Renaud, 219–42. Armonk, NY: M. E. Sharpe.

Green, R. K. 2001. Review of *Asia's financial crisis and the role of real estate,* ed. K. Mera and B. Renaud. *Journal of Housing Economics* 10 (2): 216–23.

Green, R. K., and S. Wachter. 2005. The American mortgage in historical and international context. *Journal of Economic Perspectives* 19 (4): 93–114.

Herring, R., and S. Wachter. 2003. Real estate bubbles. *Asset Price Bubbles: Implications for monetary, regulatory, and international policies,* ed. W. C. Hunter, G. G. Kaufman, and M. Pomerleano, 217–30. Cambridge, MA: MIT Press.

Ito, T. 2007. Asian currency crisis and the International Monetary Fund, 10 years later: Overview. *Asian Economic Policy Review* 2:16–49.

Mera, K., and B. Renaud. 2000. *Asia's financial crisis and the role of real estate.* Armonk, NY: M. E. Sharpe.

Miller, M., and P. Luangaram. 1998. Financial crisis in East Asia: Bank runs, asset bubbles, and antidotes. *National Institute Economic Review* 165:66–82.

Pavlov, A., and S. Wachter. 2006. The inevitability of market-wide underpriced risk. *Real Estate Economics* 34 (4): 479–96.

———. 2007. Mortgage put options and real estate markets. *Journal of Real Estate Finance and Economics,* forthcoming.

Renaud, B. 2000. How real estate contributed to the Asian financial crisis. In *Asia's financial crisis and the role of real estate,* ed. K. Mera and B. Renaud, 183–208. Armonk, NY: M. E. Sharpe.

Shun, C. 2005. An empirical investigation of the role of legal origin on the performance of property stocks. *European Doctoral Association for Management and Business Administration Journal* 3:60–75.

Thompson, R. 2006. Rebuilding commercial real estate. http://hbswk.hbs.edu/item/5156.html.

Wachter, S. 1990. The limits of the housing finance system. *Journal of Housing Research* 1 (1): 163–85.

World Bank. *World development report, 2001.* Washington, DC: World Bank.

Comment   Michael Davies

The development of bond markets (including asset-backed securities [ABS] markets) has been a key focus of Asian central banks and government agencies over the past decade (see Gyntelberg, Ma, and Remolona 2006; Gyntelberg 2007). The push to build ABS markets makes this chapter particularly relevant as it seeks to provide a robust theoretical justification for their development.

The chapter offers a theoretical model that explains how bank employees' misaligned incentives cause them to extend too much finance to the real estate sector, which destabilizes real estate prices and the broader economy. It then shows how securitization better aligns bank employees' and investors' incentives. The chapter also provides evidence from twelve countries that have experienced real estate market declines of at least 20 percent at some point during the past two decades, which shows that banks' excessive lending has a detrimental impact on real estate markets. Last, the chapter provides a discussion of current developments in ABS markets in Asia.

Overall, I thought that the chapter was good, but I have a few suggestions that might improve it.

General Comments

- The chapter argues that securitization is particularly important in Asia because it improves the transparency of the financial sector and helps lenders manage their interest rate risk and duration risk. An additional benefit of securitization is that it improves financial stability by removing risk from lenders' balance sheets and dispersing it more widely among a large number of less-leveraged domestic and nonresident institutional investors.
- The chapter discusses both residential mortgage-backed securities (RMBS) markets and commercial mortgage-backed securities (CMBS) markets and sometimes does not make a clear distinction between the two markets. It might be worth focusing on CMBS markets as this is the market for which the theoretical model and the real estate data appear best suited.
- Excess liquidity and banks' unwillingness to securitize loans are cited as reasons for why ABS markets have not developed in Asia. It might also be worth discussing how governments and market participants in

Michael Davies is head of the Institutional Markets Section in the Domestic Markets Department of the Reserve Bank of Australia.

The chapter was interesting, and I am grateful for the opportunity to discuss it. The views expressed in the following are my own and do not necessarily reflect those of the Reserve Bank of Australia.

several Asia-Pacific countries have tried to overcome these constraints and build their ABS markets:

- In Hong Kong, Japan, Korea, and Malaysia, the government-supported housing finance agencies have been issuing mortgage backed securities (MBSs) to develop a market (see Davies, Gyntelberg, and Chan 2007).
- In Singapore and Korea, government agencies have bought some of the riskier ABS tranches to help bridge the gap between the credit quality of the bonds that investors in the region would like to hold and the actual credit quality of potential corporate borrowers (see Gyntelberg and Remolona 2006)
- In Australia, new specialist mortgage lenders, that relied solely on RMBS for funding, quickly built a presence in the mortgage market and the RMBS market in the mid-1990s (see Gizycki and Lowe 2000).

Comments on the Theoretical Model

- The chapter argues that bank employees can hide losses from investors and analysts because the bank has a large, diversified loan book. I am not an expert in bank agency problems, but I have three concerns about this argument. Banks often report separate results for each division. Banks that make underpriced real estate loans would also likely underprice loans to borrowers in other industries, maybe undermining the argument that losses can be hidden in the banks' diversified loan book. Even if the additional losses on real estate loans were within the standard errors of aggregate loan losses across the whole loan book, over time, the bank's aggregate losses would always be biased upward, and eventually shareholders would realize that losses were too high.
- I agree that securitization improves the transparency of lenders' loan books, but I am not sure that it eliminates agency problems. The ability to securitize loans was an important factor in the decline in lending standards in the U.S. subprime loan market, as the companies that originated the loans did not bear the credit risk.
- The disaster scenario does not appear to impact on the profitability of safe developers. This implies that safe developers do not invest any equity in their real estate projects. If this is the case, how are safe developers different from risky developers?

References

Davies, M., J. Gyntelberg, and E. Chan. 2007. Housing finance agencies in Asia. BIS Working Paper no. 241. Basel, Switzerland: Bank for International Settlements, December.
Gizycki, M., and P. Lowe. 2000. The Australian financial system in the 1990s. Paper presented at the Reserve Bank of Australia 2000 conference, The Australian Economy in the 1990s, Sydney, Australia.

Gyntelberg, J. Developing Asia Pacific non-government fixed income markets. *State Bank of Pakistan Research Bulletin* 3 (1): 1–26.

Gyntelberg, J., G. Ma, and E. Remolona. 2006. Developing corporate bond markets in Asia. BIS Paper no. 26. Basel, Switzerland: Bank for International Settlements, February.

Gyntelberg, J., and E. Remolona. 2006. Securitisation in Asia and the Pacific: Implications for liquidity and credit risks. *BIS Quarterly Review,* (June):65–75.

Comment   Mario B. Lamberte

The authors have developed a model to explain why underpricing of risk is not detected by bank shareholders and that its persistence results in compression in the spread between lending and deposit rates, lending booms, inflated asset prices, excess building, and real estate crashes. The model may be described in figure 3C.1. There are five major players in the real estate market, namely, the bank regulator; bank shareholders; bank management; real estate developers, consisting of both risky and safe borrowers; and households who have demand for real estate, which can assume three states with associated probabilities. In this model, a principal-agent problem exists. Managers' objective function is to maximize compensation. It is assumed that managers can hide bank losses. Thus, they engage in underpricing risk, that is, lend to risky borrowers at safe rates. As the authors have pointed out, "[S]uch underpricing behavior forces a race to the bottom across lending institutions, with marketwide consequences." Under this situation, real estate markets decline more during market downturn in economies where risk is underpriced but reported bank losses are expected to be lower than real estate losses. To mitigate the principal-agent problem, the authors have offered a solution: introduce mortgage securitization that will discourage lenders from underpricing risk.

Given the title of the chapter, it is worthwhile to describe the banking system and real estate markets in Asia to see if the model and its policy implications are applicable to the region. As many analysts have observed, figure 3C.2 more accurately describes the banking system in Asia than figure 3C.1. In figure 3C.2, bank ownership is highly concentrated, and bank owners are greatly involved in the management of their banks. Thus, the principal-agent problem that exists under figure 3C.1 does not either exist or is less pronounced in Asia. Even though a number of banks are publicly listed, the listed shares as a percent of their total outstanding shares are significantly small compared to what can be found in more-developed economies. Moreover, many banks in Asia are either majority or minority shareholders of real estate companies and mortgage redemption insurance companies.

Mario B. Lamberte is director of research at the Asian Development Bank Institute.

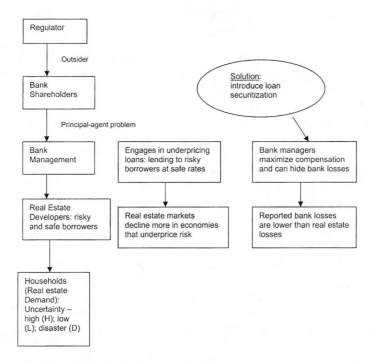

Fig. 3C.1   Model of lender and developer behavior

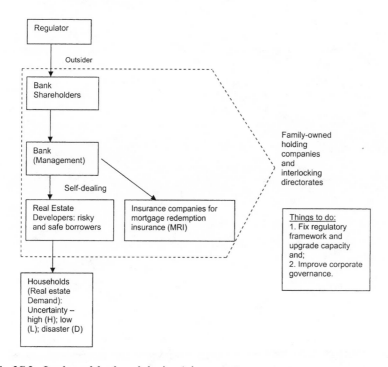

Fig. 3C.2   Lender and developer behavior: Asian context

Interlocking directorates among these institutions also abound, facilitating access of real estate companies to bank loans. Thus, the problem that arises in the Asian banking system is quite different from that described by the model. Imprudent lending to subsidiaries, affiliates, and bank directors and officers appears to be a serious problem. The solution, therefore, which many countries in the region have attempted to do in the aftermath of the financial crisis, is to strengthen banking regulations including capacities of regulators and corporate governance of banks. A strong banking sector closely monitored by regulators can fare better in times of real estate market downturn.

There are some nuances in developing mortgage securitization in Asia. In the model, P denotes the price of land for development. However, valuation of real estate properties is still a big problem in Asia. It is not unusual to find two significantly different valuations of the same property given by two real estate appraisers. Also, benchmark yield curve is not yet firmly established in Asia, making it difficult to develop the securities market rapidly.

Turning to the empirical analysis made by the authors, the sample appears to be too small to generate enough confidence in the results. More studies of this nature using a larger sample are, therefore, called for.

4

East Asia and Global Imbalances
Saving, Investment, and
Financial Development

Hiro Ito and Menzie Chinn

4.1 Introduction

The implications of persistent and widening global current account imbalances have been at the center of policy debates over the last half decade. While the concerns subside each year, as a rapid unraveling of the imbalances fails to materialize, the intellectual challenge of determining what drives these imbalances remains. To the extent that some policymakers view the configuration of imbalances to be undesirable, a salient question remains: what policies would cause those imbalances to shrink?

These imbalances are large. The U.S. deficit was 6.5 percent of gross domestic product (GDP) while China's surplus was 9.1 percent, with balances in the next two years projected at 10 percent. The rest of the developing Asian region is running an average current account surplus of 5.4 percent.[1] Finally, the sustained elevation in oil prices has added oil exporters to the list of surplus countries. Figure 4.1 highlights the lopsided nature of imbalances, with the U.S. deficit primarily financed by East Asia and the Middle East.

As a consequence of the magnitude of their surpluses, China and other Asian emerging market countries have often been identified as the main causes of the widening U.S. current account deficits. More specifically,

Hiro Ito is an associate professor of economics at Portland State University. Menzie Chinn is a professor of economics at the University of Wisconsin, and a research associate of the National Bureau of Economic Research.

We thank the discussants, Edwin Lai, Edward Robinson, and Liew Yin Sze, and the conference participants for their comments. The financial support of faculty research funds of the University of Wisconsin, Madison, and Portland State University is gratefully acknowledged.
1. Figures from IMF, *World Economic Outlook* (April 2007).

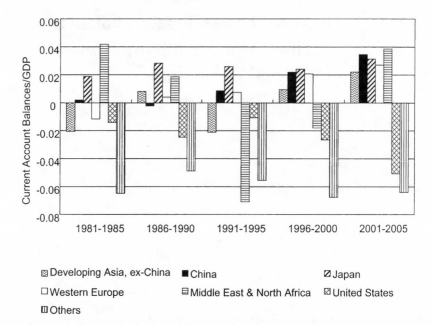

☒ Developing Asia, ex-China   ■ China   ◪ Japan
☐ Western Europe   ⊟ Middle East & North Africa   ⊠ United States
⊞ Others

Fig. 4.1   Current account balances by region (percentage of GDP)

these economies' underdeveloped and closed financial markets are alleged
to be insufficiently attractive enough to absorb the excess saving in the region, resulting in a "saving glut." Clarida (2005a,b) argues that East Asian,
particularly Chinese, financial markets are less sophisticated, deep, and
open so that Asian excess saving inevitably flows into the highly developed
U.S. financial market. Bernanke (2005) contends that "some of the key reasons for the large U.S. current account deficit are external to the United
States" and remediable only in the long run. That is, it is the saving glut of
the Asian emerging market countries, driven by rising savings and collapsing investment in the aftermath of the financial crisis, that is the direct
cause of the U.S. current account deficit. Therefore, the long-term solution
is to encourage developing countries, especially those in the East Asian region, to develop financial markets so that the saving rate would fall. Once
policies improving institutions and legal systems amenable to financial development and liberalizing the markets are implemented, "a greater share
of global saving can be redirected away from the United States and toward
the developing nations."

Standing in stark contrast to the saving glut thesis is the more parochial
view that a fall in the U.S. national saving, most notably in the form of its
government budget deficit, is the main cause of the ongoing current account deficits—the "twin deficit" argument. While the twin deficit effect
has been empirically investigated in the literature (e.g., Gale and Orszag

2004), as far as we are aware, very little investigation has been made to shed light on the effect of financial development on current account balances, with the exception of Chinn and Ito (2007a).[2] In this investigation encompassing a sample of eighty-nine countries over the 1971 to 2004 period, we found that more financial development leads to *higher* saving for countries with underdevelopment institutions and closed financial markets, which includes most East Asian emerging market countries.[3]

This chapter takes a closer look at the effect of financial development on current account balances and the saving-investment determination. Financial development cannot be defined and measured simply (see Beck, Demirgüe-Kunt, and Levine 2001). Chinn and Ito (2007a) used private credit creation (as a ratio to GDP) as a shorthand proxy measure for financial development. Clearly, this is a simplification with implications that should be investigated. Hence, in this chapter, we undertake a closer look at the effect of different *types* of financial development—whether banking, equity, bond, or insurance-market sector—to gain different insights. Additionally, we investigate various dimensions of financial development, such as size, degree of activity, and efficiency. Given the ongoing asset market booms in China and other emerging market countries in East Asia, size measures alone might lead to misleading inferences.

Other factors are suggested by the current debate. Bernanke argues that the *openness* of financial markets can also affect the direction of cross-border capital flows. Alfaro, Kalemi-Ozcan, and Volosovych (2003), on the other hand, show that institutional development may explain the Lucas paradox, that is, why capital flows from developing countries with presumably high marginal products of capital to developed countries with low ones. In short, financial development might be mediated by financial openness and institutional development. Hence, we will examine interaction effects as well.

Our empirical analysis relies upon a data set composed of nineteen industrialized countries (IDCs) and seventy developing countries for the period of 1986 through 2005. Financial development is assessed from various perspectives: different types of financial markets such as banking, equity, and bond markets, as well as different aspects of financial development such as the size, activeness, and cost performance of the industry. The analysis involves making one key trade-off: in refining the measures of financial development, we reduce the set of countries covered, as well as the time sample. We believe that the payoff to making this trade-off is on net positive.

---

2. Theoretical explanations for this phenomenon now abound. See Caballero, Emmanuel, and Pierre-Olivier (2006) and Mendoza, Quandrini, and Ríos-Rull (2006).

3. Among East Asian countries, most countries (except for Hong Kong and Singapore) could experience worsening current account balances if financial markets develop further, but that effect is achieved not through a reduction in savings rates but through higher increases in the levels of investment than those of national savings.

To anticipate our results, we find the following. First, we confirm a role for budget balances in IDCs when bond markets are incorporated. Second, empirically, both credit to the private sector and stock market capitalization appear to be equally important determinants of current account behavior. Third, while increases in the size of financial markets induce a decline in the current account balance in IDCs, the reverse is more often the case for developing countries, especially when other measures of financial development are included. However, because of nonlinearities incorporated into the specifications, this characterization is contingent. Fourth, a greater degree of financial openness is typically associated with a smaller current account balance in developing countries.

The chapter is organized as follows. Section 4.2 recaps the debate over financial development, openness, and institutions, and how those factors are related to the current pattern of current account imbalances, and saving and investment flows. Section 4.3 details the empirical methodology and results. Section 4.4 draws out the policy implications; section 4.5 concludes.

4.2   Financial and Institutional Development and the Global Saving Glut

4.2.1   Theoretical Perspectives

We adopt a medium-run prospect approach to evaluate current account behavior. Specifically, we view the current account as being driven by saving and investment behavior. Consequently, factors that affect either of these two flows—such as demographics, trend income growth, terms of trade volatility—should in principle affect the current account. The resulting empirical approach was implemented in Chinn and Prasad (2003).

The proposition that financial development or deepening influences saving and investment behavior is by now well established. Conceptually, financial development is the process of increasing efficiency in the channeling of funds from providers of capital to users of capital. In the end, the capital should be directed to activities that have the highest rate of return with the least amount of risk. Financial development might incorporate the use of new information technologies, the establishment of organized exchanges, and the other physical trappings of financial activities. But more fundamentally, it involves the reduction of information acquisition and transaction costs, overcoming or managing information asymmetries, and improving corporate governance.[4] Clearly, financial development should then have implications for both saving and investment behavior.

---

4. See King and Levine (1993), Rajan and Zingales (1998), and Wurgler (2000). This is the basis for the argument that financial development leads to economic growth. Levine (2005) provides an extensive review on the "finance-growth link."

Unfortunately, the available metrics by which the progress of financial development can be tracked are less than fully ideal. We measure the process by tabulating the size and activity of the banking sector, stock, bond, and insurance markets, with an understanding of the limitations of such indicators.

While the effect of financial development on investment is relatively unambiguous (i.e., positive), that on saving is not because higher returns and lower risk of financial investment create effects on saving akin to income and substitution effects. The traditional view on the effect of financial development on saving (such as Edwards 1996) suggests a positive association between the two variables; further financial deepening could induce more saving through more depth and sophistication of the financial system. A contrasting view suggests that more-developed financial markets lessen the need for precautionary saving and thereby lower the saving rate. This last observation is the basis for the saving glut thesis, leading to Bernanke's (2005) argument for greater financial development and liberalization as a long-run remedy to the global saving glut.[5]

Financial liberalization takes a central role in Kose et al. (2006). Liberalization can bring about more efficient allocation of capital across countries. Another key aspect of financial opening is that financial liberalization directly affects international risk sharing. In an idealized world with complete financial markets (and only tradable goods), the location of investment should be independent of saving in order to ensure state independent consumption-smoothing (Obstfeld and Rogoff 1996). However, as Feldstein and Horioka (1980) originally pointed out, investment and saving are highly correlated. Although that correlation has diminished over the years, the extent of the correlation remains nontrivial. In this environment, further international portfolio diversification afforded by greater financial liberalization could yield potentially large benefits.[6]

Most directly related to the issue at hand, financial openness can affect saving and investment determination and, hence, capital flows across borders. According to the global saving glut thesis, financial development coupled with comprehensive financial liberalization policies in East Asia would mitigate savings levels and further allow excess saving to be "recycled" within the region instead of flowing into the United States. Similarly, Dooley,

---

5. If one views the effect of financial development on saving as that of asset markets on consumption, the arguments about the wealth effect of asset market performance as well as the balance sheet effects can be relevant to our discussion. However, our main focus in this chapter is to examine the medium-run dynamics of the determinants of current account balances and saving and investment. Therefore, we focus on the comparison between the financial deepening view and the saving glut view.

6. Tesar (1995) finds that the possible gains from further international risk sharing is minimal for developed countries, where financial markets are well-developed and relatively open and whose economies are relatively more synchronized with the world economy, while the gains for developing countries are possibly significant.

Folkerts-Landau, and Garber (2005) argue that, in the absence of a well-functioning domestic or regional financial system, East Asian countries essentially lend capital to the United States at low interest rates in exchange for efficient financial intermediation. The capital returns to East Asia in the form of direct investment.

The efficacy and integrity of the legal environment and the level of institutional development should also be important determinants for saving and investment decisions. A society's legal foundations and institutions define the context wherein financial transactions and economic decisions are made. Levine, Loayza, and Beck (2000) find that the cross-country differences in legal and regulatory systems influence the development of financial intermediation.[7] The literature identifies a number of channels by which legal and institutional development can affect investment and saving decisions. Whether the legal system clearly establishes law and order, minimizes corruption, or whether the administrative branch of the government protects property rights efficiently are all important determinants of the incentives to save and invest. Decisions by foreign residents will also be affected.[8]

4.2.2   Stylized Facts: Financial Development, Openness, and Institutions

Figure 4.2 illustrates development of financial markets in terms of the market size, which we measure using SIZE, the sum of private credit creation and stock market capitalization (both measured as ratios to GDP).[9] Throughout the period, most markets, notably the U.S., Western European, and Chinese markets (relative to GDP), have steadily grown. The exceptions are the Japanese and ex-China East Asian financial markets, which experienced some retrenchment after the bursting of the bubble at the end of the 1980s and the financial crisis of 1997 to 1998, respectively. After the first half of the 1990s, U.S. financial markets have been the sole winner in terms of the market size. The relative sizes of Western European and Japanese markets are both about 58 percent of those of the United States, and those of East Asian and Chinese markets are about half of the U.S. financial markets.[10]

---

7. See also Beck and Levine (2005), Johnson, McMillan, and Woodruff (2002), and Levine (2005), among others.

8. Chinn and Ito (2006) find that financial openness leads to financial development especially when a country is equipped with developed legal systems and institutions.

9. All the measures of financial development are retrieved from the financial structure data set created and subsequently updated by Beck, Demirgüç-Kunt, and Levine (2001). Demirgüç-Kunt and Levine (2001) measures the overall size of the financial system by summing domestic assets of deposit money banks with stock market capitalization (both as ratios of GDP). However, because we want to focus on the private-sector development of financial markets that is more in line with financial development in a real sense, we use private credit creation instead.

10. Disaggregated pictures of the size of financial markets show that the relative size of financial markets in terms of either private credit creation or stock market capitalization individually are consistent with what is shown in table 4.2. However, ex-China East Asian coun-

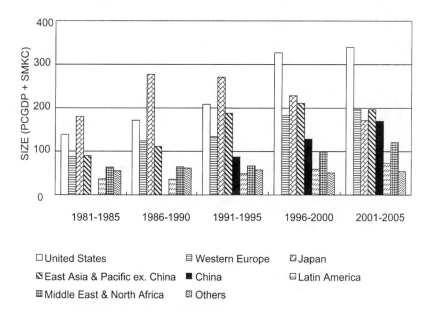

Fig. 4.2   Financial market development (size)

Beck, Demirgüe-Kunt, and Levine (2001) argue that the size of the financial system alone may not present a complete picture of financial development—a large financial market could be a relatively sedentary one, with little activity. Hence, one needs to examine the activeness of financial markets, for which we use stock market total value traded (as the ratio to GDP; SMTV). Figure 4.3 compares SMTV across different countries and regions. Also in this figure, we can make the same generalizations as we did in figure 4.2. The biggest difference from the previous figure is that the strength of U.S. financial markets is more pronounced when stock market total value is used as the measure of financial development; even the second most active financial markets, those in East Asia and Pacific, are only less than 40 percent of U.S. stock market total value (as a ratio to GDP).[11] This is clear evidence that U.S. stock markets are far more liquid than those in other regions and countries.

Figure 4.4 shows that the characterization of U.S. capital markets ex-

---

tries' and Chinese financial market developments differ from each other. While Chinese financial markets are more developed in the banking sector (its relative size to U.S. counterparts is about 63 percent), other East Asian countries are, on average, equipped with more developed equity markets (its relative size is about 81 percent).

11. Stock market turnover (SMTO) can be a measure of market activeness as well. We will use the variable later as a measure of market activeness. When SMTO is compared in the same way as other financial development measures, it is shown that China's stock market turnover was impressively high in the 1991 to 1995 and 1996 to 2000 periods, more than one and a half times as high as the U.S. figures. But this only reflects the fact that Chinese stock markets grew from a small market size.

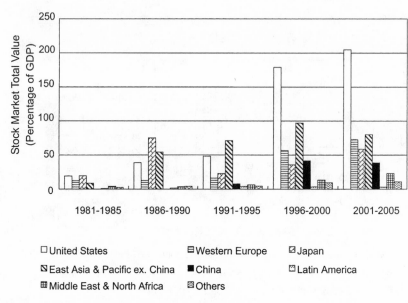

Fig. 4.3 Financial market development (activeness)

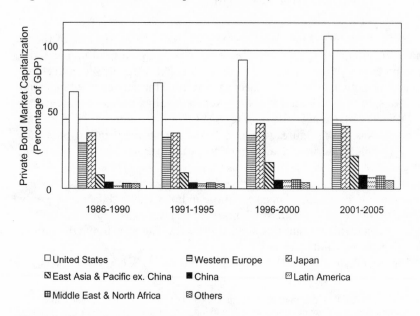

Fig. 4.4 Private bond market development

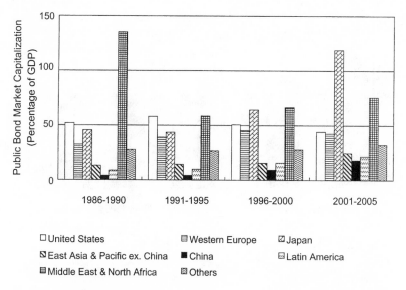

Fig. 4.5   **Public bond market development**

tends to private bond markets.[12] Even the private bond markets of Western European countries and Japan are less than half of U.S. counterparts, and only 22 percent and 9 percent for ex-China East Asia and China, respectively, showing overwhelming strength of U.S. capital markets.

Public bond market development presents a different picture, as shown in figure 4.5. While oil exporting countries have had large public bond markets, Japan's public bond market size is also increasing rapidly, reflecting the sustained period of deficit spending in response to years of stagnant growth. The U.S. public bond market is still large compared to other regions, but not as large as these two regions.[13]

Following Chinn and Ito (2007a), we measure legal and institutional development using LEGAL, which is the first principal component of law and order (LAO), corruption (CORRUPT), and bureaucracy quality (BQ).[14] Figure 4.6 compares the level of legal and institutional development of different regions and countries with the United States, whose value is normalized as 100. As one can expect, Western Europe and Japan have

12. The variables for private and public bond market capitalization (PVBM and PBBM, respectively) are only available after 1990 and for IDCs and emerging market countries.

13. In later sections, we use other measures of financial development, those pertaining to the cost performance or efficiency of the financial (mainly banking) industry. INVNETINT is an accounting value of bank's net interest revenue as a share of its interest-bearing (total earning) assets, inverted. OVERHEAD is an accounting value of a bank's overhead costs as a share of its total assets. For more details of data definitions, refer to the data appendix.

14. Higher values indicate better conditions. The choice of these variables is motivated by the literature on the finance and growth, as well as the wide coverage afforded by their use.

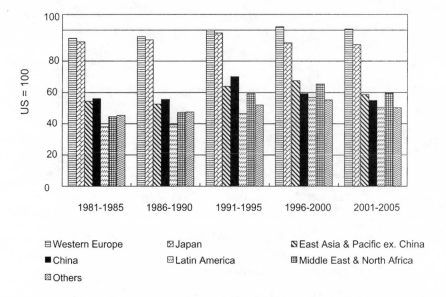

Fig. 4.6   Legal and institutional development

achieved levels of legal and institutional development comparable to the United States. The other regions lag the developed countries; their relative levels of legal and institutional development are about 60 percent at most.

The degree of financial openness is compared in figure 4.7 using the Chinn-Ito capital account openness index (KAOPEN). This index is based upon the International Monetary Fund's (IMF) categorical enumeration pertaining to cross-border financial transactions reported in *Annual Report on Exchange Arrangements and Exchange Restrictions* (AREAER). Higher values of this index indicate greater financial openness.[15] Like the LEGAL variable, financial openness is compared relatively to the United States. While East Asian countries slowed down the level of financial openness after the Asian crisis, both the Latin American and Middle East/North African regions have been steadily opening their financial markets throughout the sample period. One outlier is China. Not only is the pace of financial liberalization slow, so too is its level low.

The preceding observations lead us to conclude that China and other East Asian developing countries have achieved impressive—but uneven— financial development. Especially when it comes to the bond market sector, East Asian economies continue to lag, despite initiatives to develop these markets. Interestingly, while the extent of legal and institutional development is comparable to other developing countries, China's financial opening significantly lags behind others as is evidenced by the U.S. persis-

15. More details about the data are found in Chinn and Ito (2007b).

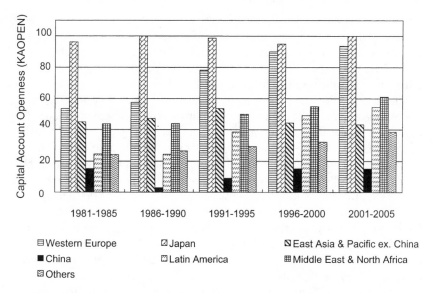

Fig. 4.7   Financial openness by region

tent demand to China for further financial opening. In the following, we will examine the effects of further development in financial markets and legal systems with an eye to drawing out the implications of further opening of financial markets in East Asian emerging market countries.

4.3   Empirics

4.3.1   Specification and Estimation

We estimate regressions of the general form:

$$
\begin{aligned}
(1) \quad y_{i,t} &= \alpha + \beta_1 FD_{i,t} + \beta_2 LEGAL_{i,t} + \beta_3 KAOPEN_{i,t} \\
&+ \beta_4 (FD_{i,t} \times LEGAL_{i,t}) + \beta_5 (LEGAL_{i,t} \times KAOPEN_{i,t}) \\
&+ \beta_6 (KAOPEN_{i,t} \times FD_{i,t}) + X_{i,t}\Gamma + u_{i,t},
\end{aligned}
$$

where three dependent variables (y), the current account balance, national saving, and investment, all expressed as a share of GDP, are regressed on FD, a measure of financial development; KAOPEN, a measure of financial openness; LEGAL a measure of legal/institutional development; and **X**, a vector of macroeconomic and policy control variables. For FD, we will include a variable pertaining to financial development depending on an analysis of our interest. Following Chinn and Prasad (2003), the vector **X** contains control variables of "usual suspects" as the determinants of current account balances, namely, net foreign assets as a ratio to GDP; relative income (to the United States); its quadratic term; relative dependency ratios on young and old population; terms of trade volatility; output growth rates; trade openness (= exports + imports/GDP); dummies for oil exporting countries; and time fixed effects. The sample for our analysis covers both industrial and developing countries. The underlying database has annual data for nineteen industrial and seventy developing countries covering the last twenty-year period, 1986 to 2005.

For our empirical analysis, we use a panel that contains nonoverlapping five-year averages of the data for each country. This approach mitigates the effect of measurement errors in annual data likely to be particularly problematic in data for developing countries. It also allows us to focus our interest in medium-term rather than business-cycle variations in current account balances.[16] All the variables, except for net foreign assets to GDP, are converted into the deviations from their GDP-weighted world mean prior to the calculation of five-year averages—net foreign asset ratios are sampled from the first year of each five-year panel as the initial conditions. The use of demeaned series controls for rest-of-world effects. In other words, a country's current account balance is determined by developments at home relative to the rest of the world.

As the preceding arguments have made clear, it is important to examine not only the effects of each of these variables, but also the interactions of these variables. Hence, we include in the estimation the interactions between financial development and legal variables (PCGDP × LEGAL), those between the financial development and financial openness variables (PCGDP × KAOPEN), and those between legal development and financial openness (LEGAL × KAOPEN). The financial and legal interaction effect is motivated by the conjecture that deepening financial markets might lead to higher saving rates, but the effect might be magnified under conditions of better-developed legal institutions. Alternatively, if greater financial deepening leads to a lower saving rate or a lower investment rate, that effect could be mitigated when financial markets are equipped with highly developed legal systems. A similar argument can be applied to the effect of financial openness on current account balances.[17]

16. Because we focus on medium-term dynamics, the predictions of the Mundell-Fleming model are of limited relevance in this framework. For the same reason, we do not control for the type of the exchange rate regime; it is not directly relevant to the *level* of current account balances, but to the *speed* of current account adjustment. However, we will examine the effect of different exchange rate regimes in the robustness checks. For the short-term current account dynamics, refer to Chinn and Lee (2006).

17. Bailliu (2000) shows that capital inflows, a proxy to capital account openness, can foster economic growth only if the level of domestic financial development is above a certain threshold, whereas Chinn and Ito (2006) find that financial openness leads to financial development especially when a country achieves a certain level of legal and institutional development. As Chinn and Ito (2006) have shown, financial development and financial openness can be highly correlated. However, inclusion of the interaction terms makes the model setting nonlinear and thereby collinearity between these variables less of an issue, thereby allowing us to identify independent effects of these variables.

4.3.2   Results from the Basic Model: Does Market Size Matter?

We first examine whether the size of financial markets (namely the sum of bank lending and equity markets as a ratio to GDP) matters for current account balances. Because these results are sensitive to the inclusion of the African countries, we also report separate sets of results with and without the African countries included for the developing country sample. We also report separate results for an emerging market group that differs somewhat from the developing country sample.[18]

Table 4.1 reports the results for the current account regressions for different subgroups. First, in contrast to the findings in Chinn and Ito (2007a), the budget balance variable is not statistically significant at conventional levels for any of the samples. A 1 percentage point increase (above the world GDP-weighted average) in the budget balance would lead to a 0.24 percentage point increase in the current account balance for IDCs and a slightly smaller effect for developing country groups, though none of them are statistically significant (with its p-value being 15 percent for IDCs and ranging from 12 percent to 17 percent for developing country groups).

This result differs from the results obtained in Chinn and Ito (2007a), where a 1 percentage point increase in the budget balance would lead to a 0.15 percentage point increase in the current account balance for IDCs and slightly higher results for developing country groups. The differing results are ascribable to the use of a different measure of financial development—private credit—and a longer sample period.[19]

SIZE exhibits a negative coefficient only in the IDCs, while its interaction with LEGAL is significantly positive for ex-Africa less-developed country (LDC) and emerging market country (EMG) groups, and its interaction with KAOPEN is significantly positive for IDCs and significantly negative for developing and emerging market countries. This finding indicates that, for IDCs, an expansion of the size of financial markets tends to decrease the current account balance. This effect is mitigated if the country is more financially open. The coefficient on the interaction term involving financial development and financial openness implies that greater financial openness will increase an IDC's propensity to export capital. Given these estimated relationships, U.S. behavior appears even more anomalous.

The dynamics between financial development, financial openness, and institutional development are different for developing countries. The estimated coefficients for both financial development and legal/institutional variables are significantly positive, while none of the SIZE coefficients are

18. The definition of emerging market countries relies upon the International Financial Corporation's (IFC) indexes. The group of emerging market countries in this study refers to the countries that were included in either the IFC's Global, Investible, or Frontier Index as of 1995.

19. Also the LEGAL variable was included as a time-invariant variable.

Table 4.1   Current account regressions with the SIZE variable

	IDC (1)	LDC (2)	LDC without Africa (3)	EMG (4)
Government budget balance	0.236	0.151	0.211	0.146
	(0.162)[15%]	(0.112)	(0.134)	(0.117)
Net foreign assets (initial)	0.058	0.042	0.037	0.043
	(0.017)***	(0.007)***	(0.012)***	(0.008)***
Relative income	0.101	−0.122	−0.028	−0.126
	(0.038)***	(0.097)	(0.098)	(0.113)
Relative income squared	−0.452	−0.123	0.012	−0.139
	(0.195)**	(0.114)	(0.118)	(0.128)
Dependency ratio (young)	0.028	−0.012	−0.02	0.011
	(0.038)	(0.020)	(0.021)	(0.023)
Dependency ratio (old)	0.07	−0.016	−0.023	−0.011
	(0.034)**	(0.017)	(0.017)	(0.023)
Financial development (SIZE)	−0.032	0.015	0.015	0.014
	(0.015)**	(0.010)	(0.012)	(0.009)
Legal development (LEGAL)	0.023	0.017	0.02	0.021
	(0.012)**	(0.009)*	(0.011)*	(0.010)**
SIZE × LEGAL	0.014	0.015	0.013	0.019
	(0.012)	(0.006)**	(0.008)[11%]	(0.007)***
Financial openness (KAOPEN)	0.016	−0.013	−0.014	−0.014
	(0.012)	(0.006)**	(0.008)*	(0.007)**
KAOPEN × LEGAL	0.01	0.001	0.001	0
	(0.008)	(0.002)	(0.002)	(0.002)
KAOPEN × SIZE	0.03	−0.006	−0.009	−0.008
	[0.014]**	(0.003)*	(0.004)**	(0.003)**
TOT volatility	0.107	0.012	0.017	0.02
	(0.071)	[0.025]	[0.024]	[0.028]
Average GDP growth	0.146	−0.04	−0.229	0.069
	[0.311]	[0.151]	[0.145]	[0.163]
Trade openness	0.024	0.032	0.021	0.037
	[0.016]	[0.011]***	[0.013]*	[0.013]***
Oil exporting countries		0.041	0.027	0.043
		[0.013]***	[0.018]	[0.013]***
No. of observations	81	156	125	125
Adjusted R^2	0.52	0.55	0.52	0.59

Notes: IDC = industrialized countries; LDC = less-developed countries; EMG = emerging market. All the variables to be included in the estimation, except for net foreign assets to GDP, are converted into the deviations from the GDP-weighted world mean before being calculated into the five-year averages. Robust standard errors in parentheses. The estimated coefficients for the time-fixed dummies and constant are not shown.

***Significant at the 1 percent level.

**Significant at the 5 percent level.

*Significant at the 10 percent level.

significant for financial development in any developing country grouping. LEGAL is marginally significant for LDC and ex-Africa LDC (its *p*-value being 12 percent and 13 percent, respectively) and significant for EMG. The level variable for financial openness is significantly negative for all developing country samples, suggesting that a financially closed country such as China is more likely to run current account surpluses (or smaller deficits). The significantly positive coefficient for the interaction between financial development and legal development indicates that a larger financial market enhances the effect of legal development. The significantly negative coefficient for the interaction between financial development and financial openness indicates that a larger financial market lessens the effect of financial openness.

The interpretation of the regression coefficients is complicated by the inclusion of the interaction terms. In the following, we will present some intuitive interpretations using some numerical examples. For now, the key stylized facts are that among developing countries, those with developed financial markets (in terms of their size), more advanced legal systems and institutions, or closed financial markets tend to run current account surpluses. With this generalization, it is unsurprising that China, with a large but closed financial market, equipped with a mediocre index of institutional development, is running a large current account surplus.[20] In this respect, China at first glance appears to fit the saving glut thesis. We return to this issue later.

The significantly positive coefficient for the oil exporting country dummy in the LDC and EMG samples are consistent with the recent rise in current account surpluses (and the accumulation foreign exchange reserves). Figure 4.1 demonstrates that the current account balances of "Middle East and North Africa" rise and fall with oil price movements.

We also estimate the regressions for both the national saving and investment equations (results not reported). While the results of the current account regression for IDCs and ex-Africa LDCs are more consistent with the national saving regression (in terms of the significance levels of the estimated coefficients of our interest and the goodness of fit of the model), those of less-developed and emerging market country groups show greater consistency with the results from the investment regressions than from those of the national saving regression. In other words, financial development and its interactions with legal development and financial openness affect current account balances through national saving for the IDC and ex-Africa LDC groups and through investment for the LDC and EMG groups.

Given that the SIZE variable is the sum of PCGDP and SMKC, we also

---

20. The estimation results for the EMG group are found to be robust to exclusion of China from the sample.

ran regressions using each of the two variables in place of FD in equation (1) to identify which of the components of SIZE is driving the results for the regressions shown in table 4.1 (results not reported).[21] In terms of the goodness of fit, it seems slightly more likely that the regressions with PCGDP have a better fit than those with SMKC. However, in terms of the statistical significance and economic magnitude of the estimated coefficients, we cannot determine which of the variables yield more consistent results with those in table 4.1. At the very least, as far as the sample period in this study is concerned, banking-sector and equity market development seem to be equally important.

4.3.3   Results for Extended Models: Activity and Efficiency

Clearly, SIZE is unlikely to convey the full complexity of financial development. To capture how *active* financial markets are, we use stock market turnover ratios (SMTO) as the measure.[22] Because an active market is not necessarily an efficient market, we also seek an efficiency measure. We are not able to obtain such a measure for equity markets but rely upon a banking-sector indicator, the net interest margin (NETINT). This variable is the banks' net interest revenues as a share of their interest-bearing (total earning) assets.[23] We invert this series (INVNETINT) and use it as a measure of market competitiveness of financial markets.[24] We reestimate the equation (1) model using these two variables. Also, because one can expect that market efficiency might affect international investors in a manner dependent upon market openness, we also include an interactive term between INVNETINT and KAOPEN.[25]

The results shown in table 4.2 are promising.[26] Interestingly, inclusion of

21. Both PCGDP and SMKC together cannot be included in the regressions because these two variables are highly correlated with each other, thereby yielding the issue of multicollinearity.

22. In the previous section, we used SMTV as the measure of stock market activeness. However, this variable is so highly correlated with SIZE that including both variables would not yield meaningful results. Stock market turnover (SMTO) can be a misleading indicator of stock market activeness because it is normalized by the market size, not the size of the economy. However, because the estimation model already controls for the size of financial markets, SMTO can be a useful indicator of market activeness.

23. The rationale for the use of this variable as the measure of banking market efficiency is that low net interest margin for a country means that banks in that country generally cannot reply too much on interest revenue, which implies that banks must compete in a more competitive market with low operating costs and low profitability. Beck, Demirgüç-Kunt, and Levine's (2001) financial structure data set also contains overhead costs (OVERHEAD) as another variable to measure market efficiency for the banking sector. Our empirical results are qualitatively unaffected when we use OVERHEAD instead of NETINT.

24. Originally, a higher value of NETINT indicates more interest margin, that is, less competitive market conditions. However, to make its interpretation easier, we inverted the variable such that a higher value of INVNETINT means less interest margin opportunities and more competitive market conditions.

25. The following results are generally unchanged if we use OVERHEAD banks' overhead costs as a share of their total assets, instead of INVNETINT.

26. To conserve space in table 4.2, we report the results only for the variables of interest. Complete results are available from the authors upon request.

Table 4.2   **Current account regressions with the SIZE, SMTO, and NETINT variables**

	IDC (1)	LDC (2)	LDC without Africa (3)	EMG (4)
Government budget balance	0.187	0.228	0.231	0.237
	(0.191)	(0.113)**	(0.152)	(0.126)*
Financial development (SIZE)	−0.03	0.019	0.02	0.02
	(0.013)**	(0.009)**	(0.011)*	(0.009)**
Stock market activeness (SMTO)	0.015	0.009	0.007	0.009
	(0.012)	(0.004)**	(0.004)*	(0.005)*
Net interest margin (INVNETINT)	−0.901	0.374	0.376	0.246
	(0.505)*	(0.152)**	(0.197)*	(0.152)[11%]
INVNETINT × KAOPEN	0.809	0.042	0.081	0.018
	(0.367)**	(0.066)	(0.076)	(0.062)
Legal/institutional development (LEGAL)	0.025	0.031	0.032	0.032
	(0.011)**	(0.009)***	(0.012)***	(0.009)***
SIZE × LEGAL	0.01	0.024	0.022	0.027
	(0.012)	(0.006)***	(0.008)***	(0.006)***
Financial openness (KAOPEN)	0.019	−0.016	−0.017	−0.019
	(0.010)*	(0.006)***	(0.008)**	(0.007)***
KAOPEN × LEGAL	0.002	0	0.002	0
	(0.008)	(0.002)	(0.002)	(0.002)
KAOPEN × SIZE	0.029	−0.009	−0.012	−0.011
	(0.013)**	(0.003)***	(0.004)***	(0.003)***
Oil exporting countries		0.054	0.05	0.048
		(0.015)***	(0.020)**	(0.016)***
No. of observations	77	140	114	112
Adjusted R^2	0.56	0.63	0.58	0.65

Notes: IDC = industrialized countries; LDC = less-developed countries; EMG = emerging market. All the variables to be included in the estimation, except for net foreign assets to GDP, are converted into the deviations from the GDP-weighted world mean before being calculated into the five-year averages. Robust standard errors in parentheses. The estimated coefficients for relative income, its quadratic term, young dependency ratio, old dependency ratio, terms of trade (TOT) volatility, output growth, trade openness, the time-fixed dummies and constant are not shown.
***Significant at the 1 percent level.
**Significant at the 5 percent level.
*Significant at the 10 percent level.

SMTO, INVNETINT, and interaction terms, has resulted in many heretofore marginally significant variables becoming more statistically and economically significant. Now the estimated coefficients for financial development in all samples are significant—negative for IDCs and positive for developing country groups.[27]

For all developing country groups, SMTO's coefficients turn out to be significantly positive. This result suggests that countries with active financial (more particularly equity) markets might become capital exporters, in-

27. The magnitude and statistical significance for the oil exporter dummy increases as well.

stead of importers, contrary to the saving glut thesis or Dooley, Folkerts-Landau, and Garber's (2005) Bretton Woods II hypothesis. When the national saving and investment regressions are examined (results not reported), the results indicate that the positive effect of stock market turnover is driven by its significantly positive entry to the national saving regression (with no corresponding effect in the investment regression). This result implies that more active financial markets can enhance national saving.

In IDCs, a reduction in the net interest margin contributes to a lower current account balance although the interaction terms seem to cancel out the linear effect for financially open countries. This means that an IDC with more competitive, but less open, financial markets tends to have smaller current account balances. For developing countries, more competitive financial markets seem to contribute to higher net saving; the level term of INVNETINT is found to be significantly positive for the LDC and ex-African LDC groups (and marginally so for EMG). This result is driven more by the results in the investment regression, where both the INVNETINT level and interaction variables turn out to have significantly negative coefficients for the LDC and ex-African LDC groups, and only the interaction term for the EMG group.[28]

Inclusion of SMTO, INVNETINT, and interaction terms increases the statistical significance and the magnitude of the variables of our main interest, especially for the LEGAL variable and its interaction with SIZE and KAOPEN. Given the obvious policy implications, we assess the sensitivity of these results more extensively in the next section.

4.3.4   Robustness Checks

Before discussing the policy implications of our regression results, we conduct a few robustness checks. These checks include accounting for endogeneity of financial development, alternative measures of financial development, accounting for the exchange rate regime, excluding periods of financial crises and aftermaths, and separating out oil exporters from our sample. We address each of these aspects in turn.

With respect to the first issue, financial development itself could be endogenous with respect to a country's political and social infrastructure. Although we have used nonoverlapping, five-year window panels to mitigate the problem of reverse causality, it may still be worthwhile to conduct some robustness checks. To examine this flow of causality, we conduct two-stage least squares (2SLS) analysis by instrumenting the SIZE variable with some variables that can be the determinants of financial development. Boyd, Levine, and Smith (2001) show that inflation significantly negatively affects both the banking-sector development and equity market activity. La Porta

---

28. The results found in this exercise are robust when the United States is removed from the IDC group and also when China is removed from the EMG group.

et al. (1998) demonstrate that the national legal origin (whether English, French, German, or Scandinavian) strongly explains cross-country differences in financial development. Therefore, we conduct 2SLS using inflation rates and the dummies for the national legal origin as instruments.[29]

The instrumental variables regression analysis yielded qualitatively similar results to those obtained before. In general, the estimation results are slightly weaker for the IDC group. For less-developed country groups, the statistical significance rose for many of the variables of our interest, so did the magnitude in some cases. At least, for developing and emerging market countries, we can safely conclude that our results shown in table 4.1 are not driven by endogeneity between the dependent variable and the financial development variable and its interactions.

There remain other types of financial markets we have not yet examined, such as private and public bond markets and insurance markets. In an effort to fill that void, we construct an index that incorporates information on other aspects of financial development; we then reestimate the regressions using this index (SIZE2) in the stead of SIZE. SIZE2 is the first principle component of private credit creation (PCGDP), stock market capitalization (SMKC), stock market total value (SMTV), private bond market capitalization (PVBM), public bond market capitalization (PBBM), inverted net interest rate margin (INVNETINT), and life insurance premium as a ratio to GDP (LIFEINS). Figure 4.8 compares regions using this financial development index while normalizing the index of the United States as 100. The historical patterns of financial development are similar to those displayed in figure 4.2. However, the underperformance of developing countries' financial markets as well as the U.S. relative strength appear more distinct, reflecting that developing countries lag behind in bond and life insurance markets.

We repeat the exercise in table 4.1, using the composite index in place of SIZE.[30] Interestingly, the estimated coefficients in the current account regressions becomes more significant for developing country groups, but not so for the regressions involving the IDC group. For the LDC groups, all the variables of our interest except for the interaction between KAOPEN and LEGAL become more than 5 percent significant.[31] We also conduct the 2SLS analysis by instrumenting in the same way as described in the preceding. Although the estimated coefficient for the composite index be-

29. All instruments were included as five-year averages of the deviations from world weighted averages. Also, the instruments found to be insignificant in the first-stage regressions were dropped.

30. The sample size is substantially reduced as PVBM and PBBM are available only after 1990 for a much smaller number of countries (especially for developing countries). Hence, the LDC group becomes the same as the EMG group.

31. The coefficient estimates in the national saving regression become more significant for the IDCs, whereas those of the investment become slightly less significant. However, the results are qualitatively the same as what we have found for IDC and LDC groups.

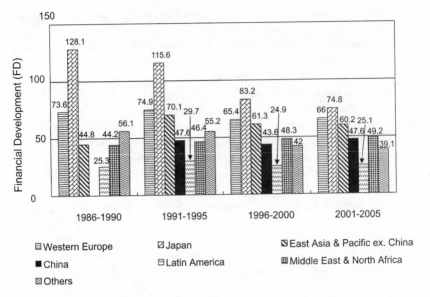

Fig. 4.8   Comparison by "financial development index"

comes insignificant, other coefficients behave similarly. The results are almost unaffected for the national saving and investment regressions.

There is a concern that one of the variables we have relied upon, private credit creation as a ratio to GDP (PCGDP), might provide an inaccurate depiction of financial development. In some economies, a large portion of financial intermediary is provided by public financial institutions, and the credit provided by such state-owned financial institutions to the private sector is included in PCGDP. This issue can become a concern when one uses this variable to proxy financial development in China, a country where the state has played a central role in the financial system. In order to address this concern, we adjust our measure by following the procedure outlined by Bekaert, Harvey, and Lundblad (2006). Specifically, we take the La Porta, Lopez-de-Silanes, and Shleifer (2002) estimates of the ratios of government ownership of banks, and interpolate data over our sample period.[32] PCGDP is then multiplied by (1 minus the ratio of government ownership of banks). Using this "adjusted" PCGDP, we reconstruct the SIZE variable (SIZE2A).

The SIZE2A series are compared across different regions and with the

32. La Porta, Lopez-de-Silanes, and Shleifer (2002) provide the estimates of the ratios of government ownership of banks for ninety-two developed and developing countries for 1970 and 1995. Bekaert, Harvey, and Lundblad (2006) use La Porta, Lopez-de-Silanes, and Shleifer's data and interpolate the ratios for their sample period. Obviously, this method is not perfect; efforts of privatization are often discrete (e.g., after experiencing a crisis) and also are not necessarily monotonic in movement.

United States in figure 4.9. The effect of the adjustment for government ownership of banks is striking for developing countries. In the 2001 to 2005 period, the size of financial markets for China, Latin America, and other countries is less than 20 percent of the United States. In fact, China's size of financial markets is merely 13.1 percent of the United States, confirming that China still has a long road to financial development.

Last, we reestimate the regressions using the adjusted SIZE variable. Interestingly, the results (not reported) are little changed, especially for developing countries. In other words, the results we have in table 4.1 are robust to the adjustment for government's involvement in the financial sector. This result is somewhat surprising.

We also assessed the importance of the exchange rate regime. In our model setting, there is no obvious reason why different exchange rate regimes should affect the level of current account balances, though they may affect the speed of current account adjustment. While we do find the estimated coefficient on the dummy for the crawling exchange rate regime to be significantly positive for emerging market countries, inclusion of two other exchange rate dummies has little quantitative or qualitative impact upon the results shown in tables 4.1 and 4.2.

Edwards (2002) argues that current account deficits are correlated with the probability of financial crises occurring, suggesting that current account dynamics surrounding crisis years might exhibit anomalous behavior. Taking the 1997 to 1998 period as one characterized as crisis years, we

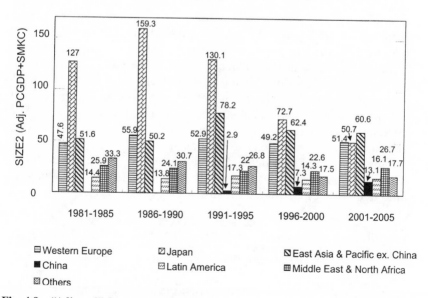

Fig. 4.9 **"Adjusted" financial market size**

reconstruct the five-year panels to exclude this period and reestimate our model. The estimation results remain intact. Similarly, we find that excluding post-1995 data does not make a substantial impact on the results.

We also consider whether oil exporters behave in a fundamentally different manner than nonoil exporters. While we included an "oil exporter" dummy variable in our basic regression specification, if being an oil exporter means that the slope coefficients are substantially different than those obtaining for nonoil exporters, then a dummy variable is not sufficient to address the issue of heterogeneity. When we exclude oil exporters from either the LDC or EMG subsample, the results are virtually unchanged.

4.4 Policy Implications

One question that immediately arises is whether one should be surprised at the current set of global imbalances, given the estimates reported in the preceding. Figure 4.10 displays both actual and predicted current account balances for the IDC group (panel A) and the emerging market group (panel B). In panel A, we can see that the United States is one of the countries that experienced a larger current account deficit than predicted by the model.[33] Panel B shows that many of emerging East Asian countries appear in the area above the 45-degree line; they experienced larger current account surpluses than predicted by the model.[34]

4.4.1 The Effects of Financial Development and Financial Opening for Emerging Asia

A second question that can be asked is what will happen to East Asian current account balances if financial development and liberalization accelerates. Thus far, we have found some evidence that financial development affects current account balances. Here, we need to interpret how the estimated coefficients on financial development variable (SIZE) would affect current account balances, national saving, and investment in interaction with other institutional variables (LEGAL and KAOPEN). Also, we examine the effect of financial opening conditional upon the levels of financial and legal/institutional development.

Panels A, B, and C in figure 4.11 shows the total effect on current account, national saving, and investment (in terms of percentage points as a ratio to GDP), respectively, if the size of financial markets (SIZE) rises by

33. The 45-degree line refers to the points where both actual and predicted values are the same. Hence, in the area above the 45-degree line, actual values are higher than predicted ones, meaning that countries' current account balances are underpredicted by the model.
34. The prediction errors shown in figure 4.10 are consistent with either model misspecification or current account behavior being delinked from the fundamentals (and, hence, being unsustainable). Determination of which interpretation is more appropriate is outside the scope of this chapter. Refer to Clarida (2007) for a debate regarding the issue of current account sustainability.

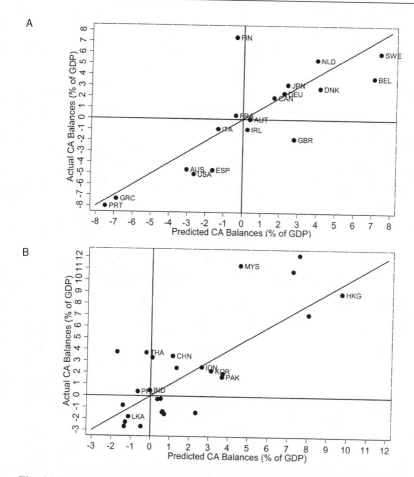

Fig. 4.10   Actual current account balances and in-sample predictions: *A,* Industrialized countries; *B,* Emerging market countries

10 percentage points above the world weighted average conditional on the levels of LEGAL and KAOPEN for emerging market countries.[35] The calculation is made based on the regression results shown in column (4) of table 4.2 and depending on whether the levels of LEGAL and KAOPEN are in the low decile, mean, or high decile in each subsample. This exercise illustrates how the impact of financial development can vary with the level

35. Between the 1996 to 2000 and 2001 to 2005 time periods, the (five-year average of *relative*) SIZE level—the level of financial deepening above or below the weighted world average—increased by 16.3 percentage points for Asian emerging market countries and an astounding 39 percentage points for China. Therefore, examining the effect of a 10 percentage point increase is not too unrealistic. This calculation holds other variables constant, including the level of stock market activeness (SMTO) and market efficiency (INVNETINT).

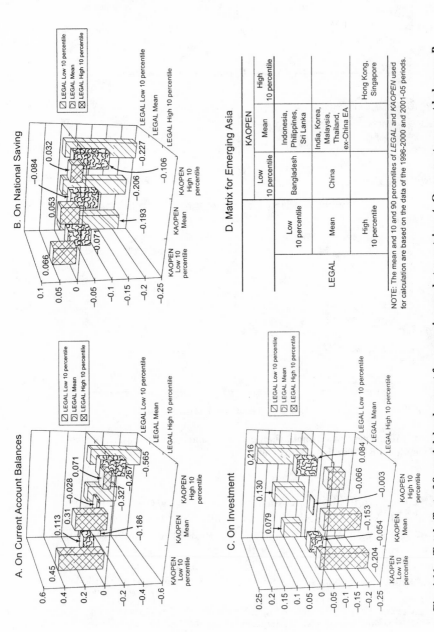

Fig. 4.11 **Total effect of financial development for emerging market countries:** *A*, **On current account balances;** *B*, **On national saving;** *C*, **On investment;** *D*, **Matrix for emerging Asia**

Note: The mean and 10th and 90th percentiles of LEGAL and KAOPEN used for calculation are based on the data of the 1996 to 2000 and 2001 to 2005 periods.

of these two variables. For example, panel A shows that a 10 percentage point increase in SIZE (expressed as the deviation from the world weighted average) can lead an emerging market country equipped with both legal development and financial openness levels above the low 10th percentile (i.e., the bar at the northwest corner on the floor) to lower its current account as a ratio to GDP by 0.186 percentage points. Examining the bars at the same location in the other two panels allows us to determine whether the effect of such a change comes from national saving or investment or both.

Theoretically, the total effects of financial development shown in the panels on national saving and investment should add up exactly to that on current account balances. However, as can be seen in the figures, this is not the case. At least two reasons can be identified for this outcome. First, while the current account regressions account for the covariance of national savings and investment, simply adding two coefficients does not.[36] Second, due to differing data conventions (balance of payments accounting versus national income accounting definition), the flows may not add up exactly. However, it is still worthwhile to examine the total effect on all three variables.

For emerging market countries, we can generalize the total effect of financial development on current account balances as that the more financially open and the less legally/institutionally developed an emerging market country is, the more negative the total effect of financial development on the current account balance is to be. The result seems to be driven by the effects on both national saving and investment. Those countries that experience current account deterioration experience both deterioration in national saving and improvement in investment (except for those with mean KAOPEN and mean LEGAL).

Panel D of figure 4.11 categorizes emerging market countries in East Asia depending on the level of legal development and financial openness. The matrix shows that only Hong Kong and Singapore are categorized as countries with highest 10th percentile legal development and highest 10th percentile financial openness, while many Asian emerging market countries, including China, are categorized in the groups with the middle or lower level of legal development and financial openness. For these economies, financial development might lead to deterioration of current account balances *if* the economy is more open than the bottom decile and its legal systems are not in the top decile.

What about financial opening? We have seen that China in particular has kept its financial markets closed, sparking considerable debate over what

---

36. If some change in one variable affects national saving and investment independently, as long as the change in national saving and investment does not affect each other, the net effect of the change ($\Delta NS - \Delta I$) would be the same as that on current account balances. However, if national saving and investment are highly correlated, as has been found in many studies such as Feldstein and Horioka (1980) and Frankel, Dooley, and Mathieson (1987), simply adding two coefficients does not yield the coefficient in the current account regression.

would occur in the event of capital account liberalization. Figure 4.12 presents a parallel analysis to what we did in figure 4.11, but this time, we examine the total effect of financial opening, a one unit increase in KAOPEN, conditional upon the level of legal/institutional development and the size of financial markets. Panels A, B, and C report the total effect of financial opening on current account balances, national saving, and investment, respectively, for emerging market countries, and panel D ranks East Asian emerging market countries by the level of financial openness measured by KAOPEN.

Panel A of figure 4.12 indicates that financial opening, holding the levels of both legal and financial development constant, would result in a typical emerging market economy experiencing a deteriorating current account balances, except when the economy is financially underdeveloped. Panels B and C show that the deterioration can be driven by either a large decrease in national saving combined with a smaller decrease in investment or a relatively smaller decrease in national saving combined with an improvement in investment. Either outcome is consistent with the saving glut hypothesis, although our results lead to a more nuanced view of the sources of the current account shift.

A one unit increase in KAOPEN is equivalent to China increasing its level of financial openness to that of Korea, Malaysia, and Thailand. If one uses the observed Chinese values of SIZE, LEGAL, and KAOPEN, the implied impact on China's current account balance would be a 1 percentage point decline. Considering that the size of current account surplus for the 2001 to 2005 period is 3.5 percent, this is not a nontrivial effect, although it must be kept in mind that the posited change in openness is very large.

One caveat involves the proper measure of financial development in China, a particularly salient issue. If one measures financial market size adjusting for government bank ownership, the effect would be considerably smaller, about 0.35 percentage points. Thus, we believe the question of how much the Chinese current account balance would be affected by capital account opening remains an open one.

4.4.2 A Magnification Effect of Bond Markets?

Our discussion thus far has focused on the Western side of the Pacific Ocean, with little reference to the United States. The observation that the United States attracts capital from the rest of the world because of its deep and sophisticated financial markets has become something of a cliché. One separate, but related, line of argument is that for such an economy, financial development can function as a magnifier for the effect of other saving-investment determinants, especially budget balances. The idea is that a country with highly developed financial markets may find its budget constraint relaxed because its highly developed financial markets make it

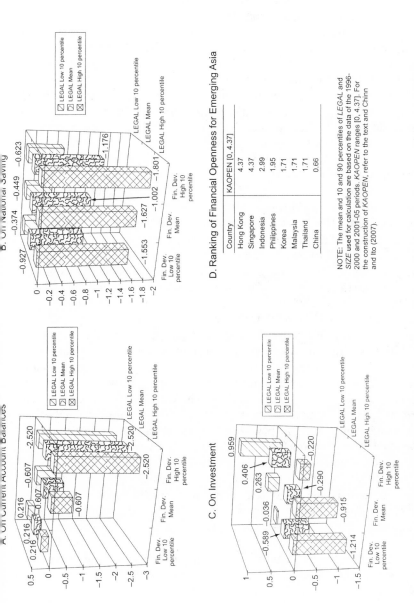

A. On Current Account Balances

0.5
0
-0.5
-1
-1.5
-2
-2.5
-3

0.216 0.216 0.216 -0.607 -0.607 -0.607 -2.520 -2.520 -2.520

Fin. Dev. Low 10 percentile
Fin. Dev. Mean
Fin. Dev. High 10 percentile

LEGAL Low 10 percentile
LEGAL Mean
LEGAL High 10 percentile

☑ LEGAL Low 10 percentile
☑ LEGAL Mean
☒ LEGAL High 10 percentile

B. On National Saving

-0.374 -0.449 -0.623
-0.927

0
-0.2
-0.4
-0.6
-0.8
-1
-1.2
-1.4
-1.6
-1.8
-2

-1.176
-1.801
-1.553 -1.627 -1.002

Fin. Dev. Low 10 percentile
Fin. Dev. Mean
Fin. Dev. High 10 percentile

LEGAL Low 10 percentile
LEGAL Mean
LEGAL High 10 percentile

☑ LEGAL Low 10 percentile
☑ LEGAL Mean
☒ LEGAL High 10 percentile

C. On Investment

0.959
0.406
0.263
-0.036
-0.589

1
0.5
0
-0.5
-1
-1.5

-0.220
-0.290
-0.915
-1.214

Fin. Dev. Low 10 percentile
Fin. Dev. Mean
Fin. Dev. High 10 percentile

LEGAL Low 10 percentile
LEGAL Mean
LEGAL High 10 percentile

☑ LEGAL Low 10 percentile
☑ LEGAL Mean
☒ LEGAL High 10 percentile

D. Ranking of Financial Openness for Emerging Asia

Country	KAOPEN [0, 4.37]
Hong Kong	4.37
Singapore	4.37
Indonesia	2.99
Philippines	1.95
Korea	1.71
Malaysia	1.71
Thailand	1.71
China	0.66

NOTE: The mean and 10 and 90 percentiles of *LEGAL* and *SIZE* used for calculation are based on the data of the 1996–2000 and 2001–05 periods. *KAOPEN* ranges [0, 4.37]. For the construction of *KAOPEN*, refer to the text and Chinn and Ito (2007).

Fig. 4.12 Total effect of financial liberalization for emerging market countries: *A*, On current account balances; *B*, On national saving; *C*, On investment; *D*, Ranking of financial openness for emerging Asia

Notes: The mean and 10th and 90th percentiles of LEGAL and SIZE used for calculation are based on the data of the 1996 to 2000 and 2001 to 2005 periods. KAOPEN ranges [0, 4.37]. For the construction of KAOPEN, refer to the text and Chinn and Ito (2007).

easier for the government to finance its budget. Chinn and Ito (2007a) were unable to find any evidence for this conjecture. Here, we take the opportunity to reexamine the magnifier effect with reference to the link between the budget and current account balances.

Table 4.3 reports the regression results that incorporate the effect of public bond market development (measured by PBBM, public bond market capitalization as a ratio to GDP) and its interactive, that is, magnifier, effect with budget balances. Columns (1) and (2) show the results for industrialized and emerging market countries, respectively, when the PBBM variable and its interaction with the budget balance variable are added to our basic model.[37] Because the PBBM data are limited, there is only an EMG group among the developing country groups. Columns (3) and (4) include stock market turnover, net interest margin, and its interaction with KAOPEN. Interestingly, for the IDC group, whether in column (1) or (3), the interaction term enters significantly. For emerging market countries, the level term for PBBM is significantly negative, but the interaction term is insignificant. The significant coefficient on PBBM for emerging market countries may reflect the tendency that emerging market countries attempt to borrow abroad to finance their budgetary programs. Using the actual five-year average of the U.S. budget balance and the estimates from columns (1) and (3), the estimated coefficient of is found to be as high as 0.487 and 0.642, respectively. These figures are around the high end of the value range of 0.10 to 0.49 found in Chinn and Ito (2007a).

As was shown in figure 4.5, Japan and oil exporting countries in the Middle East, both of which are big current account surplus countries, could be driving the results as outliers. Also, the magnifier effect of financial development can be more important for those countries that try to finance themselves from foreign capital. Therefore, we reestimated by restricting our sample to only country years when the net foreign assets (that are included only from the first year of each five-year panel) are negative. The results are shown in columns (5) and (6) for industrial and emerging market countries, respectively. Now in these specifications, the significance of the estimated coefficient on the interaction term disappears for the IDC group, though the significant coefficient for the PBBM variable remains for the EMG group. However, interestingly, the estimated coefficient on budget balances for IDCs remains significant, and its magnitude is still high, 0.48 (the p-value for the interaction term is now 22 percent). At the very least, budget balances seem to play an important role for current account balances for IDCs.

---

37. We also include a dummy for Japan because, as figure 4.5 shows, Japan, a country with not only a big public bond market, but also big current account surpluses, can be driving the results as an outlier. In fact, the estimated coefficient for the dummy is found to be significantly positive.

Table 4.3   **The impact of public bond market development in current account regressions**

	IDC (1)	EMG (2)	IDC (3)	EMG (4)	Debtor IDC (5)	Debtor EMG (6)
Government budget	0.503	0.105	0.619	0.199	0.481	0.076
balance	(0.153)***	(0.300)	(0.176)***	(0.309)	(0.241)*	(0.366)
Budget balance × PBBM	−0.767	−0.216	−1.11	0.628	−0.741	0.952
	(0.394)*	(1.116)	(0.278)***	(1.375)	(0.590)	(1.664)
Public bond market	0.005	−0.054	−0.004	−0.135	0.016	−0.144
development (PBBM)	(0.017)	(0.038)	(0.015)	(0.036)***	(0.019)	(0.038)***
Financial development	−0.022	0.013	−0.027	0.02	−0.034	0.038
(SIZE)	(0.011)*	(0.014)	(0.012)**	(0.012)	(0.015)**	(0.016)**
Stock market activeness			0.022	0.016	0.027	0.015
(SMTO)			(0.009)**	(0.006)***	(0.012)**	(0.006)**
Net interest margin	−0.332	0.686	−0.309	0.616		
(INVNETINT)	(0.445)	(0.238)***	(0.460)	(0.306)*		
NETINT × KAOPEN			−0.395	0.226	−0.327	0.208
			(0.493)	(0.083)***	(0.518)	(0.108)*
Legal/institutional	0.02	0.019	0.016	0.032	0.026	0.027
development (LEGAL)	(0.010)**	(0.013)	(0.011)	(0.010)***	(0.015)*	(0.013)**
SIZE × LEGAL	0.024	0.016	0.031	0.028	0.034	0.025
	(0.012)*	(0.009)*	(0.012)**	(0.007)***	(0.014)**	(0.010)**
Financial openness	−0.008	−0.024	−0.011	−0.026	−0.015	−0.022
	(0.009)	(0.010)**	(0.009)	(0.009)***	(0.011)	(0.010)**
KAOPEN × LEGAL	0.022	−0.002	0.022	−0.001	0.022	−0.002
	(0.006)***	(0.003)	(0.009)**	(0.003)	(0.010)**	(0.003)
KAOPEN × SIZE	0.005	−0.009	0.001	−0.017	−0.003	−0.012
	(0.011)	(0.004)**	(0.010)	(0.003)***	(0.011)	(0.006)**
No. of observations	80	72	76	65	55	58
Adjusted R^2	0.65	0.60	0.71	0.77	0.63	0.49

Notes: See table 4.2 notes. There are no oil exporting countries in any of the subsamples.
***Significant at the 1 percent level.
**Significant at the 5 percent level.
*Significant at the 10 percent level.

4.5   Concluding Remarks

In this chapter, we have taken a closer look at the effect of financial development on the present configuration of global imbalances. In particular, we scrutinized the effect of financial development from various perspectives: different types of financial markets such as equity, bond, and insurance markets as well as different aspects of financial development such as the cost performance, size, and activeness of the industry. We also examined the role of nonlinearities, in terms of interactions with financial openness and institutional development.

The empirical results from our basic model suggest that the size of financial markets does matter for saving and investment determination. Among developing countries, those with developed financial markets (in terms of their size), better legal systems and institutions, or closed financial markets tend to run current account surpluses. We also found that banking-sector and equity market development seem to be equally important.

We also extended our basic model by including variables that control for the degree of activity of financial markets, as well as for market competitiveness. Based upon the results from this extended model, we determined that that an IDC with more competitive, but less open, financial markets tends to run larger current account surpluses. For developing countries, more competitive financial markets result in a tendency to run larger current account surpluses, a finding in contradiction to the saving glut thesis. Also, developing countries with active equity markets tend to become capital exporters, largely because more active equity markets induce greater national savings. This result is again in contradiction to the saving glut hypothesis.

Generally, we found that for emerging market countries, financial development may lead to deterioration of current account balances *if* the economy exhibits greater than the average openness and a legal system not in the top decile. In other cases, this linkage is not apparent. Moreover, greater financial opening tends to make an emerging market economy run a smaller current account surplus, especially if the economy is financially underdeveloped.

We also investigated whether financial development—rather than shifting the saving and investment schedules—magnifies the impact of other determinants of saving and investment behavior. More specifically, we examined whether public bond markets contribute to relaxing budget constraints and jointly to affecting current account balances. We find some limited evidence in favor of such a magnification effect. One interesting finding is that inclusion of a bond market variable results in an estimated impact of the budget balance on the current account balance that is substantially higher than that obtained in many other studies, including our previous study (Chinn and Ito 2007a).

Overall, our investigation revealed numerous results relevant to the debate over the sources of global imbalances. At the minimum, we have demonstrated that these two hypotheses might have not be exclusionary. First, as we have shown in our previous study, budget balances should not be ruled out as a determinant of current account balances. A 1 percentage point improvement in the budget balance can lead to about half a percentage point improvement in current account balances for IDCs. Second, when we focus on the competitiveness of banking markets or the activeness of capital markets as a measure of financial development, we find the evidence against the saving glut hypothesis. That is, more competitive banking markets or more active equity markets do not necessarily lead countries to become greater capital importers. Third, in terms of the size, financial development does matter for current account balances, but the effect is conditional upon other institutional factors such as capital account openness and legal or institutional development. Fourth, greater financial openness leads to a deterioration of the current account, in a manner consistent with some aspects of the saving glut hypothesis. That is, countries with more developed legal systems and more developed financial markets (in terms of the size) tend to experience smaller current account surpluses.

Data Appendix

The data used in this chapter were drawn from a number of different sources. In the following, we provide a listing of the mnemonics for the variables used in the analysis, descriptions of these variables and the source(s) from which the primary data for constructing these variables were taken. A listing of the countries in the final sample, along with the country groupings used in the analysis, is provided in the working paper version of this chapter. For most countries, data were available from 1971 through 2005.

Table 4A.1   Data

Mnemonic	Source	Variable description
CURRENT	WDI, IFS, WEO	Current account to GDP ratio
NATL_SAVING	WDI	National saving to GDP ratio
GROSS_KF	WDI	Capital formation to GDP ratio
GSUR	WDI, IFS	General government budget balance, ratio to GDP
NFA	LM	Stock of net foreign assets, ratio to GDP
RELY	WDI	Relative per capita income, adjusted by purchasing power parity (PPP) exchange rates, measured relative to the United States, range (0 to 1)
RELDEPY	WDI	Youth dependency ratio, population under fifteen/ population between fifteen and sixty-five
RELDEPO	WDI	Old dependency ratio, population over sixty-five/ population between fifteen and sixty-five
YGRAVG	WDI	Average real GDP growth
TOTSD	WDI	Standard deviation of terms of trade
OPEN	WDI	Openness indicator: ratio of exports plus imports of goods and nonfactor services to GDP
SIZE	BDL, Authors' calculations	Financial market development in terms of its size, PCGDP + SMKC
PCGDP	BDL	Private credit creation as a ratio to GDP

(continued)

Table 4A.1   (continued)

Mnemonic	Source	Variable description
SMTV	BDL	Stock market total value as a ratio to GDP, as a measure of financial market activeness
SMTO	BDL	Stock market turnover
PVBM	BDL	Private bond market capitalization as a ratio to GDP
PBBM	BDL	Public bond market capitalization as a ratio to GDP
LIFEINS	BDL	Life insurance premium as a ratio to GDP
OVERHEAD	BDL	Accounting value of a bank's overhead costs as a share of its total assets
(INV)NETINT	BDL	Accounting value of bank's net interest revenue as a share of its interest-bearing (total earning) assets.
SIZE2	BDL, Authors' calculations	General level of financial development, first principal component of PCGDP, SMKC, SMTV, PVBM, PBBM, INVNETINT, and LIFEINS
SIZE2A	BDL, Authors' calculations	SIZE adjusted for the size of public-sector involvement
KAOPEN	Chinn-Ito	Capital account openness
BQ	ICRG	Quality of bureaucracy
LAO	ICRG	Law and order
CORRUPT	ICRG	Corruption index
LEGAL	Authors' calculations	General level of legal development, first principal component of BQ, LAO, and CORRUPT.

Sources: BDL: Beck, Demirgüc-Kunt, and Levine (2001, updated in following years); CI: Chinn and Ito (2006); ICRG: International Country Risk Guide; IFS: IMF's International Financial Statistics; IMF: Other IMF databases; LM: Lane and Milesi-Ferretti (2006); and WDI: World Development Indicator (2006).

References

Alfaro, L., S. Kalemli-Ozcan, and V. Volosovych. 2003. Why doesn't capital flow from rich to poor countries? An empirical investigation. University of Houston. Unpublished Manuscript.

Bailliu, J. N. 2000. Private capital flows, financial development, and economic growth in developing countries. Bank of Canada Working Paper no. 00-15. Ottawa: Bank of Canada.

Beck, T., A. Demirgüc-Kunt, and R. Levine. 2001. A new database on financial development and structure. In *Financial structure and economic growth: A cross-country comparison of banks, markets, and development,* ed. A. Demirgüc-Kunt and R. Levine. Cambridge, MA: MIT Press.

Beck, T., and R. Levine. 2005. Legal institutions and financial development. In *Handbook of New Institutional Economics,* ed. C. Menard and M. Shirley, 251–78. Dordrecht, The Netherlands: Kluwer.

Bekaert, G., C. R. Harvey, and C. Lundblad. 2006. Financial openness and the Chinese growth experience. Columbia University. Mimeograph.

Bernanke, B. 2005. The global saving glut and the U.S. current account. Remarks at the Sandridge lecture, Virginia Association of Economics, Richmond, Virginia.

Boyd, J. H., R. Levine, and B. D. Smith. 2001. The impact of inflation on financial sector performance. *Journal of Monetary Economics* 47:221–48.

Caballero, R., F. Emmanuel, and G. Pierre-Olivier, 2006. An equilibrium model of global imbalances and low interest rates. NBER Working Paper no. 11996. Cambridge, MA: National Bureau of Economic Research.

Chinn, M., and H. Ito. 2006. What matters for financial development? Capital controls, institutions, and interactions. *Journal of Development Economics* 82:163–92.

———. 2007a. Current account balances, financial development and institutions: Assaying the world "savings glut." *Journal of International Money and Finance* 26 (4): 546–69.

———. 2007b. A new measure of financial openness. University of Wisconsin. Mimeograph.

Chinn, M., and J. Lee. 2006. Current account and real exchange rate dynamics in the G-7 countries. *Journal of International Money and Finance* 25 (March): 257–74.

Chinn, M., and E. Prasad. 2003. Medium-term determinants of current accounts in industrial and developing countries: An empirical exploration. *Journal of International Economics* 59 (1): 47–76.

Clarida, R. 2005a. Japan, China, and the U.S. current account deficit. *CATO Journal* 25 1:111–14.

———. 2005b. Some thoughts on "The sustainability and adjustment of global current account imbalances." Speech given at the Council on Foreign Relations, Washington, DC.

Clarida, R. H., ed. 2007. *G7 current account imbalances: Sustainability and adjustment.* Cambridge, MA: National Bureau of Economic Research.

Demirgüc-Kunt, A., and R. Levine. 2001. Bank-based and market-based financial systems—Cross-country comparisons. In *Financial structure and economic growth: A cross-country comparison of banks, markets, and development,* ed. A. Demirgüc-Kunt and R. Levine, 81–140. Cambridge, MA: MIT Press.

Dooley, M., D. Folkerts-Landau, and P. Garber. 2005. *International financial stability: Asia, interest rates, and the dollar.* Frankfurt: Deutsche Bank Global Research.

Edwards, S. 1996. Why Are Latin America's saving rates so low: An international comparative analysis. *Journal of Development Economics* 51:5–44.

———. 2002. Does the current account matter?, In *Preventing currency crises in emerging markets,* ed. S. Edwards and J. A. Frankel, 21–76. Chicago: University of Chicago Press.

Feldstein, M., and C. Horioka. 1980. Domestic saving and international capital flows. *Economic Journal* 90:314–29.

Frankel, J., M. Dooley, and D. Mathieson. 1987. International capital mobility in developing countries vs. industrialized countries: What do saving-investment correlations tell us? *IMF Staff Papers* 34 (September): 503–30.

Gale, W., and P. Orszag. 2004. Budget deficits, national saving, and interest rates. *Brookings Papers on Economic Activity,* Issue no. 2:101–210. Washington, DC: Brookings Institution.

Johnson, S., J. McMillan, and C. Woodruff. 2002. Property rights and finance. *American Economic Review* 92:1335–56.

King, R. G., and R. Levine. 1993. Finance and growth: Schumpeter might be right. *Quarterly Journal of Economics* 108:717–38.

Kose, M. A., E. Prasad, K. Rogoff, and S. J. Wei. 2006. Financial globalization: A reappraisal. IMF Working Paper no. WP/06/189. Washington, DC: International Monetary Fund.

La Porta, R., F. Lopez-de-Silanes, and A. Shleifer. 2002. Government ownership of banks. *Journal of Finance* 57:265–301.

La Porta, R., F. Lopez-de-Silanes, A. Shleifer, and R. W. Vishny. 1998. Law and finance. *Journal of Political Economy* 106 (6): 1113–55.

Lane, P., and G. M. Milesi-Ferretti. 2006. The external wealth of Nations Mark II: Revised and extended estimates of foreign assets and liabilities, 1970–2004. IMF Working Paper no. WP/06/69. Washington, DC: International Monetary Fund.

Levine, R. 2005. Finance and growth: Theory and evidence. In *Handbook of economic growth,* P. Aghion and S. Durlauf, 865–934. Amsterdam: Elsevier Science.

Levine, R., N. Loayza, and T. Beck. 2000. Financial intermediation and growth: Causality and causes. *Journal of Monetary Economics* 46:31–77.

Mendoza, E. G., V. Quadrini, and J.-V. Ríos-Rull. 2006. Financial integration, financial deepness and global imbalances. Paper presented at the 7th Jacques Polak Annual Research conference, Washington, DC.

Obstfeld, M., and K. Rogoff. 1996. *Foundations of international macroeconomics.* Cambridge, MA: MIT Press.

Rajan, R. G., and L. Zingales. 1998. Financial dependence and growth. *American Economic Review* 88:559–86.

Tesar, L. 1995. Evaluating the gains from international risksharing. *Carnegie-Rochester Conference Series on Public Policy* 42:95–143.

Wurgler, J. 2000. Financial markets and the allocation of capital. *Journal of Financial Economics* 58:187–214.

Comment   Edwin Lai

My comments incorporate not just my discussion during the conference but also my reaction after reading the latest version of the chapter. This chapter is about financial development and current account balances. It looks at the effect of various aspects of financial development on current account (CA) balances and saving-investment determination. The chapter is mainly motivated by Bernanke's (2005) "global saving glut" hypothesis. The hypothesis can be briefly stated as follows:

1. The U.S. current account deficit is mainly determined by the low cost of borrowing made possible by the huge inflows of funds from emerging markets, such as China and the rest of East Asia.

2. Investment demand in the United States has been very strong (or the United States is an attractive destination for investment) in the last ten years or so because of its political stability, strong property rights, good regulatory environment, and strong performance in the equity market and later the property market (following the dot-com bubble burst).

3. The CA deficit has very little to do with the large budget deficit of the United States.

4. The U.S. current account deficit is determined by factors beyond the U.S. borders.

Bernanke thinks that the solution to this "unnatural" reversal of roles of the less-developed countries (LDCs) being lenders and developed coun-

Edwin Lai is a senior research economist and advisor at the Federal Reserve Bank of Dallas.

tries (DCs) being borrowers is for emerging markets to improve their investment environments, macroeconomic stability, property rights, and financial liberalization.

Essentially, the main point of Bernanke's (2005) speech was to explain the ballooning current account deficit of the United States in the years leading to 2005. The alternative hypothesis he focused on was the "twin deficit" hypothesis—the large current account deficit was a result of the large budget deficit.

The policy implications could not be more different. If the saving glut theory is correct, then the solution to the huge current account deficit of the United States is for emerging markets to liberalize financial sectors so that their citizens can invest their savings in domestic economies. This would possibly result in higher interest rates (or higher returns to investors) for savers and lower interest rates for borrowers (or lower cost of capital) in these countries. If the twin deficit hypothesis is correct, then the reduction of the humongous U.S. current account deficit requires a reduction of the budget deficit.

To facilitate discussion, let us write down the following simple identity:

$$CA = S - I + (T - G),$$

where CA = current account balance; S = domestic private saving; I = domestic private investment; T = tax revenue; G = government purchases. Suppose the country under discussion is the United States. Obviously, if $T - G$ is relatively stable over time, then the ballooning CA deficit cannot be due to changes in budget deficit. It must be due to a much faster increase in I relatively to that of S. On the contrary, if changes in $T - G$ more or less mirrored changes in CA, then the twin deficit hypothesis cannot be rejected.

My view of the saving glut hypothesis is that it comprises three parts. First, twin deficit hypothesis does not explain the huge current account deficit of the United States in recent years. Instead, the CA deficit must be explained by large increase in I relative to that of S in recent years. Second, the large increase in I in the United States was made possible by large influx of funds from emerging markets, whose financial development is relatively weak. Third, financial liberalization in these emerging markets can reduce the outflows of funds from these countries and, therefore, diminish this global saving glut. This will in turn help to reduce the CA deficit of the United States as cheap funds are not as easily available from overseas as before. Let us deal with each part one by one.

For the first part of the hypothesis, if one examines the data on current account balance of the United States in recent years (see table 4C.1) and compare them with data on government budget balance of the United States during the same period (see table 4C.2), one can see that the CA balance continued to deteriorate despite the gradual reduction in budget deficit. So the twin deficit hypothesis is not supported by the data. So the first part of the hypothesis seems to be right.

Table 4C.1   Current account balance in billions of U.S.$ (estimates after 2006)

Country	2000	2001	2002	2003	2004	2005	2006	2007	2008
Canada	19.715	16.213	12.605	10.486	22.369	23.074	20.792	25.603	17.909
China	20.519	17.405	35.422	45.875	68.659	160.818	249.866	379.162	453.146
France	21.968	26.086	19.8	14.74	2.641	−23.951	−27.712	−39.363	−48.885
Germany	−32.557	0.38	40.588	46.286	117.988	128.379	147.134	175.371	174.137
Italy	−5.863	−0.639	−9.483	−19.605	−15.489	−27.461	−45.215	−47.964	−48.657
Japan	119.605	87.794	112.607	136.238	172.07	165.69	170.437	195.904	195.145
Russia	46.839	33.935	29.116	35.41	59.514	84.443	95.322	72.543	49.181
Saudi Arabia	14.336	9.366	11.889	28.085	51.995	90.11	95.514	83.122	81.807
United Kingdom	−37.649	−31.512	−24.79	−24.386	−35.405	−55.435	−77.236	−96.687	−105.144
United States	−417.429	−384.701	−459.636	−522.115	−640.157	−754.852	−811.483	−784.341	−788.293

Source: International Monetary Fund (2007) World Economic Outlook Database, October 2007.

Table 4C.2   General government balance as percentage of GDP (estimates after 2006)

Country	2000	2001	2002	2003	2004	2005	2006	2007	2008
Canada	2.9	0.7	-0.1	-0.1	0.8	1.6	1	0.9	0.9
France	-1.5	-1.5	-3.1	-4.1	-3.6	-3	-2.5	-2.5	-2.7
Germany	1.3	-2.8	-3.7	-4	-3.8	-3.4	-1.6	-0.2	-0.5
Italy	-0.8	-3.1	-2.9	-3.5	-3.5	-4.2	-4.4	-2.1	-2.3
Japan	-7.6	-6.3	-8	-8	-6.2	-4.8	-4.1	-3.9	-3.8
United Kingdom	1.5	0.9	-1.8	-3.5	-3.4	-3.3	-2.7	-2.5	-2.3
United States	1.6	-0.4	-3.8	-4.8	-4.4	-3.6	-2.6	-2.6	-2.9
United States (in billions of U.S.$)	159	-39.35	-396.675	-529.775	-508.7	-446.525	-344.75	-353.169	-414.781

Source: International Monetary Fund (2007), World Economic Outlook Database, October 2007.

For the second part, if one examines data on current account balance of countries all over the world in, say, 2005 and 2006, it is clear that while the United States ran huge CA deficits (US$811 billion in 2006), a number of developed and less-developed countries ran CA surpluses. In 2006, for example, the countries that ran the largest CA surpluses were China (US$250 billion), Japan (US$170 billion) and Germany (US$147 billion).[1] Therefore, one cannot say that the capital inflows into the United States were mainly supported by capital outflows from emerging markets where the levels of financial development were low. So the second part of the hypothesis can only be partially true.

For the third part, it is not immediately clear whether financial liberalization in the LDCs that ran CA surplus can reduce the CA deficit deficit in the United States. In fact, this topic should be the main theme of the present chapter. Note that to be consistent with the saving glut hypothesis, the kind of financial liberalization that one should consider in this context should be the type that attracts domestic savers to invest in domestic markets. This would include reducing government regulation in the financial sector, improving legal infrastructure to enforce contracts and protect property rights, and maintaining macroeconomic stability. Viewed from this perspective, I can see several areas where this chapter can improve if it truly wants to test whether the global saving glut hypothesis is true. First, the chapter should focus on emerging markets. Second, one should focus on variables that capture institutional quality that improves the domestic investment environment, such as legal infrastructure, corporate governance, and independence of judiciary. The variables that the authors of this chapter use are mainly not of this nature; instead, they use data that may or may not reflect institutional quality or investment environment. For example, activity in the stock market may not reflect high level of financial development if it is only a consequence of a lack of other high-quality channels for domestic savers to invest (e.g., bonds and bank deposits), as reflected in the recent stock craze in China. Third, not all types of financial reforms help domestic capital stay at home. On the contrary, some reforms tend to increase capital outflows rather than stamping them, such as reforms that allow home citizens to invest abroad. Therefore, one should distinguish between the different types of financial liberalization and expect them to yield different effects on the CA.

It is true that China, being an emerging market, is running higher than its share of CA surplus as the United States is running higher than its share of CA deficit (especially if one looks at not only data up to 2006, but also the estimated figures for 2007 and 2008 from the International Monetary Fund [IMF]). Therefore, to test the saving glut hypothesis, one should perhaps carry out an in-depth study of China. Would financial liberalization that reduces government regulation in the financial sector, improve legal

1. They are followed by Russia (US$95 billion) and Saudi Arabia (US$95 billion).

infrastructure to enforce contracts and protect property rights, and maintain macroeconomic stability, reduce the CA surplus of China? Is it necessary for China to allow its currency to float more freely in order for its CA surplus to decrease substantially? A time series analysis or case study may be necessary to address this question.

Yet the present chapter does not seem to be directly testing the saving glut hypothesis. Instead, being inspired by the hypothesis, it carries out a cross-section analysis of the effects of financial development on current account balance. To bring the research closer to the saving glut hypothesis, I suggest focusing more on the LDCs, as these are the countries where financial reforms are more pronounced. Moreover, if one really wants to find out whether financial liberalization in general can reduce CA balance in LDCs, one should perhaps test it directly. For example, one can identify episodes of financial liberalization in the LDCs and then run a cross-section regression of lagged CA balance on dummies of episodes of financial liberalization while controlling for economic fundamentals that affect CA balance, such as exchange rate, business cycle, capital mobility, and so on. This will be less controversial than using variables that may or may not be able to capture financial liberalization.

Finally, the empirical study should be guided by theory. The Mundell-Fleming model immediately comes to mind, as it continues to be one of the most compelling models in international finance. If one adopts the Mundell-Fleming model, then how does financial liberalization affect current account balance in that context? Financial liberalization may be interpreted as an increase in the interest rate faced by lenders and a decrease in the interest rate faced by borrowers. In the Mundell-Fleming model, capital mobility and exchange rate regime affect how current account balance reacts to changes in the interest rate faced by lenders and that faced by borrowers. Therefore, both capital mobility (high, medium, low) and exchange rate regime (floating, managed, fixed) should be put on the right-hand side of the equation. To illustrate why exchange rate regime should be taken into account, note that if China continues to peg its currency to the U.S. dollar (albeit allowing it to appreciate slowly), one surmises that its current account balance would continue to be large even if it undertakes financial liberalization.

In summary, this chapter addresses a very topical and important policy issue. Its findings should provide valuable inspiration for future research.

References

Bernanke, B. 2005. The global saving glut and the U.S. current account. Remarks at the Sandridge lecture, Virginia Association of Economics, Richmond, Virginia.

International Monetary Fund. 2007. IMF World Economic Outlook Database, October 2007. http://www.imf.org/external/pubs/ft/weo/2007/02/weodata/index.aspx.

Comment   Edward Robinson and Liew Yin Sze

Professors Chinn and Ito have done a careful empirical analysis of the determinants of current account balances over the past two decades. We think their study is a useful complement to the volumes of more conceptual papers that have been written on this subject.

We will first make a few comments on the chapter's empirical findings before providing some general points on financial development in the Asian region. We close with some tentative remarks on the global imbalances.

Empirical Results

The authors set up a panel equation specification with five-year nonoverlapping data stretching from the mid-1980s. They include the usual set of conditioning variables, supplemented by a comprehensive list of other macroeconomic and institutional factors.

To begin with, there still appears to be a great deal of variation in current account balances that remained unexplained, especially for the emerging economies. In figure 4.10, the scatter plot for industrial countries shows a tighter relationship, while that for emerging economies displays a higher degree of "scatter" and more noticeable outliers.

However, the regressions do yield useful results. Allow us to comment on two of these.

Our first observation pertains to the evidence that fiscal balances do play a role in the determination of current account balances, particularly for the developed countries. Thus, the deterioration in the current account deficit in the United States in the early part of this decade coincided with a significant worsening of the fiscal position as well.

However, the relationship may not be an entirely strong one. It is noteworthy that the U.S. current account deficit continued to widen in recent years even though the fiscal shortfall has narrowed. In Asia, this "twin deficits" argument may also have been fairly weak. Many Asian governments had well-managed finances prior to the Asian crisis. The deterioration in the current account prior to the 1997 crisis was really driven by the saving-investment imbalance in the private sector, amid strong investments and capital inflows. Subsequently, although the fiscal position of many Asian nations deteriorated in the aftermath of the crisis, the current account has swung decisively into positive territory. Therefore, the fiscal bal-

Edward Robinson is executive director of the Economic Policy Department of the Monetary Authority of Singapore (MAS). Liew Yin Sze is lead economist in the Economic Policy Department of the Monetary Authority of Singapore (MAS).

The views expressed here are entirely those of the discussants and should not be attributed to the MAS.

ance may not be the dominant factor in the current account dynamics for all countries all the time.

Second, the focus of the chapter is on what the data can reveal about the role of financial variables. In general, we believe that the results and inferences in tables 4.1 and 4.2 are reasonable.

The coefficients of the financial development variables are generally considerably smaller than those for the standard macroeconomic factors such as fiscal balance, net foreign assets, and relative incomes.

Although not entirely comparable, these findings are broadly in line with similar studies by Beck et al. (2001), which find that overall financial development is positively correlated with economic growth. It is interesting to note that in the Beck et al. type studies, the *size* of the financial sector is usually not statistically significant.[1] What comes strongly through as more distinguishing across countries is financial activity and efficiency. In this study as well, the information content of efficiency/activity variables is likewise confirmed.

We would like to make two minor comments that would suggest adopting a more careful or nuanced interpretation of some results.

First, it must be said that financial variables are difficult to define and measure, especially in Asia. Furthermore, there is the potential multicollinearity between financial development and openness measures that the authors allude to. This issue is likely to be important for Asia because financial development tends to be directly correlated with being tapped into global financial markets. More broadly in Asia, the growth development strategy is an outward, export-oriented one.

Second, it is important to appreciate that the Asian economies went through an extended period of cleaning up and reform after 1997 to 1998. Against this, we may not wish to take the estimated coefficients as some form of long-term structural (or deep) parameters. For example, national savings tended to rise after the 1997 crisis as corporates and households attempted to rebuild their balance sheets. It may not have very much to do with financial openness or other institutional measures. (In other words, the coefficients could be biased by the "precautionary-rebuild-of-reserves" phase in the sample set.) This "discontinuity" may have been an important reason for the overestimation of investment in Asia (or underestimation of the current account surplus) by the Chinn-Ito model for the postcrisis period.

Relatedly, China is highlighted as an example of a country that would tend to run large surpluses given its large but closed financial market and low index of institutional development. Large current account surpluses in China are in fact a relatively recent phenomenon. Actually, its average an-

---

1. In the Beck et al. (2001) study, *finance size* is defined as the log of the sum of private credit and market capitalization.

nual current account balance was close to 1 percent of gross domestic product (GDP) between 1982 and 2004. China's current account balance only swung into a large surplus of over 7 percent of GDP in the last two years. Nonetheless, we would agree that the combination of macroeconomic, financial, and institutional developments in China is likely to sustain its current account surpluses, going forward.

Despite the preceding caveats, we have no doubt that the variation in financial development lies behind the distribution of the current account outcomes we observe. A more developed financial system allows the link between domestic savings and investments to be broken, which permits a country to optimize consumption on an intertemporal basis.

Indeed, a validation of this point is readily available from studies that considered this from the capital flow perspective. Our colleague Chew (2006) utilized an "augmented" gravity model to analyze the effect of various factors on cross-border asset holdings. She made use of the bilateral data set on financial investment of over 200 countries in the International Monetary Fund's (IMF) Coordinated Portfolio Investment Survey (CPIS) over the period 2001 to 2005.[2]

The standard gravity model was "augmented" in order to account for financial development and institutional variables and estimated for various country blocs including Asia. Chew's analysis showed that the size of cross-border financial flows increases significantly with the financial development of the domestic and foreign financial markets. Her finding is consistent with the results of the Chinn-Ito chapter as greater financial development in emerging market economies reduces the constraint on domestic investment spending. This is reflected as an increase in the dispersion of current account balances across countries. Chew also found that institutional factors, such as regulatory standards and capital controls, are important determinants of cross-border capital flows. In addition, the degree of transparency and disclosure by financial institutions is seen to have a statistically significant role in augmenting cross-border financial flows by providing a boost to investor confidence.[3]

Future Financial Development in Asia and Implications for Capital Flows

We would classify this chapter as belonging to the genre of studies that seek to understand the role of financial development in the broader context of sustainable economic growth.

---

2. This data set provides a geographical breakdown of total portfolio investment assets in a bilateral matrix displaying stocks of cross-border holdings of assets measured at market prices.

3. Restricting the data set to Asian countries as destinations for international capital flows, the results remain that financial development and other institutional factors have a significant impact on the size of financial flows into Asia. Variables such as regulatory standards are important determinants of the sources, but not destinations, of financial flows into Asia.

We believe that Professors Chinn and Ito's focus on financial development and institutional factors is timely. The Asian financial crisis ten years ago vividly brought home the fact that in the race for growth, Asian governments, and even multilateral institutions, had neglected or downplayed the "software" aspect of economic development, that is, developing the institutions, systems, infrastructure and legal framework, and human resources required for a modern market-based economy. This aspect of development is perhaps the most difficult.

In Singapore, the development of deeper and more liquid financial markets has certainly helped in raising economic efficiency via improved allocation and deployment of capital. The deepening of the financial markets has also strengthened resilience to shocks and allowed a large current account surplus to be accommodated efficiently, in this case, through fairly sizeable capital outflows.

What about the rest of Asia? It has often been said that regional integration has thus far been a "real story," that is, Asian trade integration has proceeded rapidly, driven to a large extent by the outsourcing activities of multinational corporations and the development of a highly integrated regional production network. Indeed, it has become increasingly clear that financial development has not kept pace.

Asia's bond markets, for example, constitute only 113 percent of GDP, compared to 193 percent in the United States and 151 percent in the European Union. Excluding Japan, this percentage falls to just 49 percent.

At this juncture, we would like to bring together two pieces of research we have been interested in.

First, we have been doing some work at the MAS in estimating the likely profile of current account balances for some key Asian countries. Our estimates, which use as a starting point the simulations and projections from the IMF, show that that the current account surpluses in Asia are likely to persist, led to a significant extent by the growing trade surpluses in China. For example, China's current account surplus is expected to reach some US$275 billion (or 6.5 percent of GDP) or more in 2011.

Second, there have been a number of papers revisiting the Lucas Paradox. A recent IMF study examined the experience of Europe and found that with increasing financial integration, capital in Europe flowed in the correct direction, that is, "downhill" from rich to poor (or less rich) countries within the Union (Abiad, Leigh, and Mody 2007). Poorer countries that are financially integrated run larger current account deficits, whereas the richer countries run surpluses. Thus, financial integration in Europe was a force driving the increase in current account dispersion within the region.

So for Asia, taken together, these results point toward the need for increased collaborative efforts to accelerate the pace of financial deepening and integration. A well-developed financial sector in Asia will help to raise investment spending in the region and contribute to the reduction of the saving glut. Increased financial integration could also nudge capital flow "downhill" from rich to less-rich countries within Asia itself. Professors Chinn and Ito's findings give us the basis for confidence that as financial deepening proceeds in the Asian economies, the dynamics of capital allocation are likely to improve and with it the sustainability of the current account path.

Conclusion

We conclude with some remarks on the global imbalances. It may be fair to say that, at best, the current state of affairs represents an "unholy truce" among diverse groups of financial participants, each having a vested interest in prolonging the status quo.

Indeed, at the moment, the global economy seems to be headed for an uneventful and gradual correction of the imbalances. While U.S. GDP growth has slowed, the expansion in Europe and Japan has picked up, and the growth of some of the key emerging economies, including the BRICs—namely Brazil, Russia, India, and China—has remained firm. This broadening of global growth would tend to error correct or at least stabilize the imbalances. The fall in the trade-weighted US$ since early 2002 and relatively more stable oil prices will also help.

We, therefore, suspect that Bretton Woods II may well be a passing phase rather than a stable long-term equilibrium. Asian currencies have generally become more flexible in recent years, and this is an important development in view of projections of sustained saving-investment imbalances in the region. Adjustments in exchange rates would eventually manifest themselves to restore equilibriums. Over the longer term, the scope for greater exchange rate flexibility in Asia will likely increase along with efforts to further deepen the financial infrastructure and supporting institutions.

References

Abiad, A., D. Leigh, and A. Mody. 2007. International finance and income convergence: Europe is different. IMF Working Paper no. WP/07/64. Washington, DC: International Monetary Fund, March.

Beck, T., A. Demirgüç-Kunt, R. Levine, and V. Maksimovic. 2001. Financial structure and economic development: Firm, industry, and country evidence. In *Financial structure and economic growth: A cross-country comparison of banks, markets, and development,* ed. A. Demirgüç-Kunt and R. Levine, 189–242. Cambridge, MA: MIT Press.

Chew, C. 2006. The global capital market from Singapore's perspective. Monetary Authority of Singapore. Mimeograph.

5

Consumer Credit Market in Korea since the Economic Crisis

Chang-Gyun Park

5.1 Introduction

The purpose of the chapter is twofold. One is to document the chronology of rapid growth of household credit in Korea since the foreign exchange crisis in 1997. The other is to examine the development of the credit card crisis in 2003 and evaluate the adequacy of ensuing policy responses.

Rapid increase in household debt was primarily the result of a large-scale deregulation and paradigm shift mainly driven by various efforts taken to restructure the entire financial sector after the foreign exchange crisis in 1997. The new principle adapted by financial institutions after the financial deregulation was to put most emphasis on resource allocation based on market mechanism. Price signal replaced direction government intervention as the criterion in allocation of credit resources. It was a well-known secret in the Korean financial market that household lending had been more profitable than corporate lending. Consequently, removal of government intervention coupled with a low interest rate resulted in expansion of the consumer credit market in an unprecedented pace. While one cannot deny the fact that allocation of credit resources based on price signal increased the efficiency of the economic system, recent economic history offers many examples of financial turmoil that were sparked by rapid accumulation of debts soon after deregulation of the financial sector without carefully revamping the regulatory framework. The deregulation of the financial industry in Korea after the foreign exchange crisis was not an exception in the sense that it was followed by a boom in the consumer credit market that eventually resulted in a violent crash landing.

Chang-Gyun Park is an assistant professor in the College of Business Administration at Chung-Ang University

The most serious damage was done to the credit card market. Arrears soared up and the overdue rate reached almost 30 percent. Several credit card companies went bankrupt and were bailed out by the government or parent banks. A sharp increase in the number of credit delinquents in large part due to overdue credit card debts was accompanied by an increase in unemployment and depression of consumption expenditure among the delinquents. The havoc in the credit card market also caused social problems such as disintegration of family and suicides that invited serious concerns from the general public as well as the policy circle. We discuss the development of the credit card crisis with the presumption that it is a classic example of regulatory failure. We argue that with timely and proper regulatory actions, much of the difficulty inflicted by the credit card crisis would have been alleviated, if not averted.

The next section describes the development of the consumer credit market in Korea after the foreign exchange crisis in 1997. Section 5.3 examines the causes and consequences of fast increase in household debt. Section 5.4 focuses on the credit card crisis that occurred in 2003 and evaluates the adequacy of policy measures that were taken in response to changes in market condition. The conclusion follows.

5.2   Household Debt in Korea after the Economic Crisis

5.2.1   Increase in Household Debt

While showing a clear sign of stabilization recently, household debt in Korea has grown at a spectacular pace since the foreign exchange crisis in 1997. According to figure 5.1, the household debt market seems to have gone through three distinguished phases since 1997. The first phase covers the period between 1997 and 1999 when household debt went through a period of slump following the foreign exchange crisis and the subsequent recession induced by the most part by the high interest rate policy that the Korean government vigorously pursued to restore stability in the foreign exchange market. Household debt dropped by 13 percent in 1998 and had not recovered the precrisis level until 2000. Only after 2000, it gained momentum for rapid growth observed in the following three years that constituted the second phase. Outstanding stock of household debt increased by 120 percent from 2000 to 2002, while disposable income increased only by 15.5 percent. As a consequence, debt burden soared, and households' ability to repay considerably deteriorated. For example, the debt-to-income ratio sharply increased to 113.3 percent in 2002, from just 63.8 percent in 1999, and the debt-to-asset ratio also rose by 11.7 percentage points from 40.1 in 1999 to 51.8 in 2002 (see figure 5.2).[1]

1. *Debt-to-income ratio* is defined as the ratio between total household debt and disposable income for households and private unincorporated enterprises. *Debt-to-asset ratio* is defined

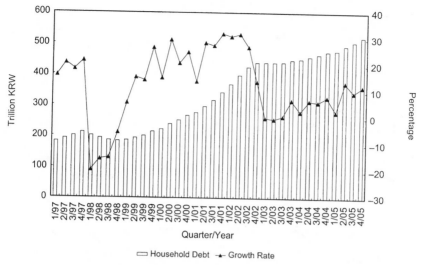

Fig. 5.1   Household debt in Korea: 1997–2005
Source: Bank of Korea.
Note: Growth rate is the annualized quarterly growth rate.

Rapid accumulation of household debt invited serious concerns from regulatory authority as well as credit providers. Alarmed with the unprecedented speed of debt accumulation, banks and credit card companies, two major credit providers to households, started to reconsider their business practices and tighten the conditions for credit provision.[2] Regulatory authority also took various policy measures to curb the explosive growth of household debt. Consequently, the annual growth rate dropped to around 10 percent that is believed to be sustainable considering the long-term trend of aggregate income growth. However, the economy paid dear for rapid accumulation of household debt. The biggest credit card company in Korea was forced to resort to an emergency loan in order to avoid bankruptcy, and the financial market underwent a couple of turbulent episodes in 2003 and 2004. The third phase started in 2003. Seemingly uncontrollable accumulation of household debt came to a halt, and a cautious atmosphere replaced the feverish race to extend lending toward the household sector. While the speed of credit expansion was slowed down and the market regained a sense

as the ratio between total individual debt and total individual assets in the Flow of Funds table published by the Bank of Korea. The individual sector in the table includes private unincorporated enterprises and various nonprofit organizations as well as households. Therefore, household debt in figure 5.1 does not coincide with individual debt in the Flow of Funds table. The change of basis is unavoidable because information on aggregate asset holdings by households is not available.

2. Most of the credit providers, especially credit card companies, tried to increase market share in the belief that larger market share would bring them a competitive edge based on network effect.

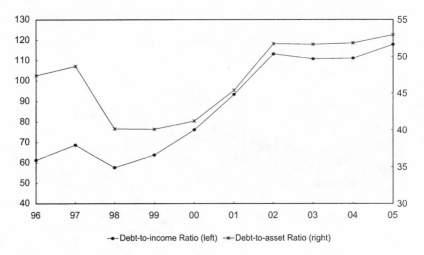

-•-Debt-to-income Ratio (left)   -*-Debt-to-asset Ratio (right)

Fig. 5.2   Trend in ability-to-repay indicators
Source: Bank of Korea.
Notes: Debt-to-income ratio is the ratio between household debt and household disposable income. Debt-to-asset ratio is the ratio between individual debt and asset in the Flow of Funds table.

of stability, financial companies in the consumer credit market were forced to undergo a turbulent restructuring process to cope with serious degradation in quality of the consumer loan portfolios they possess.

5.2.2   Household Debt by Lender Type

Banks

Banks and credit card companies played the crucial role in increasing household debt. Banks were not the biggest lenders to the household sector until the second quarter of 1999 when the bank loans to the household sector overtook loans provided by other deposit taking institutions such as savings banks, credit unions, and mutual saving cooperatives (see figure 5.3). The increase in the bank's share in the consumer credit market from 1997 to 1999 was mainly due to contraction of nonbank deposit taking institutions. They were hit especially hard by the economic crisis in 1997 and subsequent restructuring of financial industry. Banks were also seriously affected by the economic crisis, but the outstanding stock of loans households borrowed from banks has steadily increased except for the second half of 1998 when the economy was in deep recession triggered by the economic crisis and high interest rate policy pursued by the Korean government. The status of banks as the biggest lender to the household sector was further solidified between 2000 and 2002, and 56.7 percent of total debt owed by the household sector was financed by banks in 2003.

As shown in figure 5.4, the biggest share of bank loans to the household

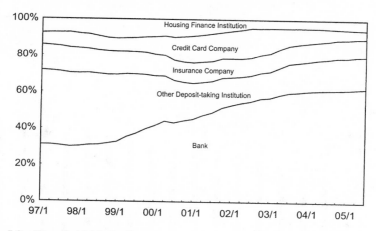

Fig. 5.3   Household debt by lender type
Source: Bank of Korea.
Notes: Housing finance institutions include the Korea Housing Finance Corporation and the National Housing Fund. Other deposit-taking institutions include savings banks, credit unions, and mutual saving cooperatives.

sector was taken up by loans to households secured by residential properties (LSRP).[3] While the proportion of LSRP in total bank loans to the household sector was 47.8 percent at the end of 2000, it had continuously risen to reach 62.4 percent in five years. During the five-year span from 2001 to 2005, a 71 percent increase in household debt provided by banks was attributable to an increase in LSRP. As discussed later, LSRP in Korea has very unique contract structure, and many commentators pointed out that the unique aspects of the loan contracts, especially short maturity and amortization scheme, could have some serious implications on the stability of the financial system.

Credit Card Companies

Another major contributor to the growth of consumer credit after the economic crisis in 1997 was credit card companies. The financial law in Korea allows financial institutions other than banks to issue credit cards and provide various supplementary services such as cash advances.[4] Sensing a

3. Except for the National Housing Fund, the long-term mortgage market had not existed in Korea until the Korea Housing Finance Cooperation was established in 2004. Because the target of the National Housing Fund was limited to low- and middle-income households, most of the mortgage financing was intermediated through short-term bank loans collateralized by residential properties (LSRP). In Korea, LSRP has several distinguished features different from the traditional long-term mortgage product in terms of maturity, repayment method, loan decision criteria, and so on. It is called a bullet mortgage due to these special aspects of the loan contract. We discuss the details later.

4. In Korea, credit card companies are treated as financial institutions and are regulated by the financial regulator. The law regulating the industry is the "Credit-specialized financial company law."

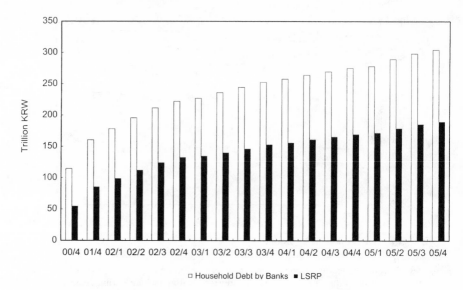

Fig. 5.4   Bank loans to household
Source: Bank of Korea.
Notes: LSRP is the loan to households secured by residential properties. Note that end-of-the-year balances are presented for 2000 and 2001 due to lack of data.

lucrative profit opportunity in the consumer credit market, several big nonfinancial companies affiliated with big industrial conglomerates entered the credit card industry in the late 1980s, and banks also established credit card companies as an independent business to bypass restrictive regulations on the banking sector.[5]

Starting from 2000, credit card companies led the early stage in the expansion of consumer credit. Credit card debt increased by 270 percent, from 13.6 trillion Korea Won at the end of 1999 to 50.6 trillion KRW in the third quarter of 2002. Loans by credit card companies constituted only 8.4 percent of the total household debt at the end of 1999. However, the proportion of credit card debt doubled in three years, and it peaked at 16.2 percent in the third quarter of 2002. The explosive growth of credit card debt came to a sudden halt in the fourth quarter of 2002, mainly due to increasing concern of the sustainability of the credit card industry and various regulatory measures to restrain the expansion of credit card debt. Contraction of credit card debt stock was so spectacular that outstanding

5. Samsung Card and LG Card were two notable examples of big nonfinancial companies. Kookmin bank, the largest commercial bank in Korea and the Korea Exchange Bank were two examples of banks that established credit card companies. There were also banks that maintained a credit card business as an inside business unit. Most of the banks internalizing a credit card business participated in the market through a credit card association, BC Card.

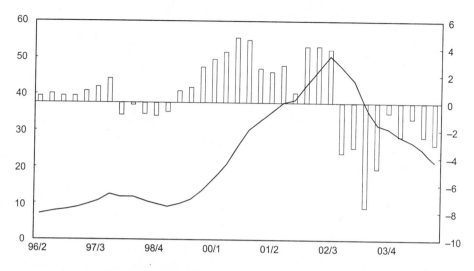

Fig. 5.5   Trend in credit card debt

Source: Financial Supervisory Service.

Notes: The bar chart indicates quarter-to-quarter change in outstanding balance and should be read by the scale on the right-hand side. Scale is in trillion Korean Won. The line graph indicates the outstanding balance at the end of each quarter and should be read by the scale on the left-hand side. Scale is in percentage.

debt stock reached 17.6 trillion KRW in the third quarter of 2005 (see figure 5.5).[6]

Credit cards typically provide three types of financial services to cardholders: full payment, installment, and cash advance services. Figure 5.6 illustrates the trend in the volume of transactions intermediated by the three categories of services. One noticeable feature we can point out from the figure is that the accumulation of credit card debt was primarily driven by cash advance services.[7] It is widely accepted conventional wisdom in the credit card industry that the cash advance service is more vulnerable to credit risk than other forms of services. Loans initiated through cash advance should bring to borrowers high enough marginal utility that can justify a very high interest rate and consequently have much larger exposure to credit risks than other forms of services. During the period between 2000 and 2002, the transactions initiated by the cash advance service occupied more than half of total transactions intermediated by credit cards. That was an unmistakable foreboding of troublesome events to follow in two or three years.

6. That is, the size of outstanding credit card debt reduced by a third in three years.
7. We treat card loan as a form of cash advance service.

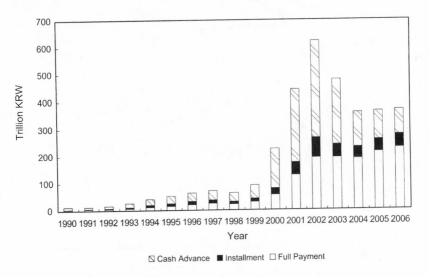

Fig. 5.6   Credit card transaction volumes by service type
Source: Credit Finance Association of Korea.

5.2.3   Distribution of Household Debt: Analysis of Microdata

In this section, we briefly present a set of micro-level analyses in order to investigate the distributional aspects of increase in household debt. The Korea Labor Institute (KLI) has maintained a panel of representative households dating back to 1998. The annual survey, the Korea Labor and Income Panel Study (KLIPS), mainly focuses on labor-related issues, but it also provides information on various financial transactions. Among seven waves of surveys that are currently available for public use, we drop the first wave for compatibility reasons and employ data from 1998 to 2002 for the analyses. The time span covered by our data set coincides with the first and the second phases in the development of the consumer credit market after the economic crisis.

Table 5.1 reports the distribution of average debt holdings classified by the age of household head. The overall pattern generally conforms to the trend we observe in aggregate-level data. After a sluggish swing in 1998 and 1999, household debt started to increase at a considerable speed from 2000. Average debt holding per household increased by 40 percent from 17.3 million KRW in 1999 to 24.2 million in 2002. Even though household debt increased in all age groups, households with heads aged in their fifties experienced the fastest accumulation of debt. The average debt for the age group doubled between 1999 and 2002. Households whose heads were aged below thirty also experienced a significant jump in debt holdings. Their average debt increased by 75 percent during the same period.

Table 5.1   Average household debt by age: 1998–2002 (thousand KRW)

			Age group			
Year	≤29	30–39	40–49	50–59	60+	Total
1998	5,540	15,198	24,718	18,836	11,598	17,301
1999	3,963	13,690	22,892	19,965	12,000	16,592
2000	4,442	13,833	25,385	20,962	11,151	17,406
2001	8,896	16,576	26,585	29,480	13,659	20,669
2002	9,217	18,533	31,811	37,759	13,972	24,226

Notes: Age group is classified by age of household head. The surveys were conducted from 1999 to 2003.

Table 5.2   Average household debt by income groups: 1998–2002 (thousand KRW)

Income percentile	1998	1999	2000	2001	2002
81–100	44,210	39,730	33,724	35,200	41,316
61–80	22,131	18,711	18,105	19,943	23,369
41–60	12,934	13,057	15,544	14,831	17,035
21–40	11,789	12,260	13,148	20,425	16,647
≤20	8,808	7,853	9,686	6,793	9,760
Total	17,301	16,592	17,406	20,669	24,226

Note: The surveys were conducted from 1999 to 2003.

Table 5.2 reports the average debt holdings by income percentiles. We can point out that low- and middle-income households experienced relatively faster growth of outstanding debt stock compared to the high-income group. Households belonging to the 21 percent to 40 percent income group saw their average debt balloon by 41 percent, from 11.8 million KRW in 1998 to 16.7 million KRW in 2002. Households belonging to the 41 percent to 60 percent income group also experienced significant increase in average debt holdings. However, it is interesting to note that debt holdings by the highest income group did not go through considerable fluctuations, and their average debt actually decreased differently from other income groups.

We can interpret the results in table 5.2 from two different perspectives. First of all, we can argue that the results provide indirect evidence for alleviation of credit constraints in the consumer credit market. The fact that lower-income households experienced faster debt accumulation may imply the alleviation of severe liquidity constraint placed on them under the practices prevailing in the financial market before the economic crisis. Before the economic crisis, direction intervention of the government in credit allocation was a common practice. The Korean government pursued the development policy to channel a disproportionately large amount of credit resources into a small group of targeted industries to promote faster growth. It was not rare that households were not able to borrow even though they did possess enough assets to offer as collateral in some cases, let alone borrowing without collateral. After the economic crisis in 1997, the Korean government gave up the traditional interventionist approach and let the market determine resource allocation in the credit market. It was then possible for financial institutions to increase the credit supply to the household sector with less concern about nonentrepreneurial factors.

While the increase of credit provision to the household sector can be used as evidence for lessening credit constraints, some critics pay particular attention to the fact that low-income households were provided credit in such a scale in such a short span of time. They argue that considering the speed and distributional feature of consumer credit expansion, it is quite difficult to justify without assuming some form of negligence from credit providers. Until recently, banks in Korea had relied on old-fashioned judgmental methods in credit evaluation and had not been equipped with formal credit risk management methods such as a credit scoring system. Moreover, credit card companies used to issue credit cards to consumers without proper checks on the ability to repay. They argue that the expansion of consumer credit after the economic crisis was at least partly attributable to an inadequate risk management system, and the seeds for turmoil in the Korean financial market in 2003 and 2004 had already started to germinate.

We can also find evidence for the mounting debt burden on households in microdata. Figure 5.7 summarizes change in average debt service ratio (DSR) from 1998 to 2004.[8] The DSR reported in figure 5.7 was calculated based on the Survey of Household Income and Expenditure (SHIE), an annual survey by the Korea National Statistical Office. The SHIE provides vast amounts of detailed information on household expenditure and income that the KLIPS does not report. The proportion of income dedicated to pay interest and principals, if not rolled over, had been consistently increased from 13.04 percent in 1998 to 22.97 percent in 2004. Even under a persistently low interest rate and generous rollover policy, repayment burden measured in DSR almost doubled in just six years. Low-income families were affected more by increased debt burden than high-income families, which is in line with the result in table 5.2, where low-income families were the main beneficiaries of extended credit opportunities.

In order to investigate the distributional aspects of debt accumulation by households in a more formal manner, we estimate the following empirical model with KLIPS panel data;

---

8. *Debt service ratio* is defined as the ratio between the amounts used to pay interest and principal, if any, to income.

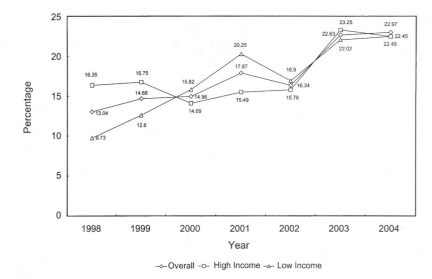

Fig. 5.7   Debt service ratio
Notes: High (low) income indicates the average DSR of households belonging to upper (lower) 50 percent of income distribution. All figures are in percentiles.

$$y^*_{iy} 1_{[y^*_{it}>0]} = \beta' \mathbf{x}_{it} + \mu_i + \varepsilon_{it},$$

where y^*_{it} is the difference between supply of debt and desired level by household i, $\mathbf{x}_{it}$ is a vector of explanatory variables, μ_i is the individual fixed effect, and ε_{it} is error term.[9] Econometricians are able to observe the amount of debt held by a household only if the desired level is lower than the level to which lenders are willing to provide credit. We have a fixed effect panel specification with a censored dependent variable and estimate the model using a trimmed least squares (TLS) estimator proposed by Honoré (1992) after imposing the usual independently and identically distributed (i.i.d.) normality assumption on the error term.[10] The explanatory variables included in the regression are all frequently cited variables in the literature.[11] Income, amount of asset holding, family size, dummies for household head's age, educational attainment, homeownership, and a dummy for type of employment are included. The estimation result is reported in table 5.3.

The estimation result conforms to previous research done in other countries.[12] Income, asset holding, family size, education attainment, and

9. For a theoretical background of the empirical model, see Crook (2001).
10. Precisely speaking, the estimator is $\hat{\beta}_4$ in the original paper, and it is obtained by optimizing the loss function defined as $T_n(b)$.
11. See Bertola, Disney, and Grant (2006).
12. See Crook (2006).

Table 5.3   Determinants of debt holdings

	Model I	Model II	Model III	Model IV
Income	0.2106***	0.2134***	0.2167***	−0.4299**
	(0.0219)	(0.02194)	(0.0218)	(0.1140)
Income squared				0.0471**
				(0.0081)
Net asset	0.0793***	0.0776***	0.0453***	0.0471**
	(0.0096)	(0.0096)	(0.0100)	(0.0100)
Family size	0.0933***	0.0892***	0.0841***	0.0785***
	(0.0189)	(0.0188)	(0.0187)	(0.0186)
Marriage (married = 1)	0.0071	0.0082	0.0151	0.0183
	(0.1235)	(0.1229)	(0.1218)	(0.1212)
Education 1 (high school = 1)	0.2196***	0.2176***	0.2269***	0.2111**
	(0.0668)	(0.0663)	(0.0658)	(0.0655)
Education 2 (college = 1)	0.2522***	0.2841***	0.2959***	0.2639***
	(0.0534)	(0.0533)	(0.0529)	(0.0529)
Age 1 (35 ≤ age < 45)	0.2015***	0.1698***	0.1396**	0.1320**
	(0.0663)	(0.0626)	(0.0678)	(0.0667)
Age 2 (45 ≤ age < 55)	0.4247	0.3694	0.2982	0.2818
	(1.4157)	(1.3682)	(0.9320)	(1.0437)
Age 3 (55 ≤ age < 65)	0.5305*	0.4698*	0.3870	0.3699
	(0.3031)	(0.2847)	(0.2513)	(0.2531)
Age 4 (65 ≤ age)	0.2111***	0.1416***	0.0417***	0.0004**
	(0.0198)	(0.0578)	(0.0151)	(0.0001)
Type of employment (self employed = 1)		0.3224***	0.3383***	0.332***
		(0.0455)	(0.0452)	(0.0450)
Unemployed (unemployed = 1)		−0.1139**	−0.1053*	−0.1021**
		(0.0558)	(.00553)	(0.0552)
Homeownership (homeowner = 1)			0.3571***	0.3554**
			(0.0335)	(0.0436)
No. of observations	6,114	6,114	6,114	6,114
Wald	615.07***	672.49***	793.27***	833.27***
	(10)	(12)	(13)	(14)

Notes: The dependent variable is in log and income; net asset are also in log. Quadratic loss function i
minimized for fixed effect Tobit model as suggested by Honoré (1992). Standard errors are in parenthe
ses. The Wald statistic is the test statistic for the joint significance of all explanatory variables except fo
the intercept. Degrees of freedom are in parentheses under the test statistics.
***Significant at the 1 percent level.
**Significant at the 5 percent level.
*Significant at the 10 percent level.

homeownership are all significantly and positively related to debt holding. On the other hand, wage earners and the unemployed are likely to hold smaller debt stocks. Other sociodemographic variables such as marriage and sex do not seem to be important factors in the determination of household demand for debt. Income elasticity of debt demand is consistently estimated to be around 0.2, which is much larger than (net) asset elasticity of debt demand. Unlike the findings for other countries in Crook (2006) that reports a concave function of income, demand for debt holding is a convex function of income in the data range.

The pattern of debt accumulation along the life cycle closely follows that of income, increasing in the thirties and forties and reaching the maximum at midfifties then decreasing afterward. The pattern is quite different from those typically found in other countries.

In most of the countries reported in Crook (2006), demand for debt decreases as the age of household head increases. However, in the Korean case, households accumulate more debts as age increases until reaching retirement age. Such a pattern may reflect the characteristic feature of the housing finance market in Korea. In the absence of a well-functioning long-term mortgage market, a typical family in Korea has to accumulate financial assets until savings can cover the down payment required to purchase a home, which is, in most cases, at least 40 percent of the housing price. The remaining amount should be borrowed from financial institutions, mainly banks, by offering the house for collateral. Therefore, the average age of a first-time home buyer in Korea is higher than that in other countries where a long-term mortgage market is well established. Because most home purchases are related to debt increase to some degree, as shown in a significantly positive correlation between debt and homeownership in table 5.3, the pattern of debt accumulation is likely to be closely correlated with that of home purchase and mortgage debt repayment. People start to buy homes in their late thirties, and the number of first-time home buyers peaks at the midforties. Moreover, because most mortgage debts are not amortized under the convention that debts are rolled over when maturities arrive, we do not observe a statistically significant drop in debt holdings even after home purchases.

5.3 Causes and Consequences

5.3.1 Causes

Changes in the Financial Market Environment

One of most obvious reasons why household debt increased at such a remarkable speed in Korea seemed to be the low interest rate environment that started in 1999 as the Korean government gave up the high interest policy.

The policy especially advocated by the International Monetary Fund was taken to restore stability in the foreign exchange market. Confronted with a severe recession in 1998 due to a high interest rate and positive signs in the foreign exchange market stability, the Korean government lowered the interest rate to stimulate the slumping economy. In line with the favorable condition in the global financial market, the low interest rate policy has been retained thereafter as shown in figure 5.8. Because a low interest

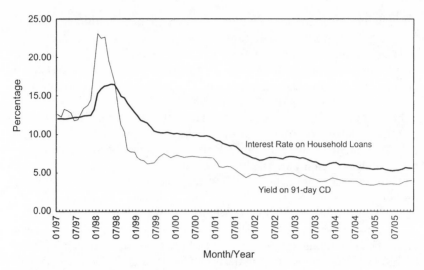

Fig. 5.8   Interest rates: 1997–2005
Source: Bank of Korea.

rate, ceteris paribus, implies lower cost for debt financing and stronger demand for borrowing, the low interest rate must have significantly contributed to rapid increase in household debt.

Another fundamental change in the financial market was the change in the financing pattern of the corporate sector. Before the economic crisis, the Korean government chose the strategy to pursue economic development by utilizing large conglomerates, *chaebols,* as the main engine. The government mobilized massive amounts of credit resources required for large-scale investment through the banking sector. Bank loans rather than bonds or equities had been the main financial vehicles through which the corporate sector raised funds for investment. However, the structural fragility of the debt-driven development strategy was clearly revealed when the economy was hit hard by sudden and massive capital outflow as the solvency of *chaebols* became suspicious. Many conglomerates were forced to declare bankruptcy or resort to a restructuring procedure. Several commercial banks suffered severe losses from large nonperforming loans concentrated on failing conglomerates and were taken over by the Korea Deposit Insurance Corporation or other less-affected banks to prevent a collapse of the financial system. Out of thirty-three commercial banks operating at the end of 1997, ten banks disappeared. Five were liquidated, and the other five were acquired by other surviving banks. Once the financial system regained stability, the Korean government accepted the reality that pursuing economic development by channeling bank credits to selected sectors was no longer viable and required the corporate sector to strengthen the financial structure by reducing debt and injecting more capital. As a result, the focus of funding for corporate investment shifted from the banking sector to the capital market.

Table 5.4 illustrates the inflow of funds to the corporate sector from banks and the capital market. We can confirm the fact that the capital market replaced the banking sector as the main funding source for the corporate sector after the economic crisis. Shrinking demand for bank loans from the corporate sector naturally put pressure on banks to pursue a more aggressive approach in promoting loans to the household sector.

The structural transformation of banks' loan portfolios is clearly illustrated in figure 5.9. The proportion of household loans in banks' total loan portfolios had stayed well below 30 percent until 1998 but increased continuously to reach 48.9 percent in 2004. In 2005, hitting the historical high

Table 5.4   Source of corporate finance (billion KRW)

Year	Bank loan	Bond and equity	Total
1996	44,977	35,191	80,167
1997	37,728	37,731	75,459
1998	–63,634	70,253	6,619
1999	–3,759	71,785	68,026
2000	19,658	73,011	92,669
2001	–27,487	99,363	71,875
2002	34,002	87,421	121,423
2003	28,129	72,909	101,038

Source: Bank of Korea.

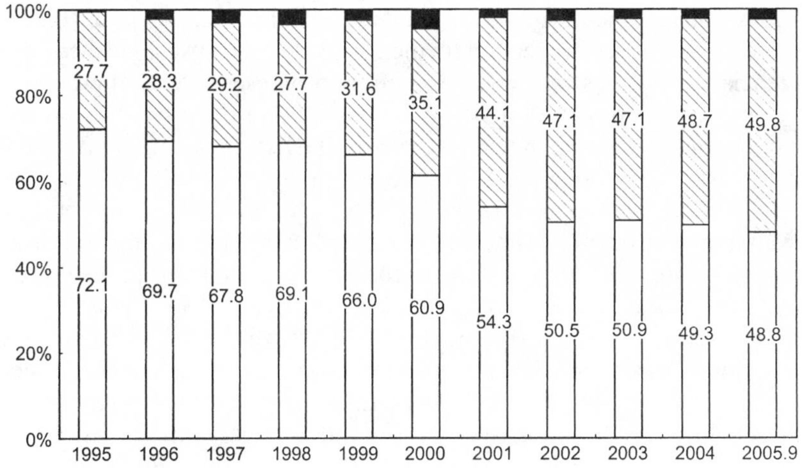

Fig. 5.9   Composition of banks' loan portfolios
Source: Bank of Korea.
Note: From bottom to top, household loans, corporate loans, and others.

at 49.8 percent, loans to the household sector finally surpassed those to the corporate sector.

Deregulation of the Financial Sector

Though deregulation of the financial sector had already begun in the 1990s, it was not until the onset of the economic crisis in 1997 that the liberalization and deregulation of the financial market was vigorously pursued. Amid various policies and actions taken during the deregulation process, the most important change was the paradigm shift in the way financial institutions are managed. Under the old regime, banks were simply regarded as instrumental agents to mobilize savings and channel them to strategically selected industries. Profitability of individual banks was not a primary concern as long as banks served the policy goals set by the government. Even banks themselves did not regard themselves as private businesses but as semipublic entities with an important mission to serve the public interest by contributing to economic development. Under the new regime, the government gave up the traditional approach to the financial sector as well as to economic development. Enhancement of the efficiency in the allocation of credit resources became the primary policy goal of financial regulation, and price mechanism replaced the government as the main player in credit resource allocation.

Aside from the fundamental paradigm shift in financial regulation, numerous measures were taken to embody the philosophical transformation at the operational level. The entry barrier to the financial industry was lowered significantly, and foreigners were allowed enter the industry by establishing a local subsidiary or acquiring the existing domestic companies. The Financial Holding Company Act was enacted to promote competition among different sectors in the financial industry. Implicit regulation on the interest rate and service fees on financial services were also abolished, and financial institutions were given discretion to choose the level of prices for the services they provide. Financial companies were allowed to be involved in numerous activities that had required authorization or consent from the regulator by simply reporting to the regulator.

As a result of fundamental changes brought by deregulation efforts, profitability was firmly established as the primary goal of all sorts of financial companies. Banks converted their attention to loans to the household sector from corporate loans they had consistently focused on. Except for intervention by the government, implicit or explicit, it is quite difficult to find justification for the large share of corporate loans before the economic crisis as shown in figure 5.9, considering the fact that loans to the household sector had consistently been, on average, more lucrative and less risky than loans to the corporate sector, at least until 2003 according to table 5.5. It was then natural in some sense to observe a sudden shift of business practice in the banking industry and fast growth of loans to the household sector.

Table 5.5   **Average loan rate and default rate**

Year	Loan rate		Default rate		
	Household	Corporate	Household	Credit card	Corporate
1997	12.30	11.75	3.3	3.3	7.3
1998	15.21	15.20	7.1	17.9	8.9
1999	10.85	8.91	3.2	6.8	4.4
2000	9.88	8.18	2.4	7.7	3.4
2001	8.20	7.49	1.3	7.5	2.1
2002	6.92	6.50	1.5	11.9	2.0
2003	6.50	6.17	1.8	10.9	2.1
2004	5.88	5.92	1.8	5.5	2.1
2005	5.64	5.75	1.4	3.9	1.9

Notes: All interest rates are average rates charged for new loans in each category. Default rate of credit card loan is for all credit card debt granted by banks.

5.3.2   Consequences

Efficiency Improvement and Welfare Gain

Because wider penetration of financial intermediation offers more opportunities for mutually beneficial voluntary exchanges, it, in general, results in more efficient resource allocation and higher welfare. Even if it is difficult to draw a firm conclusion due to a lack of hard evidence, we can offer some circumstantial evidence for the claim that the increase in household debt may have brought several positive effects. Based on the discussion in the previous section, one can argue that increased inflow of credit resources into the household sector itself reflects efficiency improvement in the allocation of credit resources. Free from government intervention, lending financial institutions were able to take the full advantage of benefits from loans to the household sector, the higher interest rate, and the lower default rate. Borrowers also benefited from a more-generous provision of credit resources. As more and more consumers free themselves from credit and liquidity constraints, it became easier for them to achieve intertemporal reallocation of consumption in pursuing a smoother lifetime consumption path. According to an extensive study by Kim (1995), the household sector had been under very severe credit and liquidity constraints before the economic crisis, and it was virtually impossible to borrow from banks without providing collateral.[13] At least to some degree, one cannot deny the fact that the large inflow of credit into the household sec-

---

13. Here is paradoxical evidence for the claim that consumer loans were severely discouraged. Two special purpose banks specializing in consumer credit were established by the government. Kookmin Bank, now privatized and the biggest commercial bank in Korea, was established to deal with the consumer and small office/home office (SOHO) loans. Another bank specializing in consumer finance was the Korea Housing Bank, merged with Kookmin Bank in 2001, whose business area was in mortgage finance.

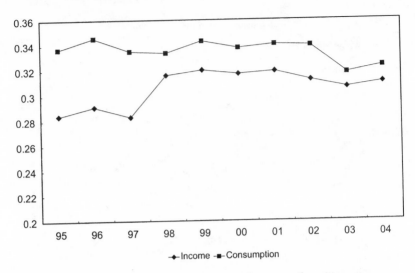

Fig. 5.10   Trend in Gini coefficient: Income and consumption
Source: Author's calculation based on the National Household Income and Expenditure Survey (NHIES).

tor contributed to alleviating restrictions imposed on intertemporal budget constraints and helped consumers achieve better resource allocation.

According to figure 5.10, while income distribution in Korea shows the tendency to worse as indicated by the rising Gini coefficient for income distribution after the economic crisis, inequality in consumption seems to be reduced. As long as the improvement in consumption equality was not totally financed by reckless loan provision by lenders who did not recognize the importance of credit evaluation in making a loan decision, this could imply that fewer consumers are affected by imperfection in the financial market and are able to attain a better position in allocating consumption in an intertemporal context.[14]

Potential Deterioration of Stability in the Financial System

In the previous section, we show that one of the main driving forces behind the explosive growth of household debt between 2000 and 2002 was the increase in LSRP supplied by banks.[15] In the five years from 1999 to 2003, LSRP quadrupled, and total loans to households by banks tripled so

14. One cannot deny that some part of the consumption was financed by debt that was recklessly extended without scrutinizing the credibility of borrowers.
15. The term LSRP is used in the Basel II accord to represent any form of loan contract collateralized by residential properties. That includes various kinds of loan contracts such as equity loans and bullet mortgages as well as conventional long-term mortgages. We use the term LSRP to indicate the bullet mortgage explained later in detail in order to distinguish it from the conventional long-term mortgage.

that the proportion of LSRPs in household loan portfolios rose from 58.1 percent in 2001 to 62.4 percent in 2005. The pace of LSRP growth in the booming period between 2000 and 2002 was especially spectacular, with an annual growth rate over 50 percent.

Compared to the conventional long-term mortgage contract, we can point out three distinguishing characteristics in the LSRP contract prevalent in Korea: short maturity, no amortization of principals, and low loan-to-value (LTV) ratio. First, LSRP has a very short maturity structure. A typical LSRP matures in three years, and the maturity is shortened further when conditions in the credit market deteriorate. According to a survey by the Financial Supervisory Service (FSS) in 2005, 47.6 percent of LSRP have a (original) maturity no longer than three years, 21.4 percent for three to five years. On the other hand, LSRP with maturity longer than ten years occupies 25.3 percent of total LSRP, and the weight increased by 15.7 percentage points compared to the previous survey in 2003. The rapid increase is mainly attributable to the establishment of the Korea Housing Finance Corporation in 2003 in the wake of rapid increase in LSRP and subsequent rising concerns on its long-term stability.[16] According to table 5.6, all countries surveyed by the Bank for International Settlements (BIS; 2006) other than Korea have long-term mortgages with maturity no shorter than ten years as the primary instrument in the housing finance market.

The second feature of LSRP in Korea is that borrowers are not required to repay the principal till maturity. Borrowers pay only interest on regular basis, and the loan is rolled over unless serious events that may harm the credibility of the borrower or collateral, such as delayed interest payment, default, and sharp decrease in housing value, happen.[17] In order to deal with possible risk factors embodied in the second feature of LSRP in Korea mentioned in the preceding, LTV is set at very low level compared to a long-term mortgage with amortization. The average LTV for LSRP in Korea is currently well below 60 percent. According to table 5.6, in most of the countries with the conventional mortgage system, LTV is set at 70 percent to 80 percent when the loan contract originates.

Literature calls the type of mortgage loan dominating the housing finance market in Korea a *bullet mortgage* to emphasize the risk factor embodied in the loan contract (Fabozzi and Modigliani 1992). Because the principal is carried to maturity without amortization, borrowers are required to pay a very large amount of money when maturity arrives. Borrowers have three ways to deal with the arrival of maturity; refinance the debt through rollover or borrow from other lenders, repay the debt by liquidating other assets, or sell the collateralized property and settle the debt.

16. The KHFC started to sell long-term mortgage loans from March 2004.
17. Monthly interest payment is the usual arrangement. In some cases, borrowers are asked to pay a very small portion (typically less than 5 percent) of the principal as a precondition for rollover of the matured loan.

Table 5.6   Features of mortgage contract in selected countries

Country	Usual length of contract (years)	Estimated average loan-to-value ratio (new loans)	% of owner-occupiers with mortgages
Australia	25	60–70%	45
Belgium	20	80–100%	56
Canada	25	75–95%[a]	54
France	15–20	78%	37.5
Germany	20–30	80–100%; 60% for Pfandbrief	n.a.
Italy	5–20	80%	n.a.
Korea	3–20	56.4%; max 70%	n.a.
Japan	20–30	n.a.[b]	n.a.
Luxembourg	20–25	80%	n.a.
Mexico	10–15	80–100%	n.a.
The Netherlands	30	87%; max 125%	85
Spain	15–20	70–80%	n.a.
Sweden	30–45	80–95%	n.a.
Switzerland	15–20	Max 80%; 65% for Pfandbrief issuance	n.a.
United Kingdom	25	70%	60
United States	30	Typically about 85%	65.1[c]

Source: BIS (2006).

[a]Seventy-five percent for convential (noninsured) mortgage loans and 95 percent for insured mortgage loans.

[b]n.a. = not available. The Government Housing Loan Corporation discloses the average loan-to-value ratio for the underlying mortgages of its mortgage backed securities (MBSs). The ratio has been approximately 70–80 percent from the first issue in March 2001 to date.

[c]2001 Survey of Consumer Finances, Board of Governors of the Federal Reserve System.

If the first option is available, no significant disruption would occur. A new debt contract will be signed, and the borrower is required to pay only interest without amortization of the principal until maturity. The maturity clock restarts. The second option is available for borrowers who have already accumulated enough assets to cover the amount of debt. Considering the high income-to-house price ratio in Korea, very few people qualify to choose the second option, especially among young borrowers.[18] Should neither the first nor the second option be available, a borrower would be forced to sell the collateralized house to meet the repayment obligation. Under the usual circumstances, the sales receipt would be large enough to cover the repayment as long as LTV was set and maintained at an accept-

18. Average income-to-house price ratio for an urban residence is known to be around 10 in Korea. Assuming that average propensity to consume is 0.3 and average LTV is 60 percent, an average worker should save at least ten years to accumulate enough assets to cover the principal repayment. With the bullet mortgage with a maturity of three years, the mortgage contract should be rolled over three or four times for an average borrower to exercise the second option in the text. In other words, no major events that make lenders refuse rollover of matured debt should occur for a very long period of time.

able level. The liquidation of collateral, voluntary or not, in most cases implies that the borrower confronts a stressful situation. When the stressful situation occurs at a personal level, borrowers would be able to execute the strategy. However, when it comes to a stressful situation at an economy-wide level, such as severe depression, they will have considerable difficulties. Under the circumstances, lenders would become very selective in granting rollover and renewing the debt contract, and a significant chunk of maturing debt would be denied renewal of contract, and most of the borrowers who are rejected in the rollover application would have to resort to liquidating the collateralized house. Enormous pressure applied to the supply side of the housing market is highly likely to result in considerable price shock or, in some cases, panic in the housing market. Disappearing liquidity, plummeting prices, and a rush to dump assets at all costs are a few examples of chaotic events we observe in a depressed-asset market. Kindleberger and Aliber (2005) documented numerous historic events when abrupt change in investors' moods or the market environment led to panic in the financial market and crisis in the economic system. With the average maturity of three years, roughly a third of total outstanding debt will mature within a year. Therefore, rapid accumulation of bullet mortgage debt has already become one of the major risk factors that might harm the stability of the financial system. Moreover, banks did not regard a borrower's income as the main variable on which the loan decision was based. In other words, as long as he or she could provide enough collateral to cover the principal, a borrower did not have difficulty obtaining a mortgage loan, even if both borrower and lender knew that the borrower did not have the ability to accumulate enough savings to repay the debt when it matured. The strategy was acceptable to both lenders and borrowers in Korea. Under a bullet mortgage contract, neither party expects the borrower to accumulate enough savings to repay the debt by the time the loan matures in two or three years. Instead, both parties expect that during the contract, the house price will increase significantly and the borrower will be able to repay the debt by using capital gain. Even if their expectation is not materialized, the borrower is easily granted a rollover of the maturing loan unless serious events occur that make it impossible to renew the loan contract, such as a delayed interest payment or a violation of the LTV condition due to a drop in the price of property offered as collateral. However, if the serious events occur on an extraordinary scale, rollover for a significant portion of matured debt will be denied, and most debtors will be forced to respond to a call for repayment by liquidating the collateral. It is highly likely that a downward spiral of the housing price will be initiated and further deterioration of the mortgage market follows, which, if not properly controlled, may lead to a disastrous collapse of the financial market and the economic system.

In a theoretical exploration on structural characteristics of the bullet mortgage contract, Park and Hur (2006) argue that the bullet mortgage contract is more robust to adverse income shock, but more vulnerable to adverse housing price shock than the conventional mortgage contract. Because borrowers under the conventional mortgage arrangement are required to pay interest and part of the principal, they have to set aside a larger portion of income to meet periodic repayment obligations than borrowers under the bullet mortgage. Affected by the same adverse shock to income, borrowers with a conventional mortgage will be more prone to default than borrowers with a bullet mortgage. On the other hand, borrowers with a conventional mortgage are less prone to adverse shock to the housing price than borrowers with a bullet mortgage because they are not subject to the LTV condition as long as they fulfill scheduled repayments. Under a bullet mortgage contract, borrowers are required to meet the LTV condition when the debt contracted is renewed after the maturity for the old contract arrives. Affected by a large adverse shock on the housing price, borrowers will have much difficulty meeting the LTV condition when they try to get a rollover granted by banks.

Fabozzi and Modigliani (1992) provided convincing historical evidence on the fragility of the bullet mortgage system. After the economy was seriously hit by the Great Depression, massive foreclosure of homes under the bullet mortgage contracts occurred as a result of the collapse of housing prices and failure to renew maturing mortgage contracts. The wealth effect made the recovery of private consumption very sluggish, and the economy suffered greatly from the delayed recovery. Fabozzi and Modigliani (1992) argue that the U.S. Congress enacted the National Housing Act of 1934 that offered the legal foundation for the Federal National Mortgage Association (Fannie Mae) in order to circumvent the structural problem embodied in the bullet mortgage system by encouraging the development of the long-term mortgage market.

It seems that policymakers started to notice the risk factor involved in rapid accumulation of bullet mortgage debt around 2002 and took various policy measures to help smooth rollover of maturing debts and introduce conventional mortgage instruments into the Korean housing finance market. The Korean Housing Finance Corporation (KHFC) was established in 2003 to promote a conventional mortgage market. The KHFC was assigned important instruments to accomplish the mission. First, unlike Fannie Mae or Ginnie Mae in the United States, the KHFC sells conventional long-term mortgage products to consumers thorough various financial institutions. Financial institutions are not legally involved in loan contracts, and they are simply agents employed by the KHFC. Second, the KHFC securitizes mortgage loans by issuing mortgage-backed securities.

It is too early to make a verdict on the effectiveness of government policies to reduce the risk factor in the housing finance market by promoting long-term mortgage products. However, it is very difficult to claim those policies showed stellar performances. Due to lack of accurate official statistics on the proportion of LSRP, we do not know how prevalent the bullet mortgage is in the Korean housing finance market. According to an FSS survey in 2005, 70.5 percent of LSRP in May 2005 were bullet mortgage loans, but the proportion declined very fast. The good news is that the proportion of LSRP with amortization doubled in two and half years. It was only 14.1 percent in 2003 but rose to 28.3 percent in May 2005.[19]

In spite of various policy efforts, the banking sector in Korea is still exposed to considerable risk factors stemming from structural fragility of bullet mortgage debts. It should also be mentioned that slow but steady progress toward a housing finance system with a more robust structure is clearly observed.

Increase in Credit Delinquents

In Korea, *credit delinquent* is the term reserved to indicate people who are in arrears for an amount larger than 0.3 million Korean Won for longer than three months and recorded at the public registry maintained by the Korea Federation of Banks.[20] The information stored at the registry is shared among the member financial institutions.

The explosive increase in household debt and the subsequent deterioration in households' ability to repay resulted in a rapid increase in household arrears and credit delinquents.

According to figure 5.11, the number of credit delinquents increased significantly in 1998 and declined slightly from 1999 to 2000. The number rose again at a rapid pace from the latter half of 2002 and continued to rise until the first quarter of 2004.

The large increase in credit delinquents in 1998 was attributable to severe depression initiated by the foreign exchange crisis at the end of 1997. Rebounding of economic conditions from the last quarter of 1998 was reflected in the slight decline in credit delinquents from 1999. The second wave of increase in registered credit delinquents started from the second half of 2002 and was closely associated with the increase in household debt between 2000 and 2002 and the sluggish economy in 2002. In the first quarter of 2003, the number of credit delinquents increased by 11.2 percent compared to the previous quarter. That was the biggest jump since the foreign exchange crisis.[21] The number of credit delinquents finally exceeded 3 million and continued to reach 3.83 million in the first quarter of 2004. The term credit delinquent was officially discarded in 2005, and the statistics on

---

19. It is conventional wisdom in the market that the proportion of conventional long-term mortgages has increased steadily since then.

20. The sum is equivalent to approximately US$300.

21. The number of credit delinquents increased by 20.4 percent in the second quarter of 2001. But the increase was due to the change in registration criteria in March 2001 and does not represent change in economic condition.

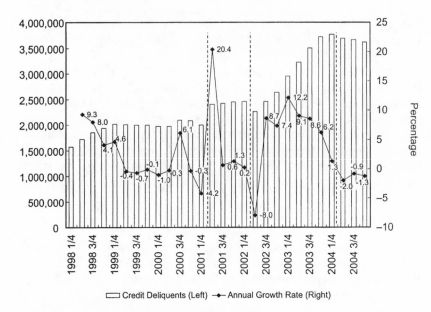

☐ Credit Deliquents (Left) —◆— Annual Growth Rate (Right)

Fig. 5.11   Trend in credit delinquents

Source: Korea Federation of Banks.

Notes: The KFB tightened the criteria of registration at the second quarter of 2001. The change was reflected in a sudden jump of number of registered credit delinquents. On the other hand, the KFB lowered the criteria of registration at the first quarter of 2002. Several administrative errors were cleared in March 2004 to lead to a slight decline in the number of credit delinquents. Many were already deceased or were registered more than twice.

credit delinquents have not been announced since then.[22] However, it is known that the decline that started in the second quarter of 2004 continued until the number dropped to approximately 3 million at the end of 2005. The decline was mainly due to active restructuring of nonperforming household loans rather than improvement of ability to repay the debt such as increased income or decreased debt burden.

Shin, Hahn, and Park (2003) pointed out four reasons for the rapid increase of credit delinquents after the second quarter of 2003; adverse macroeconomic conditions, serious moral hazard committed by credit card companies, inefficient allocation of credit resources due to the lack of an adequate scheme to share credit information, and improper and untimely financial regulation.

The slumping economy since the third quarter of 2000 generated adverse

22. Public registration of credit delinquents was discarded, but collection and sharing of credit information continued. The policy to register credit delinquents had been subject to severe criticism that the classification was not only an arbitrary one void of sound economic justification but became an obstacle that prevented individual financial institutions from developing a credit scoring system.

shock on income as well as debt burden and ultimately made ability to repay deteriorate. That would result in increase of arrears in household debt and registered credit delinquents. Equation (1) based on Shin, Hahn, and Park (2003) indicates that the number of credit delinquents is positively correlated with household debt and negatively correlated with income. The result conforms with the literature reporting the empirical findings that households' ability to repay debts is associated with income, debt burden, and interest rate.[23] Change in credit delinquents is regressed on lagged change in household debt and income employing the quarterly data from 1998 to 2004. An increase in household debt would result in an increase in credit delinquents a year later. Similarly, an increase in income measured by Gross National Income (GNI) would lead to a decrease in credit delinquents a year later.

$$(1) \quad \Delta \ln CD_t = 6.1354 + \underset{(0.8153)}{0.3199\Delta} \ln HD_{t-3} + \underset{(1.5634)}{0.6005\Delta} \ln HD_{t-4}$$

$$- \underset{(-0.7764)}{0.3232\Delta} \ln GNI_{t-1} - \underset{(-1.5039)}{0.4971\Delta} \ln GNI_{t-2}$$

$$- \underset{(-0.9082)}{0.2116\Delta} \ln GNI_{t-3} - \underset{(-1.8634)}{0.4318\Delta} \ln GNI_{t-4}$$

$$+ \underset{(2.3568)}{8.3342} D_{01/2}$$

$$R^2 = 0.5034 \quad \text{number of observations} = 28$$

In equation (1), $D_{01/2}$ indicates the dummy for change in registration criteria occurred in the second quarter of 2001, and t-values are in parentheses under the estimates.

Explosive growth of credit card loans in 2000 and 2001 and the subsequent increase in the default rate is another important factor that sparked an increase of credit delinquents. Deregulation of the credit card industry in 1999 triggered a throat-cutting competition to expand market share among credit card companies. The competition was a blind race to take the top position in size. Many borrowers with very high credit risk who would have been refused loans were allowed to access the credit market without proper credit evaluation. Owned by banks or large conglomerates, credit card companies underevaluated the possibility of their failure and charged into the competition with no prudence. They believed that they were too big to fail and the government would not be able to watch them get into trouble. That was a reckless moral hazard committed by credit card companies. Moreover, the majority of bonds issued by credit card companies to finance credit card loans were possessed by banks and money market funds that are generally regarded to be linked to system risk. That also fueled the belief that the government would not allow credit card companies to get into difficulty. Credit cards were issued recklessly without proper

---

23. For an excellent survey on the topic, see CBO (2000).

checks on credit risk, and the limits on cash advance services were raised frequently even if the borrower had already held a significant outstanding balance to repay.

As we have already seen in figure 5.6, increase in credit card debt during the boom in 2000 and 2001 was led by a cash advance service that embodied much higher credit risk than other forms of services credit cards provide. Confronting mounting arrears and accumulation of distress assets, the financial regulator took a decisive measure to stop the rapid expansion of credit card debts and prevent further deterioration of the situation.[24]

The growing concern about the viability of credit card companies and the sudden turning of policy stance resulted in a violent crash ending in the fourth quarter of 2002. Already having huge difficulty in paying monthly bills, a significant portion of credit card debtors had managed to escape falling into arrears by financing a new debt from other credit card companies or the usurious private loan market. Sudden strengthening of regulatory measures and subsequent tightening of credit risk management by credit card companies resulted in a massive increase in arrears. That could explain a lot of the steep increase of credit delinquents in 2003.

In order to see the role played by credit card companies in growing credit delinquents, we decompose the credit delinquents according to the financial institutions that reported them overdue, satisfying the registration criteria. Figure 5.12 illustrates the change in credit delinquents registered by a single type of financial institution. It is obvious that credit card companies played the most significant role in the increase of credit delinquents both in the second quarter of 2001 and in the second half of 2002.

We can draw the same conclusion from figure 5.13 that reports the changes in the number of credit delinquents registered by more than one kind of financial institution. Among the increase in the registered by multiple categories of financial institutions, nearly 90 percent were involved with credit cards in 2002 and 95 percent in 2003.

Lack of a well-functioning credit information system is pointed out as another major contributing factor to the aggravation of the problem. Roughly speaking, the credit information system consists of a credit reporting system that collects and distributes credit information among financial institutions and a credit evaluation system of individual financial institutions that evaluates the creditworthiness of individual borrowers, such as a credit scoring system (CSS) and behavior scoring system (BSS).

The current form of credit reporting system was established in Korea in 1955 when the Bank Supervisory Office introduced a compulsory reporting system that obliged all participating financial institutions to report delinquent credit information satisfying criteria set by agreement among

---

24. We will discuss the development of the credit card crisis in 2003 in the next section.

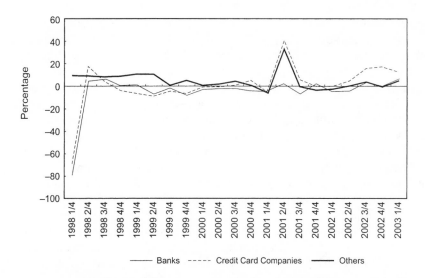

Fig. 5.12   Change in credit delinquents by financial institutions (FIs): Single registration
Source: Korea Federation of Banks.
Note: Others include insurance companies, mutual savings banks, and mutual cooperatives.

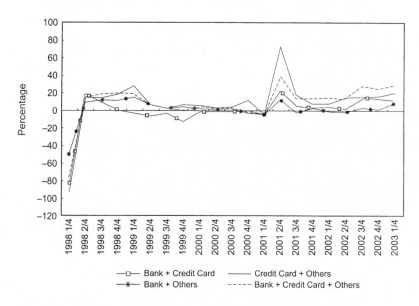

Fig. 5.13   Change in credit delinquents by financial institutions (FIs): Multiple registrations
Source: Korea Federation of Banks.
Note: Others include insurance companies, mutual savings banks, and mutual cooperatives.

participating financial institutions.[25] Under the Use and Protection of Credit Information Act (UPCIA) enacted in 1995, the Korea Federation of Banks was appointed as the agent of the Banking Supervisory Office to maintain the public registry empowered by the law.[26] The credit information gathered by the public registry and shared among participating financial institutions consisted mainly of negative information such as loan delinquency, default, and fraud. Positive information maintained by the registry was limited to outstanding loan balance and number of credit cards held. Moreover, it was not until 2001 that the limited range of positive information began to be collected by the registry. It is a well-known proposition that the use of credit information limited to negative information results in inefficient allocation of credit resources by lowering the accuracy of the credit evaluation system.[27] Therefore, the lack of adequate credit information must have, at least in part, contributed to inefficient allocation of credit resources and ultimately to an increase in credit delinquents. However, the practice to evaluate credit risk of individual borrowers was a more important reason for the serious development of the problem. According to Shin and Park (2006), it was not until 2003 that banks seriously regarded the credit scoring system as an integral part of decision making on consumer loans.[28] Moreover, credit card companies also did not have a workable credit scoring system until 2003 when the credit card crisis hit the industry very hard. In sum, we can conclude that the startling growth of household debt between 2000 and 2002 was not issued based on sound practice of evaluating borrowers' credit risk, and a huge jump in credit delinquents in 2001 and 2003 was a somewhat predictable event.

Last, we can point out the role of untimely and improper regulatory responses in the deterioration of conditions in the market. The mistakes committed by the regulatory authority during the development of events become more conspicuous when we examine the series of policy measures taken in response to development in the credit card market since 2002. We

25. The integrated body of financial regulators, the Financial Supervisory Commission (FSC) and the Financial Supervisory Service, was established after the foreign exchange crisis. Before the FSC was established in 1998, there were three main separate financial regulators, the Bank Supervisory Office in the Bank of Korea, the Securities Supervisory Office, and the Insurance Supervisory Office.

26. The Korea Federation of Banks had already performed as the de facto public registry of credit information since early 1980s through the authorization of the Bank Supervisory Office. However, the authorization was not based on the legal mandate but on the convenience of the supervisor.

27. See Barron and Staten (2003) for a detailed discussion of the value of positive information on the performance of the credit scoring system.

28. The first credit scoring system in the Korean banking sector was introduced by Hana Bank in 1996. Other banks followed in introducing a credit scoring system in the late 1990s. However, the traditional evaluation system utilizing a score card had been the primary tool used in loan decisions. The credit scoring system was not regarded as the integral part of the process and was used as a supplementary device.

will present a detailed discussion on the policy responses to credit card crisis in the next section.

5.4   Credit Card Crisis: Policy Responses and Evaluation

5.4.1   Development of the Credit Card Crisis

Even though the credit card was first introduced to Korea in 1979, the appearance of the credit card as a major financial instrument in the consumer credit market should wait about twenty more years as we discussed in previous sections.

In addition to the spectacular growth of credit card debt since 2000 we discussed in the previous sections, one can quote the following statistics in order to give more hints on how fast credit card usage penetrated the Korean economy since the foreign exchange crisis. The number of merchants accepting credit cards was less than one million in 1992, and it increased seventeen fold in just ten years to mark 17 million participating merchants in 2003. On the other hand, the average number of credit cards an economically active person in Korea possesses also increased very fast, from one in 1993, to two in 1998, and to a peak of 4.6 in 2002. The use of the credit card has become so common that about a half of total private consumption expenditure has been intermediated by the credit card since 2002. The comparable figure was only 15.5 percent in 1999.

As an almost inevitable consequence of fast credit expansion, the average quality of a loan portfolio started to drop. The overdue loan rate was already crawling up in the second half of 2001 when few raised questions about possible risk factors behind the fast loan growth. The overdue loan rate for debt by credit card companies increased very fast, reaching 10.9 percent at the end of 2002. It seemed that the steep increase in the overdue rate was temporarily halted during the first half of 2003. However, the official statistics on the overdue loan rate was quite misleading because confronted with mounting overdue loans, credit card companies tried to window-dress the quality of their loan portfolios by replacing overdue loans with additional credit to debtors in serious arrears. Official statistics did not include the overdue loans once they were replaced by new loans.[29] It is natural that we expect a very high overdue rate on that type of loan. Therefore, the temporary halt in the increase of the overdue loan rate in the first half of 2003 was the result of strategic behavior by credit card companies to disguise the seriousness of the problem. One can confirm from figure 5.14 that the overdue rate with replacement loans could be twice as high as the overdue rate without them. Hence, we can conclude that the

---

29. The Financial Supervisory Service changed the stance on the official statistics only after they faced severe criticism against the practice in 2004.

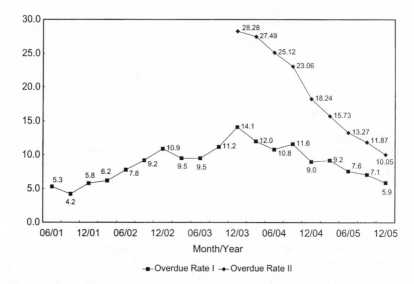

Fig. 5.14   Overdue rate of credit card loans

Source: Financial Supervisory Service.

Notes: Overdue rate I indicates the overdue loan rate excluding replacement loans. Overdue rate II indicates the overdue loan rate including replacement loans.

overdue loan rate increased steadily at least until the end of 2003. Additionally, we also find in figure 5.15 that both profitability and quality of loan portfolios showed a significant decline from the second half of 2002.

The pressure was building up in the credit card industry as the overdue loans accumulated and the quality of loan portfolios deteriorated. The momentum that brought in the turbulent crisis in the credit card industry was offered by exogenous events outside the credit card market. The accounting fraud committed by SK Global Corporation was uncovered in March 2003, which sparked the spread of a pessimistic perspective across financial market.[30] The growing concern about the strength of the financial market hit the weakest spot at the time. The liquidity of the bonds issued by credit card companies suddenly evaporated.

The most conspicuous symptom of liquidity evaporation is illustrated in figure 5.16, which depicts the change in outstanding stock of money market funds and short-term funds around the revelation of the accounting fraud by SK Global in March 2003. Those funds carried portfolios focusing on bonds issued by credit card companies. Investors rushed to secure

30. The amount of accounting fraud committed by SK Global was 1.56 trillion Korean Won. Virtually all imaginable kinds of accounting irregularities were utilized to camouflage the deterioration of the balance sheet. Liability was undervalued, while asset was grossly overvalued.

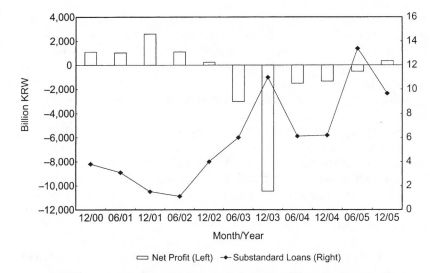

Fig. 5.15   Net profit and quality of loan portfolios of credit card companies
Source: Financial Supervisory Service.
Note: Substandard loans indicate the proportion of loans classified as substandard or below.

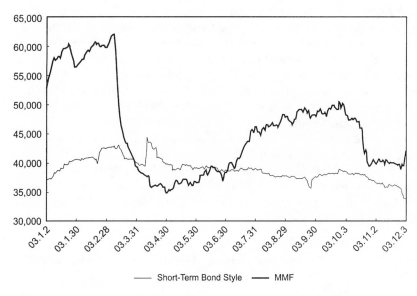

Fig. 5.16   Outstanding stock of money market fund (MMF) and short-term bond fund
Source: Korea Association of Asset Management Corporations.

their investment on those funds, and fund managers were forced to dump credit card bonds to meet the call for repurchasing from investors. Confronted with a severe liquidity crisis, credit card companies were not able to secure enough capital to meet the repayment requirement for the maturing bonds they had issued.

Alarmed by the possibility of contagion of the crisis to other sectors in the financial market, especially the banking sector, due to complex transactions among financial institutions, the Korean government promptly intervened and mediated debt rescheduling negotiations between credit card companies and lending financial institutions to avert a catastrophic collapse of the financial market. Credit card companies issued various debt instruments such as commercial paper, corporate bonds, and asset-backed securities. The total debt of credit card companies was 17.6 trillion KRW at the end of 2002. Investment trust companies that managed various kinds of funds were the biggest lender, with an outstanding balance of 25.5 trillion KRW. Banks followed at a close distance by lending 21.7 trillion KRW to credit card companies. Insurance companies, security companies, and pension funds also extended a significant amount credit to credit card companies (see table 5.7).

Considering the size of debt held by banks and insurance companies that are widely regarded to be related to system risk, some argue that the government intervention was well warranted.

Agreement between credit card companies and lending financial institutions was reached in April 2003. Credit card companies promised to strengthen their financial structure by injecting more capital, and lending financial institutions agreed to delay the redemption of matured bonds issued by credit card companies. The financial market regained a sense of stability, and credit card companies were able to secure liquidity by selling newly issued bonds and structured securities that were backed by portfolios of credit card loans.

However, the market had not retracted the doubt on the viability of credit card companies and kept a watchful eye on the fulfillment of promised injection of additional capital to strengthen the financial structure. The largest credit card company, LG Card, had become the main target in the bond market. The overdue rate on LG Card's loan portfolios stayed at very high level, and the proportion of nonperforming loans rose very fast

Table 5.7   **Lenders of credit card companies by financial institution (trillion KRW)**

	Investment trust	Banks	Insurance company	Security company	Pension fund	Total
Amount	25.5	21.7	12.7	2.1	8.0	89.4

Note: The table illustrates the position at the end of 2003.

even after the agreement in April between credit card companies and financial institutions that provided credit to them. Moreover, the fulfillment of the capital expansion plan promised by the group of large shareholders consisting of the family members controlling LG Group, then the third largest conglomerate in Korea, was delayed. When the news that the group of large shareholders had sold their shares in a discrete manner hit the market, it suddenly became impossible to trade the bonds issued by LG Card, and the company again faced severe difficulty in securing liquidity. The company was overtaken by lending financial institutions led by the Korea Development Bank, and a series of negotiations among creditors to devise a plan to bail out the company came into fruit finally in December 2003.

5.4.2   Regulatory Failures

The first regulatory misstep was committed in 1999 when the ceiling on the cash advance service was removed as a part of the deregulation and liberalization of the financial market. It is very hard to question the legitimacy of the deregulation measure in that setting the limit of the cash advance service should be left to the private contract negotiated between credit card company and customer. However, it is also true that in the absence of an adequate credit evaluation system, the uniform ceiling on the maximum amount of cash advance services played an important role in checking the uncontrollable increase in cash advance services and keeping the soundness of loan portfolios held by credit card companies. Before the deregulation measure was taken, the cash advance service was limited to 700,000 KRW, and that was not linked to creditworthiness of individual borrowers. Credit card companies did not have either the will or the resources to be equipped with a credit evaluation system. Free from harness, credit card companies plunged into brutal competition to increase market shares. Along with the removal of the ceiling on cash advance services, credit card companies made a decision not to share credit information about customers' available credit amounts and card issuances that made unfettered increase in credit card debt possible. As an inevitable result of the ill-advised deregulation measure, credit card debt accumulated in an unprecedented pace in 2001 and 2002, and a fast increase in registered credit delinquents in 2003 followed.

The second regulatory misstep was committed during the boom between 2000 and 2002. Despite increasing risks due to fast growing credit card debts, the financial regulator did not fully understand the fundamental nature of the problem. During the booming era, the credit card industry was regarded as a highly profitable sector, and many financial institutions were willing to provide credit to credit card companies by buying various debt instruments issued by them. Table 5.8 reports the amount of credit financed by various debt instruments. The outstanding stock of debt instruments issued by credit card companies increased fivefold from 1999 to

Table 5.8   Financing by various debt instruments (billion KRW)

	1999	2000	2001	2002
Commercial paper	4,084	9,649	11,324	20,888
Bonds	10,850	16,731	18,665	29,612
Asset backed security		4,476	26,712	33,535
Others	2,905	2,666	4,445	3,632
Total	17,839	33,264	61,146	87,666

2002, and most of the debts were taken by banks and investment trust companies in which banks had invested a significant portion of funds under management as shown in table 5.7.

The high profitability of credit card companies that attracted huge amount of credit into the sector was primarily based on the high interest rate charged on overdue loans. Borrowers were able to pay the high interest charged on overdue loans as long as they were allowed access to other credit provisions. In other words, debtors already in arrears were able to borrow from another credit card company to pay overdue loans. It looked as if the high profitability of credit card companies would last forever. However, that was the correct presumption only if borrowers could find another credit card company to grant credit that would be used to pay the existing overdue loan. That, however, is a form of financial pyramid that cannot be sustained and could be busted anytime.

Knowing the fragility of the scheme and observing the fast inflow of huge credit into credit card companies, the financial regulator should have intervened promptly. They should have blocked the inflow of credit by tightening supervisory activities on banks and investment trust companies. The financial regulator had the legitimate power to ask those financial institutions to stop providing further credit from the perspective of prudential regulation.

The third misstep was committed in 2002 when the financial regulator took several measures to curb rapid credit expansion by credit card companies. Giving up the laissez-faire attitude toward the credit card industry, the financial regulator suddenly changed the policy stance and imposed several very strong policy restrictions on them. The objective of the policies was to restore stability in the credit card market and to avoid realization of system risk. More specifically, the proportion of cash advance services out of total financial activities should be maintained under 50 percent, and prompt corrective action for failing credit card companies was introduced. Most notably, the provision standard for bad debts was strengthened. The new standard was even higher than the one required for banks, and credit card companies suffered loss of confidence due to a deteriorated position in income statements. The position in income statements declined simply because credit card companies were required to set aside more resources to meet the strengthened provision standard.

No one can raise a question to the necessity of the policy measures to restore stability of the market. But the timing and strength of regulatory interventions invited strong criticism from both the market and the expert commentators. Already in deep trouble in repaying monthly bills, a significant portion of credit card debtors managed to avoid falling into arrears by financing a new debt from other credit card companies or the usurious private loan market. Sudden strengthening of regulatory measures and subsequent tightening of credit risk management by credit card companies resulted in a rapid increase in arrears and a decrease in credit card debts. Consequently, the number of credit delinquents recorded at the public registry soared by more than 50 percent in a year. Many observers claim that the regulatory authority could have been able to avoid such a violent crash landing with a more cautious choice of timing and intensity of policy execution.

References

Bank for International Settlements (BIS). 2006. Housing finance in the global financial market. CGFS Paper no. 26. Basel, Switzerland: BIS, Committee on the Global Financial System.
Barron, J., and M. Staten. 2003. The value of comprehensive reports. In *Credit reporting systems and the international economy,* ed. M. Miller. Cambridge, MA: MIT Press.
Bertola, G., R. Disney, and C. Grant. 2006. *The economics of consumer credit.* Cambridge, MA: MIT Press.
Congressional Budget Office. 2000. Personal bankruptcy: A literature review. CBO Paper. Washington, DC: Congressional Budget Office.
Crook, J. 2001. The demand for household debt in the USA: Evidence from the 1995 Survey of Consumer Finance. *Applied Financial Economics* 11:82–91.
———. 2006. Household debt demand and supply: Cross-country comparison. In *The economics of consumer credit,* ed. G. Bertola, R. Disney, and C. Grant, 63–92. Cambridge, MA: MIT Press.
Fabozzi, F., and F. Modigliani. 1992. *Mortgage and mortgage-backed securities markets.* Boston, MA: Harvard Business School Press.
Honoré, B. 1992. Trimmed LAD and least squares estimation of trucated and censored regression models with fixed effects. *Econometrica* 60:533–63.
Kim, J. 1995. Liquidity constraints and consumption expenditure: A comparative analysis for Korea, Japan, and the United States. *KDI Journal of Economic Policy* 17:63–96.
Kindleberger, C., and R. M. Aliber. 2005. *Manias, panics, and crashes: A history of financial crises.* 5th ed. New York: Wiley.
Park, C., and S. Hur. 2006. Impacts of the new Basel Accord on housing finance market in Korea. Korea Development Institute. Mimeograph.

Shin, I., C. Hahn, and C. Park. 2003. *The causes of increase in credit delinquents and policy tasks* (in Korean). KDI Policy Report. Seoul: Korea Development Institute.

Shin, I., and C. Park. 2006. *Credit information system in Korea: Current condition and policy priorities* (in Korean). KDI Policy Report. Seoul: Korea Development Institute.

Comment   Winston T. H. Koh

The chapter examines the events surrounding the rapid expansion of household debt in South Korea since the foreign exchange crisis that Korea suffered in 1997, which occurred as part of the Asian Financial Crisis. A specific focus of the chapter is to investigate the developments in the housing loan market and the credit card crisis in 2003, and the government response to address the issues in both the housing loan market and the credit card industry. The chapter argues that the crisis stems from regulatory failure, and with timely and proper regulatory actions, much of the difficulties that occurred in the credit card market would have been alleviated or averted.

I will make two general comments about the chapter, before going into the specific comments. Firstly, in light of the intersecting sets of issues discussed in the chapter, it would be useful to provide, as a backdrop to the analysis, a brief discussion of the state of the South Korean economy since 1997, in terms of rate of gross domestic product (GDP) growth, foreign investment inflow, current account deficit, and so on in order that the reader can better appreciate the forces driving the economy and understand the impetus for the business strategies of the banks and credit card companies and the government's responses. In particular, it would be useful to find out if there were certain macroeconomic conditions that had prevented the authorities from taking certain preventive or corrective actions to address the developments in the credit markets.

Second, to the extent that data are available, it would be interesting to analyze the data by age of household head as well as by income/assets to gain a fuller picture. Table 5.1 and 5.2 look at household debt by age and income/asset holdings, respectively. It would be interesting to analyze the data by age of household head as well as by income/assets, if the data are available.

Winston T. H. Koh is an associate professor of economics and associate dean of the School of Economics at Singapore Management University.

Bank Lending to the Housing Market

The chapter noted that the household debt market in Korea has undergone three distinguished phases since 1997:

- The first phase was from 1997 to 1999, when household debt fell sharply due to monetary tightening in the aftermath of the 1997 economic crisis in Korea.
- The second phase was from 2000 to 2002, when household debt expanded sharply, recovering to the precrisis level. Debt-to-income ratio rose from 63.8 percent at the end of 1999 to 113.3 percent in 2002, while the debt-to-asset ratio also rose considerably, from 40.1 percent at the end of 1999 to 51.8 percent in 2002.
- The third phase was from 2003 onward, the expansion in household debt came to a grinding halt, and the financial sector went into another crisis.

As described in the chapter, three factors were behind the developments. The first and most obvious factor is the prevailing low interest rate environment. Interest rates in Korea fell since 1999, as the authorities eased monetary policy after the economy had stabilized following the economic crisis in 1997 to 1999. The low interest rates led to increased borrowings from households, particularly in collateralized housing loans.

Next, financial sector deregulation led to a shift in the business strategy of financial institutions. Before the Asian financial crisis, Korean banks were urged by the government to lend to Korean conglomerates, or *chaebols*. As the author noted, "profitability of individual banks was not a primary concern as long as banks served the policy goals set by the government." Following the Asian financial crisis, the policy stance in financial regulation shifted toward one of fostering market efficiency in the credit markets. Financial institutions are now free to set their interest rates and prices for the services they provide. Entry barriers to the financial sector have been lowered, and foreign players are now welcome to establish local subsidiaries or acquire domestic financial institutions.

Finally, driven by the need to maintain the bottom line, banks turned their attention away from loans to the corporate sector, which were deemed to be riskier, to loans to the household sector, which were considered more lucrative and less risky than loans to the corporate sector. Moreover, in the restructuring that the Korean economy went through following the 1997 financial crisis, the focus of funding by Korean corporates shifted away from bank loans to fund-raising via bond and share issuance in the capital market. Hence, the increase in attention by banks toward the household sector coincided with a reduction in demand for bank loans from the corporate sector.

During the five-year span from 2001 to 2005, it is reported that 71 percent of the increase in household debt provided by banks was attributable to increase in loans secured by residential properties (LSRP). Loans by banks to households rose from an average prevailing rate of below 30 percent of the total loan portfolio in 1998 to reach 49.8 percent in 2005, surpassing the loans to the corporate sector for the first time. Loans to households secured by residential properties rose from 47.8 percent at the end of 2000 to reach 62.4 percent in 2005.

The natural question to ask is why banks were willing to increase their exposure to the real estate sector so sharply. Was the real estate market in Korea experiencing a boom during the period under study? If there was indeed a boom in the Korean real estate market (and other asset markets) during this period, then the increase in household debt may not appear to be a problem, at least from the banks' perspective, since the net asset value of households has also increased sharply during this period. As noted in the chapter, information on the aggregate asset holdings by households is not available. Nonetheless, it would be very helpful if the author could provide some data and analysis of the real estate market during this period. In fact, there might exist an "irrational exuberance-type" explanation for the euphoria in the banking sector in increasing its exposure to the real estate market. A booming real estate market coupled with increased competition among banks to lend to households is likely to lead to an underpricing of default risk in the real estate markets—as was found to be the case in many Asian countries in the run-up to the Asian financial crisis.

Changing Structure of the Mortgage Loans

The housing market in Korea also turned out to possess several features that distinguish it from the typical long-term mortgage loan market that exists in other countries (as shown in table 5.6 in the chapter). Housing loans in Korea are short in maturity (typically one to three years) and are not amortized over the tenure of the loans. These housing loans are referred to as *bullet mortgages*. Interest payments are made monthly, and at the maturity of the housing loan, the principal is either rolled over or repaid. Loan quantum to asset value is typically less than 60 percent of the value of the properties, compared with the usual 70 percent or more in the conventional mortgage loan markets in other countries.

In taking on a bullet mortgage rather than a conventional long-term mortgage with amortization, a typical household would need to save for a long time in order to come out with a sizable downpayment of at least 40 percent of the purchase price of the property. As a result, the average age of a first-time home buyer in Korea is higher (from late thirties to the early forties) than that in other countries where the long-term mortgage market is established and the size of the initial downpayment is significantly smaller.

The chapter noted that in a booming real estate market, Korean banks were willing to "rollover" housing loans if the households were not willing or able to fully repay the loan. However, in a declining real estate market, the bullet mortgage loan structure with its short maturity structure meant that banks would generally become more selective in granting rollovers and renewing the loans. As a result, households may be forced to sell their properties to repay the loans. It is likely that the selling pressure, however weak it may be to begin with, may start to snowball, leading to depressed property values and creating a vicious cycle by inducing further reluctance on the part of the banks to renew the loans. Compared with more conventional long-term mortgages, where loan quanta are higher, and household income is the key determinant of debt-servicing ability, the bullet mortgage structure seems to have a distinct disadvantage as it gives rise to boom-bust cycles.

The interesting question is why the housing loan market in Korea did not develop mortgages with longer tenures. It is noted in the chapter that while bullet mortgage contracts are vulnerable to housing price shocks, they are more robust to adverse income shocks because there is no principal repayment during the loan tenure. It is argued that compared with the "conventional" mortgage structure, there are likely to be fewer defaults under the bullet mortgage structure. I am not sure if this claim is always true or if it has been investigated in any context before. It is not necessarily the case that households will experience greater pressure to service the housing loan under a conventional mortgage structure because households may either reduce their savings or alter their spending patterns to cope with the higher monthly mortgage payments. In fact, households may reduce their consumption and save even more to cope with contingencies when their incomes are not enough to service the monthly mortgage payments.

The chapter noted that in 2002, the Korean policymakers started to take various policy measures to help smooth the rollover of maturing debts and to introduce conventional mortgages into the housing finance market. However, the Korean financial institutions are involved merely as agents of the Korean Housing Finance Corporation (KHFC). The question is why the banks aren't marketing long-term housing terms themselves as this appears to be a profitable market segment that has found huge demand, as the proportion of LSRP with amortization has doubled from 14.1 percent in 2003 to 28.3 percent in May 2005.

Social Welfare Effects of the Increase in Household Debt

The author argues that the increase in household debt has brought about several positive effects. He cites as evidence, first, the increased inflow of credit resources into the household sector, reflecting efficiency improvements in the allocation of credit resources; and second, with easier access to credit, households were able to borrow and achieve a smoother lifetime consumption path. The caveat, of course, is proper credit evaluation and risk management have been undertaken by banks to ensure that the quality of the loan portfolio does not deteriorate. However, as it turned out, this was not the case, given the particular structure of the housing loan market in Korea.

While there are likely positive effects on social welfare from the two developments described by the author, it is also important to consider the negative effects of the severe credit contraction that were to follow in 2003, when banks (as well as credit card companies) started to curb credit supply to the household sector. Annual growth rate of household debt dropped to and stayed around 10 percent. I am not sure if the net effects would have turned out to be positive overall.

Overall, I commend Dr. Park for an interesting chapter that provides a case study of some of the issues that policymakers in Asian markets have to grapple with as they restructure the economy, particularly in the aftermath of the Asian Financial Crisis. It was a pleasure to read the chapter and to be discussant at the NBER-EASE conference.

Financial Consolidation

6

The Determinants of Cross-Border Merger and Acquisition Activity in the Financial Sector in Asia
Did the Asian Financial Crisis Change Them?

Chung-Hua Shen and Mei-Rong Lin

6.1 Introduction

Since the Asian financial crisis in 1997, the financial sector in Asian countries has been experiencing a period of consolidation. But at the time of the crisis, local currencies and equity prices plummeted, and real estate bubbles burst. Reduced collateral values, meanwhile, put banking institutions under severe stress, but worse still, the number of nonperforming loans soared, intensely shaking the financial sector. Because one of the suspected culpable factors at the root of the banking crisis was overcompetition, that is, there were too many banks in the market, policymakers were committed to reducing their number in an attempt to solve the crisis. Among the methods to accomplish this, policymakers seemed particularly to favor bank mergers (Shih 2003, 32). To cite a few examples, in 1998, the governor of the central bank of the Philippines stated, "The central bank favors mergers as a way to keep the number of bank failures to a minimum . . ." In the meantime, the Malaysian government urged that all banks be merged into six, which later became ten, and soon thereafter Taiwan's president announced the so-called Second Phase of Financial Reform, which invigorated banks to consolidate or form strategic alliances with foreign financial institutions. Thus began the welcoming of mergers and acquisitions (M&As) that were about to start their new journey across the wide financial landscape of Asia.

Before the crisis, foreign banks were, for the most part, restricted from entering Asian financial markets, but to be sure, the markets became much

Chung-Hua Shen is a professor of finance at National Taiwan University. Mei-Rong Lin is a PhD student in the Department of Money and Banking at National Chengchi University.

more open and much more accessible after the crisis.[1] It is, therefore, interesting, if not even puzzling, to try to better understand whether the determinants of mergers and acquisitions of financial institutions were different before and after the Asian crisis.

The purpose of this chapter is to empirically investigate whether the Asian crisis has changed the determinants of cross-border mergers and acquisitions among financial institutions in ten Asian countries. To the best of our knowledge, this is the first study to explore the impact of the Asian crisis on the determinants of cross-border M&A activity among financial institutions. In this line of research, most of the relevant literature has focused on Organization for Economic Cooperation and Development (OECD) countries (Fecher and Pestieau 1993; Focarelli and Pozzolo 2000, 2001, 2005), European countries (Campa and Hernando 2006; Altunbas and Marques 2004), high-income countries (Portes and Rey 2005), and the United States and four European countries (Vasconcellos and Kish 1998). Two exceptions are the works of Buch and DeLong (2004) and Giovanni (2002) who use some 150 countries in their sample, but their studies neither cover the period of the Asian crisis, nor do they take similar crises, such as the European currency crisis and the Tequila crisis, into account. Because the Asian crisis significantly changed the attitude of governments toward M&As, it is expected that the present study that focuses on Asian countries and the Asian crisis should complement existing studies considerably.

To be more specific, some parallels can be drawn between our chapter and others in the field of location choice, the study of the determinants of choosing a city to set up subsidiaries, branches, representative offices, and agents by foreign banks. Brealey and Kaplanis (1996), for example, used the location of the overseas offices of 1,000 of the world's largest banks to examine the determinants of foreign bank location. Shen and Chou (2007) recently study the determinants of foreign banks' choice of Asian cities to establish new branch offices, and they point to a significant relationship between the choice of bank location, foreign trade, and foreign direct investment. Our chapter, however, differs from those studies in that it focuses on cross-border consolidation rather than the establishment of foreign offices.[2] Our chapter differs from the past studies in three aspects. First, be-

---

1. For example, in Singapore, the authority announced a five-year program to liberalize access by foreign bank. See the appendix for the openness of each country.

2. In a broad term, our chapter is also part of foreign direct investment. Most studies of foreign direct investment is related to economic growth. For example, De Mello (1999) reported that in the first international capital flow, foreign direct investment, inflows appear to enhance economic growth in both developing and OECD countries, but Borenzstein, De Gregorio, and Lee et al. (1998) found that the positive effects of foreign direct investment can only be detected when a recipient country has a sufficiently high level of human capital. Carkovic and Levine (2005), however, concluded that foreign direct investment does not have an unconditional robust, positive effect on economic growth but that rather the effect is dependent on national in-

cause we compare the determinants before and after the Asian crisis, our sample periods cover a long span from 1990 to 2006. Past studies focus on the determinants that may affect M&As and do not consider the related important event that may change the impact of the determinants. Also, the studies commonly are limited to one particular year.

Next, our study belongs to the "from-many-to-many" category in the field of multinational enterprises, which means that acquirers are from many countries, and their targets are in many countries. In this regard, Clarke et al. (2001) have explained that from-many-to-many studies are probably fewer in number because of difficulties associated with data collection. Because our samples include "all" M&As of financial institutions, not only in Asia but also G7 countries, as the acquirers, our chapter could be the most comprehensive study of M&As in Asian financial institutions.

Third, our financial institutions contain all targets, and acquirers in the financial industry from Asian countries are included. The financial institutions include investment banks, mutual funds, insurance and security companies, banks, credit unions, credit cooperatives, and so on. Therefore, the use of firm-level data is not possible because except for banks, other firm-level data are not available. Even the bank-level data is not available before 1995, making the use of firm-level data impossible.[3]

There are very few theories about cross-border M&As among financial institutions, which explains the rationale behind the fact that most current empirical studies borrow theories from international trade. And this chapter is not an exception. We explore whether the following five existing hypotheses are related to cross-border M&A activity in Asian countries. They are the *gravity hypothesis, following the client hypothesis, market opportunity hypothesis, information cost hypothesis,* and the *regulation barrier hypothesis.* These five hypotheses are explained in detail in the following section. This chapter proceeds as follows. The next section provides a survey of the literature. Section 6.3 presents the empirical model, and section 6.4 gives the source of the data and the basic statistics. Section 6.5 summarizes the estimated results of our model, and section 6.6 presents the estimated reports of the robustness testing. Section 6.7 reviews the conclusions.

---

come, school attainment, and so on. For a survey, see Prasad et al. (2003). Wei (2001) studies the effect of taxation and corruption on international direct investment from fourteen source countries to forty-five host countries; he finds that increase in either the tax rate on multinational firms or the corruption level in the host governments would reduce inward foreign direct investment. Wei (2000b) points out the corruption can be interpreted more broadly as "poor public governance" rather than as bureaucratic corruption narrowly defined, and the corruption in a developing country may increase its chances of suffering a crisis.

3. Therefore, those using cross-border firm-level data to do the location choice studies focus only on banks. Also, because researchers' bank-level data is taken from BankScope, a data bank launched in the market in 1995, its coverage of the earlier years is limited, especially before 1996.

6.2   Literature Review on Cross-Border Consolidation

There is a paucity of studies in the literature related to the determinants of M&As of financial institutions, largely stemming from the fact that some researchers may have been impeded by problems with data collection and by the fact that cross-border M&As in the financial sector have been relatively rare. This section introduces the five hypotheses we examine.

It is noted that though the conditions discussed in the following are mostly based on bank systems or regulations, our data contains other type of financial institutions. We use only bank conditions on regulation because similar types of data for other financial institutions are released less often. Thus, our results should be interpreted cautiously.

6.2.1   Gravity Hypothesis

The gravity hypothesis, first adopted by Tinbergen (1962), explains trade flow between two countries, say i and j, using two masses, usually gross domestic product (GDP) and distance, where the former and the latter are suggested to have positive and negative effects, respectively. Most commonly, distance has been reported to have a very significantly negative impact on M&As among financial institutions. This is slightly mystifying given that most assets in financial institutions are "weightless," and distance is not a good proxy for transportation cost in transacting financial assets (Portes and Rey 2005).

As regards this conundrum, Portes and Rey (2005) suggest that distance might also be a proxy for information asymmetry. To explain, countries that are geographically near each other tend to know more about each other, either because of direct interaction between their citizens for business or tourism or because of more extensive media coverage. Thus, the significance of distance may reflect the validity of the gravity hypothesis or the asymmetric information hypothesis.

Our model considers GDP after logarithmic transformation (GDP) and distance (DISTANCE) as the measures of the gravity hypothesis.

6.2.2   Following the Client Hypothesis

Following the customer is a defensive expansionary strategy that argues that international financial institutions follow their customers when they go abroad in order to protect their existing relationship with them. See Williams (2002) for a detailed survey. The typical proxy for this hypothesis is the trade (that is, the sum of exports and imports) between two countries. However, Focarelli and Pozzolo (2005) propose a similar but broad term that they refer to as "economic integration."

This chapter follows the convention by using the degree of openness of the country, that is, the sum of exports and imports divided by GDP

(TRADE), to proxy this concept. The following the clients hypothesis suggests that TRADE should be positively related to M&As.

6.2.3   Market Opportunity

The decision to expand abroad is likely spurred by banks' search for profit opportunities beyond those offered by traditional banking activity at home. Banks in a more profitable, better-developed banking sector in their home country most probably have a competitive advantage over their competitors in the destination market. Focarelli and Pozzolo (2001) use the total credit of the banking sector (measured as the ratio of total credit to GDP) and the average return on assets (ROA) of banks in home countries as proxies for market opportunity. They find that the two variables are positively related to international expansion. Also, economic growth in the host market is important. Focarelli and Pozzolo (2001) also point out that the individual bank's size is another critical factor.

Focarelli and Pozzolo (2000) define market opportunity such that it includes the expected rate of economic growth and banks' efficiency in the destination country. The use of the former is the same as that in their 1991 paper, but the use of the latter is probably dependent on the individual banks they adopt, which allows them to estimate banks' efficiency. They then investigate those factors that affect foreign shareholding. Vasconcellos and Kish (1998) study the M&A activity between the United States and four European countries (France, German, Italy, and the United Kingdom) and find that an increase in stock returns in the United States discourages the foreign acquisition of American firms. Conversely, an increase in European country stock returns results in an escalation in the acquisition of American firms. Thus, increases in the stock returns of acquirers seem to augment acquisitions, but an increase in the stock returns of target companies has the opposite effect.

In this study, our market opportunity hypothesis comprises the expected rate of economic growth and expected stock returns effect on M&As. For the former, given the currently fast economic growth, we surmise that acquirers may continuingly feel optimistic about the future economic growth of the target market. This optimistic economic growth view suggests that the impact of the economic growth is positive. Focarelli and Pozollo's (2000) findings, for example, support the optimistic economic growth view because they find that banks prefer to invest in countries with high expected rates of economic growth.

On the other hand, given the high stock prices, the cost of acquiring costs is too high because the high stock price is not sustainable. Thus, potential acquirers likely tend to wait for the next opportunity, making the impact negative. Vasconcellos and Kish's (1998) findings support the high stock cost view. They found that a depressed U.S. stock market relative to foreign stock markets encourages the foreign acquisition of U.S. companies. The proxy for market opportunity in our chapter is the expected GDP growth rate at time $t + 1$ (GDPGROW) and expected stock returns at time $t + 1$ (STOCKRET).

6.2.4   Information Cost Hypothesis

Berger, Davies, and Flannery (2000) contend that such efficiency barriers as distance as well as differences in language, culture, currency, and regulatory/supervisory structures inhibit cross-border bank mergers within Europe. Buch and DeLong (2004) examine three different measures of information cost, that is, distance, common language, and common legal system. They find that partners in bank mergers tend to speak the same language and to be close in terms of geographical distance. DISTANCE is also the proxy for the information cost hypothesis because, as mentioned earlier, countries that are in close geographical proximity tend to know more about each other.

Many studies have shown that foreign direct investment is negatively related to information cost (Sabi 1988; Dunning 1998; Kim and Wei 1999). That is, large foreign direct investment means that firms are familiar with the transaction behavior of the host countries, which in turn reduces information cost. Therefore, foreign direct investment could also include the cost of the information. Accordingly, our information cost covers common language (**LANGUAGE**), common religion (**RELIGION**), and distance (DISTANCE). The former two are dummy variables, that is, if the shared official language is English, for instance, or the shared religion is the same, the dummy is unity; otherwise, it is zero. For example, in our sample, the official language of Singapore, Hong Kong, the Philippines and India is English (see the World Bank Web site) Thus, their **LANGUAGE** is uniform. DISTANCE refers to geographic distance, which is published in the Central Intelligence Agency (CIA) *Factbook*.

It is important to note that the movement of a variable may be the interactive outcome of more than one hypothesis. For example, DISTANCE may reflect both the gravity hypothesis and informational friction, where both indicate a pull factor for acquirers.

6.2.5   Regulatory Restrictions

It is conceivable that the attitude toward M&As by the local authority of a particular country could be a critical factor in affecting a firm's decision as to whether to engage in a cross-border M&A. On the one hand, putting explicit limits on cross-border M&As or blocking single takeovers would definitely reduce the number of the cross-border M&As, and more than that, regulatory restrictions would, in all likelihood, reduce the international competitiveness of banks, thereby hindering their opportunities for international expansion. On the other hand, restrictions could reduce the degree of information asymmetry—for example, by making the relation-ship between banks and depositors more transparent; in an environment with such regulatory restrictions, those banks would likely have a greater incentive to expand their activities abroad in order to bypass their home country's restrictions.

Two categories of regulatory restrictions are often used. The regulatory restrictions here are considered in a broad sense, and, as such, they include the rule of law as well as those governing institutional quality. Restrictions that comprise the first category of regulatory restrictions are related to the rule of law, institutional quality and government effectiveness. Thus, the proxies include legal origin (La Porta et al. 1997, 1998 [LLSV]), regulatory burden and corruption, as well as rule of law (Kaufmann, Kraay, and Zoido-Lobaton [KKZ] 2002). Focarelli and Pozzolo (2000) claim that, as a rule, countries with a relatively more efficient judicial system are pre-ferred by foreign acquirers because their market transactions would be bet-ter guaranteed. Note that Galindo, Micco, and Serra (2003) do not use these regulatory indexes to measure cross-border activities but argue that it is the differences between home and host countries that have positive effects on bilateral cross-border banking activity.

The second category of regulatory restrictions are taken from Barth et al.'s (2000, 2006) survey and comprise restrictions on banking activities in securities, insurance, and real restate, with higher values denoting more stringent restrictions. Shen and Chang (2006) hypothesize that though these restrictions may harm the performance of banks, sound government governance can reduce the adverse effects. Focarelli and Pozzolo (2000) ar-gue that these restrictions may be a proxy for actual limitations on firms from entry into a country from abroad. Both their 2000 and 2001 results show that stricter restrictions actually reduce the number of acquisitions. Focarelli and Pozzolo (2001) find similar results.

We adopt two sets of regulatory variables. The first set is related to government governance. We adopt KKZ's indexes of corruption (ΔKKZ_CORRUP), rule of law (ΔKKZ_RULELAW), quality of regula-tion (ΔKKZ_REGQUAL), and government efficiency (ΔKKZ_GOVEFF). The indexes of KKZ are renewed every two years and contain six gover-nance clusters. Wei (2000a, 2001) also mentioned the importance of gover-nance in studying cross-board capital flow. See table 6.1 for the definition of each proxy. Recall that Rossi and Volpin (2004) and Galindo, Micco, and Serra (2003) suggest using the difference of indexes as one of the de-terminates. Following their procedure, we also use the gap indexes, which are denoted as ΔKKZ. Then we proceed to examine whether these regula-tory gap indexes are related to those countries' firms' propensity to engage in cross-border M&A activity. Thus, while the original KKZ's indexes range from -2.5 to 2.5 (see table 6.1), with a higher number denoting bet-ter governance, the transformed gap indexes now range from -5 to 5. And

Table 6.1   Data specification and sources

Variable	Definition	Source
DISTANCE	Compute as the shortest line between two countries' commercial centers according to the degrees of latitude and longitude	CIA
GDP	GDP in billion US. dollar in 2000	WDI
TRADE	Bilateral trade volume (import + export) between acquirer and target country divided by GDP.	DOTSY
GDPGROW (%)	GDP growth rate	WDI
STOCKRET (%)	Stock return	DY
LANGUAGE	Dummy variable set equal to 1 if the same legal system prevails in the target and acquirer country, 0 otherwise	CIA
RELIGIOUS	Dummy variable set equal to 1 if the same religious prevails in the target and acquirer country, 0 otherwise	CIA
KKZ_CORRUP	Kaufman, Kraay, and Zoido-Lobatón (KKZ) index variable measures the Control of Corruption dimension. The KKZ index is measured in units ranging from about –2.5 to 2.5, with higher values corresponding to better governance.	WB
KKZ_RULELAW	KKZ index variable measures the Rule of Law dimension. The KKZ index is measured in units ranging from about –2.5 to 2.5, with higher values corresponding to better governance.	WB
KKZ_REGQUAL	KKZ index variable measures the Regulatory Quality dimension. The KKZ index is measured in units ranging from about –2.5 to 2.5, with higher values corresponding to better governance.	WB
KKZ_GOVEFF	KKZ index variable measures the Government Effectiveness dimension. The KKZ index is measured in units ranging from about –2.5 to 2.5, with higher values corresponding to better governance.	WB
RESTRIC_S	Index of the restrictions on Bank's operation in Securities sector; range from 1 to 4 with a higher value indicating a more restrictive environment	Barth, Caprio, and Levine (2006)
RESTRIC_I	Index of the restriction on Bank's operation in Insurance sector; range from 1 to 4 with a higher value indicating a more restrictive environment	Barth, Caprio, and Levine (2006)
RESTRIC_E	Index of the restriction on Bank's operation in Real Estate sector; range from 1 to 4 with a higher value indicating a more restrictive environment	Barth, Caprio, and Levine (2006)
RESTRIC_NF	Index of the restriction on Bank's holding in Nonfinancial Institution; range from 1 to 4 with a higher value indicating a more restrictive environment	Barth, Caprio, and Levine (2006)

Sources: CIA: Central Intelligence Agency Web site; DOTSY: Direction of Trade Statistics Yearboo published by IMF; DY: DataStream and Yahoo! WB: World Bank Web site, www.worldbank.org. WD World Development Indicator, 2006.

the better the governance in the home country is, the greater is the propensity for financial institutions in the host country to be mergered.[4]

The second set of regulatory variables comprises restrictions on banking activities that engage in securities (ΔRESTRIC_S), insurance (ΔRESTRIC_I), real estate (ΔRESTRIC_R) and nonfinancial (ΔRESTRIC_NF). (See Barth, Caprio, and Levine 2000.) We perform similar transformations to use gap indexes. In this case, the gap series range from –3 to 3. Therefore, the higher the number of the gap indexes is, the more restrictive the acquiring country is relative to the target country.

6.3   Econometric Model

We use the number of M&As as our dependent variable for the following two reasons. First, we study whether the Asian crisis has changed the attitude toward the consolidation. For example, it is generally thought that the authority is more welcome to the foreign buyers after the crisis. Thus, the number of transactions seems preferable to reflect this attitude change. The value of transaction, however, is often more related to the performance and financial condition.

Next, the data of value of transaction are often unavailable to the public because the actual money transaction is sometimes a business secret. The data of the number of M&As are complete and thus are a more accurate measure in this case.

We, therefore, employ the Poisson regression model given our dependent variable is countable numbers. That is,

(1) $$N_{ij} = \exp[\alpha + \beta_1 \mathbf{X} \mathbf{D} + \beta_2 \mathbf{X}(1 - \mathbf{D}) + \varepsilon_{ij}],$$

where i and j denote the home i and host country j, respectively, thus, N_{ij} is the number of M&As, between home country i and host country j, $\mathbf{D}$ is the dummy variable of the Asian crisis, which is equal to unity before the crisis and zero after it. $\mathbf{X}$ is the vector of the explanatory variables, β_1 and β_2 are the corresponding coefficients of the explanatory variables before and after the crisis, respectively, and ε represents errors.

Our $\mathbf{X}$ contains the five sets of variables, representing the five aforementioned hypotheses. We first examine any combination of two hypotheses and then gradually expand to three and four to avoid multicollinearity.

6.4   Data Description and Basic Statistics

Our selection of M&A data is based on the following simple rules. First, all targets and acquirers in the financial industry from Asian countries are

---

4. Note that Galindo, Micco, and Sierra (2003) also take the absolute value of the differences.

included. Furthermore, to examine the robustness, all acquirers from G7 countries are included. Next, the announcement day of M&As is used instead of the day the transaction is complete. This is simply because the former is available consistently, but the latter is often lacking the complete day and is difficult to define. Third, our financial institutions include banks, security houses, insurances, mutual funds, and so on, which help us to know the impact of the crisis on the financial industry. Fourth, the sample period covers January 1, 1990, to December 31, 2006.

We divide the whole sample into pre- and post-Asian subsample using the year of 1998 for the following reasons. Following the Thai Baht's devaluation in mid-1997, the region entered severe economic crisis. Growth was negative in 1998 in most countries in the region. The economics indexes have shown dramatical changes in 1998. Corsetti, Pesenti, and Roubini (1998) and Berg (1999) all point out a change in the Asian financial market in 1998.

Table 6.2 reports the number of M&As before (1990 to 1997) and after (1999 to 2006) the crisis. Five particularly interesting results emerge. First, the number of M&As is much higher after the crisis than before it. For example, for Singapore, the number before and after the crisis is 72 and 165, respectively; for Malaysia, 51 and 92, respectively; and for Hong Kong, 42 and 86, respectively. Therefore, Singapore, Malaysia, and Hong Kong are the three most active acquirers in the postcrisis period. Furthermore, in terms of the percentage, the acquiring rate of Singapore is the highest, up to 6 percent. The higher number after the crisis is probably because of the policy of openness toward the financial consolidation after the crisis. It is, nevertheless, difficult for the present chapter to examine the effect of policy on the consolidation. See the appendix for the policy of openness.

Second, as it has the highest number of thirty-four and forty-one in targets before and after the crisis, financial institutions in Hong Kong are the most likely targets for consolidation. Indonesia has the second largest number of targeted financial institutions.

Third, Japan shows the most asymmetric patterns as a target and an acquirer. It acquires 100 foreign banks, but only ten Japanese financial institutions are acquired in all sample periods. This asymmetric attitude that Japanese financial institutions can buy foreign banks but foreigners are not welcome to buy Japanese financial institutions is worth future study. An opposite asymmetric case can be found in Thailand. That is, seventy-five financial institutions from Thailand are the targets, but only fifteen are acquirers.

Fourth, during both periods, in India, M&A activity is almost nonexistent, while in Indonesia and Thailand, it is negligible. Furthermore, though few targets and acquirers are found in Taiwan, there is a moderate increase in the number of acquirers after the crisis. Finally, and somewhat bewildering, the number of M&As in Malaysia is relatively high.

Table 6.2   Cross-border merger number in Asian countries

Target country	Hong Kong B	Hong Kong A	India B	India A	Indonesia B	Indonesia A	Japan B	Japan A	Korea B	Korea A	Malaysia B	Malaysia A	The Philippines B	The Philippines A	Singapore B	Singapore A	Taiwan B	Taiwan A	Thailand B	Thailand A	Sum B	Sum A
												Acquiring country										
Hong Kong			0	0	2	1	9	16	2	3	14	34	0	1	20	41	7	10	5	2	59	108
India	2	4			0	1	2	2	0	0	0	0	0	0	2	9	0	0	1	0	7	16
Indonesia	1	6	0	2			7	4	2	2	10	20	1	0	13	35	1	1	0	3	35	73
Japan	0	3	0	0	0	0			0	1	0	0	0	0	3	2	0	1	0	0	3	7
Korea	0	11	0	0	0	0	4	9			0	1	0	0	1	2	0	0	0	1	5	24
Malaysia	12	14	0	0	0	0	3	6	0	0			2	0	17	24	0	0	0	1	34	45
The Philippines	4	11	0	0	0	0	5	1	0	2	10	8			8	17	2	1	1	1	30	41
Singapore	8	26	0	0	7	0	1	6	0	1	13	24	1	0			0	4	0	0	30	61
Taiwan	6	8	0	0	0	1	3	8	0	0	0	0	0	0	0	7			0	0	9	24
Thailand	9	3	0	0	0	1	4	10	0	0	4	5	0	0	8	28	0	3			25	50
Sum	42	86	0	2	9	4	38	62	4	9	51	92	4	1	72	165	10	20	7	8		686

Note: B and A denote before and after the Asian crisis, respectively.

But the financial centers that they are, Hong Kong and Singapore report the greatest amount of M&A activity. Overall, in light of the preceding basic statistics, it is abundantly clear that there is a sharp escalation in number of cross-border M&As after the Asian crisis.

Table 6.3 presents the mean of each of the explanatory variables before and after the crisis. Of particular interest here are three findings, as summarized in the following. First, the level of GDP and TRADE are two variables that are obviously higher after the crisis, in large part because of higher economic growth. If the gravity hypothesis holds, then we can surmise that, ceteris paribus, M&A activity may have also increased. Somewhat surprisingly, the values of GDPGROW and STOCKRET do not always increase after the crisis.

Third, the ΔKKZ regulatory gap indexes are overwhelmingly negative for India, Indonesia, the Philippines, and Thailand. Because these gap indexes are the indexes of acquiring countries minus those of target countries, the negative signs indicate that target countries have higher regulatory indexes than do these four countries.

Contrasting the ΔKKZ regulatory gap indexes in the preceding, the positive gap indexes for Hong Kong, Singapore, and Taiwan signify that firms in those three countries have a greater tendency to form partnerships with targets from countries with lower indexes. As much as the former four countries (India, Indonesia, the Philippines, and Thailand) have a smaller number of cross-border M&As compared with the latter three (Hong Kong, Singapore, and Taiwan), which have greater number of M&As, it seems to follow that financial institutions in countries with sound governance tend to consolidate financial institutions in countries with less-sound governance.

6.5   Empirical Results

A note must be made about the design of the methodology we employ for our estimations. In this study, we test five hypotheses, each of which contains more than two proxies; if we were to consider all of them in the regression, then we would have to estimate around twenty-two parameters. We must bear in mind that this would surely result in complex results on account of complex collinearity. The problem would be aggravated if we were to further divide the sample into two periods, as the number of unknown parameters would then be doubled. Therefore, we first take different pairs of hypotheses into account and then gradually increase the number of hypotheses.

Table 6.4 reports our estimated results based on different pairs of hypotheses. The numbers shown in the top row indicate that there are ten specifications, where the estimated results of each specification are further divided into two columns, that is, before and after the Asian crisis.

Table 6.3 **Descriptive statistics**

										Acquiring country										
	Hong Kong		India		Indonesia		Japan		Korea		Malaysia		The Philippines		Singapore		Taiwan		Thailand	
Variable	B	A	B	A	B	A	B	A	B	A	B	A	B	A	B	A	B	A	B	A
GDP	129.59	169.07	318.3	500.64	143.73	176.2	4,394.38	4,769.11	370.8	546.99	63.57	94.15	60.47	79.56	59.89	92.3	258.3	324.44	105.21	131.45
GDPGROW (%)	5.32	4.54	5.43	5.97	7.38	3.98	1.84	1.02	7.25	6.08	9.24	5.37	3.13	4.18	8.82	4.6	6.1	4.49	-3.91	4.98
STOCKRET (%)	22.82	10.36	6.7	25.86	n.a.	26.39	138.11	3.7	-16.16	23.1	-12.24	9.45	16.8	8.35	7.22	14.01	2.09	2.21	-10.07	13.49
TRADE	0.46	n.a.	0.07	0.13	0.21	0.23	0.03	0.19	0.39	0.50	0.48	0.56	0.09	0.17	0.89	1.01	0.48	0.61	0.28	0.30
FDI	n.a.	17.17	0.35	0.84	1.61	-0.94	1.83	1.60	0.32	1.14	6.29	3.23	1.61	1.45	11.15	14.43	n.a.	n.a.	1.78	2.34
ΔKKZ_CORRUP	1.18	1.24	-0.98	-0.84	-1.22	-1.59	0.83	0.89	0	-0.11	0	-0.12	-1.08	-1.05	2.01	2.15	0.27	0.26	-1	-0.81
ΔKKZ_RULELAW	1	0.94	-0.9	-0.52	-1.34	-1.63	0.89	0.99	0	0.13	0.02	-0.04	-1.02	-1.2	1.47	1.44	0.23	0.32	-0.36	-0.42
ΔKKZ_REGQUAL	1.07	1.2	-0.98	-1.1	-0.61	-1.24	-0.07	0.36	-0.22	0.02	0.02	-0.18	-0.38	-0.6	1.28	1.39	0.29	0.43	-0.39	-0.27
ΔKKZ_GOVEFF	1.16	0.74	-1.42	-0.91	-0.9	-1.36	0.51	0.43	-0.26	0.13	-0.12	0.14	-0.71	-0.86	1.63	1.71	0.47	0.47	-0.34	-0.51
ΔKKZ_CORRUP	1.64	1.53	-0.31	-0.34	-0.52	-1.01	1.32	1.22	0.57	0.31	0.57	0.3	-0.4	-0.53	2.38	2.36	0.81	0.65	-0.32	-0.31
KKZ_RULELAW	1.66	1.39	-0.05	0.06	-0.44	-0.93	1.56	1.43	0.76	0.66	0.79	0.49	-0.15	-0.54	2.09	1.83	0.97	0.82	0.43	0.15
KKZ_REGQUAL	1.73	1.71	-0.12	-0.36	0.2	-0.48	0.69	0.95	0.55	0.65	0.78	0.47	0.41	0.08	1.92	1.88	1.02	1.01	0.41	0.38
KKZ_GOVEFF	1.9	1.41	-0.42	-0.07	0.04	-0.47	1.31	1.14	0.61	0.86	0.74	0.87	0.21	-0.03	2.32	2.28	1.28	1.17	0.54	0.27
ΔRESTRIC_S	0.88		0.22		0.22		0.22		0.22		0.22		-0.88		-0.88		0.22		1.33	
ΔRESTRIC_I	0.88		0.22		1.33		-0.88		0.22		0.22		-0.88		-0.88		1.33		0.22	
ΔRESTRIC_E	2.44		0.88		0.88		0.88		0.88		-0.22		-1.33		-0.22		0.88		-0.22	
ΔRESTRIC_NF	1.11		0		1.11		0		0		0		-1.11		1.11		0		0	
RESTRIC_S	1		2		2		2		2		2		1		1		2		3	
RESTRIC_I	2		3		4		2		3		3		2		2		4		3	
RESTRIC_E	1		4		4		4		4		3		2		3		4		3	
RESTRIC_NF	2		3		4		3		3		3		2		4		3		3	

Notes: B and A denote before and after the Asian crisis, respectively. We assume that missed values are coded as n.a. (not available).

Table 6.4　　Determinants of Asian M&A: Specification I

Variable	Model 1 B	Model 1 A	Model 2 B	Model 2 A	Model 3 B	Model 3 A	Model 4 B	Model 4 A	Model 5 B	Model 5 A	Model 6 B	Model 6 A	Model 7 B	Model 7 A	Model 8 B	Model 8 A	Model 9 B	Model 9 A	Model 10 B	Model 10 A
CONST	0.63* (1.83)		1.91** (4.61)		1.3** (3.90)		0.88** (2.15)		-1.43** (11.19)		-1.88** (13.16)		-1.63**v (17.02)		-1.35** (9.52)		-1.11** (9.72)		-1.28** (9.58)	
DISTANCE	-0.62** (5.25)	-0.61** (4.75)	-0.82** (6.21)	-0.74** (5.58)	-0.78** (5.95)	-0.80** (6.02)	-0.89** (7.11)	-0.772** (5.98)												
GDP	-0.18** (2.76)	-0.09 (1.39)	-0.26** (3.57)	-0.24** (3.07)	-0.23** (3.54)	-0.15** (2.16)	-0.12 (1.44)	-0.062 (0.74)												
TRADE	0.32** (6.94)	0.35** (4.68)							0.50** (11.08)	0.51** (8.22)	0.54** (11.48)	0.68** (9.37)	0.42** (6.62)	0.52** (6.26)						
GDPGROW			-0.06** (4.33)	0.02 (0.48)					-0.04** (2.47)	0.05** (2.01)					-0.05** (2.85)	0.04 (-1.52)	-0.03** (2.36)	0.04 (1.45)		
STOCKRET			-0.00 (0.89)	-0.00 (0.20)					0.00 (0.10)	0.004 (0.87)					-0.003 (0.94)	0.000 (-0.03)	-0.004 (1.20)	-0.001 (0.28)		
LANGUAGE					0.26 (1.06)	0.56** (2.21)					0.78** (3.32)	1.17** (4.06)			0.81** (3.39)	0.86** (3.01)			0.31 (1.34)	0.85** (4.08)
RELIGIOUS					0.37 (1.73)	0.74** (3.22)					0.33* (1.66)	1.02** (5.12)			0.63** (3.02)	0.86** (4.01)			0.22 (1.12)	0.85** (4.91)
ΔKKZ_CORRUP							0.83** (2.88)	0.26 (0.78)					0.66* (1.79)	-0.06 (0.18)			0.83** (2.34)	0.18 (0.55)	0.80** (2.79)	0.23 (0.65)
ΔKKZ_RULELAW							-0.25 (0.68)	0.15 (0.62)					-0.13 (0.26)	-0.18 (0.74)			-0.41 (0.84)	0.08 (0.34)	-0.27 (0.72)	0.32 (1.56)
ΔKKZ_REGQUAL							-1.71** (3.53)	-0.60** (2.25)					-0.62 (1.03)	-1.53** (5.65)			-1.52** (2.94)	-0.79** (2.11)	-1.29** (3.10)	-0.67** (2.40)
ΔKKZ_GOVEFF							0.87* (1.94)	0.57 (1.16)					0.09 (0.16)	2.22** (5.07)			0.84* (1.73)	0.89 (1.62)	0.61 (1.59)	0.54 (1.18)
R^2	0.108		0.107		0.109		0.205		0.061		0.141		0.139		0.082		0.111		0.144	

Notes: This table presents the results of ten Poisson models estimated by maximum likelihood for the sample of Asian acquiring countries. Out of five hypotheses, two were chosen, and explained variables of those two hypotheses are used. B and A denote before and after the Asian crisis, respectively.

**Significant at the 5 percent level.

*Significant at the 10 percent level.

We first discuss the estimated results that pertain to the gravity hypothesis. The coefficients of DISTANCE are overwhelmingly significantly negative regardless of specification. For example, in the first column, they are −0.62 and −0.61 before and after the Asian crisis, respectively; hence, the gravity hypothesis gains momentum and support here.

This likely reflects the commonly-held notion that the greater the distance is, the higher the transaction cost is; if so, then this conceivably reduces the likelihood of firms engaging in transnational M&A activity. This result is similar to that of Buch and DeLong (2004). While this result is consistent with our earlier conjecture, in our case, it goes against our judgment because, as mentioned earlier, financial assets are mostly intangible, and transportation cost should not be of concern. One alternative explanation might be that distance is a proxy for the information asymmetry. When two countries are in close proximity, the extent of information asymmetry is substantially reduced, thus encouraging M&A activity.

The coefficients of GDP are mostly significantly negative both before and after the Asian crisis, compelling us to discount the gravity hypothesis in this case. The negative impact, however, is counterintuitive because GDP is the proxy for the mass in the gravity theory, and the mass attracts investors. One plausible explanation, nevertheless, is that a large GDP is typically different from GDP per capita, where the former is the proxy for the gravity hypothesis but the latter is related to the wealth of people. That is, countries with a high GDP do not necessarily attract more investors if the people in those countries are poor (i.e., GDP per capita is low). For example, there are many M&As in Singapore, but in the region, its GDP ranks second from the bottom. By way of comparison, not many M&As take place in Japan, but in the region, its GDP is the highest. The implication here could be that a lower GDP may be associated with greater M&A activity and vice versa.

Therefore, GDP per capita might be a better proxy than GDP to represent the gravity. We thus repeat the exercise but use GDP per capita as the proxy and find its coefficients are positive. We discuss this issue in the robust testing.

The coefficients of TRADE are also overwhelmingly significantly positive, lending support to the following the client hypothesis. For example, in the first column, the coefficients are 0.32 and 0.35 in the pre- and postcrisis periods, respectively, which is a strong indication that greater trade between two countries increases the tendency for their financial institutions to merge. This is similar to the situation in India and the Philippines. They have the lowest TRADE, and interestingly enough, they also have the fewest M&As. The situation in Singapore and Japan is just the reverse. The following the client effect is stronger after the crisis when TRADE is used.

The results for the market opportunity effect reveal an interesting pattern. The coefficients of GDPGROW are negative and positive for the pre- and postcrisis, respectively, regardless of specification. Three of the four specifications with negative coefficients are significant, whereas only one with a positive coefficient is significant. A negative sign before the crisis harnesses does not support the optimistic economic growth view. Recall that GDPGROW is the GDP growth rate at $t + 1$. Thus, during periods when economic growth in a host country is negative, potential acquirers likely hold the view that the downturn will be short-lived and that more promising times are ahead, prompting them not to consociate with financial institutions in the host country. Against this, a positive coefficient after the crisis seemingly supports the optimistic economic growth view but to a lesser extent.

The coefficients of STOCKRET are insignificant for most specifications, except for one that is significantly negative before the Asian crisis. Thus, the high stock cost view exists weakly. With the results of GDPGROW and STOCKRET taken together, the Asian crisis strengthens the motivation of the market opportunity hypothesis, though the effect is weak. We also use GROWTH and STOCKRET at time $t + 2$ to proxy the expectations about future economic and stock market conditions, but the results do not change qualitatively. See results in the section of robust testing.

The coefficients of **LANGUAGE,** while all positive, are dramatically different for different sample periods in the statistical sense. Before the crisis, however, only two of four are significant, but after the crisis are overwhelmingly significant. Furthermore, the coefficients are much larger after the crisis than before it. Accordingly, the problems caused by information cost are more severe after the crisis because M&A activity is more likely to go on in those countries where the same language is spoken. Before the crisis, even two firms sharing common language does not help M&A activity. However, these results may not be surprising given that, in our sample, most M&As take place in Hong Kong and Singapore, where English is the official shared language.[5]

The impact of **RELIGION** on M&A activity is similar to those of **LANGUAGE.** Before the crisis, only two of four are significant though all of the coefficients are positive. After the crisis, all of the coefficients are overwhelmingly significantly positive. It can be surmised that before the Asian crisis, it did not help firms consolidate if they come from countries that share the same religion, but after the crisis, it certainly did.

Information cost, therefore, when proxied by language and religion, receives increasing attention by investors when they engage in consolidation. This evidence is also found by Qiu and Zhou (2006), Rossi and Volpin (2004), and Buch and DeLong (2004). We conjecture that this is because the same culture could shorten the friction periods between two financial institutions, for example, whether speaking the same language is important when the targets and acquirer are from Asian countries.

---

5. Results here are based on official language announced by the Central Intelligence Agency.

The crisis evidently changed the impact of corruption on M&A activity. For both periods, the coefficients of ΔKKZ_CORRUP are overwhelmingly positive, but only those before the crisis are significant. Readers are reminded that the gap index is the difference between the corruption index of acquirers and that of targets. Hence, a significant coefficient means that there is a larger gap in the corruption index between two countries and that this does indeed encourage firms to engage in M&A activity. That is, before the crisis, financial institutions in countries with low corruption are more likely to acquire financial institutions in countries with high corruption. After the crisis, this corruption gap has no influence on firms' willingness to take advantage of M&A opportunities.[6]

The crisis evidently did not change the impact of rule of law as the coefficients of ΔKKZ_RULELAW are all insignificant in both periods.

The effect of ΔKKZ_REGQUAL is interesting from two perspectives. First, those coefficients that are significant are all negative. Second, the coefficients are about equal in size before and after the crisis. A negative coefficient means that firms in countries with efficient regulation quality are less interested in buying in those countries with poor regulation quality. Combining the results here with those obtained from corruption, we can conclude that countries with little corruption but less regulation quality tend to merge firms in the countries with greater corruption but more regulation quality. ΔKKZ_GOVEFF has no effect on M&A activity as almost none of the coefficients are significant in both periods.

The results from using the KKZ gap indexes seem to suggest that regulations are indeed *associated with* the willingness of firms from different Asian countries to partake in cross-border M&A activity. Especially pertinent here is that when corruption or regulatory quality are different in the home and host countries, it seems to prompt firms from those countries to form partnerships (M&As) before the crisis but not after.

Table 6.5 repeats the estimation procedure as those of Table 6.4, but we consider three hypotheses simultaneously. As most of the results are similar, we skip the discussion here.

Table 6.6 presents the results from using the restrictions on banks to engage in security, insurance, real estate, and the nonfinancial industry to replace the KKZ regulatory variables. Recall that these restriction variables are the restrictive indexes of acquirers minus the same indexes of targets.

The coefficients of ΔRESTRCIT_S are all insignificantly positive before the crisis and insignificant after the crisis for seven of the ten specifications. Therefore, before the crisis, financial institutions in countries that allow banks to engage in securities tend not to form partnerships with those in countries that do not allow banks to engage in that industry. Similarly put consolidation is less frequent when the target country has relatively

---

6. Wei (2000a,b, 2001) points out the corruption is similar to the tax in the foreign investment and deters the investment.

Table 6.5   Determinants of Asian M&A: Specification II

Variable	Model 1		Model 2		Model 3		Model 4		Model 5		Model 6		Model 7		Model 8		Model 9		Model 10	
	B	A	B	A	B	A	B	A	B	A	B	A	B	A	B	A	B	A	B	A
CONST	1.11**		-0.16		-0.18		1.38**		1.20**		0.41		-1.945**		-1.61**		-1.98**		-1.49**	
	(2.50)		(0.39)		(0.438)		(3.08)		(2.28)		(0.90)		(11.32)		(13.13)		(13.78)		(9.82)	
DISTANCE	-0.69**	-0.61**	-0.65**	-0.70**	-0.78**	-0.67**	-0.85**	-0.78**	-0.90**	-0.73**	-0.91**	-0.8**								
	(5.72)	(4.50)	(5.25)	(5.43)	(6.09)	(4.15)	(6.20)	(5.54)	(6.48)	(5.37)	(7.16)	(6.11)								
GDP	-0.20**	-0.217	-0.07	-0.053	0.016	0.01	-0.21**	-0.20**	-0.13	-0.14	-0.05	-0.03								
	(2.85)	(-2.593)	(1.12)	(0.66)	(0.19)	(0.12)	(2.95)	(2.32)	(1.47)	(1.52)	(-0.68)	(-0.38)								
TRADE	0.30**	0.26**	0.38**	0.48**	0.26**	0.30**							0.57**	0.58**	0.44**	0.46**	0.48**	0.57**		
	(5.49)	(3.58)	(7.34)	(6.04)	(4.14)	(3.24)							(11.51)	(8.49)	(6.51)	(5.85)	(7.20)	(6.49)		
GDPGROW	-0.06**	0.038					-0.06**	0.02	-0.04	0.01*			-0.05**	0.03	-0.02	0.011			-0.03**	0.03
	(3.54)	(0.83)					(4.57)	(0.52)	(-3.33)	(0.19)			(2.58)	(1.26)	(1.53)	(0.48)			(2.36)	(0.97)
STOCKRET	-0.001	0.004					-0.003	-0.001	-0.004	-0.002			-0.002	0.005	-0.001	0.006			-0.005	-0.001
	(0.30)	(0.87)					(0.94)	(0.15)	(1.24)	(0.46)			(0.41)	(1.15)	(0.29)	(1.71)			(1.44)	(0.30)
LANGUAGE			0.57**	0.99**			0.52**	0.64**			0.354	0.53**	1.09**	1.23**			0.82**	0.53**	0.77**	0.76**
			(2.24)	(3.21)			(1.99)	(2.21)			(1.45)	(2.04)	(4.44)	(3.73)			(3.65)	(1.88)	(3.35)	(2.75)
RELIGIOUS			0.45**	1.18**			0.63**	0.73**			0.395*	0.77**	0.52**	0.97**			0.38*	0.81**	0.58**	0.87**
			(2.02)	(4.67)			(2.77)	(2.91)			(1.86)	(3.39)	(2.40)	(4.50)			(1.86)	(3.76)	(2.79)	(4.14)
ΔKKZ_CORRUP					0.75**	-0.15			0.72**	-0.14	0.75**	0.22			0.73*	-0.43	0.60	-0.22	0.73**	-0.05*
					(2.26)	(0.40)			(2.35)	(0.44)	(2.79)	(0.65)			(1.68)	(1.35)	(1.66)	(0.61)	(2.16)	(0.16)
ΔKKZ_RULELAW					-0.04	0.17			-0.371	0.21	-0.15	0.35			-0.31	-0.05	-0.04	0.05	-0.33	0.37
					(0.09)	(0.60)			(0.96)	(0.79)	(-0.44)	(1.45)			(0.49)	(0.20)	(0.09)	(0.21)	(0.71)	(1.54)
ΔKKZ_REGQUAL					-1.38**	-1.31**			-1.485**	-0.52	-1.77**	-0.50*			-0.82	-1.63**	-0.59	-1.04**	-1.56**	-0.55*
					(2.42)	(4.15)			(2.73)	(-1.53)	(3.86)	(1.98)			(1.18)	(5.57)	(0.99)	(3.26)	(3.18)	(1.79)
ΔKKZ_GOVEFF					0.44	1.75**			0.838	0.86	0.91**	0.33			0.29	2.46**	0.06	1.73**	0.89*	0.694
					(0.80)	(2.96)			(1.71)	(1.64)	(2.04)	(0.75)			(0.44)	(5.7)	(0.10)	(4.04)	(1.90)	(1.59)
R^2	0.111		0.198		0.206		0.145		0.200		0.225		0.165		0.151		0.200		0.169	

Notes: See table 6.4 notes.

**Significant at the 5 percent level.

*Significant at the 10 percent level.

Table 6.6 **Determinants of Asian M&A: Specification III**

Variable	Model 1		Model 2		Model 3		Model 4		Model 5		Model 6		Model 7		Model 8		Model 9		Model 10	
	B	A	B	A	B	A	B	A	B	A	B	A	B	A	B	A	B	A	B	A
CONST	1.44** (3.26)		−1.53** (14.45)		−1.03** (9.30)		−1.16** (9.73)		0.59 (1.21)		1.74** (3.38)		1.26** (2.84)		−1.59 (11.84)		−1.86 (13.55)		−1.37** (10.01)	
DISTANCE	−0.80** (6.32)	−0.74** (5.87)							−0.68** (5.45)	−0.77** (5.44)	−0.85** (6.08)	−0.71** (5.41)	−0.81** (6.33)	−0.76** (5.94)						
GDP	−0.25** (2.76)	−0.17* (1.95)							−0.15* (1.68)	−0.07 (0.88)	−0.24** (2.61)	−0.23** (2.41)	−0.25** (2.73)	−0.22** (2.22)						
TRADE			0.42** (7.20)	0.38** (3.65)					0.28* (3.39)	0.048 (0.37)					0.47** (7.27)	0.34** (2.97)	0.49** (8.459)	0.51** (5.261)		
GDPGROW					−0.04** (2.69)	0.05* (1.80)					−0.05** (3.64)	0.001 (0.01)			−0.03 (1.69)	0.03 (1.34)			−0.04** (2.50)	0.03 (1.29)
STOCKRET					−0.005 (1.42)	−0.001 (0.29)					−0.004 (1.35)	−0.002 (0.47)			−0.003 (0.82)	0.004 (0.89)			−0.005 (1.60)	−0.001 (0.20)
LANGUAGE							0.23 (1.05)	0.96** (4.82)					0.27 (1.19)	0.58** (2.42)			0.68** (3.21)	0.71 (2.57)	0.67** (2.86)	0.85** (3.33)
RELIGIOUS							0.11 (0.59)	0.72** (4.22)					0.38** (1.80)	0.89** (4.07)			0.32* (1.69)	0.87** (4.07)	0.53** (2.66)	0.78** (3.90)
ΔRESTRIC_S	0.14 (1.14)	0.18* (1.67)	0.07 (0.58)	−0.19 (1.05)	0.007 (0.04)	−0.10 (0.73)	−0.04 (0.39)	−0.11 (1.02)	0.17 (1.37)	0.18 (1.32)	0.14 (1.19)	0.26** (2.23)	0.18 (1.45)	0.34** (2.88)	0.13 (0.81)	−0.06 (0.32)	0.09 (0.65)	−0.13 (0.86)	0.02 (0.13)	−0.08 (0.60)
ΔRESTRIC_I	−0.67	−0.84** (3.97)	−0.24** (5.24)	−0.53** (2.06)	−0.36** (3.33)	−0.40** (3.18)	−0.41** (3.19)	−0.53** (4.17)	−0.51** (5.11)	−1.13** (2.62)	−0.52** (3.93)	−0.74** (2.80)	−0.71** (4.24)	−1.00** (3.83)	−0.15* (5.19)	−0.38 (1.13)	−0.21** (2.31)	−0.33** (1.77)	−0.31** (2.35)	−0.35** (2.66)
ΔRESTRIC_R	0.15 (1.34)	0.01** (0.07)	0.05 (0.56)	0.35** (2.94)	0.22** (2.47)	0.14 (1.20)	0.21** (2.797)	0.18** (2.58)	0.12 (1.08)	0.29** (2.59)	0.08** (0.68)	−0.04 (0.25)	0.12 (1.17)	−0.08 (0.60)	0.02 (0.20)	0.32** (2.24)	0.02 (0.22)	0.14 (1.31)	0.19** (2.21)	0.13 (1.31)
ΔRESTRIC_NF	0.32** (2.38)	0.51** (3.53)	0.37** (2.98)	0.55** (3.36)	0.27* (1.74)	0.34** (2.19)	0.23** (2.06)	0.21** (2.04)	0.30** (2.05)	0.60** (2.96)	0.34** (2.19)	0.48** (3.00)	0.31** (2.38)	0.52** (3.50)	0.48 (3.23)	0.52** (2.81)	0.35** (3.16)	0.38** (2.90)	0.21 (1.60)	0.20* (1.82)
R^2	0.198		0.14		0.078		0.129		0.222		0.171		0.263		0.129		0.197		0.138	

Notes: This table presents the results of ten Poisson models estimated by maximum likelihood for the sample of Asian acquiring countries. The banking restriction (ΔRESTRIC) is used instead of ΔKKZ. B and A denote before and after the Asian crisis, respectively.

**Significant at the 5 percent level.

*Significant at the 10 percent level.

stiffened restrictions on banking activities. After the crisis, restrictions on banking activities are not related to cross-border M&A activity.

The coefficients of ΔRESTRICT_I are overwhelmingly significantly negative for both periods, which indicates that financial institutions from relatively less-restrictive countries with regard to insurance have a propensity to engage in M&A activity with those from relatively more-restrictive countries. Because the coefficients in the two periods are similar, the crisis does not affect this pattern.

The pattern vis-à-vis ΔRESTRICT_R is ambiguous given that there are both positive and negative coefficients. Owing to the fact that the most of the significant coefficients are positive, we are inclined to say that, on balance, the variable has a positive effect. That is, financial institutions from countries that are relatively more restrictive when it comes to real estate tend to engage in M&A activity with those from countries that are relatively less restrictive. Because the coefficients are similar in both periods, once again, the crisis does not affect this pattern.

The coefficients of ΔRESTRICT_NF are all significantly positive. Thus, financial institutions from countries that are relatively more restrictive when it comes to real estate tend to engage in M&A activity with those from countries that are relatively less restrictive. Again, the crisis seems to not have had too much impact on this pattern as the coefficients in the two periods are roughly the same or there is no clear pattern.

6.6   Robustness Testing

6.6.1   Using GDP per Capita as Proxy

Tables 6.7 and 6.8 report the estimated results using GDP per capita as the proxy for the mass in the gravity hypothesis. Results, however, are sensitive to different specifications. When KKZ and bank restrictive variables are not present in the regression, the coefficients are insignificantly negative. However, the results change to become significantly positive when they are added in.

6.6.2   Market Opportunity Using $t + 2$

Tables 6.9 and 6.10 report the estimated results when GDPGROW and STOCKRET use the future growth rate of $t + 2$. Results change dramatically because coefficients of STOCKRET become almost all significantly positive. Therefore, the market opportunity hypothesis gains strong support if the acquirers look at the long-run effect stock return two years ahead. Results of GDPGROW, however, remain the same.

6.6.3   Acquirers from G7 Countries

Tables 6.11, 6.12, and 6.13 add the estimated results by adding G7 countries. Results do not change significantly except for the coefficients of

Table 6.7   **Determinants of international financial mergers: Poisson estimates (1-1 robustness testing)**

Variable	1		2		3		4		5		6		7	
	B	A	B	A	B	A	B	A	B	A	B	A	B	A
CONST	0.03 (0.14)		0.62** (-.88)		0.49** (2.32)		-0.01 (0.05)		-0.35 (1.48)		0.36 (1.60)		-0.72** (-3.07)	
DISTANCE	-0.75** (6.16)	-0.54** (5.91)	-0.90** (7.47)	-0.80** (7.37)	-0.95** (7.58)	-0.80** (8.01)	-0.71** (6.00)	-0.66** (5.73)	-0.71** (6.05)	-0.70** (6.47)	-0.94** (7.51)	-0.85** (7.22)	-0.77** (7.03)	-0.74** (7.09)
GDPPER	-0.03 (0.44)	-0.04 (0.46)	0.03 (0.51)	0.02 (0.27)	-0.03 (0.59)	-0.05 (0.84)	0.03 (0.43)	0.02 (0.27)	-0.04 (0.64)	-0.15* (1.86)	0.01 (0.21)	-0.02 (0.32)	0.51** (5.56)	0.64** (7.06)
TRADE	0.32 (6.65)	0.41** (5.74)					0.35** (6.34)	0.29** (4.13)	0.39** (7.61)	0.53** (6.86)				
GDPGROW			-0.06** (3.80)	0.04 (0.92)			-0.05** (3.15)	0.04 (1.05)			-0.06** (4.13)	0.03 (0.74)		
STOCKRET			-0.00 (0.51)	-0.001 (0.19)			0 (0.03)	0.004 (0.92)			-0.003 (0.72)	-0.001 (0.20)		
LANGUAGE					0.34 (1.40)	0.69** (2.75)			0.61** (2.46)	1.18** (3.79)	0.63** (2.48)	0.74** (2.52)		
RELIGIOUS					0.35* (1.65)	0.82** (3.61)			0.46** (2.08)	1.31** (4.98)	0.64** (2.95)	0.75** (3.08)		
ΔKKZ_CORRUP													0.71** (2.28)	-0.13 (0.39)
ΔKKZ_RULELAW													0.53 (1.12)	1.04** (4.13)
ΔKKZ_REGQUAL													-1.26** (3.04)	-0.44* (1.80)
ΔKKZ_GOVEFF													0.31 (0.60)	0.57 (1.45)
R^2	0.100		0.097		0.114		0.102		0.206		0.144		0.232	

Notes: This table presents the results of ten Poisson models estimated by maximum likelihood for the sample of Asian acquiring countries. The GDP per capita (GDPPER) is used instead of GDP. B and A denote before and after the Asian crisis, respectively.

**Significant at the 5 percent level.

*Significant at the 10 percent level.

Table 6.8 Determinants of international financial mergers: Poisson estimates (1-2 robustness testing)

	1		2		3		4		5		6		7	
Variable	B	A	B	A	B	A	B	A	B	A	B	A	B	A
CONST	-0.88** (3.33)		-0.68** (2.32)		-0.79** (3.36)		0.10 (0.47)		-0.17 (0.65)		0.22 (0.86)		-0.04 (0.18)	
DISTANCE	-0.71** (6.27)	-0.71** (5.95)	-0.77** (6.24)	-0.755 (-6.647)	-0.781 (-6.890)	-0.811 (-7.310)	-0.843 (-7.770)	-0.71 (-7.282)	-0.74 (6.16)	-0.68** (6.32)	-0.85** (6.90)	-0.74** (6.55)	-0.83** (7.55)	-0.80** (7.80)
GDPPER	0.44** (4.18)	0.53** (5.44)	0.54** (4.89)	0.60** (6.04)	0.492** (5.55)	0.58** (6.51)	0.13* (1.78)	0.22** (2.77)	0.08 (0.92)	0.11 (1.43)	0.16* (1.98)	0.21** (2.45)	0.11* (1.68)	0.15* (1.88)
TRADE	0.18** (2.87)	0.15 (1.60)							0.22 (3.20)	0.07 (0.62)				
GDPGROW			-0.04** (2.54)	0.016 (0.324)							-0.05** (3.31)	0.004 (0.07)		
STOCKRET			-0.004 (1.09)	0.000 (0.024)							-0.003 (1.05)	-0.001 (0.29)		
LANGUAGE					0.23 (1.20)	0.33* (1.67)							0.27 (1.21)	0.58** (2.54)
RELIGIOUS					0.20 (1.01)	0.60** (2.86)							0.30 (1.49)	0.79** (3.66)
ΔKKZ_CORRUP	0.62* (1.84)	-0.27 (0.70)	0.85 (2.55)	-0.37 (1.05)	0.61** (1.99)	-0.15 (0.44)								
ΔKKZ_RULELAW	0.57 (1.05)	0.88** (3.22)	0.26 (0.54)	1.07** (3.93)	0.60 (1.27)	1.15** (4.76)								
ΔKKZ_REGQUAL	-1.03** (2.01)	-0.89** (3.06)	-1.30 (3.08)	-0.45 (1.35)	-1.26** (3.09)	-0.31 (1.37)								
ΔKKZ_GOVEFF	0.10* (0.16)	1.29 (2.77)	0.35 (0.64)	0.72* (1.73)	0.35 (0.68)	0.33 (0.90)								
ΔRESTRIC_S							0.15 (1.21)	0.21 (1.64)	0.19 (1.48)	0.19 (1.24)	0.15 (1.21)	0.30** (2.29)	0.18 (0.42)	0.33** (2.63)
ΔRESTRIC_I							-0.74** (4.78)	-1.01** (6.84)	-0.56** (2.93)	-1.16** (4.21)	-0.61** (3.53)	-0.89** (5.43)	-0.77** (4.65)	-1.10** (6.41)
ΔRESTRIC_R							0.14 (1.47)	-0.005 (0.04)	0.12 (1.22)	0.23** (2.10)	0.07 (0.74)	-0.04 (0.30)	0.13 (1.35)	-0.05 (0.45)
ΔRESTRIC_NF							0.36** (2.58)	0.57** (3.86)	0.31* (1.95)	0.65** (3.32)	0.43** (2.58)	0.54** (3.15)	0.33* (2.53)	0.52* (3.52)
R	0.260		0.233		0.277		0.191		0.219		0.169		0.257	

Notes: This table presents the results of seven Poisson models estimated by maximum likelihood for the sample of Asian acquiring countries. The GDP per capita (GDPPER) is used instead of GDP. B and A denote before and after the Asian crisis, respectively.

**Significant at the 5 percent level.

*Significant at the 10 percent level.

Table 6.9 Determinants of international financial mergers: Poisson estimates (2-1 robustness testing)

Variable	1		2		3		4		5		6		7	
	B	A	B	A	B	A	B	A	B	A	B	A	B	A
CONST		1.97** (5.46)		-1.52 (12.40)		-1.42** (9.76)		-1.23** (10.77)		1.19** (2.66)		1.48** (3.72)		1.16** (2.51)
DISTANCE	-0.86** (6.31)	-0.76** (5.58)							-0.71** (5.67)	-0.66** (4.21)	-0.88** (6.27)	-0.80** (5.68)	-0.93** (6.70)	-0.75** (5.72)
GDP	-0.29** (4.29)	-0.20** (2.36)							-0.24** (3.16)	-0.16* (1.91)	-0.24** (3.52)	-0.18* (1.83)	-0.14* (1.71)	-0.08 (0.82)
TRADE			0.48** (11.46)	0.48** (7.33)					0.29** (5.60)	0.23** (2.86)				
GDPGROW	-0.04** (2.77)	-0.08 (1.55)	-0.02 (1.23)	0.01 (0.80)	-0.02 (1.03)	0.01 (1.14)	-0.01 (0.72)	0.029 (1.009)	-0.04** (2.59)	-0.07* (1.19)	-0.04** (2.53)	-0.08 (1.62)	-0.02 (1.49)	-0.08* (1.19)
STOCKRET	0.006** (2.28)	0.01** (2.53)	0.006** (2.17)	0.01* (1.75)	0.005* (1.94)	0.01** (2.04)	0.004* (1.69)	0.003 (0.68)	0.006** (2.22)	0.01** (2.31)	0.006** (2.14)	0.01** (2.95)	0.005* (1.88)	0.008* (1.72)
LANGUAGE					0.59** (2.21)	0.94** (3.35)					0.33 (1.26)	0.68** (2.24)		
RELIGIOUS					0.52** (2.44)	0.87** (4.20)					0.54** (2.37)	0.73** (2.77)		
ΔKKZ_CORRUP							0.82** (2.28)	0.31 (0.74)					0.76** (2.36)	-0.02 (0.06)
ΔKKZ_RULELAW							-0.27 (0.54)	0.11 (0.42)					-0.40 (0.93)	0.34 (1.29)
ΔKKZ_REGQUAL							-1.26** (2.37)	-0.75** (1.97)					-1.48** (2.64)	-0.48 (1.54)
ΔKKZ_GOVEFF							0.57 (1.12)	0.77 (1.15)					0.88* (1.68)	0.61 (0.87)
R^2	0.110		0.049		0.074		0.110		0.124		0.153		0.206	

Notes: This table presents the results of seven Poisson models estimated by maximum likelihood for the sample of Asian acquiring countries. The period of GDP growth rate and stock return changed from $(T + 1)$ to $(T + 2)$. B and A denote before and after the Asian crisis, respectively.
**Significant at the 5 percent level.
*Significant at the 10 percent level.

Table 6.10   Determinants of international financial mergers: Poisson estimates (2-2 robustness testing)

Variable	1 B	1 A	2 B	2 A	3 B	3 A	4 B	4 A	5 B	5 A	6 B	6 A	7 B	7 A
CONST	-2.02** (11.78)		-1.77** (13.39)		-1.58 (10.16)		-1.15 (11.00)		1.88 (3.87)		-1.71** (13.52)		-1.46** (10.32)	
DISTANCE									-0.87 (6.21)	-0.70** (5.34)				
GDP									-0.30 (3.16)	-0.21** (2.03)				
TRADE	0.55** (11.30)	0.51** (7.46)	0.44** (6.67)	0.38** (5.39)							0.46** (7.47)	0.25** (2.59)		
GDPGROW	-0.01 (0.92)	0.004 (0.38)	0 (0.01)	-0.001 (0.06)	-0.01 (0.47)	0.01 (0.66)	-0.01 (1.06)	0.03 (1.46)	-0.02* (1.94)	-0.11* (1.77)	-0.009 (0.44)	0.006 (0.51)	-0.01 (0.69)	0.01 (1.17)
STOCKRET	0.006** (2.20)	0.01* (2.03)	0.006** (2.24)	0.008* (1.75)	0.005* (1.69)	0.004 (1.04)	0.004 (1.58)	0.008 (1.48)	0.005* (1.87)	0.01* (2.24)	0.005* (1.72)	0.01* (-1.82)	0.005 (1.57)	0.008* (1.79)
LANGUAGE	0.90** (3.42)	1.24** (3.47)			0.56** (2.18)	0.81** (2.69)							0.48** (1.96)	0.93** (3.48)
RELIGION	0.434** (1.99)	1.038** (4.73)			0.50** (2.34)	0.89** (4.08)							0.43** (2.10)	0.77** (3.64)
ΔKKZ_CORRUP			0.71* (1.71)	-0.56 (1.41)	0.74** (2.13)	-0.01 (0.04)								
ΔKKZ_RULELAW			-0.18 (0.30)	0.051 (0.18)	-0.19 (0.39)	0.43 (1.63)								
ΔKKZ_REGQUAL			-0.57 (0.84)	-1.66** (6.323)	-1.31** (2.51)	-0.49 (1.44)								
ΔKKZ_GOVEFF			0.04 (-0.063)	2.68** (5.75)	0.62 (1.22)	0.62 (1.14)								
ΔRESTRIC_S							-0.05 (0.40)	-0.13 (0.86)	0.11 (0.86)	0.30** (2.37)	0.07 (0.44)	-0.16 (0.72)	-0.05 (0.35)	-0.11 (0.76)
ΔRESTRIC_I							-0.37** (3.30)	-0.40** (3.09)	-0.57** (3.08)	-0.72** (4.27)	-0.15 (1.16)	-0.44** (3.04)	-0.34** (2.97)	-0.35** (2.86)
ΔRESTRIC_R							0.21** (2.51)	0.08 (0.54)	0.07 (0.63)	-0.14 (0.74)	0.01 (0.16)	0.40** (2.81)	0.20** (2.37)	0.08 (0.65)
ΔRESTRIC_NF							0.24* (1.66)	0.40** (2.28)	0.32** (2.21)	0.60** (3.50)	0.44** (3.07)	0.60** (3.27)	0.20 (1.55)	0.24* (1.77)
R^2	0.138		0.146		0.159		0.073		0.179		0.136		0.127	

Notes: See table 6.9 notes.

**Significant at the 5 percent level

Table 6.11   Determinants of international financial mergers: Poisson estimates (3-1 robustness testing)

	1		2		3		4		5		6		7		8		9		10	
Variable	B	A	B	A	B	A	B	A	B	A	B	A	B	A	B	A	B	A	B	A
CONST	-1.76** (4.68)	0.04 (1.43)	-0.40 (1.085)		-0.81** (2.16)		-0.68* (1.65)		-1.13** (11.30)		-1.44 (14.53)		-1.43** (17.77)		-1.01** (10.11)		-0.98** (10.48)		-1.09** (12.50)	
DISTANCE	-0.07** (2.08)		-0.05 (1.136)	0.06 (1.63)	-0.04 (1.08)	0.05* (1.77)	-0.17** (2.64)	-0.02 (0.645)												
GDP	0.08 (1.38)	0.18** (2.83)	-0.07 (1.297)	0.00 (0.02)	-0.07 (1.184)	0.02 (0.26)	-0.02 (0.299)	0.03 (0.45)												
TRADE	0.45** (11.17)	0.45** (9.01)							0.36** (8.85)	0.46** (9.84)	0.37** (9.61)	0.62** (13.73)	0.38** (10.37)	0.55** (9.72)						
GDPGROW			-0.06** (3.82)	-0.01 (0.24)					-0.05* (5.10)	0.06** (3.42)					-0.06** (5.31)	0.05** (2.47)	-0.05** (4.01)	0.04* (1.95)		
STOCKRET			-0.002 (0.59)	-0.005 (1.39)					-0.001 (0.515)	-0.004 (0.896)					-0.003 (1.366)	-0.005 (1.28)	-0.003 (1.42)	-0.006* (1.72)		
LANGUAGE					0.60** (3.44)	0.95** (5.48)					0.41** (2.56)	1.60** (9.35)								
RELIGIOUS					0.31 (1.62)	0.16 (0.87)					0.05 (0.27)	0.36** (2.10)			0.63** (3.86)	1.27** (7.30)				
ΔKKZ_CORRUP							-0.07 (0.29)	0.46 (1.27)					0.04 (0.22)	0.54 (1.43)	0.16 (0.88)	0.18 (1.00)	-0.33* (1.75)	0.36 (0.95)	0.32** (2.07)	1.15** (8.19)
ΔKKZ_RULELAW							0.44* (1.78)	-0.53** (2.512)					0.31 (1.40)	-1.16** (5.06)			0.70** (2.95)	-0.63** (2.79)	-0.27* (1.734)	0.13 (0.40)
ΔKKZ_REGQUAL							-0.59* (1.70)	-0.30 (1.474)					0.30 (1.59)	-0.65** (2.26)			-0.05 (0.233)	-0.15 (0.551)	0.69** (3.64)	-0.22 (1.016)
ΔKKZ_GOVEFF							0.40 (1.46)	0.65* (1.74)					-0.35 (1.57)	1.62** (4.01)			-0.06 (0.244)	0.79* (1.94)	-0.29 (1.534)	0.75** (2.18)
R^2	0.072		0.044		0.072		0.077		0.036		0.125		0.062		0.073		0.068		0.095	

Notes: This table included data of cross border merger & acquisition activities of Asian and G7 nations before and after the Asian crisis. B and A denote before and after the Asian crisis, respectively.

**Significant at the 5 percent level.

*Significant at the 10 percent level.

Table 6.12 Determinants of international financial mergers: Poisson estimates (3-2 robustness testing)

Variable	M1 B	M1 A	M2 B	M2 A	M3 B	M3 A	M4 B	M4 A	M5 B	M5 A	M6 B	M6 A	M7 B	M7 A	M8 B	M8 A	M9 B	M9 A	M10 B	M10 A
CONST	-1.65** (4.05)	0.06* (1.89)	-2.29** (5.68)	0.05* (1.94)	-2.35** (5.35)	0.00 (0.12)	-0.79** (2.12)	0.07** (2.05)	-0.48 (1.08)	0.00 (0.01)	-1.05** (2.32)	-0.01 (0.350)	-1.43** (11.07)	0.55 (10.84)	-1.36** (12.81)	0.50** (7.93)	-1.66** (15.53)	0.60** (11.11)	-1.17** (10.58)	0.02 (1.21)
DISTANCE	-0.08** (2.33)		-0.06* (1.92)		-0.15** (3.19)		-0.03 (0.79)		-0.17** (2.55)		-0.16** (2.36)									
GDP	0.10 (1.61)	0.16** (2.26)	0.13** (2.17)	0.19** (2.56)	0.20** (2.64)	0.22** (2.98)	-0.07 (1.17)	0.02 (0.31)	-0.02 (0.22)	0.01 (0.07)	0.00 (0.03)	0.05 (0.62)	0.40** (9.95)	0.03* (1.74)	0.40** (9.52)	0.03 (1.25)	0.42** (10.75)			
TRADE	0.48** (10.60)	0.38** (7.46)	0.51** (11.51)	0.53** (9.64)	0.47** (10.36)	0.52** (9.46)														
GDPGROW	-0.05** (2.92)	0.00 (0.13)					-0.07** (4.34)	-0.02 (0.66)	-0.05** (3.28)	-0.02 (0.421)			-0.05** (4.67)		-0.04** (3.519)				-0.05** (4.32)	
STOCKRET	0.001 (0.48)	-0.003 (0.814)					-0.003 (1.07)	-0.005 (1.22)	-0.003 (1.28)	-0.006 (1.665)			-0.002 (0.802)	-0.003 (0.733)	-0.001 (0.34)	-0.003 (0.877)			-0.004* (1.72)	-0.006 (1.57)
LANGUAGE			0.75** (4.13)	1.27** (6.09)			0.89** (4.87)	1.04** (5.49)			0.58** (3.29)	0.83** (4.60)	0.68 (3.97)	1.57** (8.15)			0.48** (3.04)	1.13** (6.15)	0.63** (3.95)	1.05** (5.98)
RELIGIOUS			0.26 (1.31)	0.34* (1.68)			0.45** (2.36)	0.07 (0.35)			0.29 (1.53)	0.20 (1.09)	0.19 (1.01)	0.26 (1.37)			0.19 (1.06)	0.28 (1.54)	0.25 (1.40)	0.23 (1.37)
ΔKKZ_CORRUP					0.21 (0.97)	0.35 (0.89)			-0.14 (0.578)	0.27 (0.62)	-0.09 (0.39)	0.42 (1.15)			0.06 (0.27)	0.35 (0.83)	0.08 (0.44)	0.32 (0.91)	-0.34* (1.82)	-0.35 (1.51)
ΔKKZ_RULELAW					0.28 (1.05)	-0.69** (2.92)			0.33 (1.10)	-0.48** (2.08)	0.57 (2.12)	-0.32 (1.49)			0.21 (0.72)	-1.12** (4.871)	0.30 (1.23)	-0.83** (3.38)	0.68** (2.68)	-0.11 (0.42)
ΔKKZ_REGQUAL					-0.65** (2.06)	-0.68** (2.75)			-0.68* (1.89)	-0.07 (0.25)	-0.62* (1.799)	-0.29 (1.55)			0.14 (0.68)	-0.48** (1.417)	0.23 (1.26)	-0.50* (1.80)	-0.08 (0.46)	0.62 (1.62)
ΔKKZ_GOVEFF					0.25 (0.86)	1.32** (3.15)			0.59 (1.84)	0.59 (1.32)	0.31 (1.16)	0.45 (1.22)			-0.17 (0.65)	1.55** (3.58)	-0.34 (1.597)	1.34** (3.50)	-0.02 (0.07)	
R²	0.072		0.152		0.109		0.101		0.079		0.103		0.130		0.059		0.137		0.102	

Notes: See table 6.11 notes.

**Significant at the 5 percent level.

*Significant at the 10 percent level.

Table 6.13   Determinants of international financial mergers: Poisson estimates (3-3 robustness testing)

Variable	Model 1		Model 2		Model 3		Model 4		Model 5		Model 6		Model 7		Model 8		Model 9		Model 10	
	B	A	B	A	B	A	B	A	B	A	B	A	B	A	B	A	B	A	B	A
CONST	-1.36** (2.68)		-1.11** (13.97)		-0.79** (9.70)		-0.92** (10.84)		-2.26** (4.43)		-1.16** (2.36)		-1.50** (2.87)		-1.09** (10.52)		-1.38** (12.44)		-0.99** (9.14)	
DISTANCE	-0.03 (1.039)	0.06** (2.21)																		
GDP	0.06 (0.68)	0.15* (1.67)							-0.04 (1.344)	0.08** (2.44)	-0.04 (0.974)	0.07** (2.48)	-0.04 (1.20)	0.05 (1.74)						
TRADE			0.24** (4.95)	0.48** (8.24)					0.18** (2.05)	0.25** (2.83)	0.06 (0.79)	0.14 (1.53)	0.06 (0.64)	0.14 (1.39)	0.30** (6.01)	0.39** (6.41)	0.32** (6.83)	0.54** (9.56)		
GDPGROW					-0.05** (5.00)	0.05** (3.15)			0.37** (6.86)	0.29** (4.57)	-0.04** (3.02)	-0.04 (0.92)			-0.05** (4.196)	0.05** (2.62)			-0.05** (4.58)	0.03* (1.71)
STOCKRET					-0.00** (2.073)	-0.01* (1.759)					-0.00 (1.06)	-0.01* (1.92)			-0.00 (1.28)	-0.01* (1.19)			-0.01** (2.13)	-0.01* (1.67)
LANGUAGE							0.12 (0.74)	1.26** (9.80)												
RELIGIOUS							-0.17 (0.99)	0.25* (1.80)					0.48** (2.67)	0.77** (4.22)			0.30* (1.78)	1.41** (7.84)	0.52** (3.02)	1.19** (7.19)
ΔRESTRIC_S	0.12 (1.13)	0.09 (1.06)	0.05 (0.65)	-0.04 (0.38)	0.11 (1.25)	0.01 (0.14)	0.05 (0.56)	-0.15* (1.68)	0.13 (1.15)	0.07 (0.75)	0.19* (1.78)	0.11 (1.17)	0.24 (1.23)	0.15 (0.84)	0.07 (0.84)	-0.01 (0.12)	0.01 (0.03)	0.33* (1.89)	0.11 (0.60)	0.05 (0.91)
ΔRESTRIC_I	-0.71** (6.53)	-0.75** (7.76)	-0.27** (3.71)	-0.49** (4.79)	-0.34** (4.72)	-0.54** (5.97)	-0.39** (5.87)	-0.53** (7.05)	-0.52** (3.97)	-0.67** (5.85)	-0.67** (5.21)	-0.73** (6.89)	-0.70** (6.10)	-0.71** (6.98)	-0.19** (2.352)	-0.39** (3.79)	0.01 (0.10)	-0.25** (2.31)	0.05 (0.51)	-0.18 (1.62)
ΔRESTRIC_R	0.23** (3.56)	0.09 (1.53)	0.08* (1.68)	-0.02 (0.250)	0.19** (3.82)	0.14** (2.21)	0.18** (4.10)	0.23** (4.75)	0.12* (1.68)	0.04 (0.57)	0.25** (3.87)	0.08 (1.28)	0.25** (3.87)	0.30** (3.21)	0.04 (0.81)	0.00 (0.03)	-0.24 (2.872)	-0.23** (2.48)	-0.30** (3.73)	-0.43** (5.14)
ΔRESTRIC_NF	0.29** (2.56)	0.45** (4.42)	0.31** (4.21)	0.25** (2.56)	0.20** (1.98)	0.18* (1.84)	0.27** (3.26)	0.11 (1.49)	0.28** (2.37)	0.48** (4.46)	0.22 (1.54)	0.42** (3.77)	0.21* (1.86)	0.14** (2.43)	0.32** (3.45)	0.22** (2.24)	0.29** (3.64)	0.10 (1.28)	0.16* (1.65)	0.08 (0.95)
R^2	0.133		0.056		0.061		0.135		0.155		0.138		0.167		0.054		0.145		0.125	

Notes: See table 6.11 notes.

**Significant at the 5 percent level.

*Significant at the 10 percent level.

LANGUAGE. Recall that its coefficients are only significant for two specifications before the crisis without considering G7 countries. The coefficients now become overwhelmingly significantly positive. This, thus, further strengthens the importance of information cost, especially when targets are from Asian countries.

6.7 Conclusions

We study the motivation that drives financial institutions to engage in cross-border M&A activity in Asian countries prior to and subsequent to the Asian crisis. In other words, we delve into the impact of the Asian crisis on the determinants of cross-border M&As in Asian countries. Before discussing the conclusions, one caveat should be pointed out. While we posit five hypotheses, their multiple proxies may yield mixed results. Furthermore, some proxies may belong to more than one hypothesis. Thus, it is uneasy to decisively reject or not reject the hypotheses by simply examining the significance of proxies (which are also referred to as determinants here). One way to overcome this shortcoming is to discuss more about the influence of each determinant and less about whether each hypothesis is supported or rejected. The conclusion can be highlighted in the following.

First, some determinants have an equal impact on M&A activity before and after the Asian crisis. For example, DISTANCE has a negative impact in both periods, which supports the gravity hypothesis and information cost hypothesis. Gross domestic product also has a negative impact during both periods, contrary to the gravity hypothesis in this case. The following the client hypothesis is supported for both periods too, but only when TRADE is employed as the proxy. When the value of the regulatory gap is relatively small between two countries in terms of the number of restrictions on the banking industry engaging in insurance, then firms seem to be encouraged to partake in cross-border M&A activity. By contrast, when the value of the regulatory gap is relatively large between two countries in terms of restrictions on nonfinancial activities, it encourages firms to engage in M&A activity.

Next, some determinants are only effective before the Asian crisis. For example, GDP growth rate at $t + 1$ has a negative impact before the Asian crisis but no effect after it. Thus, the market opportunity hypothesis was at play before the crisis but was not important after it. Also, the gap in regulation barriers between two countries, when proxied by the differences of corruption, is also important before the crisis but is no longer crucial after it. Thus, the regulation barrier hypothesis may have become less in force after the crisis.

Third, some determinants are only effective after the Asian crisis. For example, sharing a common language and being of the same religious faith become more and more important in determining the extent of M&A activity after the crisis. That is, the information cost hypothesis based on these two determinants gains momentum after the crisis. Last, some determinants seem to have no effect whatsoever in both periods. For example, future stock return does not have any impact in our sample.

Appendix

Indonesia

By the end of January 1998, further steps were taken on bank restructuring with the granting of a full guarantee for all bank depositors and creditors, together with the introduction of the Indonesian Bank Restructuring Agency (IBRA).

The foreign holdings in domestic financial institutions would be eased.

Korea

The government has been encouraging mergers between banks that are both sound and of substantial size.

In 1998, regulation of 4 percent of commercial banks controlled by foreigners is lifted.

Malaysia

In 1998, Malaysia requests fifty-eight financial institutions merger into ten large anchor banks.

The Philippines

In 1998, development cooperation, development assistance, and other such topics were key, and they should not be hijacked by discussions of new financial system. There was a need for the international community to create partnerships that met development needs. The international community should also create the required resources for implementing the proposals and commitments made in the major United Nations conferences.

In 1999, nine mergers involving twelve commercial banks, four thrift banks, and two rural banks have taken place. All these measures promoted the mobilization of more resources that will be made available to the market.

Singapore

In May 1999, MAS announced a five-year program to liberalize access by foreign banks to the domestic banking industry. The first package of measures was deliberately calibrated to give local banks time to build their capabilities and minimize the risk of destabilizing the financial system.

On 29 June 2001, MAS announced the second phase of the liberalization program, which will enable the broadening of access to the domestic wholesale banking industry. This will allow offshore banks and qualifying offshore banks to develop their restricted bank status.

Taiwan

On December 13, 2000, Taiwan passed the Law of M&As of Financial Institutions to encourage M&As. Foreign M&As are also allowed.

Thailand

In 1997, the Bank of Thailand said that restrictions on foreign holdings in domestic financial institutions would be eased. Domestically incorporated banks and finance companies "with sound financial status" would be allowed to hold 49 percent of other financial institutions for ten years, the central bank said. These measures will apply to fifteen commercial banks, thirty-three active finance companies, and twelve property finance companies that have not been suspended, the central bank said.

Foreign holdings in fifty-eight bankrupt finance companies, whose activities were suspended this year, will be unlimited for ten years. Currently, foreign companies may hold no more than 10 percent of a bank and 25 percent of a property finance company.

References

Altunbas, Y., and D. Marques. 2004. Mergers and acquisitions and bank performance in Europe: The role of strategic similarities. ECB Working Paper no. 398. Frankfurt, European Central Bank.

Barth, J., G. Caprio, and R. Levine. 2000. Bank regulation and supervision. What works and what doesn't. Washington, DC: World Bank. http://info.worldbank .org/etools/docs/library/83681/caprio.pdf.

———. 2006. *Rethinking bank regulation: Till angel govern.* Cambridge, UK: Cambridge University Press.

Berg, A. 1999. The Asia crisis: Cause, policy responses, and outcomes. IMF Working Paper no. WP-99-138. Washington; DC: International Monetary Fund.

Berger, A. N., S. M. Davies, and M. J. Flannery. 2000. Comparing market and supervisory assessments of bank performance: Who knows what when? *Journal of Money, Credit and Banking* 30 (3): 641–47.

Borenzstein, E., J. De Gregorio, and J.-W. Lee. 1998. How does foreign direct investment affect economic growth? *Journal of International Economics* 45:115–35.

Brealey, R., and E. Kaplanis. 1996. The determination of foreign banking location. *Journal of International Money and Finance* 15 (4): 577–97.

Buch, C. M., and G. L. DeLong. 2004. Cross-border bank mergers: What lures the rare animal? *Journal of Banking and Finance* 28:2077–2102.

Campa, J. M., and I. Hernando. 2006. The reaction by industry insiders to M&As in the European financial industry. IESE Research Paper no. D/689. Barcelona: IESE Business School.

Carkovic, M., and R. Levine. 2005. Does foreign direct investment accelerate economic growth? In *Does foreign direct investment promote development?*, ed. T. H. Moran, E. M. Graham, and M. Blomström, 195–220. Washington, DC: Peterson Institute for International Economics.

Clarke, G., R. Cull, M. Peria, and S. Sanchez. 2001. Foreign bank entry: Experience, implications for developing countries, and agenda for future research. World Bank Policy Research Paper no. 2698. Washington, DC: World Bank.

Corsetti, G., P. Pesenti, and N. Roubini. 1998. What caused the Asian currency and financial crisis? Part 1: A macroeconomic overview. NBER Working Paper no. 6834. Cambridge, MA: National Bureau of Economic Research.

De Mello, L. R. Jr. 1999. Foreign direct investment-led growth: Evidence from time series and panel data. *Oxford Economic Papers* 51 (1): 133–51.

Dunning, J. 1998. Location and the multinational enterprise: A neglected factor? *Journal of International Business Studies* 19:45–66.

Fecher, F., and P. Pestieau. 1993. Efficiency and competition in O.E.C.D. financial services. In *The measurement of productive efficiency: Techniques and applications*, ed. H. O. Fried, C. A. Knox Lovell, and S. S. Schmidt, 374–85. New York: Oxford University Press.

Focarelli, D., and A. F. Pozzolo. 2000. The determinants of cross-border bank shareholdings: An analysis with bank-level data from OECD countries. Bank of Italy, Working Paper.

———. 2001. The patterns of cross-border bank mergers and shareholdings in OECD countries. *Journal of Banking and Finance* 25:2305–37.

———. 2005. Where do banks expand abroad? An empirical analysis. *Journal of Business* 78 (6): 2435–64.

Galindo, A., A. Micco, and C. Sierra. 2003. Better the devil that you know: Evidence on entry costs faced by foreign banks. IDB Working Paper no. 477. Washington, DC: Inter-American Development Bank.

Giovanni, J. 2002. What drives capital flows? The case of cross-border M&A activity and financial deepening. eScholarship Repository, University of California. http://repositories.cdlib.org/iber/cider/C01-122.

Kaufmann, D., A. Kraay, and P. Zoido-Lobatón. 2002. Governance matters II: Updated indicators for 2001–01. World Bank Policy Research Working Paper no. 2772. Washington, DC: World Bank.

Kim, W., and S. J. Wei. 1999. Foreign portfolio investors before and during a crisis. NBER Working Paper no. 6968. Cambridge, MA: National Bureau of Economic Research.

La Porta, R., F. Lopez-de-Silanes, A. Shleifer, and R. Vishny. 1997. Legal determinants of external finance. *Journal of Finance* 52:1131–50.

———. 1998. Law and finance. *Journal of Political Economy* 106:1113–55.

Portes, R., and H. Rey. 2005. The determinants of cross-border equity flows. *Journal of International Economics* 65:269–96.

Prasad, E., K. Rogoff, S. J. Wei, and M. A. Kose. 2003. Effects of financial globalization on developing countries: Some empirical evidence. IMF Occasional Paper no. 20. Washington, DC: International Monetary Fund.

Qiu, L. D., and W. Zhou. 2006. International mergers: Incentives and welfare. *Journal of International Economics* 68 (1): 35–38.

Rossi, S., and P. F. Volpin. 2004. Cross-country determinants of mergers and acquisitions. *Journal of Financial Economics* 74:277–304.

Sabi, M. 1988. An application of the theory of foreign direct investment to multinational banking in LDCs. *Journal of International Business Studies* 19:433–47.

Shen, C. H., and Y. H. Chang. 2006. Do regulations affect banking performance? Government governance may matter. *Contemporary Economic Policy* 24 (1): 92–105.

Shen, C. H., and H. H. Chou. 2007. Foreign banks in Asian markets: The determinants of location choice. National Taiwan University, Working Paper.

Shih, S. H. M. 2003. An investigation into the use of mergers as a solution for the Asian banking sector crisis. *Quarterly Review of Economics and Finance* 43:31–49.

Tinbergen, J. 1962. Shaping the world economy: Suggestions for an international economic policy. New York: The Twentieth Century Fund.

Vasconcellos, G. M., and R. J. Kish. 1998. Cross-border mergers and acquisitions: The European-US experience. *Journal of Multinational Financial Management* 8:431–50.

Wei, S. J. 2000a. How taking is corruption on international investors? *Review of Economics and Statistics* 82 (1): 1–11.

———. 2000b. Local corruption and global flows. *Brookings Papers on Economic Activity,* Issue no. 2:303–54. Washington, DC: Brookings Institution.

———. 2001. Corruption in economic transition and development greaser or sand? United Nations Economic Commission for Europe, Working Paper.

Williams, B. 2002. The defensive expansion approach to multinational banking: Evidence to date. *Financial Markets Institutions & Instruments* 11 (2): 127–203.

Comment   Mario B. Lamberte

The authors have observed a significant increase in mergers and acquisitions (M&As) in Asia after the Asian financial crisis. Thus, they have attempted to empirically investigate the determinants of cross-border M&As among financial institutions in ten Asian countries and to find out whether the determinants have changed after the Asian financial crisis. They have offered five hypotheses, namely, the gravity hypothesis, following the client hypothesis, market opportunity hypothesis, information cost hypothesis, and regulatory restrictions hypothesis. Their empirical results confirm some of these hypotheses and also show some changes in effects of the determinants of M&As after the crisis.

These comments will focus on two areas, namely, data and interpretation of the empirical results.

Data

The data used by the authors need some clarification as they affect the results as well as the interpretation of the results. First, they have classified M&As by acquiring and target countries. It may be worthwhile to look at nationalities of these financial institutions as they provide additional information why a financial institution in an acquiring country has merged with a financial institution in a target country. For example, a U.S.-registered financial institution owned by Hong Kong investors may merge

Mario B. Lamberte is director of research at the Asian Development Bank Institute.

with a financial institution in Hong Kong because of better information it has regarding market opportunities and relative ease dealing with regulatory restrictions that it is familiar with. Second, the authors have divided the number of M&As into two: before the crisis (1990 to 1997) and after the crisis (1999 to 2006). They should provide an explanation why M&As in 1998 have been excluded from the analysis. Some of the M&As during the 1999 to 2006 period could have been arranged well before the crisis but completed and consummated only after the crisis. Hence, the crisis might not have been a factor determining such M&As, although the data showed that such M&As occurred after the crisis. Third, the variable **RELIGION** needs to be elaborated further, especially because this variable became a statistically significant factor determining M&As after the crisis. For instance, 90 percent of the people in Hong Kong have eclectic religions, a phenomenon that makes it almost impossible to claim that Hong Kong has the same religion as another country of which the majority of the population follows a certain religion. Fourth, in this age of greater connectivity, the variable DISTANCE may be defined differently. For instance, bank executives usually travel by air; hence, the number of commercial flights between two countries may be a better description of distance than physical distance as commonly used in gravity models. Fifth, which is a relatively minor comment, the variable **LANGUAGE** described in table 6.1, which refers to the legal systems prevailing in the target and acquirer countries, does not match with the description of the variable in the text. And, last, it is not clear how the variable TRADE is measured as can be gathered from sections 6.2.2 and 6.5 of the chapter. Does it refer to the country's total trade (as percent of gross domestic product [GDP]) or bilateral trade between acquiring and target countries?

Interpretation of the Results

The authors should have exerted more effort to explain the results of their empirical analysis, especially those that seem to be surprising results. Here, I would like to mention a few examples.

The authors have found that "the crisis evidently changed the impact of corruption on M&A activity." More specifically, before the crisis, financial institutions in countries with low corruption are more likely to acquire financial institutions in countries with high corruption, but after the crisis, such tendency has gone. The authors should expound more on this result to clarify some issues and policy implications. For instance, why would a financial institution in a country with less corruption target another financial institution in a country with high corruption before the crisis and stop doing it after the crisis? Is it because return on bribes is significantly higher before the crisis than after the crisis? For a country that encourages foreign investments in various modalities including M&A, how can such results be of use to policymakers? Some explanations are also needed with respect to the findings that financial institutions from relatively less-restrictive countries with regard to insurance and real estate have propensity to engage in M&A activities with those from relatively more-restrictive countries. What's the reason for obtaining such results, and why do such results hold before and after the crisis? Is the barrier to entry into these sectors not binding in target countries, or is the return for overcoming such a barrier, like enjoying monopoly status, very attractive?

The results generated by the variable **LANGUAGE** are quite interesting, but they also need to be elaborated. Languages in the countries being analyzed, like those variables that represent information cost, have not changed before and after the crisis, but the variable is found to have significant effect on M&A activities after the crisis. It could be that certain laws and regulations of target countries have been changed after the crisis, and financial institutions of acquiring countries find those new laws and regulations easier to access and understand if written in the same language as theirs than those written in languages different from theirs.

Comment   Wimboh Santoso

In the last few years, financial sector structure and competition has changed in global perspective, especially in the post-Asian crises. New regulatory standards, financial innovations, competition strategies, and information technology are the main drivers for banks to reposition their competition strategy to improve efficiency among others by mergers and acquisitions (M&A). The growth of M&A is 25 percent per year since 2003 in Asia Pacific. This note will provide different perspectives on the main rationale and driving forces of mergers and acquisitions in the banking industry in the Asia-Pacific region.

Mergers and acquisitions are considered part of strategic management to respond to the environment evolution of the industry with the main objective to improve competitive advantages. Three main reasons behind M&A from a strategic management point of view are (1) competition; (2) responses to changing environment; and (3) private equity and financial investors. Merger and acquisitions cases in some countries may provide additional information to the authors. The note will also comment on the hypotheses and model before a summary recommendation.

Wimboh Santoso is head of the Financial Stability Bureau at the Directorate of Banking Research and Regulation, Bank Indonesia.

Competition Driver

Competition in the banking industry changes over time due to product innovations and technology developments. Banks always try to gain competitive advantages against other banks in the market. Increasing markets and monopoly powers seems to be the strategy of improving the competitiveness. With this strategy, the synergy to improve economics of scope and scale will be achieved; then the banks will be more efficient as transaction and information cost will be reduced. M&A is the way to execute the strategy. The merger of two large banks is a good example for the competition driver.

Regulatory Environment Driver

The development of a regulatory regime over the globe is the main driver of M&A. With this regime, governments and regulators tend to develop a stronger banking industry to enable them to be champions in global competition. Consolidation policies have been the main policy platform in most Association of Southeast Asian Nations (ASEAN) countries such as Singapore, Malaysia, Indonesia, and Thailand. The feature of this policy is to have a small number of banks with high economies of scale and scope. For the weak and small banks, seeking a stronger partner is the only way to be champions in local and global markets. For stronger banks, enhancement of economies of scope and scale is the only way to be more efficient and competitive in the global market. Merger and acquisitions transactions between those two create mutual benefits for both parties and provide benefits for industry as the merged firms will be stronger and more efficient in their operations. For the postcrisis countries, M&A is also one of strategies in problem bank resolutions. The evidence of the regulatory environment driver on M&A has been clearly visible in the Republic of Korea, the People's Republic of China, Taipei, and Indonesia.

Private Equity and Financial Investor Driver

In recent years, many investors in developed markets enlarged their focus of investments in overseas and emerging markets to diversity their risks and returns. Mergers and acquisitions are the most preferable transaction for investors to lock-up a longer horizon of their investment. Short-term investment in financial markets is mainly for global liquidity management and also for trading purposes. The difference between those two is very distinct. Mergers and acquisitions provide returns from income after tax and, hence, increase the equity prices at the end of the day with medium- or long-term horizons, while trading is to earn spread between buying and selling price of the instruments. The latter is less relevant to M&A matters. With M&A, the cost of each unit product will be lower in post-M&A, and the banks will provide broad-base customers to improve economies of scale and scope. The case of Newbridge's sale of Korea First Bank to Standard Chartered, Carlyle's sale of Koram Bank to Citigroup, and also the sale of Jinro to Hite Brewery are good examples of private equity drivers.

Cases of M&A in Selected Countries

Indonesia

Cross-border M&A occurred in the postcrisis when the government divested its stake in bank takeover. During the crisis, the government closed thirty-eight banks as the owners were unable to invest more capital for problem banks, and sixteen banks were taken over by government for restructuring. These banks eventually privatized in 2004 and 2005. Most of the investors were overseas banks or financial holdings such as Temasek, Faralon Capital, Khazanah, OCBC Overseas Investment, United Overseas Bank, Sorak Holding, and Standchart. The acquisition cases in Indonesia were driven by government policy to privatize former problem banks in the postcrisis. The acquirer motives could be private equity investment and also responses to the environment. The number of banks in Indonesia is still very large in the postcrisis (131 banks). The top fourteen banks account for approximately 80 percent of market share in loans. Bank Indonesia announced the consolidation of small banks (with capital less than IDR 100 million) in 2004. Failing to satisfy the capital threshold will downgrade their operation as limited banks.

Malaysia

Malaysian authorities announced a plan in September 1999 for fifty-eight local banks and finance companies to merge into six large groups. In October, these banks and finance companies were allowed to voluntarily decide their partners. By end of January 2000, all financial institutions submitted their proposals, and in February 2000, the central bank announced the ten core banking groups, which consist of six appointed anchor banks and four newcomers. By August 2000, the ten banking groups completed the signing of the merger agreements. The M&A in Malaysia was considered the most successful government-driven bank consolidation effort.

Thailand

Since the introduction of the Financial Sector Master Plan in 2003, M&A has begun turning some of the country's top financial institutions into even stronger economic powers. Though these changes precede full implementation of the Plan, they are expected to continue and even intensify over the next decade.

Hypotheses

The authors employ five hypotheses to identify the determinants of M&A: gravity, following the client, market opportunity, information cost, and regulatory restriction. Five determinants employed in this study are highly correlated and can be simplified into two groups, market and regulatory driven. The cost of each component of these market-driven determinants is the appropriate measure to identify efficiency. The M&A objective is achieved because cost indicators reduce in the post-M&A. Regulatory restriction or the regulatory driven determinant is another important point in the M&A for acquired banks. In postcrisis countries, privatization of government stakes on bailed-out banks has been the main driver from a policy perspective. The result shows the number of M&As in the postcrisis countries is extremely high. In certain circumstances, investors are interested in acquiring banks just because there is a high opportunity to create profit by selling shares to other buyers.

The authors will be benefit from outlining the structure of determinants of M&A by considering the preceding information and providing strong arguments before determining the hypothesis.

Model

The data in this study consists of cross-country and time series. Most studies using panel data must consider the different response of each country due to country-specific issues such as politics or public pressure to support or disagree with the policy of privatization. Time-specific issues may also affect the decision of M&A. Three issues must be addressed by the authors in this study:

1. How to ensure that the model ignores or accommodates the issues of country-specific determinants.

2. How the model ignores or accommodates time-specific determinants in the model.

3. How to deal with heteroskedastic variances in the regression model.

Even though the authors ignores the three preceding points, the reason and argument must be clearly stated on the chapter.

Concluding Remarks

The driving force of M&A is difficult to precisely define in some cases. The decision on M&As is not specifically based on only a single reason. In many cases, M&As have multiple objectives, such as to comply with regulatory authority policy, to improve efficiency, and to obtain capital gain.

The drivers affect the decisions simultaneously; sometimes the private equity or financial investor drivers are also the reason behind why a bank tries to acquire other banks. No single answer can respond to the question with respect to what the driving force of M&As is. The cases of Indonesia, Malaysia, and Thailand make it very clear that government policy is the main reason behind M&A. But one may come up with different answers as to why M&A occurs because of a different reason. More analysis on the reason behind M&A in both acquired and acquirer bank is very important before coming up with a hypothesis. A detailed model must be explored to satisfy general rules on regression analysis using panel data such as fixed effect and random effect.

7

Merger Activities and Stock Market Valuation in China

Ho-Mou Wu

7.1 Introduction

The stock markets of China have been developed quickly and in a very different way from other country's stock markets. Since establishment of the markets, China has adopted a dual-track equity system (or so-called parallel market) with nontradable and tradable shares. The nontradable shares are owned by the government agencies of various levels, who are frequently the controlling shareholders of many listed companies. A major feature of the dual-track equity system might be the privatization of these state-owned companies over the least ten years in the stock market. By 2002, it was estimated that 11 percent of listed companies were privately owned. And to the end of 2005, private individuals controlled about 26 percent of listed companies. The changes are brought forth by thousands of transactions, including management buy outs and negotiated transfers of control rights.

The purpose of this chapter is to examine the nature of merger and acquisition (M&A) activity and analyze how it affects a company's value in China's stock markets. The study of China's M&A markets can help us to understand better how the stock markets function with the special institutional arrangement of the dual-track equity system. We focus on the most recent period from 2004 to 2005 because M&A activities have been growing rapidly in this period. The total value of M&A activities reached 211 bil-

Ho-Mou Wu is the executive director and Langrun Chair Professor of Economics at the China Center for Economic Research, Peking University.

I am grateful to Julian Wright, Kaoru Hosono, Andy Rose, Taka Ito, and participants of the NBER-EASE conference for helpful suggestions. I also want to thank Yu Zhang and Yun Bai of the China Center for Economic Research (CCER) for research assistance.

lion RMB in 2004, about twice the M&A value in 2003, and three times the M&A value in 2002. In addition, China's stock markets also experienced institutional changes in recent years, with the reform of the dual-track equity system first implemented in mid-2005. As China's stock market went through fundamental changes and the M&A activities also became very lively in this period, it will be interesting to assess whether M&As can bring value for listed companies for the period from 2004 to 2005.

In the first part of the chapter, we adopt the event-study method (see Brown and Warner 1985; Bruner 2002) to assess the effects of M&As in China. We use estimates of abnormal returns, the difference between actual and expected stock returns, to measure the economic effects of M&As. The expected returns are based on the capital asset pricing model (CAPM), with the market index serving as the benchmark to summarize the influence of marketwide events on the returns of individual stocks. After reviewing thirteen studies of U.S. market data, Jensen and Ruback (1983) found that targets of successful mergers earn significantly positive returns around 20 to 30 percent, but returns to bidding firm shareholders are zero. Their conclusions are also confirmed by more recent works, as summarized by Bruner (2002).

It will be interesting to study whether such a pattern of returns also emerges in China's M&A market. Loaded with heavy computation of the CAPM models for these individual stocks, this chapter only concentrates on the M&A activities from 2004 to 2005. In 2004, we collect data of 611 M&A events involving 499 companies, and in 2005, we find 752 M&A events involving 587 companies listed on the Shanghai and Shenzhen stock exchanges. We then examine the cumulative abnormal returns (CAR) of M&A events in depressed markets and upbeat markets.

Because privatization is an important feature in China's stock market, we will study how the ownership structure may affect the CAR of M&A events. After separating M&A activities into those initiated by state holding companies and those initiated by privately owned companies, we can find that M&A activities were value-creating for both private- and state-controlled firms in 2005, but only for private-controlled firms in 2004. We also try to explain why this might be so. In addition, we also examine the CAR of acquiring and target firms. We can find that the positive returns of M&A in 2005 were evenly shared by acquiring and target firms.

The validity of the event-study method relies much on the stock market being efficient such that the CAPM can be used to capture the market influence on individual stocks. However, there exist doubts about the efficiency of China's stock markets as they are in a flux of institutional transformation. And our event studies also lead to mixed results. The alternative avenue of investigation is to use the accounting method. Using the return on assets (ROA), Meeks (1977) found that merger activities brought ROA down for bidding firms. Mueller (1980) found that profitability of acquiring firms declines and economic gains from mergers appear to be small. Other related works include Healy, Palepu, and Ruback (1992) and Clark and Ofek (1994), who adopt various accounting indicators to study M&A events.

In the second part of the chapter, we use accounting indicators as a complementary way to understand the effects of M&As in China. We obtain financial indicators for four years and study whether the financial conditions of M&A companies demonstrated a deteriorating or improving trend after the M&A event. We examine how earning per share (EPS), return on assets (ROA), return on equity (ROE), operating cash flows (OCF), free cash flows (FCF), and other indicators change during and after M&A. We also obtain from financial statements the current ratio, quick ratio, equity multiplier, and liability to equity ratio to study their ability to repay debt before and after merger.

In the next section, we describe M&A activities in China's stock markets. The economic effects of M&A as analyzed by the event-study method are discussed in section 7.3. The results from using accounting methods are examined in section 7.4. Section 7.5 provides concluding remarks about our findings.

7.2 Merger Activities in China's Stock Market

As of June 2007, China's stock market has a capitalization of US$2,400 billion, with an upward trend in transaction volume and relative importance in the global financial market. About 900 of the 1,300-plus list companies have their controlling parties from government agencies of various levels. Many of the merger activities involve decisions by government agencies, which is a special feature of China's M&A market. The dollar amounts of merger activities occurring in the stock market have been growing in recent years, with a significant increase in total values of M&A activities after 2004 (table 7.1). The total values of M&A in 2004 and 2005 are about 1 percent of China's gross national product (table 7.2).

We collect all M&A announcements with values exceeding 10 million RMB and obtain 1,363 events involving 1,086 companies in 2004 and 2005. In 2005, there are 587 firms involved in 752 merger activities (table 7.3).

Table 7.1   **The size of merger activities, 2002–2005**

Year	Events	Total amount (billion RMB)
2002	951	77.78
2003	934	92.31
2004	1,541	211.69
2005	1,219	132.32

In 2004, there are 499 firms involved in 611 events of M&A (table 7.4). As for the ownership structure, there were 503 events in 2005 with state holding companies as the controlling shareholders and 211 events with privately owned enterprises as the controlling shareholder (table 7.5).

In year 2004, there were 426 events with state holding companies as the controlling shareholders and 142 events with privately owned enterprises as the controlling shareholders (table 7.6).

The reform of the dual-trade equity system was first implemented in May 2005. The stock market also went through a cyclical phase for the period from 2004 to 2005, with Shanghai composite stock index dropping to below the 1,000-point level on June 6, 2005, returning to the level of eight years prior. The market index has been rising ever since then (figure 7.1 and figure 7.2).

During the first half of 2005, before June 3, 300 events of M&A occurred together with a downward market. For the second half of 2005, there were

Table 7.2   Relative importance of merger activities (billion RMB)

	2004	2005	Growth rate (%)
Total amount	211.69	132.32	−37.5
GDP	13,651.5	18,232.1	9.9
Total amount/GDP (%)	1.55	0.73	−52.9

Table 7.3   Sample of merger activities in 2005

	Shanghai stock exchange	Shenzhen stock exchange	Total
Firms	361	226	587
Events	468	284	752

Table 7.4   Sample of merger activities in 2004

	Shanghai stock exchange	Shenzhen stock exchange	Total
Firms	312	187	499
Events	397	214	611

Table 7.5   Types of controlling shareholders in 2005

Type	State holding company	Privately owned enterprise	Foreign-owned company	Others	Total
Shanghai	312	127	4	25	468
Shenzhen	191	84	0	9	284
Total	503	211	4	34	752

Table 7.6   **Types of controlling shareholders in 2004**

Type	State holding company	Privately owned enterprise	Foreign-owned company	Others	Total
Shanghai	278	91	3	25	397
Shenzhen	148	51	0	15	214
Total	426	142	3	40	611

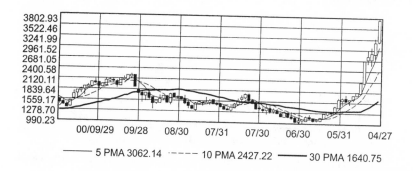

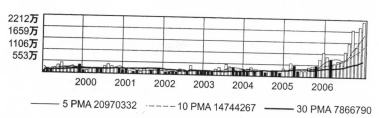

Fig. 7.1   Shanghai Composite Index, 2000–2007

452 events of M&A in the market with an upward trend (table 7.7). This period also coincided with the early phase of reforming the dual-track equity system. As for year 2004, all M&A events occurred during a downward market.

In the next section, we will use the factors of ownership structures (as in table 7.5 and table 7.6) and aggregate market performance (as in table 7.7, for 2005) to divide our sample and examine whether the returns of M&A events may depend on these factors.

7.3   Stock Market Valuation of M&A Events

We divide the event period (t_0, t_2) into the preannouncement subperiod $(t_0, t_1 - 1)$, and postannouncement subperiod (t_1, t_2), with t_1 as the date of announcement (see figure 7.3).

In order to use the event-study method, we need to estimate the expected

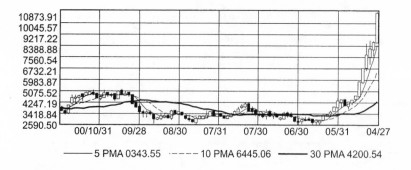

------- 5 PMA 0343.55   ----- 10 PMA 6445.06   ------- 30 PMA 4200.54

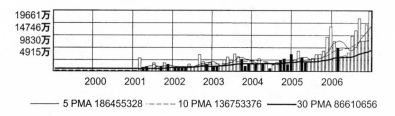

------- 5 PMA 186455328   ----- 10 PMA 136753376   ------30 PMA 86610656

Fig. 7.2   Shenzhen Component Index, 2000–2007

Table 7.7   Merger activities in upward and downward markets in 2005

	Period of downward index (2005.1.1–2005.6.3)	Period of upward index (2005.6.6–2005.12.31)	Total Total
Shanghai	178	290	468
Shenzhen	122	162	284
Total	300	452	752

returns from holding the stocks of M&A companies if the M&A event did not occur, which are then used as the benchmark for computing the abnormal returns. The period $(t_0, t_1 - 1)$ before announcing the M&A at $t = t_1$ is used as the basis to estimate the daily expected returns in the CAPM framework:

(1) $R_{it} = \alpha_i + \beta_i R_{mt} + \varepsilon_{it}$ for $t = t_0$ to $t = t_1 - 1$, $i = 1, \ldots, N$,

where R_{mt} is the returns on market index in period t. We define $r_{it} = (P_{it} - P_{it-1})/P_{it-1}$ and adopt the continuously compounded rate of return $R_{it} = \ln(1 + r_{it})$ and $R_{mt} = \ln(1 + r_{mt})$. Then daily abnormal returns (AR) before and after the announcement, that is, $t = t_0$ to $t = t_1 - 1$ and $t = t_1$ to $t = t_2$, can be computed as:

(2) $AR_{it} = R_{it} - E(R_{it})$,

with

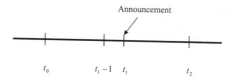

Fig. 7.3   Time line of the event

(3) $E(R_{it}) = \alpha_i + \beta_i R_{mt}$, for $t = t_0$ to $t = t_2$.

Then we can aggregate across securities to obtain average abnormal returns (AAR). The associated average cumulative abnormal returns (CAR) is:

(4) $$CAR_t = \sum_{t=t_0}^{t} AAR_t,$$

with

(5) $$AAR_t = \frac{1}{N} \sum_{i=1}^{N} AR_{it}.$$

In our study, the preannouncement period (–50, –1) corresponds to (t_0, $t_1 - 1$), and the postannouncement period (0,39) corresponds to (t_1, t_2) in the preceding formulation.

We first analyze the data for 2004 and find that the AAR and CAR of all merger activities (611 events, see table 7.8) were significantly negative (table 7.9).

It is quite surprising to find that the AAR and CAR of M&A events were significantly negative in 2004. We next analyze the CAR of all merger activities in 2005 (752 events, see table 7.10). In contrast, we discover that AAR and CAR were significantly positive (table 7.11).

In order to better understand how average abnormal returns (AAR) and cumulative abnormal returns (CAR) evolved over time, we also plot them for 2004 and 2005 separately (figure 7.4 and figure 7.5). This constitutes a very interesting phenomenon for China's M&A activities: either small positive returns or significantly negative returns, as in 2005 and 2004. It is quite different from the experiences of other countries (see Bruner 2002; Bris and Cabolis 2003; Agrawal, Jaffe, and Mandelker 1992; Datta, Pinches, and Narayanan 1992; Dodd and Ruback 1977; Gillan, Kensinger, and Martin 2000; Jarrell, Brickley, and Netter 1988; Leeth and Borg 2000; Mulherin and Boone 2000; Schwert 1996).

In addition, we find that transaction volume of the stocks involved in M&A jumped at the date of announcement ($t = 0$) and stayed quite stable on other days in 2005, and the situation was also similar in 2004 (figure 7.6). One may conclude that the stock market more or less treated the announcement of M&A events as a piece of new information in this period.

In order to understand why the CAR is negative in 2004, we separate all events into various industries, but do not find significant differences across

Table 7.8   Descriptive statistics of all merger activities in 2004

	Minimum	Maximum	Mean	Standard deviation
AAR	−0.0020412	0.0018957	−0.0002216	0.0009668
CAR	−0.0199465	0.0011907	−0.0066257	0.0058423

Table 7.9   Significance test of all merger activities in 2004 (test value = 0)

	t	Significance (2-tailed)	Mean difference	95% confidence interval of the difference Lower	Upper
AAR	−2.1747762	0.032299	−0.0002216	−0.0004241	−1.914E-05
CAR	−10.75884	8.799E-18	−0.0066257	−0.0078493	−0.005402

Table 7.10   Descriptive statistics of all merger activities in 2005

	Minimum	Maximum	Mean	Standard deviation
AAR	−0.002816	0.0055395	0.0001699	0.0011215
CAR	−0.007585	0.0189335	0.0057595	0.0078968

Table 7.11   Significance test of all merger activities in 2005 (test value = 0)

	t	Significance (2-tailed)	Mean difference	95% confidence interval of the difference Lower	Upper
AAR	1.429	0.157	0.0001699	−6.64E-05	0.0004061
CAR	6.881	0	0.0057595	0.0040961	0.007423

industries. However, we discover that the major source of the negative returns might be due to the ownership structure. Those events with state holding companies as the final shareholder (called the *first kind*) had a large negative CAR (figure 7.7), while those privately owned enterprises as the final shareholder (called the *second kind*) demonstrated a significantly positive CAR (figure 7.8). Because the weight of the first kind (426 out of 611 events) is larger than the second kind (142 out of 611 events), we have a combined impact of negative returns for 2004. This may lead us to consider the M&A events initiated by state holding companies as not so focused on enhancing the value of the firm, while those done by privately owned enterprises might be more motivated by efficiency concerns. It may be due to the fact that the government may want to achieve a different objective.

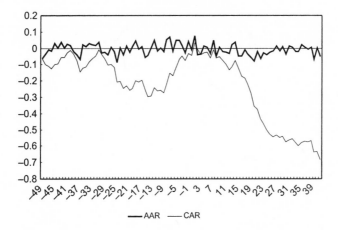

— AAR — — CAR

Fig. 7.4   CAR of all merger activities (average CAR = –0.662%) in 2004

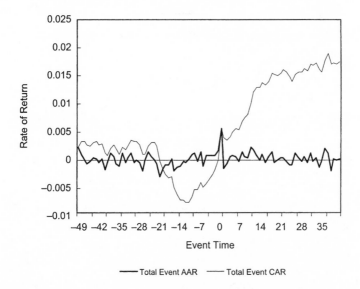

—— Total Event AAR —— Total Event CAR

Fig. 7.5   CAR of all merger activities (average CAR = 0.575%) in 2005

In 2005, we also examine whether ownership structures had influence on the value created through M&A. We find that M&A activities with the state as the controlling party (CAR at $t = 40$ is 1.83 percent) and those with the private enterprises as the controlling party (CAR at $t = 40$ is 1.11 percent) all produced positive returns (figure 7.9 and figure 7.10). This may demonstrate that the state holding companies paid more attention to value creation in their M&A activities and that the ownership structure was not such a significant factor in influencing the values of M&A events in 2005.

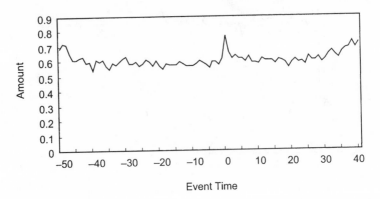

Fig. 7.6   Transaction volume, 2005

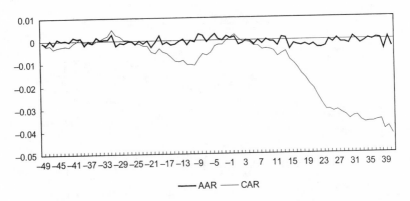

Fig. 7.7   State holding companies as the controlling party, 2004

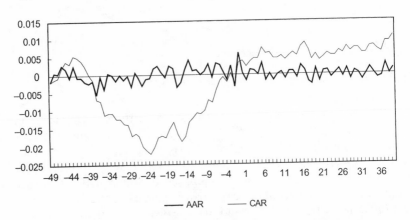

Fig. 7.8   Privately owned enterprises as the controlling party, 2004

In order to understand better how the stock market evaluates merger activities when they produce positive returns, we separate the sample into acquiring firms and target firms in 2005. The average CARs of both types are less than 1 percent (table 7.12 and table 7.13).

In contrast to the findings with U.S. data, with the sample of China's 2005 M&A events, the bidders in China obtained a significantly positive but small return (CAR at $t = 40$ is 1.68 percent). Also in contrast to the U.S. market, the target firms' returns (CAR at $t = 40$ is 2.03 percent) were

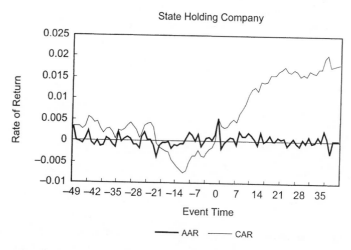

Fig. 7.9   State holding company as the controlling party (average CAR = 0.625%), 2005

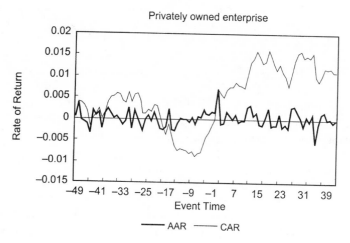

Fig. 7.10   Privately owned enterprise as the controlling party (average CAR = 0.504%), 2005

Table 7.12   CAR of acquiring firms, 2005 (test value = 0)

	t	df	Significance (2-tailed)	Mean difference	95% confidence interval of the difference	
					Lower	Upper
AAR	0.958	88	0.341	0.0001666	−0.000179	0.0005124
CAR	8.948	88	0	0.0064602	0.0050255	0.0078949

Table 7.13   CAR of target firms, 2005

	t	df	Significance (2-tailed)	Mean difference	95% confidence interval of the difference	
					Lower	Upper
AAR	1.185	88	0.239	0.000227	−0.000154	0.0006076
CAR	4.946	88	0	0.0051033	0.0030527	0.0071539

also much smaller than their counterparts in the United States, where the target firms can earn up to 20 to 30 percent (figure 7.11 and figure 7.12).

The other possible deciding factor for the different M&A performances in 2004 and 2005 may be the aggregate market performance. While the market in 2004 had a downward trend over the whole period, the market in 2005 witnessed both a depressed market (before June 3) and an upbeat market. As a possible channel to discern the different M&A performances between 2004 and 2005, we separate our 2005 sample into a period with downward index and another with upward index (figure 7.13 and figure 7.14). We find that merger activities increase a company's value both in a depressed market (CAR at $t = 40$ is 3.19 percent) and in an upbeat market (CAR at $t = 40$ is 0.78 percent). Because we use the CAPM as the benchmark to compute excess returns, this demonstrates that after correcting market conditions, M&A events had positive returns in both depressed and upbeat markets in 2005. It is different from the performance of 2004, when M&A activities produced negative returns in a depressed market.

Because the period with upward trend coincided with the early phase of reforming the dual-track equity system, our results (from figure 7.13 and figure 7.14) may demonstrate that the reform itself did not have a direct impact on M&A performance. However, the reform might have indirect and lasting influences on the improvement of efficiency in China's stock market.

Besides using the event period $(-49,40)$, we also tried different windows such as $(-24,20)$ and $(-12,10)$. We also tried to set the preannouncement period to $(t_0, t_1 - 5)$, allowing the possibility of leak of information before announcement. However, the results are quite similar, and we omit them in this version of the paper.

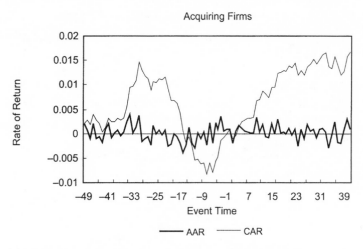

Fig. 7.11   CAR of acquiring firms (average CAR = 0.641%), 2005

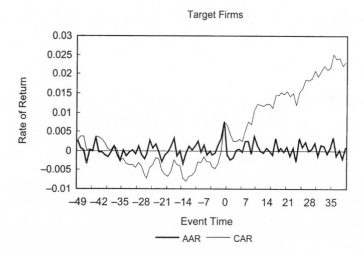

Fig. 7.12   CAR of target firms (average CAR = 0.508%), 2005

We can conclude this section by noting that the event-study method produces some rather interesting results for the valuation of merger activities in China. We found that the M&A activities produced negative returns in 2004, but positive, although small, returns in 2005. Although China's stock market may not have reached the level of efficiency in advanced economies, our preliminary investigation demonstrates that its efficiency has been improved from 2004 to 2005. This chapter also shows that stock market valuation of all merger activities in China is mildly positive in 2005, which may also help to enhance the allocative role of China's stock market in the future.

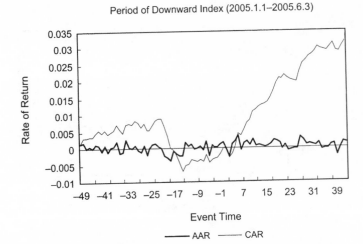

Fig. 7.13   **Period of downward index (average CAR = 0.963%), 2005**

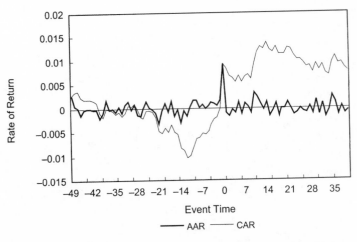

Fig. 7.14   **Period of upward index (average CAR = 0.312%), 2005**

7.4   Accounting Indicators Before and After Mergers

In this section, we study the financial conditions of merging firms. Because the returns on M&A events in 2004 are negative, we only concentrate on verifying whether financial conditions also improve for the M&A events with positive returns in 2005. We collect accounting information from 2002 to 2006 for the 587 firms involved in the M&A activities in 2005. First, we obtain EPS, earning before interest and taxes (EBIT) per share, and cash flow per share of all firms we studied in the last section. From table 7.14 and

Table 7.14   Earnings per share (EPS), EBIT, cash flow per share, 2002–2006

	2002	2003	2004	2005	2006
EPS	0.161864	0.13994	0.13541	0.09876	0.153206
EBIT per share	0.291789	0.284257	0.291105	0.267955	0.329258
Cash flow per share	0.073534	0.043986	0.040717	−0.01556	0.027136

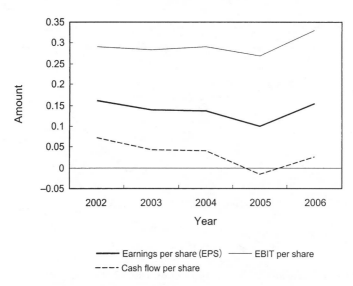

Fig. 7.15   Accounting information (per share) for all merging firms

figure 7.15, we can see clearly that all three indicators decline in 2005, the year of the merger, and improve in 2006, the year after the merger. The growth rates of the last two years are –27 percent and 55 percent for EPS, –8 percent and 23 percent for EBIT per share, and –138 percent and 270 percent for cash flow per share. These three indicators demonstrate a consistent pattern before, during, and after the merger.

Next, we study the earning ability of these firms, which forms the basis of a firm's strong financial condition. From table 7.15 and figure 7.16, we can find that EBIT increases over the whole period but ROE and ROA both decrease in 2005 and then improve in 2006. The growth rates for the last two years are –71 percent and 273 percent for ROE and –14 percent and 25 percent for ROA. In contrast to the findings in the U.S. market, our results show a clear pattern for the 587 firms combined together.

The ability to service debt is another way to measure the firm's financial conditions. We first study the current ratio, which is current asset (cash, cash equivalent, accounts receivable, and inventory) divided by current liability (short-term loans and accounts payable). Because inventory is not

Table 7.15   **Earning ability, 2002–2006**

	2002	2003	2004	2005	2006
EBIT (billion RMB)	0.214956	0.253167	0.331346	0.368624	0.447996
Return of equity	4.769542	4.070747	3.650489	1.049658	3.917524
Return of assets	4.943371	4.563602	4.337534	3.726122	4.671156

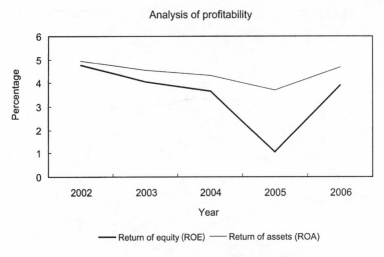

Fig. 7.16   Earning ability of all merging firms, 2002–2006

easy to convert into cash, the quick ratio, which does not include inventory in the numerator, is also computed for our data set. These two ratios measure the firm's ability to repay short-term debt.

The normal range of the current ratio is within 0.5 to 2.0. For our 587 firms, their average is within the safe range, but it clearly declines over time. The quick ratio should have its ideal range around 1. We can see that the average of quick ratio fell below 1 after the merger in 2005. Both ratios of these merging firms clearly become worse after 2005. So the short-term ability of these merging firms to repay debt has declined after the merger (see table 7.16).

We use the liability to equity ratio and the equity multiplier to represent the long-term ability to repay debt. As the liability to equity ratio increases, the ability to repay debt has declined, as shown in figure 7.17, before and after the merger. In the mean time, as the equity multiplier, which is defined to be the ratio of asset to equity, rises in the firm's reliance on debt has also increased (figure 7.18).

Before closing this section, we present the cash flows of these firms over

Table 7.16	Ability to repay debt, 2002–2006				
	2002	2003	2004	2005	2006
Liability to equity ratio	44.8117	47.34732	50.01123	52.28126	52.64088
Current ratio	1.632192	1.525752	1.427801	1.333356	1.32292
Quick ratio	1.240658	1.123622	1.021103	0.933706	0.889238
Equity multiplier	2.0863	2.151938	2.229744	2.466456	2.89927

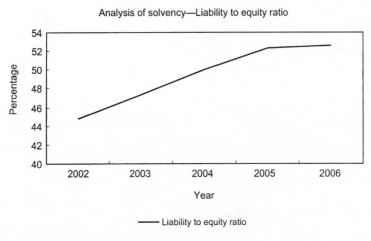

Fig. 7.17   Liability equity ratios

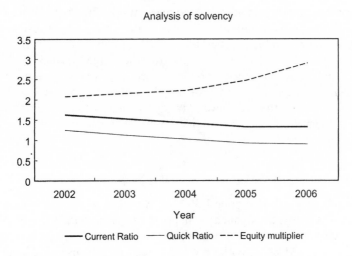

Fig. 7.18   Ability to repay debt

Table 7.17   Cash flows, 2002–2006 (100 million RMB)

	2002	2003	2004	2005	2006
Operating cash flow	3.244178	3.807216	4.599242	5.102536	5.91053
Free cash flow of firm	0.373923	0.417455	−0.25308	0.549061	0.815731

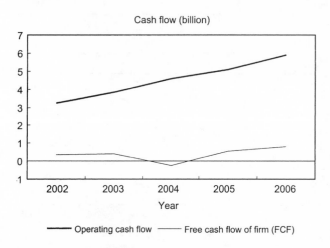

Cash flow (billion)

——— Operating cash flow   ——— Free cash flow of firm (FCF)

Fig. 7.19   Cash flows, 2002–2006

the four-year horizon. Both operating cash flows (OCF), which is EBIT plus depreciation minus taxes, and free cash flows (FCF), which is OCF minus any expenditures necessary to maintain the firm's operating assets, measure the firm's profitability before or after deducting investment expenditures. From table 7.17 and figure 7.19, we can see that the profitability of the merging firms has improved after the merger in 2005.

By using the accounting method in this section, we can conclude that the financial conditions of the M&A firms showed a certain degree of decline in the first year of the M&A event, but improve in the next year. However, the short-term and long-term ability to repay debt declined without a clear sign of improvement after the merger.

7.5   Concluding Remarks

In this chapter, we examine 1,363 M&A events involving 1,086 companies traded on the Shanghai and Shenzhen stock exchanges from 2004 to 2005. Our event-study analysis indicates that within the event period (–50 days, 40 days), M&A activities produced negative returns in 2004, but positive, although small, returns in 2005. For the 2004 data with negative returns in aggregate, we discover that M&A activities controlled by state holding companies were responsible for producing those negative returns, while the M&A events initiated by privately owned enterprises had positive returns. For the 2005 data with positive returns in aggregate, both types of M&A activities produced positive but small returns.

We also separate the 2005 data into acquiring and target firms and discover that the acquiring firms and target firms received, respectively, 1.68 percent and 2.03 percent in China, while the target firms often received over 20 percent of returns in the U.S. market. In addition, we found that the M&A companies' industries and the market's aggregate performance did not have significant impacts on the returns of M&A events.

Our results may demonstrate that China's stock market might not have reached the level of efficiency of the more-advanced economies, but its efficiency in assessing the value of M&A activities might have been improved from 2004 to 2005. The stock market valuation of M&A events became mildly positive in 2005, which may help to enhance the allocative role of China's stock market in the future.

Analyzing accounting indicators within a longer observation period (four years), we also discover that the financial conditions of companies involved in M&A in 2005 showed a certain degree of decline in the first year of the M&A event, but an obvious improvement in the following year. However, the short-term and long-term ability to repay debt declined without a clear sign of improvement after the merger.

This chapter serves as a pioneering study for China's M&A activities. There are many interesting phenomena discovered in this preliminary study. However, precise measurements and more studies with control groups to disaggregate the total effects should be included in the future work. As China's stock market grows rapidly with fundamental institutional changes, more in-depth studies will help us to understand how this major market functions in transition.

References

Agrawal, A., J. F. Jaffe, and G. N. Mandelker. 1992. The post-merger performance of acquiring firms: A re-examination of an anomaly. *Journal of Finance* 47:1605–21.

Bris, A., and C. Cabolis. 2003. Adopting better corporate governance: Evidence from cross-border mergers. Paper presented at European Finance Association conference. Glasgow, Scotland.

Brown, S. J., and J. B. Warner. 1985. Using daily stock returns: The case of event studies. *Journal of Financial Economics* 14:3–31.

Bruner, R. 2002. Does M&A pay? A survey of evidence for the decision-maker. *Journal of Applied Finance* 12:48–68.

Clark, K., and E. Ofek. 1994. Mergers as a means of restructuring distressed firms: An empirical investigation. *Journal of Financial and Quantitative Analysis* 29 (4): 541–65.

Datta, D. K., G. E. Pinches, and V. K. Narayanan. 1992. Factors influencing wealth creation from mergers and acquisitions: A meta-analysis. *Strategic Management Journal* 13:67–86.

Dodd, P., and R. Ruback. 1977. Tender offers and stockholder returns: An empirical analysis. *Journal of Financial Economics* 5:351–74.

Gillan, S. L., J. W. Kensinger, and J. D. Martin. 2000. Value creation and corporate diversification: The case of Sears, Roebuck & Co. *Journal of Financial Economics* 55:103–37.

Healy, P. M., K. G. Palepu, and R. S. Ruback. 1992. Does corporate performance improve after mergers? *Journal of Financial Economics* 31:135–75.

Jarrell, G. A., J. A. Brickley, and J. M. Netter. 1988. The market for corporate control: The empirical evidence since 1980. *Journal of Economic Perspectives* 2 (1): 49–68.

Jensen, M. C., and R. S. Ruback. 1983. The market for corporate control: The scientific evidence. *Journal of Financial Economics* 11:5–50.

Leeth, J. D., and J. R. Borg. 2000. The impact of takeovers on shareholder wealth during the 1920's merger wave. *Journal of Financial and Quantitative Analysis* 35 (2): 217–38.

Meeks, G. 1977. *Disappointing marriage: A study of the gains from merger.* Cambridge, UK: Cambridge University Press.

Mueller, D. 1980. *The determinants and effects of mergers: An international comparison.* Cambridge, MA: Oelgeschlager, Gunn & Hain.

Murlherin, J. H., and A. L. Boone. 2000. Comparing acquisitions and divestitures. *Journal of Corporate Finance* 6:117–39.

Schwert, G. W. 1996. Markup pricing in mergers and acquisitions. *Journal of Financial Economics* 41:153–62.

Comment   Kaoru Hosono

Using merger and acquisition (M&A) events involving listed companies in China during the 2004 to 2005 period, the author found the following facts:

1. The cumulative abnormal return (CAR) of the M&A firms was significantly negative in 2004, while it was significantly positive in 2005.

2. In 2004, M&A activities initiated by state-owned companies had negative returns, while those done by privately owned companies had positive returns. In 2005, both types of companies had positive returns from M&As.

3. In 2005, the CARs of acquiring and target firms were both significantly positive, though small.

4. For the companies involved in 2005 M&A events, return on assets (ROA) and other financial conditions showed a decline in the year of M&A, but recovered in the following year. On the other hand, leverage increased after M&A.

Kaoru Hosono is a professor of economics at Gakushuin University.

To my knowledge, this is the first paper that has ever analyzed M&As implemented by Chinese firms. In general, event studies using abnormal stock returns have the merit of using forward-looking measures but require assumptions of stock markets' efficiency. Accounting studies using financial statements have the merit of using credible (audited) statements but have the drawbacks of backward-looking properties. Given these strengths and weaknesses of the two approaches, it is good to do both, as the author does in this chapter. In addition, we can check whether stock market reactions are consistent with the following financial performances.

I have several comments that I expect to improve this chapter.

First, background information concerning M&As in China may be useful to readers outside China. In particular, information on the types of M&As that are most popular in China would be useful: mergers versus tender offers, focused versus diversified (like conglomerates), paying with stock versus cash, domestic versus cross-border. Experiences of the United States show that tender offers, focused M&As, and paying with cash are more likely to create values (Bruner 2002). In Japan, out-in cross-border mergers are found to be more likely to improve productivity (Fukao et al. 2006). Information on regulations and restrictions imposed on M&As would also be useful to understand the results.

Second, analyses of accounting indicators can be improved in several ways. Most important, the author does not control for macroeconomic or industrial shocks to the profitability and other financial conditions. It might be better to subtract off the industrial (or market) average from the financial ratios of the consolidating firms. In addition, the author looks at the simple average of merging firms without taking into consideration the differences in sizes of acquiring and target firms. It might be better to use weighted average of acquirers and targets in the premerger period. Finally, the author shows only the average values of accounting ratios over time. It would be useful to test statistically whether postmerger accounting ratios change significantly as compared with the premerger values.

Third, the author can elaborate why the stock price responses to M&A announcements are small in China relative to the U.S. stock market responses. The U.S. evidences show that target shareholders receive average abnormal returns in the 20 to 30 percent range, while the estimates of bidder shareholders' returns are negligible or mixed (Bruner 2002). On the other hand, this chapter shows that the CARs for acquiring firms and target firms were 1.68 percent and 2.03 percent, respectively. Why is the CAR for target firms so small and that for acquiring firms significant in China? The differences of the types of M&As, regulations on M&As, or the efficiency of stock market between the United States and China may help explain the differences in the CARs.

Fourth, the author can clarify what hypothesis the event study tests in this chapter. Usually, event studies using stock prices test whether events (e.g., M&As) increase firm value based on the assumption that the stock market is efficient. On the other hand, in this chapter, the author says in the conclusion, "Our results may demonstrate that China's stock market might not have reached the level of efficiency of the more-advanced economies, but its efficiency in assessing the value of M&A activities might have been improved from 2004 to 2005." Does this chapter test whether China's stock market is efficient given that M&As increase economic values?

Finally, the author may want to test formally whether the differences of CARs by ownership structures and by stock market's boom-and-bust periods are statistically significant.

In sum, this chapter tackles a very challenging and important topic that no one else has ever investigated: the stock market responses to M&A announcements in China. Further improvements of analytical methods and the interpretations of the results based on Chinese regulations and practices will make this chapter more valuable to all that are interested in the functioning of emerging markets.

References

Bruner, R. 2002. Does M&A pay? A survey of evidence for the decision-maker. *Journal of Applied Finance* 12:48–68.
Fukao, K., K. Ito, H. U. Kwon, and M. Takizawa. 2006. Cross-border acquisitions and target firms' performance: Evidence from Japanese firm-level data. NBER Working Paper no. 12422. Cambridge, MA: National Bureau of Economic Research.

Comment   Julian Wright

Let me first provide some additional context and background to the chapter. The research question addressed by this chapter is quite simply "do mergers create or destroy value?" This is an important question for finance, industrial organization, and antitrust. There is a large literature that has looked at the question using data mainly from the United States but also from some other developed countries. The literature adopts two main approaches. One is to measure the abnormal stock return associated with merger announcements, and the other is to look at the change in accounting earnings following merger announcements.

The consensus from this literature is that the abnormal stock return to acquiring firms is not significantly different from zero, the abnormal stock return to target firms is significantly positive, and that the combined ab-

Julian Wright is an associate professor of economics at the National University of Singapore.

normal return is about 2 percent of the total initial value. This 2 percent estimate is probably downward biased. Any equity financed merger involves two events—a merger and an equity issue. The latter may have a negative effect on stock returns for standard reasons, including that it may reveal negative information about the value of the acquirer. For example, an acquirer may use equity financing when it expects lower growth than the market does. Thus, cash- or debt-based mergers should reveal higher returns to acquirers. More generally, the fact a firm wishes to acquire another reveals some information about the acquirer (perhaps that it has few options to grow organically), and so the stock returns associated with the merger announcement will partly reflect this release of information.

So what are the innovations of this chapter? Put simply, the innovation is that this is the first study of mergers using Chinese data. Specifically, the author uses Chinese data from 2005, looking at 752 M&A events involving 587 companies.

Why is this interesting? One possible reason is the lack of formal antitrust law against mergers in China. Antitrust laws that make anticompetitive mergers illegal exist in the other countries that have been used to consider whether mergers increase firm value. This is potentially important because these laws mean the most profitable mergers are likely to be blocked. The absence of laws against anticompetitive mergers mean mergers in China could be substantially more profitable. A second reason this is interesting is that in China a large number of mergers involve public ownership, with 503 mergers involving state holding companies as the controlling shareholders (211 involved privately owned enterprises as the controlling shareholder). Because the government may have different objectives (such as bailing out failing firms) and may have more bargaining power with respect to private firms, this could also mean mergers have different implications for value creation in China.

So what are the main findings of the chapter? Compared to evidence from the existing literature, the combined return to mergers is surprisingly similar. What is more interesting is that the authors find the acquirers obtain a significantly positive abnormal return and that this is about equal to the target firm return. Recall this is in contrast with the United States and other countries, where the existing literature finds the entire positive return from mergers is generated from the return to the target firm.

If this difference in findings remains robust to considering a longer sample of Chinese mergers, it naturally raises the question of why acquiring firms do so much better in China compared to other countries. A possible answer is that in China, many acquiring firms are state firms, and they may have greater bargaining power, thereby extracting more of the surplus than would otherwise be the case. This could be tested by breaking up the results on abnormal returns to acquirers into private and state-controlled acquirers. Here the author finds that state controlled mergers have a slightly higher abnormal return, but they do not break this up into acquirer and target firm returns. More generally, an interesting avenue for investigation is to explore the role of bargaining between acquirers and target firms. Does competition between acquirers or market position of the acquirer play a role? This could be addressed empirically, not just for this Chinese data set, but more generally.

There are, of course, several strong assumptions that are needed for the results of the stock market valuation approach to be valid. One always worries the market cannot efficiently calculate the change in value of firms as a result of a merger. If there is any bias in the market's perceptions of mergers, this will be directly reflected in the calculated abnormal returns. I mention this because at present, there are particular concerns about the rationality of the Chinese stock market. The alternative is to use the accounting methodology instead, but this raises more serious problems in my view—are the accounts reliable in China and are they comparable pre- and post-merger? Typically researchers do not put much weight on this accounting approach due to the large measurement errors involved, especially because a merger involves the firms merging their accounts. This measurement error problem is likely to be even more acute in China.

I have more serious concerns about the specific application of the accounting methodology in the chapter. The author compares whether earnings per share (and other accounting measures) increase in 2006 compared to 2005 for the 587 firms merging in 2005. This is meaningless unless there is some counterfactual of what earnings per share would otherwise have done in 2006. Otherwise, the increase in earnings per share after 2005 could well be an aggregate country-level effect. This indeed seems likely given the substantial rise in stock values in China since July 2005. Rather, in line with standard practice, the author should control for industry (or at the very least country-level) effects here.

Finally, I mention two important ways in which the chapter needs to be improved. For both accounting and stock return results, the author should follow the existing literature and break the results down into equity-based versus cash- debt-based transactions. As mentioned at the start, equity-based transactions involve an additional bias so that focusing on cash-debt-based transactions will give cleaner results. More critically, the author needs to extend the study to obtain more than one year of merger data. In doing so, the robustness of the results can be considered, and the analysis based on accounting indicators can be done properly.

8

Consolidation of Banks in Japan
Causes and Consequences

Kaoru Hosono, Koji Sakai, and Kotaro Tsuru

8.1 Introduction

Mergers and acquisitions (M&As) among financial institutions have been accelerating over the last two decades across the world. These waves of mergers and acquisitions in the banking industries raise important questions of whether mergers enhance the efficiency of surviving banks and contribute to the stabilization of the banking sector or just increase their market power in setting prices. A large number of studies attempt to resolve these questions by examining profitability, cost efficiency, and market performance of merger survivors. However, most of the existing studies examine the consolidation among the U.S. or European financial institutions, and little is known about the causes and consequences of financial consolidation outside the United States or Europe.

This chapter investigates the causes and consequences of the consolidation among Japanese banks. In Japan, a variety of banks have been consolidated since the 1990s when most banks suffered from a huge amount of nonperforming loans. The number of city banks, which operate nationwide and internationally, remained at thirteen during the 1980s but decreased almost by half to seven in 2005. While the number of first-tier regional banks, which operate in one or a few prefectures, virtually did not change over the last two decades (sixty-three in 1980 and sixty-four in 2005), the number of second-tier regional banks, which are smaller than first-tier regional banks

Kaoru Hosono is a professor of economics at Gakushuin University. Koji Sakai is a research fellow of the Japan Society for the Promotion of Science. Kotaro Tsuru is a senior fellow at the Research Institute of Economy, Trade, and Industry.
We appreciate valuable comments from Andy Rose, Taka Ito, Hiro Ito, Barry Williams, and other participants at the NBER-EASE eighteenth annual conference.

and operate mainly within a prefecture, decreased from seventy-one in 1980 to forty-eight in 2005. The number of cooperative (*shinkin*) banks, which are deposit-taking cooperatives operating within a prefecture and specializing in small- and medium-sized enterprise (SME) loans, also dropped from 462 in 1980 to 301 in 2005.[1]

Using a rich data set of bank M&As in Japan, this chapter comprehensively analyzes the causes and consequences of bank mergers in the following ways. First, we analyze motives of bank mergers as well as their consequences. Using ex-ante bank characteristics, we investigate what type of a bank was more likely to be a target or an acquirer. Looking at the postmerger performance of a consolidated bank, we examine the effects of mergers on cost efficiency, profitability, and healthiness. Though many preceding studies focus on profitability and cost efficiency, it would be important to examine whether bank consolidation improved bank healthiness, if regulatory authorities promote bank consolidation to stabilize the banking system. We measure long-run postmerger performance based on accounting ratios rather than stock market returns. Though market returns are relatively free from measurement errors associated with accounting ratios, analyzing them would severely reduce the sample size, given that a small number of regional banks and no *shinkin* bank are publicly traded. In addition, accounting ratios enable us to analyze important components of performance (e.g., cost efficiency or market power).[2] Finally, our observations are comprehensive. We use data of major banks (i.e., city banks, trust banks, and long-term credit banks, which operate nationwide and internationally) and regional banks (i.e., first-tier regional banks and second-tier regional banks) over the period of fiscal years 1990 to 2004, and data of *shinkin* banks over the period of fiscal years 1990 to 2002. Our sample universe accounts for more than 80 percent share of deposits in all the depository institutions in Japan.[3] During the period of fiscal years 1990 to 2004, there were ten mergers by major banks, nine mergers by regional banks, and

---

1. City banks and regional banks are both corporations licensed under Bank Law, while *shinkin* banks are cooperatives of small- and medium-sized enterprises (SMEs) licensed under Shinkin Bank Law. Regional banks are classified into first-tier and second-tier regional banks according to the associations they belong to. There are usually one relatively large first-tier regional bank and some relatively small second-tier regional banks in one prefecture.

2. We could analyze the impact of merger announcement on abnormal returns for the mergers of listed major banks (e.g., Okada 2005). However, it would still be difficult to analyze the long-run performance of stock returns even for the mergers of listed major banks because most of the consolidated major banking firms newly established holding companies that owned the share of other financial institutions (e.g., nonbanks, securities companies, and credit card companies). For the pitfalls of using short-run responses of stock market prices to merger announcement when mergers are a relatively new phenomenon, see Delong and DeYoung (2007).

3. As of March 2001, for example, the share of deposits at city banks, first-tier regional banks, second-tier regional banks, and *shinkin* banks are 29.2 percent, 25.5 percent, 8.2 percent, and 15.1 percent, respectively. Data source is the Bank of Japan Web site: http://www.boj.or.jp.

ninety-seven mergers and two transfers of business among *shinkin* banks, besides the mergers and transfer of business from failed banks.[4] The rest of the chapter is organized as follows. Section 8.2 briefly reviews the existing literature on bank mergers. Section 8.3 discusses the hypotheses on the motivations of bank mergers. Section 8.4 analyzes the M&A waves in Japan using aggregate data at the prefectural level. Section 8.5 describes our bank-level data set. Section 8.6 analyzes the motivation of bank mergers using premerger bank characteristics data. Section 8.7 presents the postmerger performance concerning profitability, market power, cost efficiency, healthiness, and portfolio. Section 8.8 concludes.

8.2   Literature Review

In the United States, a large number of commercial and savings banks were taken over by other depository institutions during the 1980s, especially after restrictions on intrastate and interstate banking were removed by the Riegle-Neal Interstate Banking and Branching Efficiency Act of 1994. Recently, financial conglomerates have emerged through a series of M&As after restrictions on securities and insurance businesses by banks were lifted by the Gramm-Leach-Bliley Financial Service Modernization Act. In Europe, the emergence of the European Union in 1999 spurred consolidation of the financial services industry. In the crisis-hit Asian countries, foreign capital entry into the banking industry and government recapitalization promoted bank consolidation. These merger waves generated a vast literature on bank M&As, especially for U.S. and European banks.

Berger, Demsetz, and Strahan (1999) review existing research concerning the causes and consequences of the consolidation of the financial services industry. They point out that the evidence is consistent with increases in market power, especially in the case of consolidation within the same market (in-market M&As); improvements in profit efficiency, and diversification of risks, but little or no cost efficiency improvement on average; and potential costs to the financial system from increases in systemic risk or expansion of the financial safety net.

As for the consolidation of banks in Japan, Okada (2005) studied ten megamergers among city banks during 1989 to 2000 and found that no improvement in X-inefficiency was observed but increases in cumulative excess stock returns and decreases in perceived default probability were found. Her results suggest that the motivation of megamergers was not to improve efficiency but to take advantage of the government's too-big-to-fail policy. Yamori, Harimaya, and Kondo (2003) studied financial holding

---

4. No merger was conducted across different types of banks during the sample period, and there was one sale of business of a failed bank across bank types: the business of the failed city bank, Hokkaido Takushoku Bank, was sold to a regional bank, Hokuyo Bank, and a trust bank, Chuo Trust Bank, in 1997.

companies of regional banks and found that profit efficiency tended to increase when the market share in the region increased. Hosono, Sakai, and Tsuru (2006) analyzed the motives and consequences of credit corporative (*shinkin*) banks during the period of 1984 to 2002.[5] Their major findings are as follows. First, less profitable and cost efficient banks were more likely to be an acquirer and a target. Second, acquiring banks improved cost efficiency but still deteriorated their capital-to-asset ratio after consolidation. Finally, the consolidation of *shinkin* banks tended to improve profitability when the difference in the ex-ante profitability between acquiring banks and target banks were large. This chapter extends Hosono, Sakai, and Tsuru (2006) to cover most Japanese banks, including city banks, first-tier regional banks, second-tier regional banks, and *shinkin* banks. Compared with the preceding studies on the consolidation of Japanese banks, this chapter comprehensively analyzes the causes and consequences of bank mergers, as we mention in the introduction.

8.3   Hypotheses on the Motives of Bank Consolidation

This section reviews four major hypotheses on the motives of bank consolidation.

8.3.1   Improving Efficiency

As Berger, Demsetz, and Strahan (1999) point out, the primary motive for consolidation would be maximizing the value of shares owned by existing shareholders. Banks can maximize value either by increasing their efficiency or by increasing their market power in setting prices. Cost efficiency will be improved if an efficient bank spreads its superior managerial skills to an inefficient bank by acquiring the latter. Profitability will be enhanced by superior risk management.

The efficiency improvement hypothesis suggests that an efficient bank tends to acquire or purchase the business of an inefficient bank.

8.3.2   Strengthening Market Power

Market power can be strengthened if two or more banks operating in the same market are consolidated and, consequently, the market becomes more concentrated. Existing evidences from the U.S. bank M&As suggest that in-market M&As, that is, M&As of banks operating in the same market, may increase market power in setting prices.

According to this hypothesis, banks operating in the same region are more likely to be consolidated. Actually, most of the M&As among regional banks were conducted by banks operating in the same prefecture. Although all of the M&As among corporative (*shinkin*) banks were also conducted by

---

5. See also Yamori and Harimaya (2004) for the study of the mergers of *shinkin* banks.

banks operating in the same prefecture, this fact does not necessarily imply the market power motive but may simply reflect the regulatory restriction under which *shinkin* banks are allowed to operate only in a region that is usually defined within a prefecture.

8.3.3   Taking Advantage of a Too-Big-to-Fail Policy

The government policy directly or indirectly affects banks' M&A decisions. In particular, if regulatory authorities are expected to pursue a too-big-to-fail policy, weak banks have a strong incentive to be consolidated with each other because bank managers may want to keep their positions. Bank shareholders can also gain from the value of deposit insurance by surviving through mergers.

The government can promote bank consolidations among weak banks in some ways. First, the government can "arrange" consolidations, persuading (or sometimes forcing) relatively healthy banks to acquire unhealthy banks. Second, the government can give weak banks incentives to be consolidated with each other by establishing a scheme for recapitalizing consolidated banks.

In Japan, the government's "arrangements" were sometimes used before the 1980s when the financial markets were heavily regulated, and even in the first half of the 1990s, as is known as the "convoy system" (see the next section for details). The "market-based" consolidation through public money injection has become an alternative tool since 1998 when the banking crisis culminated and the government first recapitalized banks. When Japanese authorities recapitalized banks first in 1998, they did so toward major banks and the two largest regional banks. This fact may have fostered banks' anticipation for bailouts as long as they were large. Not only a large bank that operates nationwide, regional banks and corporative (*shinkin*) banks that are relatively large in a prefecture may also have anticipated bailouts because the Japanese regulatory authorities have often worried about the stability of regional financial systems, though the notion of a regional systemic risk had not been stipulated until the Deposit Insurance Act was revised in 2001 (Article 102).[6]

If the government's anticipated too-big-to-fail policy and local market stabilization policy affect the decision of M&As, unhealthy banks or banks recapitalized by the government tend to be consolidated with each other.

---

6. For example, when the largest regional bank in Tochigi Prefecture, Ashikaga Bank, was failing, the government temporarily nationalized it to avoid a regional systemic risk. Though the government has not recapitalized *shinkin* banks so far, this does not necessarily mean that the government does not care about the stability of the local financial market. It has not been necessary for the government to recapitalize *shinkin* banks because the central financial institution of *shinkin* banks, called Central Shinkin Bank, recapitalized member *shinkin* banks when necessary.

8.3.4   Managerial Empire Building

When corporate governance structures are weak, managers may be willing to acquire other banks for the purpose of empire building. They may gain personal financial and nonfinancial gains from consolidated institutions. Managerial hubris may also drive bank mergers (Bliss and Rosen 2001).

Weak governance structures allow managers to spend on activities with scope for generating managerial private benefits, such as advertisement or entertainment expenditures (Yafeh and Yosha 2003). Therefore, we may expect that banks that spend more on advertisement or entertainment tend to acquire other banks. In addition, if the managerial empire building motive drives M&As, then a consolidated bank cannot realize efficiency gains and is not willing to downsize or restructure the business. Managers of consolidated banks may increase advertisement expenditures for their private benefits.

8.4   Bank Merger Wave in Japan

8.4.1   Overview

A very small number of mergers occurred in the banking industry until the 1980s after World War II in Japan. The number of city banks, which operate nationwide and internationally, had been thirteen until 1990.[7] Mergers among regional banks, which operate mainly within a prefecture, also had been rare until the 1990s. Only one mutual bank (former second-tier regional bank) was acquired in the 1970s, and two mutual banks were acquired in the 1980s.[8] Mergers among credit corporative banks (*shinkin*) did not occur frequently, either. A small number of mergers until the 1980s reflected the government's so-called convoy system policy.[9] Under this policy, the regulatory authorities tried to stabilize the banking system by restricting competition among banks and bailing out failing banks. The government restricted banks' opening new branches and prohibited banks from engaging in securities business to control competition. When a weak bank fell into financial distress, the government requested a healthy bank to rescue the weak bank by injecting capital and sending directors. Healthy banks responded to the government's request because they could obtain the branch networks of the failing banks. Until the 1980s, M&As in the banking industry occurred only when the government requested healthy banks to acquire failing banks.

---

7. Mitsui Bank acquired Taiyo Kobe in 1990.

8. Hirosaki Sogo Bank was acquired by Seiwa Bank in 1976. Takachiho Sogo Bank was acquired by Nishinippon Sogo Bank in 1984. Heiwa Sogo Bank was acquired by Sumitomo Bank in 1986.

9. For the details of the convoy system, see Hoshi and Kashyap (2001). For a typical example, the Ministry of Finance asked Sumitomo Bank to acquire the failing Heiwa Sogo Bank, and Sumitomo responded to it so as to obtain the branch network of Heiwa Sogo.

Table 8.1   Number of banks and number of mergers and acquisitions

	Major banks			Regional banks			*Shinkin* banks		
	Total	Merger	Sale of business	Total	Merger	Sale of business	Total	Merger	Sale of business
1990	22	1	0	132	0	0	451	3	0
1991	21	1	0	132	1	0	440	3	0
1992	21	0	0	130	1	1 (1)	435	4	0
1993	21	0	0	129	1	0	428	5	0
1994	21	0	0	129	0	0	421	8	0
1995	21	0	0	129	0	1 (1)	416	4	0
1996	20	1	0	128	0	0	410	5	1
1997	19	0	1 (1)	126	0	1 (1)	401	8	0
1998	19	0	0	124	0	3 (3)	396	3	0
1999	19	0	0	123	0	1 (1)	386	5 (1)	1 (1)
2000	18	1	0	119	1	1 (1)	371	7 (2)	9 (8)
2001	15	3	0	117	0	0	349	11 (2)	5 (5)
2002	13	3	0	116	0	0	326	15	6 (6)
2003	13	0	0	110	2	0	306	14	0
2004	13	0	0	107	3	0	298	7	0
Total	276	10	1 (1)	1,851	9	8 (8)	5,834	102 (5)	22 (20)

Notes: Major banks include city banks, long-term credit banks, and trust banks. Regional banks include first-tier regional banks and second-tier regional banks. The numbers in the parentheses denote the numbers of mergers or acquisitions of the business of a failed bank. No merger was implemented across bank type during the sample period, and one sales of business of a failed bank was conducted across bank types (in the case of the failure of a major bank, Hokkaido Takushoku Bank in 1997).

As financial liberalization made progress in the 1980s, the regulatory authorities found it more and more difficult to maintain the convoy system; healthy banks had little incentive or capability to rescue failing banks. In the early 1990s, stock prices and land prices fell sharply, which hit hard banks' asset quality. Risk-based capital requirements based on the Basel capital standards, introduced in fiscal year 1992, spurred consolidation of weak banks. Two mergers among city banks and three mergers among regional banks occurred in the first half of the 1990s (table 8.1).[10] Mergers among *shinkin* banks also occurred more frequently in the 1990s than before. Despite the introduction of the Basel capital standards, which were supposed to be rule-based regulations, financial regulations and supervisions by the Ministry of Finance were still affected by political pressure until a banking crisis occurred in 1997.[11]

A banking crisis occurred in 1997, when three large financial institu-

10. Taiyo Kobe Bank was acquired by Mitsui Bank in 1990, and Saitama Bank was acquired by Kyowa Bank in 1991.
11. The government's resolutions of the failed "Jusen," nonbank finance companies that specialized in housing and real estate loans, were severely criticized by the public to the extent that the government rescued agricultural cooperatives that had invested in Jusen and had a strong political influence (see Hoshi and Kashyap 2001).

tions, including a city bank named Hokkaido Takushoku Bank, failed. In 1998, two long-term credit banks named the Long-Term Credit Bank of Japan and the Nippon Credit Bank failed. In response to the severe banking crisis, the Japanese regulatory authorities introduced prompt corrective actions in 1998, applied stringent accounting standards in implementing the Basel capital standards, and recapitalized banks to promote their restructuring. The Financial Supervision Agency (FSA) was built and took over financial supervisions from the Ministry of Finance in 1998. The FSA refrained from "arranging" mergers, not intervening in bank mergers to rescue weak banks.

Major banks tried to survive through mergers, resulting in the merger wave in the early 2000s. The Financial Rehabilitation Plan, released by Takenaka, Minister of Financial Services Agency, in October 2002, forced major banks to apply strict accounting standards and to reduce their nonperforming loan share to a half, urging weak banks to be consolidated.

Seven mergers among major banks occurred from fiscal year 2000 to fiscal year 2002. Megabanks are now reorganized into three groups (Mizuho, Mitsui-Sumitomo, and Mitsubishi-UFJ). The government also promoted consolidation of regional banks and *shinkin* banks. New legislation has enabled the government to recapitalize a consolidated bank since 2002.[12] Six mergers among regional banks occurred from fiscal year 2000 to fiscal year 2004. Mergers among *shinkin* banks also accelerated in the early 2000s (table 8.1).

8.4.2   Empirical Analysis

We first investigate the reasons for the recent merger wave using the M&A ratios, that is, the numbers of M&As divided by the total number of banks existing in the previous year, sorted by prefectures and bank types. The hypotheses concerning the motives of bank mergers discussed in section 8.3 have some implications concerning the time when and the space where M&A waves occur.

First, if M&As are driven by the motivation for improving efficiency, then merger waves result from shocks to an industry's economic, technological, or regulatory environment (e.g., Mitchell and Mulherin 1996). These shocks lead to industry reorganization. Analyzing the U.S. industrial merger waves in the 1980s and the 1990s, Harford (2005) found that operational performances measured by return on assets (ROA), sales growth, and others, were high prior to merger waves. He also found that higher market valuations relaxed financing constraints and made it easier

---

12. The Special Measures Law for the Promotion of Financial Institutions Reorganization was enacted in October, 2002. Under this law, the government recapitalized Kanto Tsukuba Bank in September 2003. The Financial Function Reinforcement Law was enacted in April 2004 to enable the government to preemptively capitalize healthy regional and *shinkin* banks. Under this law, Kiyo Holdings and Howa Bank were recapitalized in 2006.

to implement efficiency-driven M&As.[13] Following Harford (2005), we use the average ROA for each bank type to capture the economic shocks to the industry's operating environment and the stock price index for the banking industry to capture the degree of financial constraints.

Second, if M&As are driven by the motivation for strengthening market power, banks operating in a less-concentrated and more competitive market are more willing to merge each other. Given that banks often compete within a region, we use the Herfindahl index for the deposits of regional banks and *shinkin* banks calculated for each prefecture.[14]

Third, if M&As are driven by the motivation for taking advantage of a too-big-to-fail policy or a local market stabilization policy, then merger waves occur when the overall bank health is deteriorated. To capture the bank healthiness, we use the average capital-to-asset ratio for each bank type. The change in the stock price index for the banking industry also serves as a proxy for bank healthiness. Unlike the efficiency-motive hypothesis, the hypothesis concerning a too-big-to-fail policy suggests that a lower stock price triggers a bank merger. A low ROA may also lead to a merger under the too-big-to-fail-policy hypothesis because a low ROA deteriorates bank health.

Finally, if M&As are driven by the managerial motives for private benefits, then M&As are more likely to occur when and where the average expenditures for managerial private benefits such as advertisement expenditures or entertainment expenditures are high. While major banks and regional banks disclose advertisement expenditures, *shinkin* banks do not disclose the components of operational costs such as advertisement expenditures. Therefore, we cannot test the managerial motives hypothesis using the prefecture-level data here.

To control for regional shocks that affect banks' operating environment, financial constraints for M&As, and bank healthiness, we add the growth rate of prefectural gross domestic product (GDP) to the explanatory variables.[15] We also include a time dummy that takes the value of unity in and after fiscal year 1998 and zero before fiscal year 1997 to capture the regulatory changes stated in the previous section. The estimation period is from fiscal year 1990 to fiscal year 2004.

We estimate the following equation.

---

13. Shleifer and Vishny (2003) argue that stock market overvaluation promotes corporate managers to acquire relatively undervalued firms. This "behavioral" hypothesis also suggests that higher share prices cause merger waves. However, most of bank mergers in Japan have not been carried out through tender offers (take-over-bids) paying with stocks. So we do not discuss the possibility of the behavioral hypothesis in detail in this paper. For the empirical evidences of the "neoclassical" and "behavioral" hypothesis applied to Japanese nonfinancial firms, see Arikawa and Miyajima (2007).

14. For the empirical evidences in Japan, see, for example, Kano and Tsutsui (2003).

15. Major banks had head offices in Tokyo, Nagoya, Sapporo, or Osaka.

(1)   M&A Ratio$_{i,j,t}$ = β_1 Average Performance$_{i,j,t-1}$
       + β_3 Herfindahl Index$_{i,t-1}$ + β_4 GDPGrowth$_{i,t-1}$
       + β_5 PostCrisisDummy$_t$ + β_6 PostCrisisDummy$_t$
       * Average Performance$_{i,j,t-1}$ + $\varepsilon_{i,j,t}$,

where indexes i, j, t, are a prefecture, a bank type, and a fiscal year, respectively. Average Performance is either the average ROA, the average capital-to-asset ratio calculated for each prefecture, or the change in the stock price index for the banking industry. We do not enter those three variables at a time because they are highly correlated. The Herfindahl Index is calculated based on the shares of deposits of regional and *shinkin* banks in a prefecture. Gross domestic product growth is the growth rate of the GDP of the prefecture where the head office locates. Because GDP growth is highly correlated with the stock price index, we do not enter them at the same time. We allow for the change in the coefficients of the bank performance variables after the crisis using the interaction term of the postcrisis dummy and the performance variables.

Table 8.2 reports the pooled-ordinary least squares (OLS) regression estimates of equation (1). Though we also estimate the model with a fixed or random prefectural effect, we report the pooled-OLS model based on the specification tests. First, when the average ROA is included as a performance measure (column [1]), the coefficients on ROA and its interaction term with the postcrisis dummy are both negative, though neither is significant. This is not consistent with the efficiency-driven hypothesis. Next, looking at the case where the average capital-to-asset ratio is used (column [2]), we see that the coefficients on the capital-to-asset ratio and its interaction term with the postcrisis dummy are both negative, though only the interaction term is significant. Finally, using the stock price index yields the result (column [3]) that its coefficient is negative and significant, while its interaction term is positive but not significant. These results suggest that M&As tended to occur when the overall bank health was deteriorated, consistent with the too-big-to-fail or stabilization policy hypothesis. The coefficients on the Herfindahl index are negative and significant, regardless of the bank performance measures, suggesting that M&As tended to occur where the market was less concentrated, which is consistent with the market-power hypothesis. The coefficients on the GDP growth are significantly negative, which is again consistent with the too-big-to-fail or the financial stabilization policy hypothesis. Finally, the postcrisis dummy is positive and significant, suggesting that the regulatory changes triggered bank consolidations.

We will examine the relevance of the four hypotheses concerning the motives of M&As more closely using bank-level data in the following sections.

Table 8.2   Pooled OLS regression results for merger wave

	1985–2004		
	(1)	(2)	(3)
Return of assets (ROA)	−0.352		
	(0.628)		
Postcrisis Dummy • ROA	−0.586		
	(0.648)		
Capital-to-Asset Ratio		−0.022	
		(0.070)	
Postcrisis Dummy • Capital-to-Asset Ratio		−0.450***	
		(0.122)	
Industrial Stock Price			−0.008**
			(0.004)
Postcrisis Dummy • Industrial Stock Price			0.008
			(0.015)
Herfindahl Index	−1.625**	−1.509**	−2.077***
	(0.736)	(0.740)	(0.735)
GDP Growth	−0.099**	−0.109***	
	(0.040)	(0.040)	
Postcrisis Dummy	0.840***	3.214***	1.377***
	(0.324)	(0.641)	(0.365)
Cons	1.665***	1.668***	1.421***
	(0.362)	(0.453)	(0.313)
No. of observations	1,963	1,963	1,963
Adjusted R^2	0.039	0.034	0.022

Notes: The dependent variable is the numbers of mergers and acquisitions divided by the total number of banks. Pooled OLS regression results are reported. Standard errors are in parentheses.
***Significant at the 1 percent level.
**Significant at the 5 percent level.

8.5   Bank-Level Data

The data source of financial statements of major banks and regional banks is Nikkei Financial Quest and that of *shinkin* banks is *Financial Statements of Shinkin Banks in Japan,* edited by Financial Book Consultants, Ltd. (*Kinyu tosho konsarutanto sha*). We identify an acquirer if the bank is legally surviving and a target if the bank has legally disappeared. We focus on the M&As of surviving banks by excluding from our data set the transfers of business from a failed bank because the latter is likely to be conducted for different motives and to have different consequences.[16] Our

16. The transfer of business from a failed bank is identified if the deposit insurance made financial assistance (not recapitalization) to the bank that acquired or purchased the business of another bank.

data set covers the period of fiscal year 1990 to 2004 (i.e., from March 1991 to March 2005) for major and regional banks and fiscal year 1990 to 2002 (i.e., from March 1991 to March 2003) for *shinkin* banks. For the details of the variables we use, see the data appendix.

In Japan, financial holding companies were allowed to be built since 1998 when the Antimonopoly Act was revised. Some consolidated banks, especially major banks and large regional banks, took that opportunity to form a financial holding company that held insurance companies and non-bank financial companies as well since 2000. In the case of holding companies, we use the financial statements of the subsidiary banking companies. We do not use the stock prices of the financial holding companies because they reflect the performance of the other subsidiary companies as well. By using the financial statement of the subsidiary banking companies, we focus on the effects of mergers on the banking company. If there is a synergy effect from the security companies to the banking company within the same holding company, it is reflected by the financial statement of the banking company.

In the following analyses, we divide the sample banks into major banks (city banks, long-term credit banks, and trust banks), regional banks (first-tier regional banks and second-tier regional banks), and *shinkin* banks for the following reasons.[17] First, a *shinkin* bank is a cooperative depository institution specialized to small- and medium-sized enterprise (SME) finance. Therefore, the motives and consequences of M&As might be different from corporations like major banks and regional banks. Second, while major banks operate nationwide, regional banks and shinkin banks operate mainly within a prefecture. Most of the M&As among regional banks and *shinkin* banks were conducted by those banks that operated within the same prefecture (in-market merger).[18] The effects of mergers on market power might be different between major banks and regional or *shinkin* banks. Third, regulatory authorities' attitudes toward the nonperforming loan problems were different between major banks, on one hand, and regional and *shinkin* banks, on the other hand, in the late 1990s and the early 2000s. The government aimed at quickly reducing the nonperforming loans of major banks, while the government, afraid from the adverse effect of the write-off of nonperforming loans on SME finance, did not force regional and *shinkin* banks to reduce nonperforming loans quickly. Because the number of mergers by major banks and regional banks are small (ten

---

17. Long-term credit banks are those banks that were established for the purpose of long-term corporate finance and permitted to issue long-term bonds exclusively under Long-Term Credit Bank Law. Though three long-term credit banks were established after WWII, two of them (i.e., Long-Term Credit Bank of Japan and the Nippon Credit Bank) failed in 1998, and one (i.e., Industrial Bank of Japan) was merged with city banks (Fuji Bank and Daiichi-Kangyo Bank) and reorganized in 2002.

18. Among the M&As by regional banks or *shinkin* banks, only four (two M&As by regional banks and two M&As by *shinkin* banks) were conducted across prefectural borders.

and nine, respectively), separating them may yield relatively weak statistical results. However, we choose not to pool the major banks and regional banks because of the preceding reasons.

Table 8.3 shows the descriptive sample statistics of the bank and market characteristics that we use in the following analyses. We compare the bank characteristics variables among the acquirers, targets, and the average of each bank type: major banks, regional banks, and *shinkin* banks. The variables of the acquirers and the targets are as of one year before the mergers. Though we do not control for macroeconomic shocks across different years in table 8.3, it provides some useful information concerning the ex-ante characteristics of acquires and targets.[19] First, targets and acquirers are less capitalized than the average of each bank type, and the differences in the risk-based capital ratios are significant in the case of the mergers of regional banks and *shinkin* banks. Second, the acquirer tends to be larger and the target tends to be smaller than the bank-type average, with the exception of the major banks' targets, though the differences in the logarithm of total assets are significant only in the case of *shinkin* banks. Finally, in the case of the M&As of *shinkin* banks, the targets' ROA are significantly lower than the average.

Figures 8.1, 8.2, and 8.3 compare some characteristics of acquirers and targets as compared with the average of each bank type. We follow the following three-step process to draw the figures. First, observing the financial statements of the acquirer and the target for the five years preceding the merger, we combine these statements to create pro forma financial ratios for a hypothetical combined bank. To calculate hypothetical premerger financial ratios, we calculate the weighted average of the acquirer and the target, where the total assets of the acquirer and the target are used as a weight.[20] Second, we calculate the postmerger bank's financial ratios for the actual combined bank using its financial statements for five years after the merger. Third, we normalize both the premerger and postmerger financial ratios of the acquirer and the combined bank, respectively, by subtracting off the same-year, bank-type average.

Those banks whose data are available at the merger year and a premerger year are included in the sample here. Similarly, those banks whose data are available at the merger year and a postmerger year are included in the sample here. In figures 8.1, 8.2, and 8.3, simple averages of bank characteristics are depicted. Because we cannot compare accounting variables as of the year of M&As with the premerger or postmerger periods, we just

19. The differences in the interest rates on deposits and loans, in particular, seem to reflect the fact that a large number of M&As occurred in the latter half of the 1990s, when Bank of Japan conducted an extremely low interest rate policy.

20. If three or more banks merged, the series of the targets are a weighted sum of the targets, and the series of the hypothetical combined bank are a weighted sum of the targets and acquirers. In both series, we use total assets as weights.

Table 8.3   Descriptive sample statistics

	Major banks					Regional banks					Shinkin banks				
	Acquirer	Target	All	Acquirer – All	Target – All	Acquirer	Target	All	Acquirer – All	Target – All	Acquirer	Target	All	Acquirer – All	Target – All
Return of assets (ROA)	-0.32 (1.08)	-0.36 (0.79)	-0.27 (1.13)	-0.19 (0.85)	0.00 (0.65)	0.13 (0.37)	-0.06 (0.49)	-0.17 (2.16)	0.23 (0.31)	0.06 (0.17)	0.11 (0.47)	-0.27 (0.96)	0.19 (1.03)	-0.01 (0.44)	-0.37*** (0.89)
Cost Ratio	0.85 (0.35)	0.95 (0.66)	0.86 (0.41)	0.01 (0.32)	0.12 (0.64)	1.43 (0.25)	1.48 (0.17)	1.45 (0.26)	0.03 (0.22)	0.07 (0.16)	1.61 (0.20)	1.69 (0.36)	1.64 (0.24)	-0.01 (0.20)	0.07 (0.36)
Fees and Commissions	0.26 (0.13)	0.29 (0.26)	0.26 (0.16)	-0.01 (0.13)	0.01 (0.26)	0.25 (0.10)	0.20 (0.10)	0.19 (0.06)	0.03 (0.08)	-0.02 (0.07)	0.16 (0.04)	0.15 (0.04)	0.15 (0.04)	0.00 (0.04)	0.00 (0.04)
Loan-to-Asset Ratio	56.60 (6.50)	57.83 (6.62)	56.12 (8.81)	1.38 (7.53)	2.29 (8.57)	70.85 (5.28)	71.82 (4.43)	69.33 (7.03)	2.44 (5.15)	3.36 (4.93)	61.29 (6.95)	57.77 (10.26)	58.84 (8.53)	3.17*** (6.55)	-0.19 (10.27)
Loans to SMEs	28.53 (7.68)	24.22 (6.12)	27.84 (7.75)	2.07 (6.84)	-1.89 (7.49)	47.98 (8.11)	52.13 (6.43)	47.96 (9.52)	2.73 (7.24)	6.34 (7.75)					
Loan Growth Rate	5.99 (10.03)	0.08 (9.31)	2.32 (18.58)	0.11 (12.39)	-5.34 (8.97)	9.48 (23.32)	-0.41 (5.33)	2.81 (8.01)	7.57 (23.15)	-2.36 (3.91)	2.12 (5.72)	-2.35 (5.78)	4.09 (8.72)	-0.38 (3.93)	-4.46*** (4.86)
Deposit Interest Rate	2.29 (2.08)	1.87 (2.01)	3.04 (2.26)	-0.23 (0.54)	-0.13 (0.92)	1.49 (2.08)	1.79 (2.28)	1.75 (1.67)	-0.06 (0.11)	0.07 (0.23)	1.39 (1.47)	1.25 (1.47)	1.91 (1.57)	0.00 (0.18)	0.02 (0.13)
Loan Interest Rate	3.47 (2.19)	3.14 (1.87)	3.96 (2.06)	-0.06 (0.27)	0.03 (0.42)	3.85 (2.22)	4.51 (2.16)	4.05 (1.76)	-0.04 (0.38)	0.43*** (0.24)	4.24 (1.57)	4.08 (1.60)	4.78 (1.64)	0.01 (0.34)	0.02 (0.49)
Capital-to-Asset Ratio	3.75 (1.37)	4.02 (1.57)	3.95 (1.47)	-0.46 (1.02)	-0.19 (1.19)	3.27 (0.68)	3.11 (1.36)	3.67 (3.19)	-0.73 (0.96)	-0.81 (1.09)	4.92 (1.44)	4.11 (1.99)	5.34 (2.16)	-0.51*** (1.45)	-1.34*** (2.03)
Risk-Based Capital Ratio (BIS)	10.31 (1.70)	10.55 (1.55)	11.50 (2.58)	-1.36 (1.37)	-0.89 (1.54)	7.30 (1.31)	6.15 (1.70)	8.77 (3.80)	-1.72** (1.27)	-2.86** (1.76)	8.86 (3.15)	7.18 (3.44)	9.65 (4.11)	-1.12** (2.87)	-2.98*** (3.45)
Nonperforming Loan Ratio (BL)	8.72 (4.46)	8.99 (6.72)	10.32 (7.87)	-1.46 (3.66)	-1.74 (7.13)	9.40 (3.03)	9.59 (2.62)	7.15 (5.15)	1.56 (2.63)	1.74 (2.06)	9.69 (6.42)	14.15 (6.69)	7.81 (5.75)	0.50 (4.98)	4.67*** (6.05)
Nonperforming Loan Ratio (FRL)	8.92 (4.53)	9.17 (6.80)	9.77 (6.79)	-1.40 (3.71)	-1.75 (7.25)	9.48 (3.19)	10.33 (3.56)	8.01 (4.93)	1.71 (2.98)	2.40 (2.95)					
Advertisement Expenses	1.76 (0.93)	1.47 (0.77)	1.91 (1.07)	0.00 (1.02)	-0.19 (0.76)	1.68 (0.90)	1.99 (0.94)	1.60 (0.65)	0.21 (0.90)	0.50 (1.00)					
Stock Price	-17.58 (16.15)	-22.60 (10.61)	-10.77 (28.79)	-4.28 (15.49)	6.83 (10.61)										
Ln Asset	17.03 (0.84)	16.87 (1.15)	16.85 (0.96)	0.18 (0.82)	0.00 (1.13)	14.27 (0.56)	13.67 (0.74)	14.19 (0.89)	0.04 (0.54)	-0.54 (0.71)	19.38 (0.86)	18.20 (0.93)	18.82 (0.97)	0.49*** (0.84)	-0.70*** (0.89)
Asset Growth Rate	9.57 (10.63)	-0.60 (10.63)	1.35 (17.57)	3.02 (6.86)	-5.32 (9.80)	9.17 (21.63)	1.99 (4.55)	2.30 (8.82)	7.71 (21.21)	0.64 (4.84)	2.63 (4.37)	-0.68 (8.88)	4.06 (8.17)	-0.62 (3.32)	-3.84*** (8.35)
No. of observations	8	11	286			9	8	1,876			64	80	5,928		

Notes: "Acquirer – All" and "Target – All" are calculated for each merger and acquisition (M&A) and only for the years when there are at least one M&A, while "All" is a simple average over the whole sample years. This is the reason why the differences between "Acquirer" (or "Target") and "All" do not coincide with "Acquirer – All" (or "Target – All"). Values are means (standard deviation). Numbers in parentheses are standard errors.

***Significant at the 1 percent level.

**Significant at the 5 percent level.

connect a line for one year before M&As and one year after M&As. We look at the financial ratios that represent bank efficiency, market power, healthiness, and portfolio.

Figure 8.1 depicts the premerger and postmerger financial ratios of major banks, suggesting some interesting facts. First, target banks were less cost efficient than the average, and consolidated banks' ROA recovered slowly from an immediate deterioration after mergers. Second, consolidated banks increased the share of SME loans at least for the first three years after mergers. Third, the loan interest rate did not show a clear increasing tendency. Fourth, poorly capitalized banks tended to be an acquirer or a target, and consolidated banks suffered from decreasing capital ratios and increasing nonperforming loans at least for three to four years after mergers.[21] Finally, both acquirers and targets spent less on advertisement expenses before mergers, and consolidated banks continued to spend less on them after mergers than the average.

Figure 8.2 depicts the premerger and postmerger bank characteristics of regional banks. Like major banks, target banks were inefficient and poorly capitalized and profitability and efficiency once deteriorated and then slowly recovered after consolidation. The recovery of bank health, measured by capital ratios or nonperforming loans, after consolidation was also slow. Unlike major banks, consolidated banks decreased the share of loans to SMEs after mergers. Consolidated banks also decreased the advertisement expenses after mergers from a relatively high level before mergers.

Figure 8.3 shows the premerger and postmerger bank characteristics of *shinkin* banks. Like major banks and regional banks, target banks were inefficient and unhealthy. The recovery of profitability, cost efficiency, or healthiness could not be seen clearly after M&As. Acquirers and targets tended to focus on traditional loan business before M&As, and a consolidated bank tended to focus more on loan business, unlike major banks. A consolidated bank raised the loan interest rate after M&As.

In the following sections, we statistically examine how the premerger bank characteristics affected the M&A decision and how M&As changed bank performance.

8.6   Ex-Ante Characteristics and the Decision of Consolidation

If efficiency improvement motives drive consolidation, relatively profitable and efficient banks would tend to acquire relatively unprofitable and inefficient banks in order to spread superior expertise and management

---

21. Nonperforming loans (NPLs) defined by Bank Law are the sum of loans to failed borrowers, delinquent loans, loans delinquent for more than three months, and loans with the terms alleviated, all classified by each loan. The NPLs defined by the Financial Rehabilitation Law are all the claimable assets other than the normal ones whose debtors have no financial problems, classified by debtors' financial conditions. Banks are required to disclose both types of NPLs.

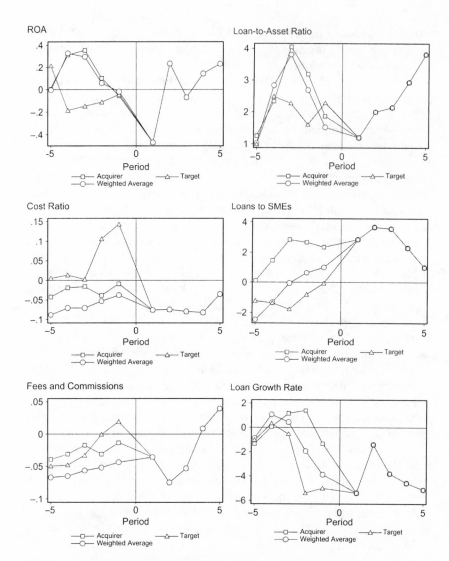

Fig. 8.1 Premerger and postmerger performances of major banks

Notes: Period zero designates the year when the bank merger occurred. Negative periods denote premerger years, and positive periods denote postmerger years. We connect the period (–1) value and period (+1) value with a straight line. *Weighted average* denotes the hypothetical premerger combined bank, calculated as a weighted average of the acquirer and the target with their total assets being used as weights.

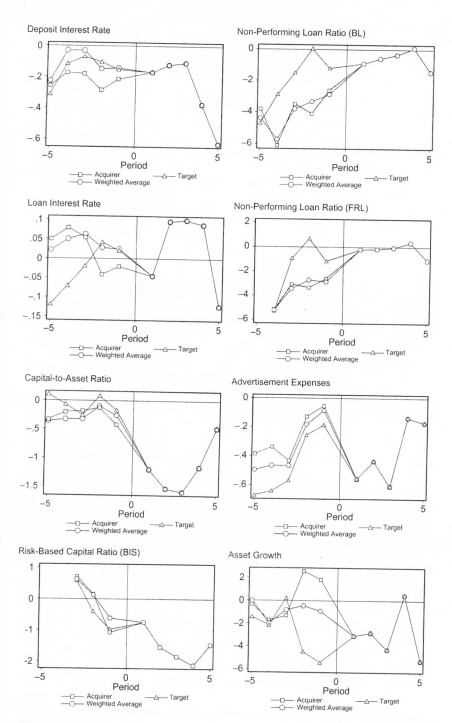

Fig. 8.1   (cont.)

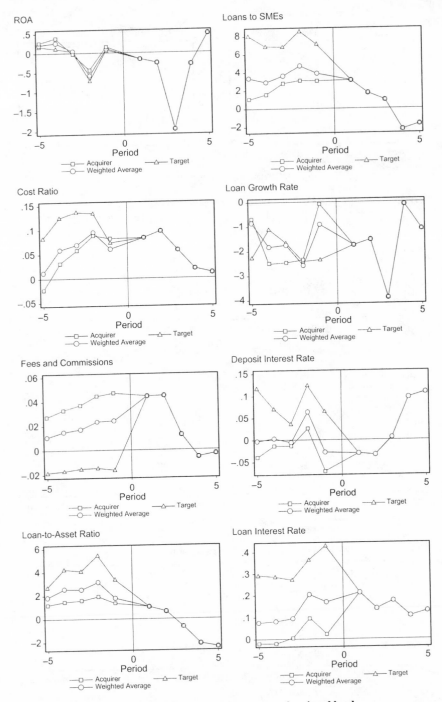

Fig. 8.2 Premerger and postmerger performances of regional banks

Notes: See notes to figure 8.1.

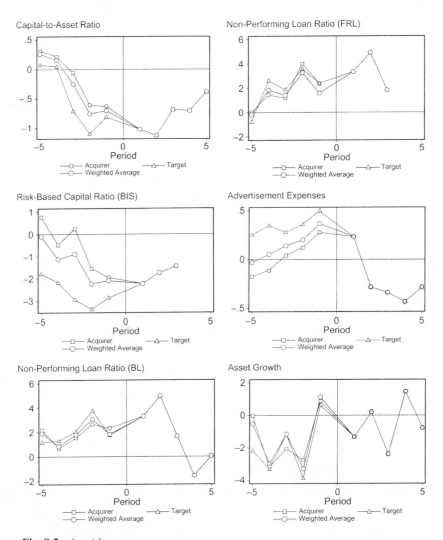

Fig. 8.2   (cont.)

skills over the target bank. On the other hand, if the government's too-big-to-fail policy or its motives of stabilizing the nationwide or local banking system drive consolidation, relatively unhealthy banks tend to be consolidated with each other. The government may also promote consolidations through recapitalization. If managerial private incentive for empire building is a major motive for mergers, banks that spend more on private benefits like advertisement expenditures are more likely to acquire other banks.

To analyze the motives for consolidation, we estimate the multinomial logit model:

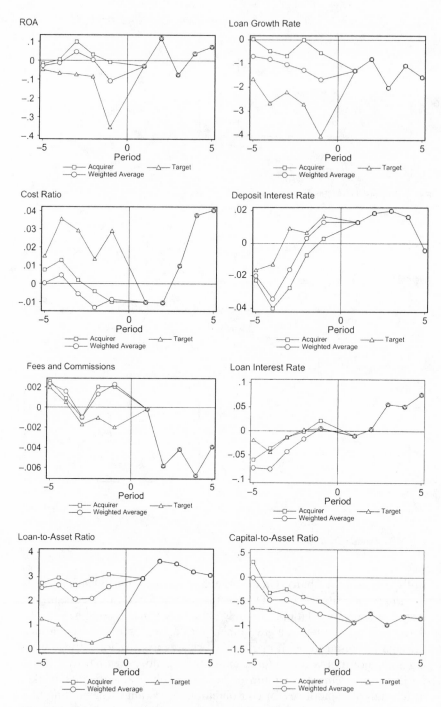

Fig. 8.3 Premerger and postmerger performances of *shinkin* banks

Notes: See notes to figure 8.1.

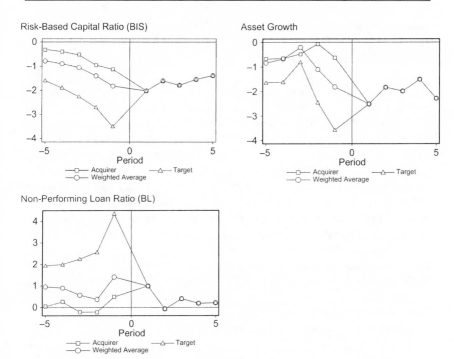

Fig. 8.3   (cont.)

$$(2) \qquad P_{t,j} = \frac{\exp(\beta' \mathbf{X}_{t-1,j})}{\sum_{j=1}^{3} \exp(\beta' \mathbf{X}_{t-1,j})} \, for \, j = 1,2,3,$$

where $P_{t,j}$ is the probability of the bank's choosing the variable j at time t, with j being an acquirer, a target, or neither. The explanatory variable vector $\mathbf{X}_{t-1,j}$ consists of bank profitability, efficiency, healthiness, governmental recapitalization, managerial private benefits, and size, as well as other control variables including market concentration and macroeconomic variables. We choose the ROA and the cost ratio for the efficiency variables and the capital-to-asset ratio and the nonperforming loans as a proportion of total loans as bank health measures. Nonperforming loans are available only after 1998. We also use the yearly change in the stock prices as bank health measures in the case of major banks, though the stock price data of individual banks are available only up to 2001 because since then major banks established holding companies whose subsidiaries include security companies and nonbanks as well. The governmental recapitalization is captured by a dummy variable that takes the value of one if the bank has been recapitalized that year or before and zero otherwise. As a measure of private benefits, we use advertisement expenses as a proportion of total cost. For the size variables, we use the logarithm of total assets and the growth rate of total assets. As a degree of market concentration, we use the Herfindahl index for regional banks and *shinkin* banks. Though major banks had head offices in Tokyo, Osaka, Nagoya, or Sapporo and had some operational advantages over the areas where the head offices were located, they had branches and operated nationwide. This is why we do not use the prefectural Herfindahl index in the case of major banks. We control for the experience of M&As using a dummy variable that takes the value of one if the bank has experienced an M&A before and zero otherwise. A bank that has experienced a M&A before may not want to carry out another M&A if it takes a long time to consolidate information systems and other business cultures. On the other hand, a bank that has experienced M&As may have knowledge and skills how to efficiently integrate different business practices. In that case, the M&A experience dummy has a positive effect on the probability of being an acquirer. Finally, to control for industrial or macroeconomic shocks, we add the change in the stock price index for the banking industry and the growth rate of GDP in the case of major banks and the growth rate of prefectural GDP in the case of regional and *shinkin* banks. All the explanatory variables are lagged by one year.

We checked the correlation among the explanatory variables and found that ROA and the capital-to-asset ratio are strongly correlated for regional banks and *shinkin* banks (The correlation coefficients are 0.045, 0.853, and 0.615 for major banks, regional banks, and *shinkin* banks, respectively). To check the robustness, we also estimate equation (2) by entering ROA and the capital-to-asset ratio one by one into the explanatory variables. In addition, to take into consideration the possibility that it took more than one year to prepare for mergers, we also present the estimation results in the case of two-year lagged explanatory variables.[22]

We estimate equation (2) for each bank type: major banks, regional banks, and *shinkin* banks. In addition to the full sample period (fiscal year 1990 to 2004), we divide the sample period into the precrisis period (fiscal year 1990 to 1997) and the postcrisis (fiscal year 1998 to 2004). The regulatory authorities did not intervene in bank mergers to rescue weak banks in the postcrisis period. Furthermore, their attitudes toward major banks' nonperforming loan problems became much more severe in the postcrisis period than in the precrisis period. It would be useful to see whether there would be a difference in the motives of bank mergers between the pre- and postcrisis periods.

8.6.1   Major Banks

Table 8.4 shows the estimation results for major banks. Column (1) shows the estimated coefficients and column (2) shows the estimated

---

22. Two-year lagged dependent variables may be appropriate in case a bank that is to be acquired by a relatively healthy bank in two years gambles on high-risk, high-return investment and finally deteriorates its balance sheet one year before mergers. This potential moral hazard problem was pointed out by Hiro Ito.

Table 8.4 Multinomial logistic regression results for merger and acquisition (M&A) choices among major banks

	1990–2004						1990–2001		1990–2004		1990–1997		1998–2004	
	Coefficient (1)	Marginal effect (2)	Coefficient (3)	Marginal effect (4)	Coefficient (5)	Marginal effect (6)	Coefficien (7)	Marginal effect (8)	Coefficient (9)	Marginal effect (10)	Coefficient (11)	Marginal effect (12)	Coefficient (13)	Marginal effect (14)
Acquirer														
Return of assets (ROA)	-0.200 (0.470)	-0.0000	-0.267 (0.342)	-0.0000					0.284 (0.843)	0.0000	17.817 (19.158)	0.0000	0.079 (0.900)	0.0001
Cost Ratio	3.157 (2.207)	0.0028	2.451 (2.073)	0.0000	3.138 (2.201)	0.0000	0.433 (2.475)	-0.0046	1.734 (2.065)	0.0020	1.907 (4.665)	0.0000	5.054 (2.820)	0.0155
Capital-to-Asset Ratio	-0.421 (0.426)	-0.0003			-0.478 (0.416)	-0.0000			0.313 (0.369)	0.0004	-4.355 (3.079)	-0.0727	-0.954 (0.716)	-0.0323
Advertisement Expenses	0.218 (0.497)	0.0000	0.129 (0.500)	0.0000	0.195 (0.499)	0.0000	0.092 (0.524)	0.0052	-0.275 (0.539)	-0.0000	-0.505 (0.880)	-0.0000	2.062 (1.179)	0.0030
Ln Asset	1.255 (0.936)	0.0437	1.284 (0.918)	0.0437	1.178 (0.916)	0.0072	0.766 (1.025)	0.0043	0.937 (0.909)	0.0026	-0.200 (1.561)	0.0024	2.015 (1.607)	0.0641
Asset Growth	0.017 (0.018)	0.0000	0.018 (0.017)	0.0000	0.017 (0.018)	0.0000	0.024 (0.017)	0.0000	0.019 (0.017)	0.0000	-0.001 (0.044)	-0.0000	0.011 (0.021)	0.0000
Industrial Stock Price	-0.031 (0.033)	-0.0000	-0.038 (0.033)	-0.0000	-0.028 (0.032)	-0.0000			0.019 (0.031)	0.0000	0.747 (0.595)	0.0000	-0.150 (0.096)	-0.0018
GDP Growth	0.527 (0.279)	0.0000	0.455 (0.266)	0.0000	0.508 (0.274)	0.0000			0.578 (0.324)	0.0000	5.310 (4.326)	-0.0011	0.189 (0.793)	0.0002
M&A Experience	-2.783 (1.600)	-0.0506	-2.402 (1.479)	-0.0435	-2.729 (1.589)	-0.0499	-1.768 (1.537)	-0.0311	-1.941 (1.390)	-0.0345			-3.447 (1.977)	-0.1163
Governmental Capital	2.987** (1.338)	0.1209	2.247** (1.024)	0.0745	3.076** (1.349)	0.1271	1.685 (0.894)	0.0650	2.617 (1.353)	0.1054				
Stock Price							-0.005 (0.016)	-0.0000						
Nonperforming Loan Ratio													-0.019 (0.269)	0.0024
Cons	-28.848 (18.148)		-29.828 (17.845)		-27.195 (17.645)		-17.567 (19.683)		-23.765 (17.740)		-5.595 (30.763)		-42.340 (31.100)	

(continued)

Table 8.4 (continued)

	1990–2004						1990–2001		1990–2004		1990–1997		1998–2004	
	Coefficient (1)	Marginal effect (2)	Coefficient (3)	Marginal effect (4)	Coefficient (5)	Marginal effect (6)	Coefficien (7)	Marginal effect (8)	Coefficient (9)	Marginal effect (10)	Coefficient (11)	Marginal effect (12)	Coefficient (13)	Marginal effect (14)
Target														
Return of assets (ROA)	-0.082 (0.401)	-0.0000	-0.092 (0.366)	-0.0000					0.001 (0.284)	0.0000	7.495 (9.127)	0.0000	0.323 (0.915)	-0.0001
Cost Ratio	2.134 (1.637)	0.0010	2.110 (1.626)	0.0000	2.119 (1.629)	0.0000	6.011 (4.998)	0.0574	1.821 (1.640)	0.0039	-1.494 (3.793)	-0.0000	7.484** (3.292)	0.3149
Capital-to-Asset Ratio	-0.051 (0.355)	0.0001			-0.075 (0.334)	0.0000			0.613** (0.305)	0.0090	-2.184 (1.778)	-0.0272	0.209 (0.702)	0.0153
Advertisement Expenses	-0.286 (0.519)	-0.0000	-0.294 (0.516)	-0.0000	-0.297 (0.515)	-0.0000	-11.020 (6.692)	-0.0692	-0.645 (0.527)	-0.0000	-0.545 (0.641)	-0.0000	0.344 (0.970)	-0.0024
Ln Asset	0.868 (0.792)	0.0082	0.895 (0.762)	0.0103	0.832 (0.769)	0.0116	3.524 (3.155)	0.0282	1.195 (0.789)	0.0596	-1.689 (1.586)	-0.0288	1.513 (1.718)	0.0518
Asset Growth	-0.028 (0.032)	-0.0000	-0.028 (0.031)	-0.0000	-0.029 (0.032)	-0.0000	0.094 (0.071)	0.0000	0.001 (0.022)	0.0000	0.018 (0.054)	0.0000	-0.055 (0.064)	-0.0000
Industrial Stock Price	-0.083** (0.042)	0.0000	-0.084** (0.042)	-0.0000	-0.083 (0.042)	-0.0000			-0.021 (0.027)	-0.0000	0.458 (0.383)	0.0000	-0.427 (0.315)	-0.0203
GDP Growth	0.499 (0.282)	0.0000	0.493 (0.277)	0.0000	0.495 (0.284)	0.0000			0.351 (0.242)	0.0000	3.305 (2.837)	0.0064	1.204 (1.870)	0.0039
M&A Experience	-1.164 (0.972)	-0.0290	-1.146 (0.965)	-0.0292	-1.142 (0.967)	-0.0287	-2.962 (3.029)	-0.0275	-1.283 (0.978)	-0.0337			-1.744 (1.359)	-0.0495
Governmental Capital	1.792 (1.010)	0.0576	1.721** (0.844)	0.0610	1.838 (0.986)	0.0586	2.525 (3.004)	0.0178	1.011 (0.930)	0.0281				
Stock Price							-0.035 (0.055)	-0.0000						
Nonperforming Loan Ratio													-0.399 (0.281)	-0.0090
Cons	-21.920 (15.593)		-22.526 (14.882)		-21.181 (15.110)		-60.254 (54.140)		-27.602 (15.501)		23.337 (29.490)		-42.943 (34.366)	
No. of observations	279		280		279		225		279		170		90	
Pseudo R^2	0.168		0.162		0.167		0.272		0.166		0.277		0.446	
Log-likelihood	-68.457		-69.027		-68.547		-34.234		-68.641		-21.780		-25.370	

Notes: The probability of being an acquirer or a target as compared with being neither of them is estimated using the maximum-likelihood estimator. Standard errors are in parentheses. Independent variables are lagged one year for columns (1)–(8) and (11)–(14), while they are lagged two years for columns (9) and (10).

***Significant at the 1 percent level.

**Significant at the 5 percent level.

marginal effects for the full sample period.[23] Looking at the results of the acquirer equation, we see that the coefficient on the governmental capital injection dummy is positive and significant, suggesting that those major banks that had been recapitalized by the government were more likely to be consolidated. This result is consistent with the too-big-to-fail policy or stabilization policy hypothesis. It should be noted, however, that because all the major banks were recapitalized by the government in 1998, the coefficient on the governmental capital injection dummy may reflect any structural changes after 1998. The other bank characteristics variables and macroeconomic variables are not significant. Turning to the target equation, we see that the coefficient on the industrial stock price index is negative and significant, suggesting that a bank was more likely to be acquired when the equity values of the banking industry were deteriorated. These results are consistent with the too-big-to-fail policy or the stabilization policy hypothesis.

Entering ROA and the capital-to-asset ratio one by one into the explanatory variables, we obtain similar results (shown in columns [3] to [6]), though the coefficient on the governmental capital injection dummy is positive and significant in the target equation when only ROA is entered.

Columns (7) and (8) show the results when the changes in individual banks' stock prices are used as a bank health measure. We see that its coefficient is not significant in the acquirer or target equation. In the case of major banks, the overall worsening of bank health and the government's response to a systemic risk may have driven the merger waves rather than the individual bank health.

Using two-year lagged explanatory variables, we see (in columns [9] and [10]) that no explanatory variable is significant in the acquirer or the target equation, except for the capital-to-asset ratio in the target equation that is positive and significant. Though this result is not consistent with the too-big-to-fail policy hypothesis, the two-year lagged explanatory variable may not be suitable in the case of the mergers of major banks because every major bank seemed to hasten to choose the bank to consolidate or to be consolidated by, especially in the postcrisis period.

The subperiod estimation results are presented in columns (11) to (14). While no premerger variable is significant in the precrisis period, the coefficient on the cost ratio is positive and significant in the target equation in the postcrisis period. The fact that a less cost-efficient major bank tended to be acquired by other banks in the postcrisis period is consistent with the efficiency-improving hypothesis.

8.6.2 Regional Banks

Table 8.5 shows the estimation results for regional banks. Looking at the full sample period estimation result, we see that the coefficients on the

---

23. The average marginal effects are reported here (Wooldridge 2001, 467).

Table 8.5   Multinomial logistic regression results for merger and acquisition choices among regional banks

	1990–2004								1990–1997		1998–2004	
	Coefficient (1)	Marginal effect (2)	Coefficient (3)	Marginal effect (4)	Coefficient (5)	Marginal effect (6)	Coefficien (7)	Marginal effect (8)	Coefficient (9)	Marginal effect (10)	Coefficient (11)	Marginal effect (12)
Acquirer												
Return of assets (ROA)	0.321 (0.171)	0.0000	0.258 (0.227)	0.0000	-0.567 (2.116)	-0.0000	-0.086 (0.394)	-0.0000	1.231 (4.907)	0.0000	5.329*** (1.724)	0.0000
Cost Ratio	-0.643 (2.184)	-0.0000	-0.308 (2.218)	-0.0000			0.276 (2.346)	0.0000	0.258 (4.026)	0.0000	3.284 (3.314)	0.0063
Capital-to-Asset Ratio	-0.173 (0.103)	-0.0000			-0.043 (0.077)	-0.0000	0.063 (0.300)	0.0000	-0.663 (1.065)	-0.0000	-1.622*** (0.575)	-0.0000
Advertisement Expenses	0.219 (0.459)	0.0000	0.212 (0.441)	0.0000	0.224 (0.446)	0.0000	-0.018 (0.577)	-0.0000	0.042 (1.091)	0.0000	-0.028 (0.421)	-0.0000
Ln Asset	-0.145 (0.631)	0.0001	-0.110 (0.639)	0.0001	-0.143 (0.615)	0.0001	-0.045 (0.680)	0.0001	0.161 (1.259)	0.0000	1.190 (1.083)	0.0037
Asset Growth	0.017 (0.012)	0.0000	0.018 (0.012)	0.0000	0.018 (0.012)	0.0000	-0.048 (0.072)	-0.0000	0.033 (0.050)	0.0000	0.001 (0.016)	0.0000
Herfindahl Index	0.480 (2.195)	0.0000	0.170 (2.175)	0.0000	0.216 (2.161)	0.0000	-0.066 (2.165)	-0.0000	5.948 (4.042)	0.0000	-1.046 (3.063)	-0.0000
GDP Growth	0.016 (0.096)	0.0000	0.022 (0.097)	0.0000	0.022 (0.097)	0.0000	0.085 (0.115)	0.0000	-0.007 (0.157)	-0.0000	-0.052 (0.235)	-0.0000
Governmental Capital	2.125** (0.894)	0.0257	2.106** (0.891)	0.0258	1.983** (0.878)	0.0227	1.965** (0.874)	0.0221			1.080 (1.082)	0.0112
Nonperforming Loan Ratio											0.201 (0.180)	0.0000
Cons	-2.570 (11.904)		-4.073 (11.983)		-3.089 (11.524)		-5.609 (13.038)		-9.029 (23.551)		-21.882 (18.934)	

Target

	(1)	(2)	(3)	(4)	(5)	(6)	(7)	(8)	(9)	(10)	(11)	(12)
Return of assets (ROA)	0.279	0.0000	0.095	0.0000		0.0000	-0.145	-0.0000	1.892	0.0000	2.221	0.0000
	(0.226)		(0.385)				(0.376)		(2.142)		(1.491)	
Cost Ratio	-3.315	-0.0000	-3.083	-0.0000	-3.227	0.0000	-1.951	-0.0000	-2.785	-0.0000	-4.467	-0.0053
	(2.242)		(2.256)		(2.167)		(2.006)		(3.671)		(4.473)	
Capital-to-Asset Ratio	-0.177	-0.0000		-0.0000	-0.057	-0.0000	0.123	0.0000	-1.708	-0.0021	-0.543	-0.0000
	(0.117)				(0.084)		(0.300)		(0.969)		(0.517)	
Advertisement Expenses	0.441	0.0000	0.457	0.0000	0.459	0.0000	0.454	0.0000	-0.440	-0.0000	0.674	0.0000
	(0.396)		(0.379)		(0.388)		(0.439)		(1.241)		(0.480)	
Ln Asset	-1.497**	-0.0028	-1.482**	-0.0029	-1.484**	-0.0028	-1.317**	-0.0032	-1.732	-0.0021	-1.435	-0.0069
	(0.625)		(0.621)		(0.613)		(0.622)		(1.347)		(0.991)	
Asset Growth	-0.017	-0.0000	-0.022	-0.0000	-0.014	-0.0000	-0.093	-0.0000	0.013	0.0000	-0.073	-0.0000
	(0.060)		(0.072)		(0.061)		(0.060)		(0.099)		(0.125)	
Herfindahl Index	-1.399	-0.0000	-1.725	-0.0000	-1.547	-0.0000	-1.725	-0.0000	-0.435	-0.0000	1.334	0.0000
	(2.227)		(2.195)		(2.203)		(2.288)		(3.479)		(4.129)	
GDP Growth	0.006	0.0000	0.019	0.0000	0.014	0.0000	0.114	0.0000	-0.051	-0.0000	0.083	0.0000
	(0.115)		(0.119)		(0.115)		(0.109)		(0.167)		(0.306)	
Governmental Capital	2.511***	0.0324	2.418***	0.0300	2.405***	0.0297	2.442***	0.0297			1.643	0.0133
	(0.929)		(0.920)		(0.906)		(0.914)				(1.311)	
Nonperforming Loan Ratio											0.245	0.0001
											(0.209)	
Cons	20.334		19.234		19.589		14.645		28.199		19.328	
	(11.402)		(11.261)		(11.057)		(11.030)		(23.502)		(18.866)	
No. of observations	1,869		1,869		1,869		1,866		1,039		628	
Pseudo R^2	0.100		0.089		0.088		0.092		0.130		0.308	
Log-likelihood	-97.683		-98.878		-99.034		-98.603		-35.724		-40.175	

Notes: The probability of being an acquirer or a target as compared with being neither of them is estimated using the maximum-likelihood estimator. Standard errors are in parentheses. Independent variables are lagged one year for columns (1)–(6) and (9)–(12), while they are lagged two years for columns (7) and (8).

***Significant at the 1 percent level.

**Significant at the 5 percent level.

governmental capital injection dummy are positive and significant in both the acquirer and target equations, which supports the too-big-to-fail policy or stabilization policy hypothesis. In the target equation, the coefficient on the (logarithm of) asset is negative and significant, suggesting that a smaller regional bank was more likely to be a target. These results hold even if we enter ROA and capital-to-asset ratio one by one and if we use two-lagged explanatory variables (columns [3] to [8]). Looking at the subsample period estimation results (columns [9] to [12]), we see that no premerger variable is significant in the precrisis period. On the other hand, in the postmerger period, the coefficient on ROA is positive and significant, and the coefficient on capital-to-asset ratio is negative and significant in the acquirer equation, while none is significant in the target equation. The result for the acquirer equation in the postcrisis period is consistent both with the efficiency-improving hypothesis and the too-big-to-fail policy or stabilization policy hypothesis.

8.6.3   Shinkin Banks

Table 8.6 displays the estimation results for *shinkin* banks. We exclude advertisement expenses from the explanatory variables because *shinkin* banks do not disclose them. Looking at the full sample period estimation result of the acquirer equation (columns [1] and [2]), we see that the coefficients on the (logarithm of) asset and the M&A experience dummy are positive and significant. A larger *shinkin* bank is more likely to acquire another *shinkin* bank. In the target equation, the coefficient on ROA is positive and significant, and the coefficient on the cost ratio is negative and significant. Efficient *shinkin* banks tended to be a target, though the efficiency-improving hypothesis posits that efficient banks tend to be an acquirer. The coefficient on the capital-to-asset ratio is negative and significant, which is consistent with the too-big-to-fail or stabilization policy. The coefficient on the Herfindahl index is negative and significant, suggesting that a *shinkin* bank tends to be consolidated if it operates in a less-concentrated market, which is consistent with the market power hypothesis. The coefficients on the (logarithm of) asset and the asset growth are both negative and significant, suggesting that a small or slowly growing *shinkin* bank tended to be a target.

Most of these results still hold even if we enter ROA and the capital-to-asset ratio separately (columns [3] to [6]) or if we use two-year lagged explanatory variables (columns [7] and [8]), though the coefficients on ROA and the capital-to-asset ratio become insignificant in the target equation when we enter them separately.

Though the subsample period estimation results yield similar results both in the premerger and postmerger periods, it is notable that the coefficient on the capital-to-asset ratio is negative and significant in the target equation only in the postcrisis period, suggesting that the too-big-to-fail or

Table 8.6   Multinomial logistic regression results for merger and acquisition (M&A) choices among *Shinkin* banks

	1990–2002								1990–1997		1998–2002	
	Coefficient (1)	Marginal effect (2)	Coefficient (3)	Marginal effect (4)	Coefficient (5)	Marginal effect (6)	Coefficien (7)	Marginal effect (8)	Coefficient (9)	Marginal effect (10)	Coefficient (11)	Marginal effect (12)
Acquirer												
Return of assets (ROA)	0.113 (0.151)	0.0000	0.050 (0.115)	0.0000			0.089 (0.159)	0.0000	−0.447 (1.528)	0.0000	0.072 (0.238)	0.0000
Cost Ratio	0.397 (0.655)	0.0000	0.504 (0.631)	0.0000	0.443 (0.648)	0.0000	0.571 (0.640)	0.0000	0.859 (0.856)	0.0000	0.036 (1.076)	0.0000
Capital-to-Asset Ratio	−0.055 (0.083)	−0.0000			−0.014 (0.055)	−0.0000	−0.039 (0.085)	−0.0000	−0.143 (0.168)	−0.0000	0.051 (0.110)	0.0000
Ln Asset	0.521*** (0.168)	0.0000	0.546*** (0.165)	0.0000	0.534*** (0.167)	0.0000	0.573** (0.166)	0.0000	0.541** (0.215)	0.0000	0.536** (0.274)	0.0071
Asset Growth	−0.029 (0.022)	−0.0000	−0.029 (0.022)	−0.0000	−0.025 (0.020)	−0.0000	−0.016 (0.019)	−0.0000	−0.021 (0.034)	−0.0000	−0.033 (0.028)	−0.0000
Herfindahl Index	0.495 (0.789)	0.0000	0.441 (0.785)	0.0000	0.439 (0.786)	0.0000	0.451 (0.784)	0.0000	0.746 (1.082)	0.0000	−0.138 (1.209)	−0.0000
GDP Growth	−0.021 (0.039)	−0.0000	−0.018 (0.039)	−0.0000	−0.019 (0.039)	−0.0000	0.007 (0.031)	0.0000	0.006 (0.038)	0.0000	−0.149 (0.093)	−0.0000
M&A Experience	0.989*** (0.334)	0.0161	1.030*** (0.328)	0.0171	0.998*** (0.334)	0.0164	1.009*** (0.332)	0.0163			1.280*** (0.422)	0.0268
Nonperforming Loan Ratio											0.061 (0.035)	0.0000
Cons	−14.915*** (4.074)		−15.837*** (3.858)		−15.422*** (4.000)		−16.361*** (4.045)		−15.626*** (5.276)		−15.662** (6.735)	
Target												
Return of assets (ROA)	0.445*** (0.110)	0.0000	0.079 (0.055)	0.0000			0.505*** (0.122)	0.0000	−3.783*** (1.336)	−0.0000	0.549*** (0.132)	0.0000

(continued)

Table 8.6 continued

	1990–2002								1990–1997		1998–2002	
	Coefficient (1)	Marginal effect (2)	Coefficient (3)	Marginal effect (4)	Coefficient (5)	Marginal effect (6)	Coefficien (7)	Marginal effect (8)	Coefficient (9)	Marginal effect (10)	Coefficient (11)	Marginal effect (12)
Cost Ratio	-1.167***	-0.0002	-1.265***	-0.0001	-1.356***	-0.0001	-1.111***	0.0000	-1.398**	-0.0000	-0.943	-0.0008
	(0.416)		(0.437)		(0.437)		(0.403)		(0.590)		(0.694)	
Capital-to-Asset Ratio	-0.284***	-0.0000			-0.043	-0.0000	-0.304***	-0.0000	-0.087	-0.0000	-0.236**	-0.0000
	(0.072)				(0.040)		(0.073)		(0.136)		(0.093)	
Ln Asset	-0.955***	-0.0014	-0.876***	-0.0012	-0.944***	-0.0013	-0.868***	-0.0010	-1.157***	-0.0011	-0.911***	-0.0170
	(0.141)		(0.137)		(0.138)		(0.136)		(0.216)		(0.212)	
Asset Growth	-0.129***	-0.0000	-0.141***	-0.0000	-0.098***	-0.0000	-0.121***	-0.0000	-0.037	-0.0000	-0.158***	-0.0000
	(0.026)		(0.027)		(0.025)		(0.025)		(0.031)		(0.046)	
Herfindahl Index	-2.588***	-0.0003	-2.701***	-0.0000	-2.890***	-0.0000	-2.450***	-0.0000	-2.426**	-0.0000	-3.663***	-0.0000
	(0.753)		(0.756)		(0.753)		(0.736)		(1.180)		(1.105)	
GDP Growth	-0.066	-0.0000	-0.048	-0.0000	-0.065	-0.0000	-0.004	-0.0000	-0.054	-0.0000	-0.052	-0.0000
	(0.040)		(0.041)		(0.039)		(0.036)		(0.057)		(0.088)	
M&A Experience	-0.369	-0.0042	-0.166	-0.0022	-0.398	-0.0045	-0.369	-0.0043			-0.282	-0.0051
	(0.663)		(0.641)		(0.721)		(0.622)				(0.666)	
Nonperforming Loan Ratio											0.112***	0.0000
											(0.028)	
Cons	17.821***		15.151***		16.835***		16.125***		21.240***		15.637***	
	(2.971)		(2.926)		(2.972)		(2.865)		(4.288)		(4.763)	
No. of observations	5,626		5,626		5,626		5,758		3,432		2,167	
Pseudo R^2	0.098		0.087		0.086		0.085		0.098		0.158	
Log-likelihood	-681.741		-690.583		-691.122		-706.882		-327.212		-320.765	

Note: See notes to table 8.5.

***Significant at the 1 percent level.

**Significant at the 5 percent level.

stabilization policy hypothesis is valid in the postcrisis period. The coefficient on the nonperforming loan ratio is also positive and significant in the target equation in the postcrisis period. The evidences on the effects of the premerger bank efficiency on the likelihood of being a target are mixed; the signs of the coefficients on ROA change from negative in the precrisis period to positive in the postcrisis period, and the coefficient on the cost ratio is negative and significant in the precrisis period.

In sum, the efficiency-improving hypothesis seems to be valid in the case of the postcrisis period's consolidations among major banks and among regional banks. The market power hypothesis seems to be valid in the case of the consolidations among *shinkin* banks. The government's too-big-to-fail or financial stabilization policy hypothesis also seems to be valid, especially in the case of the postcrisis period's consolidations. We find no evidence that supports the managerial empire-building hypothesis, though we cannot test that hypothesis in the case of the consolidations among *shinkin* banks due to the lack of suitable data.

8.7   Postmerger Performance

8.7.1   Background

Consolidation may have various effects on the consolidated bank's efficiency, market power, services provided, healthiness, and expenses for managerial private benefits.

First, consolidation may increase or decrease efficiency in various ways. A consolidated bank may be able to achieve a scale or scope economy. It may also improve X-efficiency by spreading superior acquirers' managerial skills over targets. On the other hand, it may take considerable time and costs to integrate different accounting and information systems, ways of doing business, and corporate cultures.

Second, consolidation may change the availability of loans and other financial services to small- and medium-sized enterprises (SMEs), though such changes may not be intended either by acquirers or targets. If consolidation improves efficiency, a more efficient consolidated bank may be able to serve more customers, including SMEs. On the other hand, if a large bank finds it costly to process relationship-based information due to its organizational complexity, a consolidated bank may reduce loans to the SMEs that are informationally opaque (Berger, Demsetz, and Strahan 1999). Consolidated banks may also increase or reduce other services, including fee businesses, according to their comparative advantages.

Third, consolidation may strengthen market power, enabling the consolidated bank to raise loan interest rates or lower deposit interest rates. This is likely to occur when acquirers and targets operate within the same local market (e.g., Berger, Demsetz, and Strahan 1999).

Fourth, consolidation may improve or deteriorate healthiness. Although regulators may promote consolidations by weak banks, it is not clear whether weak banks can restore healthiness just through consolidation. On one hand, a consolidated bank may gain from risk diversification through investing various areas and industries (Berger, Demsetz, and Strahan 1999). In addition, an acquirer may apply its superior risk management skills to a target. However, if poorly-capitalized banks are consolidated, a consolidated bank must be highly profitable to fill in the initial shortage of capital and then to recover its capital to a normal level, unless it raises capital from outside. In addition, a consolidated bank may be exposed to the risk of an unproportionally large amount of loans to some specific large borrowers as compared with other banks as a result of the consolidation.[24]

Finally, consolidation may increase or decrease expenses for the purpose of managerial private benefits, like advertisement expenses. If a bank acquires another bank for the purpose of increasing private benefits, a consolidated bank may increase expenses for private benefits. On the other hand, if a bank becomes a target due to its weak governance structures that allow large amounts of spending for private benefits, a consolidated bank may decrease such spending.

8.7.2   Methodology

We investigate the consequences of M&As by comparing the bank financial variables of premerger and postmerger periods.[25] From the viewpoint of existing shareholders (or members of *shinkin* banks) of acquirers, it is natural to compare premerger acquiring banks and postmerger consolidated banks. On the other hand, from the viewpoint of regulators that care about the banking system, it is useful to compare hypothetical premerger combined banks (that is, a weighted average of an acquirer and a target) and postmerger consolidated banks. We perform both comparisons.

Specifically, we first construct the financial ratios of the premerger hypothetical combined bank and the postmerger consolidated bank in the same way as we depicted in figures 8.1 through 8.3. Note that we normalize all the premerger and postmerger financial ratios by subtracting off the same-year, bank-type average. Next, we take the premerger average of the hypothetical combined bank over the five years before mergers. If the pre-

---

24. The following example may be useful. Tokai Bank, Sanwa Bank, Fuji Bank, and Sumitomo Bank each had almost equal amounts (more than 500 billion yen) of loans outstanding to a large retail company, Daiei, which was in financial distress. It is said that UFJ Bank, formed from the consolidation of Tokai Bank and Sanwa Bank, was saddled with a distinguished amount (more than one trillion yen) of loans to Daiei for a long time after the consolidation.

25. The approach here is similar to Delong and Deyoung (2007).

merger data are available for less than five years, we take the premerger average over the maximum years for which we can observe the data. Finally, we take the difference between the normalized premerger bank financial ratios and the normalized postmerger bank financial ratios. We look at the changes of the bank financial ratios for one to five years after mergers, respectively, though we report in tables 8.7, 8.8, and 8.9 only three and five years after mergers to save space. Focarelli and Panetta (2003), Focarelli and Pozzolo (2005), and Rhoades (1998) show that a two- to three-year postmerger period is needed to determine if there are any postmerger gains. We also take the average of the postmerger financial ratios of the consolidated bank over the (at most) five years after mergers and take the difference between the premerger five-year average and the postmerger five-year average.

We perform the t-test for the null hypothesis so that the difference between a normalized premerger financial ratio and a normalized postmerger financial ratio has mean zero. We also performed the Wilcoxon signed-rank test (z-statistic) for the null hypothesis so that the difference between them has median zero and obtained qualitatively similar results for most financial ratios. So we mainly report the t-test results in the following.

In this section, we select a sample where data on bank financial ratios are available for the merger year, one or more premerger years, and one or more postmerger years. The data set here is slightly different from that used in figures 8.1 through 8.3, where we choose sample banks whose data were available for the merger year and one or more premerger years but not necessarily available for postmerger years and sample banks whose data were available for the merger year and one or more postmerger years but not necessarily available for premerger years.

8.7.3   Results

Major Banks

Table 8.7 shows the changes in the financial ratios of the consolidated major banks. The first column shows the changes from the hypothetical premerger combined bank for the full sample period.

Looking at the efficiency variables, we see that the changes in ROA are negative three years after mergers and then turn to positive five years after mergers, though none of the changes is significant. The changes in the cost ratio are not significant, either, though consolidated banks seem to have decreased the cost ratio. It seems to take considerable time for a consolidated bank to realize cost savings or gain economies of scale or scope.

Market power variables show that the changes in the average deposit interest rate and the changes in the loan interest rate are not significant. A consolidated major bank did not seem to be able to exert market power in

Table 8.7   Postmerger performance of major banks

Change from:	Premerger combined bank			Premerger acquirer
	1990–2004	1990–1997	1998–2004	1990–2004
Return of assets (ROA)				
ΔROA (3-year postmerger)	−0.200			−0.212
ΔROA (5-year postmerger)	0.149			0.125
ΔROA (postmerger average)	−0.219	0.150	−0.377	−0.230
Cost Ratio				
ΔCost Ratio (3-year postmerger)	−0.015			−0.054
ΔCost Ratio (5-year postmerger)	−0.058			−0.124
ΔCost Ratio (postmerger average)	−0.018	0.015	−0.033	−0.058
Fees and Commissions				
ΔFees and Commissions (3-year postmerger)	0.079			−0.032
ΔFees and Commissions (5-year postmerger)	0.110			0.048
ΔFees and Commissions (postmerger average)	0.006	0.065	−0.024	−0.029
Loan-to-Asset Ratio				
ΔLoan-to-Asset Ratio (3-year postmerger)	−0.235			−0.398
ΔLoan-to-Asset Ratio (5-year postmerger)	2.498			1.817
ΔLoan-to-Asset Ratio (postmerger average)	−1.037	0.580	−1.730	−1.200
Loans to SMEs				
ΔLoans to SMEs (3-year postmerger)	1.700[b]			−1.850
ΔLoans to SMEs (5-year postmerger)	−0.384			−4.909
ΔLoans to SMEs (postmerger average)	1.727[b**]	1.064[b]	2.390	−2.047
Loan Growth Rate				
ΔLoan Growth Rate (3-year postmerger)	−2.760			−3.784
ΔLoan Growth Rate (5-year postmerger)	−4.478			−6.387
ΔLoan Growth Rate (postmerger average)	−3.058[b**]	0.014	−4.375[a**]	−4.082[b**]
Deposit Interest Rate				
ΔDeposit Interest Rate (3-year postmerger)	0.008			0.114
ΔDeposit Interest Rate (5-year postmerger)	−0.354			−0.249
ΔDeposit Interest Rate (postmerger average)	−0.058	0.023	−0.093	0.048
Loan Interest Rate				
ΔLoan Interest Rate (3-year postmerger)	0.062			0.075
ΔLoan Interest Rate (5-year postmerger)	−0.057			−0.010
ΔLoan Interest Rate (postmerger average)	−0.001	0.167	−0.073	0.012
Capital-to-Asset Ratio				
ΔCapital-to-Asset Ratio (3-year postmerger)	−1.319[a**]			−1.342[a**]
ΔCapital-to-Asset Ratio (5-year postmerger)	−0.509			−0.498
ΔCapital-to-Asset Ratio (postmerger average)	−1.158[a***]	−0.432	−1.470[a***]	−1.181[a***]
Risk-Based Capital Ratio (BIS)				
ΔRisk-Based Capital Ratio (BIS) (3-year postmerger)	−2.108[b]			−1.788[b]
ΔRisk-Based Capital Ratio (BIS) (5-year postmerger)				
ΔRisk-Based Capital Ratio (BIS) (postmerger average)	−1.376		−1.376	−1.104
Nonperforming Loan Ratio (BL)				
ΔNonperforming Loan Ratio (BL) (3-year postmerger)	4.118[b]			4.301[a***]

Table 8.7   (continued)

	Premerger combined bank			Premerger acquirer
Change from:	1990–2004	1990–1997	1998–2004	1990–2004
ΔNonperforming Loan Ratio (BL) (5-year postmerger)				
ΔNonperforming Loan Ratio (BL) (postmerger average)	3.697[b]		3.697[b]	3.880[b]**
Nonperforming Loan Ratio (FRL)				
ΔNonperforming Loan Ratio (FRL) (3-year postmerger)	3.589[b]			3.835[b]**
ΔNonperforming Loan Ratio (FRL) (5-year postmerger)				
ΔNonperforming Loan Ratio (FRL) (postmerger average)	3.202		3.202	3.448[b]**
Advertisement Expenses				
ΔAdvertisement Expenses (3-year postmerger)	−0.268			−0.339
ΔAdvertisement Expenses (5-year postmerger)	0.243			0.038
ΔAdvertisement Expenses (postmerger average)	−0.164	0.240	−0.337	−0.234
Asset Growth				
ΔAsset Growth (3-year postmerger)	−3.450			−4.497
ΔAsset Growth (5-year postmerger)	−3.891			−5.557
ΔAsset Growth (postmerger average)	−2.617	1.973	−4.585[a]**	−3.665

Notes: The columns under the heading of "Premerger combined bank" denote the average change from the premerger hypothetical combined bank that is a weighted average of an acquirer and a target. The column under the heading of "Premerger acquirer" denotes the average changes from the premerger acquirer. ΔX (t-year postmerger) is the difference of the variable X between t-year postmerger and the premerger average over five years (or less if data is not available). ΔX (postmerger average) is the difference between X(postmerger average) and X(premerger average), where X(postmerger average) is the postmerger average of the variable X over five years (or less if data is not available) and X(premerger average) is the premerger average of the variable X over five years (or less if data not available).

[a]Significant at the 1 percent level for the null hypothesis that ΔX (or X) has zero mean.
[b]Significant at the 5 percent level for the null hypothesis that ΔX (or X) has zero mean.
***Significant at the 1 percent level for the Wilcoxon signed-rank test for the null hypothesis that ΔX (or X) has median zero.
**Significant at the 5 percent level for the Wilcoxon signed-rank test for the null hypothesis that ΔX (or X) has median zero.

the deposit or loan market. This is not surprising, given that both acquiring major banks and target major banks operated nationwide.

Business scope variables suggest that the share of SME loans significantly increases three years after mergers. One possible reason is that acquirers may have spread the skills necessary to make SME loans to targets. However, more a plausible reason is that when the government recapitalized banks, it required banks to increase SME loans. Because banks tended to be consolidated after the government recapitalization, consolidated banks increased SME loans. This result is different from U.S. bank merger evidences, especially for the mergers of large banks (Berger, Demsetz, and Strahan 1999, 170). The changes in fees and commissions and in the loan-to-asset ratio are not significant.

Bank health measures suggest that the changes in the capital-to-asset ratios are negative and significant three years after mergers and the changes in the risk-based Bank for International Settlements (BIS) capital ratios are also negative and significant (for t-statistics) for three years after mergers. The improvement of ROA after the merger was not quick or sufficient enough to offset the initial gap of the capital ratios between consolidated banks (i.e., acquirers and targets) and their peers. In addition, the changes in the nonperforming loan ratios, based either on Bank Law or the Financial Rehabilitation Act, are positive and significant three years after mergers. Consolidated banks may have applied a stricter standard to recognize nonperforming loans than before, resulting in the increase in disclosed nonperforming loans. It is well known that Japanese banks often manipulated the amounts of disclosed nonperforming loans so that they could satisfy the Basel capital standards before the Financial Rehabilitation Plan (i.e., Takenaka Plan) in 2002. In addition, a consolidated bank may have been exposed to the risk of an unproportionally large amount of loans to some specific large borrowers as a result of the consolidation. When those borrowers fell in financial distress, the consolidated bank may have continued to lend to them in order to avoid their failures, which would cause a sharp decrease in the bank's own capital.[26]

Finally, private benefit variables suggest that the change in the advertisement expenses as a proportion of total assets is not significant. The consolidated bank did not significantly increase advertisement expenses. In addition, the change in the average loan growth rate over the postmerger five years is significantly negative. The change in the average asset growth rate is also negative, though not significant. These results suggest that mergers triggered asset restructuring. Considering these results together, we may say that no evidence is found that supports the managerial empire building hypothesis.

The second and third columns of table 8.7 report the changes in the postmerger performance from the hypothesized premerger combined bank for the subperiods of the precrisis period (fiscal year 1990 to 1997) and the postcrisis period (fiscal year 1998 to 2004), respectively. In the premerger period, the change in the share of SME loans is significantly positive. On the other hand, in the postmerger period, the changes in the loan growth rate, the asset growth rate, and the capital ratio are significantly negative, and the change in the nonperforming loan ratio based on the Bank Law is significantly positive. The mergers in the postmerger crisis period seem to

26. Such a behavior is called "ever-greening" (Peek and Rosengren 2005) or "zombie lending" (Caballero, Hoshi, and Kashyap 2006).

have been more directed to asset restructuring and yet to have resulted in a worse bank health, though the long-run effects of the mergers in the early 2000s may not have been realized yet.

The last column of table 8.7 shows the changes of the performance of consolidated banks from the premerger acquirer's level for the full sample period. Most of the changes from the premerger acquirer's level are qualitatively the same as the changes from the premerger hypothetical combined bank, except that the changes in the share of SME loans is not significant, reflecting the fact that the premerger acquirer's share of SME loans was higher than the average of major banks.

Regional Banks

Table 8.8 shows the changes in the financial ratios of the consolidated regional banks. The first column shows the changes from the premerger hypothetical combined bank for the full sample period. Like major banks, the changes in ROA are negative, though not significant, three years after mergers and then turn to be positive and significant (for t-statistics) five years after mergers. This increase in ROA is caused partly by a strengthened market power of a consolidated bank in the loan market, which can be seen by the positive and significant change in the loan interest rate three and five years after mergers. Though the increase in the loan interest rate may reflect the change in the riskiness of the portfolio, the share of SME loans, which can be considered to be relatively risky, tended to decrease, if anything, rather than to increase after mergers. Furthermore, examining the correlations of the change in the loan interest rate with the Herfindahl Index and with the SME loan share, we find that the former is 0.571, while the latter is 0.243. A relatively high correlation between the change in the loan interest rate and the Herfindahl Index is consistent with the market power hypothesis. Though there is a possibility that consolidated banks implemented more stringent risk management, it would be difficult to charge higher loan rates without a strengthened market power. The changes in the capital-to-asset ratio are negative up to five years after mergers, though significant only in the five-year average after mergers. The improvement of ROA after the merger was too slow and small to offset the initial gap of the capital ratios between consolidated banks and their peers. The advertisement expenses as a proportion of total costs decrease significantly three and five years after mergers, which is not consistent with the managerial empire-building hypothesis.

Dividing the sample period into the precrisis period and the postcrisis period (the second and third columns, respectively), we see that the changes in the capital-to-asset ratio are negative for both periods but significant only for the postcrisis period, while the change in the fees and commissions is positive and significant in the postcrisis period (for the z-statistics).

Table 8.8   Postmerger performance of regional banks

	Weighted average			Acquirer
	1990–2004	1990–1997	1998–2004	1990–2004
Return of assets (ROA)				
ΔROA (3-year postmerger)	−1.869			−1.934
ΔROA (5-year postmerger)	0.504[b]			0.481[b]
ΔROA (postmerger average)	−0.471	0.067	−0.793	−0.530
Cost Ratio				
ΔCost Ratio (3-year postmerger)	−0.003			0.021
ΔCost Ratio (5-year postmerger)	−0.084			−0.045
ΔCost Ratio (postmerger average)	0.009	−0.064	0.053	0.021
Fees and Commissions				
ΔFees and Commissions (3-year postmerger)	0.013			−0.001
ΔFees and Commissions (5-year postmerger)	−0.003			−0.010
ΔFees and Commissions (postmerger average)	0.034	−0.005	0.057**	0.014
Loan-to-Asset Ratio				
ΔLoan-to-Asset Ratio (3-year postmerger)	−2.131			−0.623
ΔLoan-to-Asset Ratio (5-year postmerger)	−3.387			−2.100
ΔLoan-to-Asset Ratio (postmerger average)	−2.163	−2.299	−2.082	−1.303
Loans to SMEs				
ΔLoans to SMEs (3-year postmerger)	−1.556			−1.079
ΔLoans to SMEs (5-year postmerger)	−1.320			−0.721
ΔLoans to SMEs (postmerger average)	−0.335	−1.310	0.249	0.415
Loan Growth Rate				
ΔLoan Growth Rate (3-year postmerger)	−3.471			−3.587
ΔLoan Growth Rate (5-year postmerger)	−1.928			−2.549
ΔLoan Growth Rate (postmerger average)	−0.846	−0.974	−0.768	−0.818
Deposit Interest Rate				
ΔDeposit Interest Rate (3-year postmerger)	−0.010			0.015
ΔDeposit Interest Rate (5-year postmerger)	0.125			0.143
ΔDeposit Interest Rate (postmerger average)	−0.006	0.025	−0.024	0.023
Loan Interest Rate				
ΔLoan Interest Rate (3-year postmerger)	0.187[b]			0.269
ΔLoan Interest Rate (5-year postmerger)	0.177[b]			0.221
ΔLoan Interest Rate (postmerger average)	0.069	0.174	0.007	0.178[b]**
Capital-to-Asset Ratio				
ΔCapital-to-Asset Ratio (3-year postmerger)	−0.371			−0.416
ΔCapital-to-Asset Ratio (5-year postmerger)	−0.202			−0.283
ΔCapital-to-Asset Ratio (postmerger average)	−0.892[b]**	−0.135	−1.347[a]**	−0.995[b]**
Risk-Based Capital Ratio (BIS)				
ΔRisk-Based Capital Ratio (BIS) (3-year postmerger)				
ΔRisk-Based Capital Ratio (BIS) (5-year postmerger)				
ΔRisk-Based Capital Ratio (BIS) (postmerger average)	−0.543		−0.543	−0.718
Nonperforming Loan Ratio (BL)				
ΔNonperforming Loan Ratio (BL) (3-year postmerger)				

■ble 8.8   (continued)

	Weighted average			Acquirer
	1990–2004	1990–1997	1998–2004	1990–2004
ΔNonperforming Loan Ratio (BL) (5-year postmerger)				
ΔNonperforming Loan Ratio (BL) (postmerger average)	0.813		0.813	0.870
onperforming Loan Ratio (FRL)				
ΔNonperforming Loan Ratio (FRL) (3-year postmerger)				
ΔNonperforming Loan Ratio (FRL) (5-year postmerger)				
ΔNonperforming Loan Ratio (FRL) (postmerger average)	1.478		1.478	0.560
dvertisement Expenses				
ΔAdvertisement Expenses (3-year postmerger)	−0.353[a]			−0.300
ΔAdvertisement Expenses (5-year postmerger)	−0.251[b]			−0.154
ΔAdvertisement Expenses (postmerger average)	−0.052	−0.203	0.038	0.064
sset Growth				
ΔAsset Growth (3-year postmerger)	−2.223			−2.018
ΔAsset Growth (5-year postmerger)	−1.652			−2.126
ΔAsset Growth (postmerger average)	0.242	−0.158	0.482	0.298

ote: See notes to table 8.7.
■gnificant at the 1 percent level for the null hypothesis that ΔX (or X) has zero mean.
ignificant at the 1 percent level for the null hypothesis that ΔX (or X) has zero mean.
Significant at the 5 percent level for the Wilcoxon signed-rank test for the null hypothesis the ΔX (or
■ has median zero.

The last column shows the changes of the performance of a consolidated bank from the premerger acquirer for the full sample period. The changes from the premerger acquirer are qualitatively the same as the changes from the premerger hypothetical combined bank except for the change in the advertisement expenses from the premerger acquirer, which is negative but not significant.

Shinkin Banks

Table 8.9 shows the changes in the financial ratios of the consolidated *shinkin* banks for the full sample period. The first column shows the changes from the hypothetical premerger combined bank. Some financial ratios change in similar ways to those of major and regional banks. First, the changes in ROA are negative three years after mergers and then turn to positive, though not significant. Second, the changes in the loan interest rate are positive, though not significant. The correlation of the change in the loan interest with the change in the Herfindahl Index is positive (0.356) and significant, suggesting that the increase in the loan interest rate, if any,

Table 8.9   Postmerger performance of *Shinkin* banks

	Weighted average			Acquirer
	1990–2002	1990–1997	1998–2002	1990–2002
Return of assets (ROA)				
ΔROA (3-year postmerger)	−0.032			−0.047
ΔROA (5-year postmerger)	0.107			0.093
ΔROA (postmerger average)	0.003	0.064	−0.098	−0.019
Cost Ratio				
ΔCost Ratio (3-year postmerger)	−0.002			−0.011
ΔCost Ratio (5-year postmerger)	0.011			−0.014
ΔCost Ratio (postmerger average)	0.000	0.018	−0.029	0.000
Fees and Commissions				
ΔFees and Commissions (3-year postmerger)	0.004			0.003
ΔFees and Commissions (5-year postmerger)	0.007			0.005
ΔFees and Commissions (postmerger average)	0.003	0.003	0.003	0.003
Loan-to-Asset Ratio				
ΔLoan-to-Asset Ratio (3-year postmerger)	0.718			−0.120
ΔLoan-to-Asset Ratio (5-year postmerger)	1.127			0.186
ΔLoan-to-Asset Ratio (postmerger average)	0.765	0.328	1.492	0.178
Loan Growth Rate				
ΔLoan Growth Rate (3-year postmerger)	−0.916			−1.833[a]***
ΔLoan Growth Rate (5-year postmerger)	−0.971			−2.029[b]**
ΔLoan Growth Rate (postmerger average)	−0.823	−0.744	−0.956	−1.940[a]***
Deposit Interest Rate				
ΔDeposit Interest Rate (3-year postmerger)	0.037			0.052
ΔDeposit Interest Rate (5-year postmerger)	0.039			0.064
ΔDeposit Interest Rate (postmerger average)	0.022	0.049	−0.021	0.029
Loan Interest Rate				
ΔLoan Interest Rate (3-year postmerger)	0.084			0.052
ΔLoan Interest Rate (5-year postmerger)	0.088			0.045
ΔLoan Interest Rate (postmerger average)	0.062	0.079	0.033	0.040
Capital-to-Asset Ratio				
ΔCapital-to-Asset Ratio (3-year postmerger)	−0.547[b]**			−0.659[a]***
ΔCapital-to-Asset Ratio (5-year postmerger)	−0.476			−0.551
ΔCapital-to-Asset Ratio (postmerger average)	−0.510[a]***	−0.487[b]**	−0.548[a]***	−0.625[a]***
Risk-Based Capital Ratio (BIS)				
ΔRisk-Based Capital Ratio (BIS) (3-year postmerger)	−1.508			−1.801[b]**
ΔRisk-Based Capital Ratio (BIS) (5-year postmerger)	−3.331[b]			−3.354[b]
ΔRisk-Based Capital Ratio (BIS) (postmerger average)	−0.969[a]***	−1.820	−0.733[a]***	−1.311[a]***
Nonperforming Loan Ratio (BL)				
ΔNonperforming Loan Ratio (BL) (3-year postmerger)	0.697			1.565
ΔNonperforming Loan Ratio (BL) (5-year postmerger)	0.842			1.338
ΔNonperforming Loan Ratio (BL) (postmerger average)	0.625	0.094	0.782	1.426[b]**

Table 8.9   (continued)

	Weighted average			Acquirer
	1990–2002	1990–1997	1998–2002	1990–2002
Asset Growth				
ΔAsset Growth (3-year postmerger)	−1.070			−1.358[b]**
ΔAsset Growth (5-year postmerger)	−1.844[b]**			−2.011[a]**
ΔAsset Growth (postmerger average)	−1.904[a]***	−1.462[b]**	−2.640[a]***	−2.543[a]***

Note: See notes to table 8.7.

[a]Significant at the 1 percent level for the null hypothesis that Δ*X* (or *X*) has zero mean.

[b]Significant at the 1 percent level for the null hypothesis that Δ*X* (or *X*) has zero mean.

***Significant at the 1 percent level for the Wilcoxon signed-rank test for the null hypothesis the Δ*X* (or *X*) has median zero.

**Significant at the 5 percent level for the Wilcoxon signed-rank test for the null hypothesis the Δ*X* (or *X*) has median zero.

may be caused by a strengthened market power. Third, the capital-to-asset ratio and the risk-based capital ratio (BIS) are both negative and significant for most of the postmerger years. Fourth, the changes in the asset growth rate are negative and significant five years after mergers.

The second and third columns show the results for the precrisis and postcrisis periods, respectively. The changes in the capital-to-asset ratios and the asset growth rate are negative and significant in both periods, while the change in the risk-based capital ratio is negative in both periods but significant only in the postcrisis period.

The last column shows the changes in the financial ratios of a consolidated bank from the premerger acquirer. The changes in the capital-to-asset ratio, the risk-based capital ratio, and the asset growth rate are similar to the changes from the hypothetical combined bank, while the changes in the loan growth rates are negative and significant up to five years after M&As, and the change in the nonperforming loan ratio is positive and significant for the five-year postmerger average.

We may summarize the postmerger performance of consolidated banks as follows. First, consolidated banks tended to go through a decline in ROA at first and then to increase ROA about five years after mergers, though this recovery was significant only for the mergers of regional banks. It seems to take considerable time and cost to integrate different information systems and other business methods. Second, in the case of the M&As by regional banks or *shinkin* banks, consolidated banks tended to raise interest rates on loans, though this is significant only for the mergers by regional banks, suggesting that their market power was strengthened within the prefecture they operated in. This is consistent with the U.S. evidence, showing that in-market consolidation strengthens market power. Third, the changes in services provided are different by bank type and by period. Consolidated major banks tended to expand SME loans in the precrisis period, while consolidated regional banks tended to expand fees and commissions business in the postcrisis period. Fourth, consolidated banks did not recover bank health after mergers. The capital-to-asset ratio tended to decrease rather than to increase regardless of bank type. The recovery of ROA was too slow and small to fill in the initial gap of the capital-asset-ratio between consolidated banks and their peers. In addition, consolidated banks did not decrease nonperforming loans. Finally, consolidated banks tended to decelerate the loan growth rate and the asset growth rate, suggesting that consolidated banks tried to restructure assets and to downsize. Consolidated banks did not increase the advertisement expenses. The managerial empire-building hypothesis does not seem to be valid in Japan.

8.8   Conclusion

The recent waves of M&As in the banking industries across the world raise important questions of whether mergers enhance the efficiency of consolidated banks and contribute to the stabilization of the banking sector. We investigate the motives and consequences of the consolidation of banks in Japan during the period of fiscal year 1990 to fiscal year 2004. In particular, we test the four hypotheses concerning the motives for bank mergers: efficiency improving, strengthening market power, taking advantage of a too-big-to-fail policy, and managerial empire building.

We first investigated the reasons for the recent merger wave using the aggregate data at the prefecture level. Our results suggest that M&As tended to occur when the overall bank health was deteriorated and where the market was less concentrated. These results are consistent with the too-big-to-fail or stabilization policy hypothesis and the market power hypothesis, respectively.

Our analysis concerning the relationship between ex-ante bank characteristics and the decision of M&As suggests the following. First, in the postcrisis period (1998 to 2004), efficient banks tended to acquire an inefficient bank except for the M&As of corporative (*shinkin*) banks. This finding is consistent with the efficiency-improving hypothesis. Second, unhealthy banks tended to be consolidated with each other, especially in the postcrisis period, which is consistent with the too-big-to-fail policy or stabilization policy hypothesis.

Our investigation of postmerger performance suggests the following. First, consolidated banks tended to go through a decline in ROA at first and then to increase ROA about five years after mergers, though these changes are not necessarily significant. Second, in-market consolidation enabled consolidated banks to raise the loan interest rate. Third, consolidated banks tended to decrease the capital-to-asset ratio and not to decrease nonperforming loans. Finally, consolidated banks tended to restrain loan and asset growths and not to increase advertisement expenses.

In sum, our analysis suggests that the government's too-big-to-fail policy or its attempt at stabilizing the local financial market through consolidations played an important role in the M&As, though its attempt does not seem to have been successful. The efficiency-improving motive also seems to have driven the M&As conducted by major banks and regional banks in the postcrisis period, while the market-power motive seems to have driven the M&As conducted by regional banks and corporative (*shinkin*) banks. We obtain no evidence that supports managerial motives for empire building.

Japanese banking industries are still in the midst of an ongoing merger wave. Future research incorporating new data that will be available in coming years would help us fully understand its eventual consequences.

Data Appendix

- ROA = Current Profit/Total Asset × 100
- Cost Ratio = (Personnel Expenditure + Nonpersonnel Expenditure + Taxes)/Total Asset × 100
- Fees and Commisions = Fees and Commisions/Total Asset × 100
- Loan-to-Asset Ratio = Loans Outstanding/Total Asset × 100
- Loans to SMEs = Loans to SMEs/Total Asset × 100
- Loan Growth Rate = Growth Rate of Loans Outstanding × 100
- Deposit Interest Rate = Interest on Deposits/Deposits Outstanding × 100
- Loan Interest Rate = Interest on Loans/Loans Outstanding × 100
- Capital-to-Asset Ratio = Equity Capital/Total Asset × 100
- Risk-Based Capital Ratio (BIS) = Regulatory Capital/Risk Asset × 100 (Based on BIS)
- Nonperforming Loan Ratio (BL) = Nonperforming Loan Based on Banking Law/Total Asset × 100
- Nonperforming Loan Ratio (FRL) = Nonperforming Loan Based on Financial Revitalization Law/Total Asset × 100
- Ln Asset = ln(Total Asset)
- Asset Growth = Growth Rate of Total Asset × 100
- Herfindahl Index = Prefectural Herfindahl Index (calculated by deposits outstanding of regional and shinkin banks)
- GDP Growth = Growth Rate of GDP × 100
- Stock Price = Growth Rate of the Stock Price × 100
- Industrial Stock Price = Growth Rate of the Stock Price Index of banking industry × 100

• Advertisement Expenses = Advertisement Expenses/Operating Cost
  × 100

References

Arikawa, Yasuihiro, and Hideaki Miyajima. 2007. Understanding M&A booms in Japan: What drives Japanese M&A? RIETI Discussion Paper no. 07-E-042. Tokyo: Research Institute of Economy, Trade, and Industry.
Berger, Allen N., Rebecca S. Demsetz, and Philip E. Strahan. 1999. The consolidation of the financial services industry: Cause, consequences, and implications for the future. *Journal of Banking and Finance* 23:135–94.
Bliss, Richard T., and Richard J. Rosen. 2001. CEO compensation and bank mergers. *Journal of Financial Economics* 61:107–38.
Caballero, Ricardo J., Takeo Hoshi, and Anil A. Kashyap. 2006. Zombie lending and depressed restructuring in Japan. MIT Economics Working Paper no. 06-06. Cambridge, MA: Massachusetts Institute of Technology.
Delong, Gayle, and Robert Deyoung. 2007. Learning by observing: Information spillovers in the execution and valuation of commercial bank M&As. *Journal of Finance* 52 (1): 181–216.
Focarelli, Dario, and Fabio Panetta. 2003. Are mergers beneficial to consumers? Evidence from the market for bank deposits. *American Economic Review* 93:1152–72.
Focarelli, Dario, and Alberto Franco Pozzolo. 2005. Where do banks expand abroad? An empirical analysis. *Journal of Business* 78:2435–63.
Harford, Jarrad. 2005. What drives merger waves? *Journal of Financial Economics* 77:529–60.
Hoshi, Takeo, and Anil Kashyap. 2001. *Corporate finance and governance in Japan: The road to the future.* Cambridge, MA: MIT Press.
Hosono, Kaoru, Koji Sakai, and Kotaro Tsuru. 2006. Consolidation of corporative banks (*Shinkin*) in Japan: Motives and consequences. RIETI Discussion Paper no. 06-E-034. Tokyo: Research Institute of Economy, Trade, and Industry.
Kano, Masaji, and Yoshiro Tsutsui. 2003. Geographical segmentation in Japanese bank loan market. *Regional Science and Urban Economics* 33 (2): 157–74.
Mitchell, Mark L., and J. Harold Mulherin. 1996. The impact of industry shocks on takeover and restructuring activity. *Journal of Financial Economics* 41 (2): 193–229.
Okada, Tae. 2005. Consequences of bank mergers (in Japanese). Paper presented at the Japanese Economic Association Spring Meeting, Kyoto, Japan.
Peek, Joe, and Eric S. Rosengren. 2005. Unnatural selection: Perverse incentives and the misallocation of credit in Japan. *American Economic Review* 95 (4): 1144–66.
Rhoades, Stephen A. 1998. The efficiency effects of bank mergers: An overview of case studies of nine mergers. *Journal of Banking and Finance* 22:273–91.
Shleifer, Andrei, and Robert W. Vishny. 2003. Stock market driven acquisitions. *Journal of Financial Economics* 70:295–311.
Wooldridge, Jefferey M. 2001. *Econometric analysis of cross-section and panel data.* Cambridge, MA: MIT Press.
Yafeh, Yishay, and Oved Yosha. 2003. Large shareholders and banks: Who monitors and how? *Economic Journal* 113 (484): 128–46.

Yamori, Nobuyoshi, and Kozo Harimaya. 2004. Governance of shinkin banks and choice of mergers (in Japanese). Paper presented at the symposium on the Governance and Contemporary Meaning of Cooperative Financial Institutions at Hokkaido University, Sapporo, Japan.

Yamori, Nobuyoshi, Kozo Harimaya, and K. Kondo. 2003. Are banks affiliated with holding companies more efficient than independent banks? The recent experience regarding Japanese regional BHCs. *Asia Pacific Financial Markets* 10 (4): 359–76.

Comment   Hiro Ito

Before the 1990s, bank mergers were hardly seen in Japan except for a very few cases of rescue mergers. Even those rare mergers were initiated by the Ministry of Finance (MOF) with help of keiretsu-related companies and banks of the rescued bank. At present, bank merger is no longer uncommon in Japan. In retrospect, two events led to a significant increase in bank mergers in Japan. One is a series of deregulation/liberalization policies in the financial sector that started in the early 1980s, and the other is the 1990s recession.

Deregulation/liberalization policies contributed to thinning profit margins, which used to be guaranteed by the government through financially repressive policies, and thereby intensifying market competitions for the financial institutions. The recession that started in 1991 hurt financial institutions' balance sheets through severe asset deflation and weakened loan demand. Inevitably, in the early 1990s, merging with other institutions started to be viewed as one of the means to survive the severe conditions in the Japanese financial industry. In the aftermath of the banking crisis of 1998, which broke out with several major bank failures, as the Japanese banking industry became fluid, so did the number of bank mergers drastically increase.

With this background, this chapter investigates a fundamental question pertaining to banking consolidations in Japan: "What motivates banks to decide to merge?" More specifically, the authors investigate whether banks decide to merge so as (1) to increase market power; (2) to improve cost efficiency; (3) to merely follow government's financial stabilization policy; or (4) to build a managerial empire. The authors categorize the first two views as the "value maximization view" because these two consequences can lead to increasing the value of shares and the last two as the financial stabilization view and the managerial empire building view.[1]

Hiro Ito is an associate professor of economics at Portland State University.

1. As Andy Rose pointed out at the presentation, I also agree that points one and two should not be considered to be one view. Although both of the two points may lead to in-

With these questions in mind, the authors conduct an empirical analysis on what kind of premerger conditions motivate banks, either acquirers or acquirees, to merge, and on what bank consolidations could do to the merged banks in terms of cost efficiency, profitability, and healthiness of the financial conditions.

There is no question that this chapter investigates an interesting question. When bank mergers started becoming more commonplace in the late 1990s, many discussions arose both within the policy community and in the general public about the efficacy of bank consolidations. Many wondered if bank mergers merely mean big amalgamations of feeble banks or the creation of slimmer and more efficient banks. While there are very few studies on mergers and acquisitions (M&A) in the Japanese banking industry—simply because it is only recently that they started appearing in the Japanese banking scene—this chapter nicely fills the void.

Using a sample of major banks, regional banks, and *shinkin* banks for fiscal year 1990 to 2004 (fiscal year 1990 to 2001 for *shinkins*), the authors find empirical evidence as follows. As for the premerger determinants of bank mergers, efficient banks, among major and regional banks, but not *shinkin* banks, tend to acquire inefficient ones. The authors argue that this result is in line with the value maximization view. They also find that large, but unhealthy regional or *shinkin* banks tend to acquire small and unhealthy ones, which they believe is suggestive of the government's stabilization efforts. As for the postmerger conditions, they find that merged banks tend to experience a short-term decline, but a long-term gain, in their return on assets (ROA) in the aftermath of consolidations. Merged banks also tend to raise loan rates, which they believe evidence that merged banks exert more market power but also are more likely to fail to increase the capital-to-asset ratio or to decrease the volume of nonperforming loans (NPLs). They also find that merged banks tend to experience loan growth.

This chapter presents an interesting set of results and adds important information to the debate on the efficacy of bank consolidations in Japan. It should help financial administrators as well as bankers in Japan to self-evaluate their policies. However, because of its potential policy implications, this chapter deserves careful scrutiny. Let me make three comments on the estimation of the premerger determinants of bank mergers and one on the postmerger estimation.

First, on the premerger estimation, the authors may need to be more careful about theoretical interpretation of the estimation results. When empirical findings are analyzed, the authors often argue whether the estimated coefficients are indicative of banks' market-driven motivations (i.e., the "value

---

creasing the value of shares, these points are about completely opposite issues in terms of the competitiveness of market conditions. That is, while point one indicates an increasing markup for a bank, that is, more gains from less-competitive market conditions, point two refers to more-competitive conditions for the bank.

maximization view") or reflecting the government's stabilization efforts. However, these two views are by no means mutually exclusive, especially in the case of Japanese banking industry where, historically, the MOF has heavily intervened with the industry. Although a series of deregulation/ liberalization policies and the creation of the Financial Services Agency (FSA) have lessened the government's meddling since the late 1990s, it is still the case that bank consolidations in Japan are a function of what the government or FSA thinks. In other words, political-economic factors play an important role in banks' decision makings about potential mergers regardless of the type and size of the banks. Hence, the value maximization view and the government stabilization view are not an *either/or* issue and, therefore, the empirical results should not be interpreted one way or the other. That said, from a different angle, it may not be sufficient to have only economic factors as explanatory variables for the estimation as the authors have done. They may need to include some political variables to incorporate the political-economic factors of the decision makings.

Second, the timing of the dependent and explanatory variables appears to be questionable. To avoid bidirectional causality, the authors lag the explanatory variables by one year. However, lagging the right-hand-side variables by one year may not capture appropriately the effects of the determinants of bank mergers. In other words, conditions in one year before a merger may not properly reflect the motivations on the side of merging banks. This concern arises due to the following two reasons. First, it usually takes a long time, possibly more than a year, for Japanese banks to implement a merger after its announcement. Hence, in the year prior to a merger, it is often the case that the merging banks are preparing and working toward the merger, not determining the merger. Therefore, the business or economic conditions in one year prior do not represent as the determinants of the merger. Second, using one-year lagged variables for the explanatory variables may involve a risk of capturing moral hazard behavior. That is, a bank that is to be acquired by a relatively healthy or bigger bank may behave on contrary to the benefit of the future shareholders of the merged bank by taking unnecessarily risky investment. Especially, if a to-be-acquired bank is riddled with severely weakened balance sheets, it may as well take the long-bomb strategy—gamble on high-risk, high-return investment to improve balance sheets—because it has small net worth to lose anyway. The U.S. savings and loan crisis witnessed such moral hazard cases. One cannot rule out the possibility for Japanese mergers and acquisitions. In this sense also, lagging the explanatory variables for one year may not be appropriate to examine the motivations for Japanese banks' mergers.

Last, on the premerger estimation, the results of the determinants of bank mergers (shown in table 8.3) are generally not that significant. The weakness in the results is suspected to be due to multicollinearity. In the estimation, the authors attempt to incorporate different aspects of banking business, namely, cost performance, size, and healthiness of the banks, and include several variables for each aspect as explanatory variables. For example, the ROA and the cost ratios are included to capture the market efficiency levels of the banks, whereas the capital-to-asset ratio and the asset growth rate are to capture their size. However, one can suspect that these variables for each aspect of banking business are highly correlated. Furthermore, these different aspects of banking business can also be highly correlated with each other. Either or both of cost performance and the operation size of banks usually affect the healthiness of the banks, or vice versa. At the very least, the authors may need to be careful about the choice of variables and avoid unnecessary multicollinearity.

Finally, on the postmerger estimation results, the authors find that merged banks tend to raise loan rates and interpret that as evidence that merged banks strengthen their market power. However, this result can also be interpreted as that newly merged banks tend to implement more stringent risk management and, therefore, charge higher rates on their loans. It has been discussed that a merger plan is often approved—implicitly or explicitly—by the MOF or FSA with a condition that the new bank will improve balance sheets and capital adequacy. If that is the case, it is not surprising that a newly merged bank implement more stringent risk management and charge higher loan rates.

After all, this chapter can convey important messages to financial administrators and bankers. For that purpose, careful interpretation of the empirical results and some refinement in the model construction may be necessary. It seems that the NPLs problem is finally history; as of the spring of 2007, among the six major city banks, the ratio of NPLs to total loans is around 1.5 percent, a significant fall from 8 percent in 2002. As the NPL problem is over, fluidity in the banking industry may end as well. However, given the current M&A boom and ample liquidity on the global scale, restructuring of Japanese banks may not end soon. Given that, the implications this chapter presents can be quite significant.

Comment   Barry Williams

I appreciate the opportunity to discuss this chapter as it provides an insight into the merger process in a country I do not make a focus of my research. Thus I found the chapter both informative and interesting. I do have a few comments to make that I feel can possibly improve the chapter.

Barry Williams is a professor of finance and head of the Department of Finance at Bond University.

Motivation

The chapter raises some interesting questions, but I feel that much of the material in the second paragraph (and some of the third paragraph) should be promoted to the first paragraph, in order to strengthen the attractiveness of this chapter. Further, I feel that some of the literature review material in the first few paragraphs should be moved to a separate literature review section.

Literature Review

I feel that the literature review should be separated from the introduction and motivation, as it will make the transition between these two components of the chapter clearer. At the moment the motivation and literature review are a bit too intermingled for my tastes.

Managerial Empire Building

Given that one of the interesting results of this chapter is the lack of managerial empire building, I feel that the literature discussion here should be a bit more detailed. This could provide a stronger foundation for the rejection of this hypothesis. As stated, "If managerial private incentive for empire building is a major motive for mergers, bank efficiency or healthiness is not associated with the M&A decision." I am always cautious of any hypothesis that involves testing a null hypothesis and would prefer this issue explored with a different test.

Major Bank Measure of Market Power

It is stated in the chapter that the measure of market power for regional and *shinkin* banks is the Herfindahl index. I assume that this is the prefecture Herfindahl index. I would like to see some discussion of the omission of this variable for the major banks. In a similar vein, given that the major banks operate nationally, how was the prefectural gross domestic product (GDP) chosen?

Choice of Significance Level

I would like to see the discussion focus upon the use of a 5 percent significance level, with results at the 10 percent level not considered significant. In this vein, I feel that the tables presenting the results should be tidied up; they are a bit messy, and removing the 10 percent significant level would help, as would perhaps the use of boldface font for significant variables.

Choice of Postmerger Window for Analysis

In the interests of simplification, I feel a focus upon the three- five-year postmerger period would be valuable. As shown by studies such as Focarelli and Panetta (2003), Focarelli and Pozzolo (2005) and Rhoades (1998), a two- three-year postmerger period is needed to determine if there are any postmerger gains.

Impact on Small- and Medium-Sized Enterprise Lending

The chapter has an interesting result that postmerger share of major bank lending to small- and medium-sized enterprises (SME) increases; this is opposite to the result of Berger, Demsetz, and Strahan (1999), and I would like to see a discussion addressing why this opposite is obtained.

I appreciate the chance to review this chapter and thank the authors for an interesting chapter that raises a number of valuable and topical issues. Like all interesting papers, this one raises a number of questions while also answering some other questions.

References

Berger, Allen, N., Rebecca S. Demsetz, and Philip E. Strahan. 1999. The consolidation of the financial services industry: Causes, consequences, and implications for the future. *Journal of Banking and Finance* 23:135–94.
Focarelli, Dario, and Fabio Panetta. 2003. Are mergers beneficial to consumers? Evidence from the market for bank deposits. *American Economic Review* 93:1152–72.
Focarelli, Dario, and Alberto Franco Pozzolo. 2005. Where do banks expand abroad? An empirical analysis. *Journal of Business* 78:2435–63.
Rhoades, Stephen A. 1998. The efficiency effects of bank mergers: An overview of case studies of nine mergers. *Journal of Banking and Finance* 22:273–91.

IV

Reform and Dynamism

Did the Japanese Stock Market Appropriately Price the Takenaka Financial Reform?

Masaya Sakuragawa and Yoshitsugu Watanabe

9.1 Introduction

The financial crisis and nonperforming-loan problem effectively ended in 2005, after one decade since its onset. The Japanese government continued a policy of forbearance until October 2002, when the government released the aggressive financial reform, the so-called Takenaka Plan, in order to accelerate the disposal of nonperforming loans. The Takenaka Plan was remarkable in that it was the first reform in Japan that strongly requested that banks improve bank governance.

Bank governance becomes effective through market discipline and the government's supervision. Behind the release of the Takenaka Plan were undercapitalized banks and the weak supervision to accommodate them. The government continuously took a policy of forbearance that allowed banks to keep financing almost insolvent firms and to understate the amount of nonperforming loans. Minimum capital requirements had been formally introduced, but did not work effectively. A number of papers point out that the government allowed banks to engage in various accounting discretions in meeting capital requirements, including Ito and Sasaki (2002), Shrieves and Dahl (2003), Hosono and Sakuragawa (2003), Peek and Rosengren (2005), and Skinner (2005). The stock market also played little disciplinary role on bank governance.

What the government chose was to strengthen supervision to banks

Masaya Sakuragawa is a professor of economics at Keio University. Yoshitsugu Watanabe is a research associate at the Global Security Research Institute of Keio University.

We greatly appreciate our two referees, Takatoshi Ito and Randall Morck; Ken Koibuchi; Andrew Rose; and participants of East Asia Seminar on Economics held in Singapore and the eighth Macro-Conference held in Keio University. This project is supported by Nijyuuis- seiki Bunka Gakujyutsu Zaidann.

rather than to use market discipline. The Takenaka Plan strongly requested banks to accelerate the disposal of nonperforming loans and, hence, to improve the transparency of financial information. However, the perverse link of the stock market with the banking sector made things complicated. If investors thought the reform was too tough and reacted contagiously, it would have been difficult to implement the reform that requested banks meet capital requirements because Japanese banks held substantial amounts of equities so that they were vulnerable to declines in stock prices. The policymakers came to understand strongly the necessity for the policy coordination between the government and Bank of Japan (BOJ). In March 2003, the new governor of BOJ, Toshihiko Fukui, announced a package of monetary policies to accommodate the Takenaka Plan, including the continuation of the ample supply of liquidity to banks and an increase in the maximum amount of equity holdings that BOJ purchases from banks.

The purpose of this chapter is to study the market evaluation of the Takenaka Plan, using event study methodology. We investigate several financial events that occurred in 2002 and 2003, including the release of the Takenaka Plan, the announcement of the work schedule for implementing that plan, the release of a package of monetary policies, and the failures of Resona Bank and Ashikaga Bank. We hope to understand how market participants perceived the implementation of the Takenaka Plan through these events that will be closely related to the effectiveness of supervision to banks. For each of the events, we examine three questions. The first question is if the impact of each event on the stock market return is positive or negative to the banking sector as a whole. The second question is if the impact on the stock market return, if it exists, is uniform across banks, regardless of possible differences of the financial condition of individual banks. The third question is if the impact reflects more than pure contagion across banks, and if market participants differentiate the riskiness of individual banks by their financial conditions. The answer to the third question may uncover possible improvement of financial supervision.

We believe that the estimation for the market reaction to each event that occurred after the introduction of the Takenaka Plan contributes to evaluating the financial reform and bank governance in Japan. By estimating several events sequentially, we can investigate how market participants changed their expectation for the implementation of the financial reform over time. In addition, we can evaluate the role of the policy coordination by comparing estimations between, before, and after the monetary policy.

Brewer et al. (2003), a paper that is closely related to ours, estimate how the stock market prices financial conditions of individual banks for the failures of four commercial banks and two securities firms that occurred for the period from 1995 to 1998. Their finding reports that to some extent the stock market incorporates information on financial conditions of individual banks into prices although the ability of the Japanese stock market to price the riskiness of financial firms was recognized to have been low due to the poor transparency of bank information. The methodology and some of financial variables used in the present analysis are common and comparable to theirs.

A number of other papers have studied the effectiveness of Japanese financial supervision using an approach of an event-study analysis. Peek and Rosengren (2001) study the government reaction to Japan's premium problem that occurred from 1995 to 1998 and report that the announcement by the government was not effective in the reduction of the premium, but capital injections to banks were effective.[1] Spiegel and Yamori (2003) study the stock market response to two financial regulatory reforms passed in 1998, the Financial Reconstruction Act and the Rapid Recapitalization Act, and report that shareholders of regional banks responded favorably to the legislation of these acts, while those of large banks did adversely. Spiegel and Yamori (2004) argue that market participants perceive the financial supervisory policy as a too-big-to-fail policy, but that the tendency to favor large banks has been diminishing over time. Yamori and Kobayashi (2007) study the effect of the nationalization of Resona Bank on the stock market and report that as the government announces the protection of shareholders of Resona, market participants come to regard the injection of public funds for the nationalization as a too-big-to-fail policy.

This paper is organized as follows. Section 9.2 surveys the financial supervisory policy in Japan since 1998. Section 9.3 explains the methodology. Section 9.4 explains data. Section 9.5 reports the empirical results. Section 9.6 examines other related events. Section 9.7 concludes.

9.2   Financial Supervisory Policy in Japan

In 1997, three large financial institutions, Sanyo Securities, Hokkaido Takushoku Bank, and Yamaichi Securities, failed, and Japanese financial supervision came to the turning point.[2] In July 1998, the Financial Supervisory Agency was founded as an independent agency of the fiscal authority, which was reorganized in June 2000 as Financial Services Agency (hereafter, FSA). In October 1998, two financial reforms, the Financial Reconstruction Act and the Prompt Recapitalization Act, were passed. These two acts were aimed to inject public funds into weak banks, to nationalize failing banks, and to protect depositors. Soon after their enactment, two major banks, the Long-Term Credit Bank of Japan and Nippon Credit Bank, were nationalized for insolvency. Financial supervision was formally arranged.

---

1. Ito and Harada (2004), since 2001, credit derivative swaps as a good indicator of Japanese bank risk.
2. See also Hoshi and Kashyap (2004), which is a good overview for the Japanese banking problem.

In March 1998 and March 1999, the government injected public funds into large banks in an attempt to avoid a possible financial crisis and its associated economic stagnation. As figure 9.1 illustrates, just after the legislation of the Financial Reconstruction Act done in October 1998, the stock market rapidly recovered. The stock market seems to have priced the de facto establishment of financial supervision favorably.

In January 1999, Mr. Yanagisawa was appointed as financial supervisory minister. However, Minister Yanagisawa was conservative in the disposal of nonperforming loans and even opposed to the nationalization of banks for the reason that Japanese banks were recovering. The FSA started to inspect bank assets in order to promote the disposal of nonperforming loans. The FSA made the first-round special inspection from 2000 to 2001, reporting that the total amount of nonperforming loans disclosed by individual banks was 34 trillion and over, whereas the total amount made by the FSA inspection was 47 trillion and over. The gap amounted to 13 trillion yen. This observation suggests that even after the legislation of the two acts for financial reforms, the FSA did not evaluate bank assets accurately.

The government continued a policy of regulatory forbearance in helping banks that were severely undercapitalized. In 1998, banks were allowed to account for "deferred tax assets" as Tier 1 core capital. Deferred tax assets are tax credits from past loses that banks expect to claim in the future. This accounting treatment of deferred tax assets provided bank managers with much discretion on its estimation that should be subjective. Skinner (2005) reports that Japanese banks have used deferred tax assets to compensate for declines in bank capital that arose from unrealized losses on the holdings of stocks.

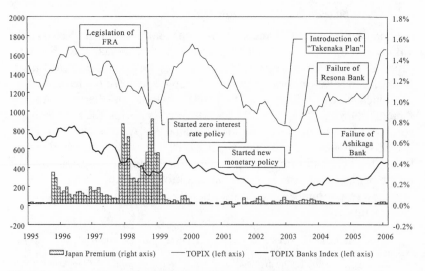

Fig. 9.1   Changes in stock price index and Japan premium

Subordinated debt is allowed to account for as Tier 2 complementary capital in the Japanese local rule of capital requirements. In Japan, subordinated debt is, however, held mainly by insurance companies, while banks hold a significant amount of debt issued by insurance companies so that banks and insurance companies are under the relationship of "double gearing" (e.g., Fukao and the Tokyo Center for Economic Research [TCER] 2003). Consequently, subordinated debt was used as a tool of regulatory-capital arbitrage. Ito and Sasaki (2002) and Hosono and Sakuragawa (2002) report that banks with poor capital tended to issue more subordinated debt in order to inflate their bank capital.

Fukao and TCER (2003) estimate the "true" bank capital by excluding problematic capital from the regulatory capital and report that, as of March 2002, the true capital ratio in the Bank for International Settlements (BIS) standard amounted only to 1.36 percent even after including public funds injected as bank capital. The stock market also seems to have questioned the government's ability to supervise banks. Spiegel and Yamori (2003) report that market participants perceived the Financial Reconstruction Act as a tool of forbearance. These observations suggest that in the period of 1998 to 2002, the FSA had poor ability to supervise banks. Stock prices began to decline again in October 1999.

Bank of Japan continued monetary expansion in order to avoid further decline in stock prices and the consequent financial crisis. Despite the huge amount of liquidity supply, however, stock prices continued to decline.

In October 2002, Minister Yanagisawa had to take responsibility for a possible financial crisis and was replaced by Heizo Takenaka. He released the Financial Revitalization Program, the so-called, Takenaka Plan in order to accelerate the disposal of nonperforming loans. Behind this policy change was recognition that a continued policy of forbearance led to huge amounts of bad loans and nonperforming loans and made the stagnation severe and prolonged.

The regulatory forbearance in helping undercapitalized banks allowed banks to roll over loans to nearly insolvent firms (e.g., Hosono and Sakuragawa 2002; Peek and Rosengren 2005; and others). The subsidized lending led to credit misallocation from manufacturing firms with high productivity to nonmanufacturing firms with low productivity (e.g., Caballero, Hoshi, and Kashyap 2003). The "evergreen" has been recognized to be one important source of the slowdown of economic growth in the Japanese economy.

At the end of November 2002, the government announced the detailed work schedule for implementing the Takenaka Plan. The Takenaka Plan had three main parts. First, the government requested banks to disclose the amount of nonperforming loans on a stricter standard than before. Second, the government stopped a policy that allowed banks to engage in regulatory-capital arbitrage for meeting minimum capital requirements.

Specifically, the government requested banks not to overstate deferred tax assets as bank capital. Third, the government arranged a scheme for injecting public funds into weak but solvent banks by adopting the Deposit Insurance Law, Article 102 that is intended to help banks in order to prevent a possible financial crisis.

The government appealed strongly for the implementation of the financial reform, but some observers have been disappointed with the announced work schedule. Before the release of work schedule, the tighter schedule of assessment rules on deferred tax assets was expected but remained unspecified. In addition, the detailed rule for applying Deposit Insurance Law was expected but not settled. To the end of this year, stock prices continued to decline.

In early 2003, the persistent decline in stock prices continued. The government came to fear a possible financial crisis that might be triggered by the decline in stock prices. Japanese banks were vulnerable to stock market risk because they held substantial amounts of equities. The policymakers came to understand strongly the necessity of strengthening policy coordination between the government and BOJ.

On March 25, 2003, the new governor of BOJ, Toshihiko Fukui, announced a package of new monetary policies. New policies had three main parts: first, BOJ continued the ample supply of liquidity to banks; second, BOJ applied the Lombard-type lending facility to the official discount rate by suspending the restriction on the maximum number of days; and third, BOJ extended the maximum amount of equity holdings that BOJ purchases from banks from 2 trillion yen to 3 trillion yen.[3] The third pillar is a so-called nontraditional monetary policy that was intended to interrupt the transmission of risk from the stock market to the banking sector.[4] The stock market got out of the bottom in March.

In May 2003, the failure of Resona, one of the Japanese largest banks, was revealed. This failure was triggered by its auditors who did not agree to the excessively estimated deferred tax assets, but requested the write-off of part of these assets. The capital ratio on the BIS standard was reported to be about 2 percent at the earnings report as of March 2003, below the minimum requirement for ordinary domestic operation of 4 percent. An immediate emergency meeting of the Government's Financial Service Management Council, headed by Prime Minister Koizumi, decided a subsequent massive injection of public funds following the Deposit Insurance Law, Article 102-1-1. The bankruptcy proceeding following Article 102-1-1 involves the injection of public funds and the restructuring by the government initiative. This procedure is not followed by liquidation, unlike in the

---

3. Governor Fukui stated before the press that BOJ was ready for purchasing all the equities held by banks if the worst scenario came.
4. On November 29, 2002, BOJ implemented the first-round purchase of equities from banks.

case of Long-Term Credit Bank of Japan and Nippon Credit Bank. Article 102-1-1 is applied to a failing bank whose net asset is positive, but a possible negative net asset for Resona was revealed from the FSA inspection done later.

Just two days following the announcement of nationalization, the government, fearing a possible decline in stock prices, announced protection for the existing shareholders of Resona. Some observers criticized the government's statement for the reason that this policy weakens market discipline. Although the unclear government attitude led to much controversy, stock prices apparently reversed the trend upward in May.

The FSA pursued Ashikaga Bank, one of the largest regional banks, and disclosed the inappropriate loan classification, the shortage of loan loss reserves, and the overstatement of differed tax assets of that bank. The net asset of Ashikaga was reported to be negative in the earning report as of September 2003. Using this report, November 29, 2003, an immediate emergency meeting of the Government's Financial Service Management Council decided on a subsequent injection of public funds following Deposit Insurance Law, Article 102-1-3. The bankruptcy proceeding following Article 102-1-3 involves the acquisition of all stocks at zero by the government while protecting all deposits, the restructuring on the government initiative, and the sale of bank assets to other banks. Unlike the case of Resona, shareholders bear the substantial costs. Stock prices kept the upward trend.

From 2003 to 2004, the FSA conducted the third-round special inspection. The total amount of nonperforming loans disclosed by individual banks was 34 trillion and over, while the total amount by the FSA inspection was 36 trillion and over, and the discrepancy reduced to 2 trillion yen. This observation seems to reveal that the financial supervision improved to some extent.

By the introduction of the Takenaka Plan, the accuracy of evaluating bank assets and the transparency of financial conditions seems to have improved, but the market reaction to each individual event varied. In the following, we examine the market response to the Takenaka Plan using an event-study approach.

9.3   Methodology

In this section, we examine three important events that occurred in 2003, the release of a package of monetary policies, and failures of Resona Bank and Ashikaga Bank. For each of the three events, we examine three questions. The first question is if the impact of each event on the stock price is positive or negative to the whole banking sector. The second question is if the impact on the stock market return, if it exists, is uniform across banks, regardless of possible differences of financial conditions or other characteristics of individual banks. The third question is if the impact reflects more than pure contagion, and if market participants differentiate the riskiness of individual banks by their financial conditions.

The estimation basically takes the form:

$$(1) \qquad R_{it} = \alpha_i + \beta_i R_{mt} + \sum_{k=0}^{1} \gamma_{ik} D_k + \varepsilon_{it},$$

where R_{it} is the stock return of bank i on day t; α_i is the intercept coefficient for bank i; R_{mt} is the market index for day t; β_i is the market risk coefficient for bank i; D_k is a binary variable that equals 1 if day t is equal to the event day or window $k \in [0, +1]$, zero otherwise; γ_{ik} is the event coefficient for bank i; and ε_{it} is a random error. Thus, the estimated parameters γ_{ik} capture any daily intercept shifts on event day (window) k and provide an estimate of abnormal (excess or unexpected) returns associated with the event announcement on day (window) k.

Each of events occurred on the same day for all the banks. It is likely that the abnormal returns are correlated contemporaneously among the individual banks. Thus, we do not estimate each of individual equations independently, but estimate equation (1) as a system of separate equations in the sample using generalized least squares (GLS).[5] To permit the variance of the residuals to vary across banks, we apply seemingly unrelated regression (SUR).[6]

The values of the parameters in equation (1) are estimated using daily data before and after each event date over an observation period sufficiently long to obtain meaningful results. However, because the three events that

---

5. When the abnormal returns in the individual banks have contemporaneous correlation with one another, there are two different approaches: the first is the "portfolio approach," in which the bank-level analysis can be applied to a portfolio into which the abnormal returns are aggregated using event time. This approach has the advantage of allowing for cross-correlation of the abnormal returns. The second is an application of a multivariate regression model with dummy variables for the event date. Comparing the two approaches, the latter methodology has the advantage of testing the null hypothesis that the event has no impact using individual bank data.

6. Because the events occurred on the same day for all the banks, it is likely that the residuals in the individual bank equations are correlated contemporaneously. Thus, we adjust for contemporaneous correlation. The methodology used in this article makes the standard assumptions that the residuals are independent and identically distributed within each equation and independent of the market return and the binary event variables; the noncontemporaneous correlation of residuals across banks is zero; and there is no event-induced heteroskedasticity. Thus, the covariance matrix of the residuals in equation (8) has the following structure:

$$E(\varepsilon\varepsilon') = \begin{bmatrix} \sigma_1^2 I & \sigma_{12} I & \cdots & \sigma_{1n} I \\ \sigma_{21} I & \sigma_2^2 I & \cdots & \sigma_{2n} I \\ \vdots & \vdots & \ddots & \vdots \\ \sigma_{n1} I & \sigma_{n2} I & \cdots & \sigma_n^2 I \end{bmatrix},$$

where I is the identity matrix, and N is the number of banks in the sample.

occurred in 2003 are reasonably close to one another, we have to be careful to possible effects of a specific event on the subsequent events. To avoid this problem, following Brewer et al. (2003), equation (1) is modified so as to permit a shift in both the intercept (α) and the market index coefficient (β) after the first event:

$$(2) \qquad R_{it} = \alpha_i + \beta_i R_{mt} + \alpha_i P + \beta_i P R_{mt} + \sum_{e} \sum_{k=0}^{1} \gamma_{ik,e} D_{ke} + \varepsilon_{it},$$

where e is the number representing each of events, the announcement of new monetary policy ($e = 1$), the failure of Resona ($e = 2$), and the failure of Ashikaga ($e = 3$); $\gamma_{ik,e}$ is the coefficient for bank i for the event $e (= 1,2,3)$; and P is a binary variable that is equal to 1 for the period after the first event window, the announcement of new monetary policy, and zero otherwise.

We first assess the impact of each event on the stock market return as a whole in the banking industry. In doing so, we test the following hypothesis using the estimated coefficients in equation (2).

$$(3) \qquad H_0^{\text{mean}}: \frac{1}{N} (\gamma_{1k,e} + \gamma_{2k,e} + \ldots + \gamma_{Nk,e}) = 0.$$

Equation (3) represents the hypothesis that the simple average of the individual abnormal returns is zero. If market participants perceive the impacts of each event favorably on the whole banking industry, the average will be positive, while otherwise, it will be negative. Be careful that large banks may have a great impact on the market price for the whole banking industry. To take into account the possible impacts of large banks, we test also the hypothesis with an asset-weighted coefficient.

$$(4) \qquad H_0^{W\text{mean}}: v_1 \gamma_{1k,e} + v_2 \gamma_{2k,e} + \ldots + v_N \gamma_{Nk,e} = 0,$$

where v_i is the weight on bank i that is calculated by dividing the total market value of bank i by the sum of total market values of all banks. Additionally, in order to compute the cross-sectional median of abnormal returns, we test the hypothesis that the number of banks with positive abnormal returns is greater than 50 percent in the sample:

$$(5) \qquad H_0^{\text{median}}: \text{median} = 0.$$

If market participants perceive the impacts of each event favorably, the median is expected to be positive, while otherwise, it is expected to be negative. For testing this hypothesis, we compute the t-test statistic and check the sign test.

Second, we test the pure contagion hypothesis by assessing if the impact of each of the events is equal across all banks. We examine the following hypothesis

$$(6) \qquad H_0^{AR}: \gamma_{1k,e} = \ldots = \gamma_{Nk,e}.$$

Equation (6) represents the hypothesis that the coefficients of the individual abnormal returns in the sample are equal across banks. If shareholders differentiate the riskiness of individual banks, the hypothesis is rejected, while otherwise, the pure contagion hypothesis will be supported. For testing this hypothesis, we compute the standard asymptotic χ^2 test statistic and the F-statistic.

Third, given that the pure contagion hypothesis is rejected, we test if the evidence of cross-sectional variation reflects their own financial conditions. In doing so, we expand equation (2) to include a number of conditioning variables that reflect financial characteristics of each bank and two other control variables:

$$(7) \quad R_{it} = \alpha_i + \beta_i R_{mt} + \alpha_i P + \beta_i P R_{mt} + \sum_e \overline{\gamma}_{ke} D_{ke} + \sum_e \phi_e D_{ke} \text{COND}_i$$
$$+ \sum_e \theta_e D_{ke} \text{SH}_i + \sum_e \lambda_e D_{ke} \text{TA}_i + \mu_{it},$$

where $\overline{\gamma}_{ke}$ is the coefficient for all banks for the event e ($= 1,2,3$); COND_i is a variable that describes the financial condition of bank i at the time of the event and is explained in detail in the following; TA_i is the log of total assets for bank i at the time of the event, and controls for bank size; and SH_i is a variable that measures the shareholding between banks and controls for the exposure of bank i to the failed bank through equity holding.[7] The positive coefficient of TA_i may reveal the evidence of a too-big-to-fail policy. If the response of the stock market to the event reflects individual bank conditions, the coefficient of either COND_i or SH_i is statistically different from zero. We test the following hypotheses:

$$(8) \qquad\qquad H_0^{\text{cond}}: \phi_e = 0,$$

and

$$(9) \qquad\qquad H_0^{\text{SH}}: \phi_e = 0,$$

for each of the three events and a number of measures of COND_i and SH_i. The coefficient of SH_i, θ_e, may reflect the government's attitude toward the existing shareholders of the failed bank. If shareholders bear substantial costs in the event of bank failure, the coefficient of SH_i is expected to be significant and negative.

We investigate nine descriptive variables as representing financial conditions of banks: (1) the ratio of nonperforming loans to total loans outstanding (NPL); (2) the ratio of reported loan loss reserves to risk-weighted regulatory capital (LLR); (3) the ratio of domestic loans to firms

---

7. The variable SH_i is defined as $\text{SH}_i = \rho_i \text{TA}_j / \text{TA}_j$, where ρ_i is the percent of outstanding shares of the failed institution j that was owned by bank i, TA_j is the total assets of the failed institution j, and TA_i is the total assets of the surviving bank i.

in the three industries of construction, real estate, and finance and insurance, which are typically deemed to be riskier than other loans, to total domestic loans (RISKY); (4) the ratio of bank capital to total bank assets calculated based on either international or domestic standard (CAPITAL); (5) the ratio of subordinated debt to risk-weighted regulatory capital (SUB); (6) the ratio of deferred tax assets debt to risk-weighted regulatory capital (DEF); (7) the ratio of liquid assets to total bank assets (LIQ); (8) the ratio of the market value of stocks to total bank assets (STO), and (9) the ratio of the latent gains (losses) of stocks to total bank assets (GAIN).

If the disclosure of nonperforming loans by banks is accurate, banks with high values of NPL are then supposed to be financially weak. The marginal impact of each event is expected to be greater for banks with a higher NPL, and the sign is expected to be positive ($\phi_1 > 0$) for the announcement of new monetary policy and negative ($\phi_2 < 0$, $\phi_3 < 0$) for failures of banks. Loan loss reserves are, in principle, provisions for nonperforming loans so that banks that hold a higher number of nonperforming loans should account for greater loan loss reserves and, thus, should be associated with a higher value of LLR. The expected signs are the same as NPL so that $\phi_1 > 0$, $\phi_2 < 0$, and $\phi_3 < 0$.

As we have discussed extensively in section 9.2, however, it has been widely believed that nonperforming loans were understated. If the stock market incorporated this information into pricing, the two variables, NPL and LLR, may not appropriately reflect the soundness of banks. As a complementary variable, we use RISKY. A number of works, including Hoshi (2000), Sakuragawa (2002), and Hosono and Sakuragawa (2002), report that banks helped many of nearly bankrupt firms in the three industries of construction, real estate, and finance and insurance by rolling over loans to them. Banks should account for loan loss reserves against loans extended to these almost bankrupt firms, but they could dress up their balance sheets by classifying these problem loans as good because the FSA did not inspect nonperforming loans closely. For this reason, we use RISKY as a proxy to potential nonperforming loans. Banks with a higher value of RISKY tend to hold a higher number of nonperforming loans. The expected signs are $\phi_1 > 0$, $\phi_2 < 0$, and $\phi_3 < 0$.

We consider variables that capture the effect of minimum capital requirements. Banks with a smaller value of CAPITAL tend to be constrained more severely by capital requirements and will be affected more strongly by each of the events. The expected signs are $\phi_1 > 0$, $\phi_2 < 0$, and $\phi_3 < 0$.

As explained in section 9.2, the government implicitly allowed banks to use subordinated debt and deferred tax assets as tools of regulatory-capital arbitrage for meeting capital requirements. We use SUB and DEF as measures of regulatory-capital arbitrage in meeting capital requirements. Banks with a higher value of SUB or DEF will be perceived as banks that relied more on subordinated debt because they had scarce true capital. Those banks will be affected more strongly by each of the events. The expected signs for SUB and DEF are $\phi_1 > 0$, $\phi_2 < 0$, and $\phi_3 < 0$.

The variable LIQ is expected to have a great impact at the event of the package of new monetary policy. If shareholders think that the shortage of liquidity is a serious banking problem, an announcement for monetary expansion should affect stock prices favorably. Banks with a lower value of LIQ are more likely to suffer from the liquidity shortage and will be affected more strongly by the monetary expansion. The expected sign is $\phi_1 < 0$.

The variables STO and GAIN are expected to capture the influence of the change in stock prices on banks. Purchasing stocks by BOJ is supposed to weaken the adverse effect of the stock market decline on banks. Banks with a higher value of STO tend to be more vulnerable to the stock market risk and will be affected more favorably by this policy. The expected sign is positive ($\phi_1 > 0$). Banks with greater losses of stock holding tend to be more vulnerable to the stock market risk and will be affected more favorably by this policy. The expected sign is negative ($\phi_1 < 0$).

The stock price of banks that hold a greater proportion of the stock of the failed bank is expected to decline more sharply. The coefficients of SH_i are expected to be $\theta_2 < 0$ and $\theta_3 < 0$.

9.4 Data

Daily stock prices and returns for our sample of eighty publicly traded and surviving banks are obtained from the *Toyo Keizai Kabuka* CD-ROM for 307 business days from October 1, 2002 to December 30, 2003. All dates are Japanese dates. Market returns are measured by the TOPIX index, which includes seasoned shares of over 1,000 major companies including both banks and nonbanks (First Section) traded on the Tokyo Stock Exchange, from the CD-ROM of the *Toyo Keizai* Inc.'s stock price database. The data on the financial condition of individual banks are obtained from the *Nikkei* NEEDS financial statement database.

For financial data of individual banks, we use the earning reports released as of March 2003. The announcement dates of new monetary policy and the two failures are obtained through a search of the statement released by BOJ and a search of the *Nihon Keizai Shimbun*. Actually, BOJ announced a package of new monetary policies on March 25, 2003. At this stage, earning reports as of March 2003 were not yet released, but banks usually released the prediction of their earning in the interim period. It will be conceivable to think that market participants use this information in order to form the expectation on the financial condition of individual banks.

If each announcement is made during a trading day in Japan, that date is used as the event day. If an announcement was made after the market was closed or over the weekend, we use the next trading date as the event date.

Following this criterion, we set the event days of the release of a package of monetary policies as March 25, 2003, the failure of Resona Bank as May 19, 2003, and the failure of Ashikaga Bank as December 1, 2003.

The number of banks used in the analysis is eighty for which stock market data is available, except for Resona and Ashikaga, both of which are excluded from the sample to avoid the survivorship bias. Note that in this sample period, a number of large banks are established by merger. We exclude Mitsui-Sumitomo Bank that is established by the merger of Sumitomo Bank and Sakura Bank for the reason that the stock market data is available only after November 29, 2002.

9.5   Empirical Results

Table 9.1 reports estimation results on equations (3), (4), and (5). The first column in the table reports the result for the estimated abnormal returns of individual banks for Day0 of each event window, the second column for Day+1, and the third column for the [0, +1] window.

For the new monetary policy, the first row, denoted, "Simple Mean," reports the average of the individual abnormal returns, and beneath the first row reports t-values.[8] The average of abnormal stock market returns is positive and significant for Day0, negative and insignificant for Day+1, and positive and significant for the [0, +1] window. The third row, denoted, "Weighted Mean," reports the asset-weighted average of the individual abnormal returns and reports t-values beneath the third. The abnormal returns are positive and significant for Day0, negative and significant at the 10 percent level for Day+1, and positive and significant for the [0, +1] window. The two alternative estimations both seem to show that market participants perceive the monetary policy as favorable.

The row denoted "Median" reports the median of the abnormal returns of individual banks. The row denoted "Positive" reports the number of banks whose abnormal return is positive, and the row denoted "Negative" reports the number of banks whose abnormal return is negative. The row denoted "sign-test" reports z-values on the statistical significance for the median. On the event Day0, among eighty surviving banks, abnormal returns are positive for sixty-two banks, and the median is positive and significant. On the event Day+1, the number of banks whose abnormal return is negative is more than a half (forty-six banks), and the median is

8. On November 29, 2002, BOJ implemented the first-round purchase of equities held by banks. But we do not examine this event because there were some reasons to support that some impacts of this policy were already incorporated into stock prices. For example, TOPIX shot up 1.66 percent on news that BOJ first announced the stock purchasing plan on September 18, 2002 and 3.32 percent on news that BOJ released "Stock Purchasing Guidelines" in October 11, 2002. On the other hand, it moved up only 0.52 percent on November 29, 2002. On the other hand, on the second-round purchase of equities, no information was leaked beforehand.

Table 9.1   Abnormal returns of surviving banks

	Day 0	Day +1	[0,+1]
New monetary policy (March 25, 2003)			
Simple mean	0.011	−0.001	0.01
t-statistic	5.55***	−0.51	4.09***
Weighted mean	0.017	−0.004	0.006
t-statistic	2.62**	−1.41*	2.37**
Median	0.011	−0.002	0.011
Positive	62	34	60
Negative	18	46	20
Sign-test; z-statistic	5.45***	−0.79	4.56***
$H_0 : \gamma_1 = \ldots = \gamma_{80}$			
F-statistic	2.61***	2.60***	5.21***
χ^2-statistic	208.92***	208.07***	416.51***
Failure of Resona Bank (May 19, 2003)			
Simple mean	−0.011	−0.004	−0.015
t-statistic	−5.95***	−2.00**	−5.10***
Weighted mean	−0.015	−0.006	−0.011
t-statistic	3.19***	−1.46*	−2.55**
Median	−0.008	−0.002	−0.008
Positive	16	32	20
Negative	64	48	60
Sign-test; z-statistic	−5.82***	−1.91*	−5.27***
$H_0 : \gamma_1 = \ldots = \gamma_{80}$			
F-statistic	1.35**	1.76***	3.16***
χ^2-statistic	108.23**	141.50***	252.79***
Failure of Ashikaga Bank (December 1, 2003)			
Simple mean	−0.013	0.008	−0.004
t-statistic	−4.64***	3.91***	−1.30*
Weighted mean	−0.019	−0.002	−0.011
t-statistic	−2.16**	−0.33	−1.56*
Median	−0.007	0.006	0.002
Positive	25	55	45
Negative	55	25	35
Sign-test; z-statistic	−4.94***	3.78***	0.15
$H_0 : \gamma_1 = \ldots = \gamma_{80}$			
F-statistic	2.87***	1.89***	4.81***
χ^2-statistic	229.79***	151.75***	384.80***

***Significant at the 1 percent level.
**Significant at the 5 percent level.
*Significant at the 10 percent level.

negative but insignificant. On the two-day window, the median is positive and significant. The results for the three event days suggest that stockholders of banks evaluate new monetary policy favorably to the banking industry.

The estimation of the failure of Resona Bank shows that the row denoted "Simple Mean" reports that the average of the coefficients on the abnormal return is negative and significant in any of the three windows. The results on "Weighted Mean" also report that the average is negative and significant in any of the three. In more than half of the banks, abnormal returns are negative, and the medians are negative and significant in any of the three windows. Market participants seem to incorporate new information on Resona Bank negatively into stock prices.

On the other hand, for the failure of Ashikaga Bank, the row denoted "Simple Mean" reports that the average of the individual abnormal returns is negative and significant for Day0, but positive and significant for Day+1. For the [0,+1] window, the estimated value is negative but slightly significant. The results on "Weighted Mean" report that the average is negative and significant for Day0, and negative but insignificant for Day+1. The results on the median report that the number of banks whose abnormal return is negative is more than half on the window [0], but less than half on the window [+1].

In the case of Ashikaga, the average of the individual abnormal returns is positive for Day+1. This finding is contrasted with the case of Resona in which the average abnormal stock returns are negative for both Day0 and Day+1. In addition, the stock price of more than half the number of banks rises for Day+1. Market participants do not seem to perceive that the failure of Ashikaga transmits to other surviving banks. In other words, market participants may have anticipated the rapid government response.

Table 9.1 reports estimation results on equation (6). Rows beneath "$H_0 : \gamma_1 = \ldots = \gamma_{80} = 0$" report the χ^2-statistic and F-statistic. In any of the events, the pure contagion hypothesis is rejected. For each of the events, market participants seem to differentiate the riskiness of individual banks by financial condition and other characteristics.

We turn to the investigation for individual financial conditions. The upper part of table 9.2 reports estimation results for the event of new monetary policy. None of the financial variables is significant. Particularly, the coefficient of LIQ is expected to be significant, but it is insignificant. Neither STO nor GAIN is significant. Market participants perceive the monetary package as favorable to the whole banking industry, but they do not seem to regard it as a tool of differentiating banks by their conditions.

The central part of table 9.2 reports estimation results for the case of Resona. Among variables of financial conditions, RISKY, CAPITAL, DEF, and GAIN are significant. The statistical significance of CAPITAL and DEF will reveal that market participants came to perceive the Takenaka Plan as an effective tool to strengthen supervision. Particularly, the negative and significant coefficient of DEF will reflect the fact that the government did not allow Resona to overestimate differed tax assets as bank capital and finally nationalized Resona. Market participants seem to perceive that banks with greater deferred tax assets will be more severely disciplined through a stricter standard of capital requirements.

Neither NPL nor LLR is significant, while RISKY is significant. Market

Table 9.2   Effects of bank financial conditions for event day or event window $k \in (0,1)$

	NPL	LLR	RISKY	CAPITAL	SUB	DEF	LIQ	STO	GAIN
	New monetary policy (March 25, 2003)								
Cond	-0.045	0.002	-0.002	0.011	0.02	-0.005	-0.028	-0.121	-0.058
	(1.09)	(0.19)	(0.20)	(0.16)	(1.03)	(0.82)	(1.25)	(1.12)	(0.26)
TA	-0.002	-0.001	-0.001	-0.001	-0.002	-0.001	-0.001	-0.001	-0.001
	(0.87)	(0.71)	(0.67)	(0.70)	(0.87)	(0.58)	(0.72)	(0.72)	(0.70)
	Failure of Resona Bank (May 19, 2003)								
Cond	-0.048	0.001	-0.035	0.146	-0.009	-0.02	0.01	-0.108	0.508
	(1.15)	(0.14)	(2.96)***	(2.09)**	(0.46)	(3.11)***	(0.44)	(0.99)	(2.25)**
TA	-0.002	-0.002	-0.002	-0.003	-0.002	-0.001	-0.002	-0.001	-0.002
	(1.27)	(1.02)	(0.95)	(1.43)	(0.91)	(0.62)	(1.07)	(0.77)	(0.92)
SH	-0.017	0.042	0.065	0.051	0.04	0.084	0.035	0.036	0.056
	(0.11)	(0.27)	(0.41)	(0.32)	(0.25)	(0.53)	(0.22)	(0.23)	(0.35)
	Failure of Ashikaga Bank (December 1, 2003)								
Cond	-0.139	-0.038	-0.006	0.346	-0.053	-0.031	0.012	-0.075	-0.058
	(3.35)***	(4.01)***	(0.38)	(4.95)***	(2.79)***	(4.87)***	(0.50)	(0.69)	(0.26)
TA	-0.002	-0.002	-0.001	-0.003	0.000	0.001	-0.001	0.000	-0.001
	(0.94)	(0.83)	(0.42)	(1.37)	(0.14)	(0.28)	(0.43)	(0.23)	(0.51)
SH	-1.928	-2.219	-1.995	-1.904	-1.948	-1.645	-2.073	-1.983	-1.965
	(3.68)***	(4.22)***	(3.82)***	(3.65)***	(3.70)***	(3.13)***	(3.80)***	(3.79)***	(3.76)***
No. of observations	24,560	24,560	24,560	24,560	24,560	24,560	24,560	24,560	24,560
No. of banks	80	80	80	80	80	80	80	80	80

Note: See text for explanation of variables (column heads).

***Significant at the 1 percent level.

**Significant at the 5 percent level.

participants seem to perceive that nonperforming loans are still understated. Indeed, the government nationalized Resona by following Deposit Insurance Law, Article 102-1-1, which is intended to be applied to the bank whose net asset is positive, but later the FSA inspection detected a possible negative net asset of Resona. The measure of bank size, TA, is insignificant. We do not find any result to support for the too-big-to-fail policy.[9] The variable SH is insignificant in all of the estimations. This result may reflect the fact that market participants accurately anticipated the protection of the existing shareholders of Resona following nationalization.

The lower part of table 9.2 reports estimation results for the case of Ashikaga. Among variables of financial conditions, five variables, NPL, LLR, CAPITAL, DEF, and SUB are significant. In terms of variables on nonperforming loans, NPL and LLR are significant. On the other had, RISKY is insignificant, while it is significant in the case of Resona. Market participants come to perceive that the FSA came to inspect nonperforming loans more accurately than before. In terms of variables on bank capital, DEF and SUB are significant. Market participants seem to perceive that the FSA came to force banks to meet capital requirements in a stricter standard. The variable SH is, unlike the case of Resona, negative and significant in all of the estimations. This result seems to reflect the fact that the government adopts the bankruptcy proceeding under which the existing shareholders bear the substantial costs. The variable TA is insignificant in all of the estimations.

Brewer et al. (2003) study a similar analysis using the failures of six financial institutions that occurred from 1995 to 1998, including Hyogo Bank, Sanyo Securities, Hokkaido Takushoku Bank, Yamaichi Securities, Long-Term Credit Bank of Japan, and Nippon Credit Bank. Four comparable variables of NPL, LLR, RISKY, and CAPITAL are used for their analysis and ours. Limiting cases on their four bank failures, the proportion of significant coefficients is about 31 percent (five among sixteen). On the other hand, the percentage rises to 63 percent in the present analysis. Market participants seem to perceive that the FSA supervision considerably improved after the introduction of the Takenaka Plan.

9.6   Other Related Events

In this section, we examine three other related events. The first event is the release of the Takenaka Plan, the second the announcement of the work schedule for implementing the Takenaka Plan, and the third is the announcement of the protection of existing shareholders of Resona Bank.

---

9. We never deny other possible methodologies to verify the evidence of a too-big-to-fail policy. For example, a nonlinear relationship between abnormal return and bank size might uncover the presence of a too-big-to-fail protection.

We first examine the two events on the Takenaka Plan. We estimate equations (2) through (9) using the event day of the release of the Takenaka Plan as October 30, 2002, and the event day of the announcement of work schedule for implementing the Takenaka Plan as November 28, 2002.[10]

Table 9.3 reports the estimation results for equations (3), (4), and (5). For the estimation of the release of the Takenaka Plan, the row denoted "Simple Mean" reports that the average of the individual abnormal returns is positive and significant in any of the three windows. The results on "Weighted Mean" also report that the average is positive and significant for Day1 and the [0, +1] windows. In more than half of the banks, abnormal return is positive, and the median is positive and significant in any of the three windows. Market participants seem to perceive the release of the Takenaka Plan as favorable.

On the other hand, for the announcement of schedule for implementing the Takenaka Plan, the row denoted "Simple Mean" reports that the average of the individual abnormal returns is negative and significant for Day0 and the [0, +1] window. The results on "Weighted Mean" also report that the average is negative and significant for Day0 and the [0, +1] window. The results on the median report that the number of banks whose abnormal return is negative is more than half for Day0 and the [0, +1] window. Market participants seem to be disappointed with the announced details of the work schedule.

Table 9.3 reports estimation results for equation (6). Rows beneath "$H_0 : \gamma_1 = \ldots = \gamma_{80} = 0$" report the χ^2-statistic and F-statistic. In any of the events, the pure contagion hypothesis is rejected. For each of the events, market participants seem to differentiate the influence of the Takenaka Plan on individual banks by financial conditions and other characteristics.

We turn to the investigation for individual financial conditions. For the event of the release of the Takenaka Plan, the upper part of table 9.4 reports estimation results. The measure of bank size, TA, has positive and significant coefficient in any of the estimations. This result may support the too-big-to-fail hypothesis. At first, market participants seem to be afraid if the financial reform is appropriately implemented. Among variables of financial conditions, NPL is significant but positive, contrasted sharply with the estimations of the three events examined in the previous section. On the release of the Takenaka Plan, market participants may have evaluated banks with great nonperforming loans as "strong" banks by conjecturing that strong banks can differentiate themselves from other banks by revealing the amount of nonperforming loans accurately. Behind this interpretation is that, as of 2002, it was widely believed that the number of nonperforming loans was understated.

10. We use daily stock prices data over 246 business days from January 4, 2002 to December 30, 2002. On financial data of individual banks, we use the earning reports released as of March 2002.

Table 9.3   **Abnormal returns of banks for release of the Takenaka Plan and announcement of work schedule**

	Day 0	Day +1	[0,+1]
Release of Takenaka Plan (October 30, 2002)			
Simple mean	0.005	0.003	0.008
t-statistic	2.36**	1.64*	2.33**
Weighted mean	0.010	0.019	0.015
t-statistic	1.00	1.76**	1.59*
Median	0.002	0.001	0.002
Positive	50	43	50
Negative	30	37	30
Sign-test; *z*-statistic	1.86*	0.79	2.25**
$H_0: \gamma_1 = \ldots = \gamma_{80}$			
F-statistic	1.81***	2.17***	3.99***
χ^2-statistic	145.08***	174.12***	319.20***
Announcement of work schedule (November 28, 2002)			
Simple mean	−0.018	0.002	−0.016
t-statistic	−13.04***	0.93	−6.46***
Weighted mean	−0.016	0.000	−0.008
t-statistic	−5.00***	0.13	−3.16***
Median	−0.018	0.003	−0.013
Positive	5	49	16
Negative	75	31	66
Sign-test; *z*-statistic	−7.37***	1.89*	−5.92***
$H_0: \gamma_1 = \ldots = \gamma_{80}$			
F-statistic	1.88***	2.68***	4.76***
χ^2-statistic	151.16***	214.46***	381.24***

***Significant at the 1 percent level.
**Significant at the 5 percent level.
*Significant at the 10 percent level.

The lower part in table 9.4 reports estimation results for the event of the announcement of the work schedule. The variable TA is negative and insignificant. Among variables of financial conditions, two variables, CAPITAL and SUB, are significant. Market participants seem to have anticipated that the government took a first step to prevent banks from engaging in regulatory-capital arbitrage to meet minimum capital requirements. The variable DEF is insignificant. This result may reflect the fact that the time table of tightening assessment rules on deferred tax assets was still not specified. We have several comments from the comparison between the failure of Resona and the one of Ashikaga. First, market participants perceive the Takenaka Plan as a too-big-to-fail policy only in the first event of the release of that plan. Second, the market perception to deferred tax assets differs quite a bit between events of 2002 and 2003. In the two events that occurred in 2002, DEF is not significant. As of 2002, market participants do not seem to perceive that the government forces banks

Table 9.4   Effects of release of the Takenaka Plan and announcement of work schedule for event day or event window $k \in [0,1]$

	NPL	LLR	RISKY	CAPITAL	SUB	DEF	LIQ	STO	GAIN
				Release of Takenaka Plan (October 30, 2002)					
Cond	0.065	−0.047	0.003	0.000	−0.724	0.002	0.021	0.015	−0.106
	(2.62)***	(0.15)	(0.21)	(0.25)	(0.74)	(0.54)	(1.30)	(0.26)	(1.18)
TA	0.005	0.005	0.005	0.005	0.005	0.005	0.005	0.005	0.005
	(3.92)***	(3.96)***	(4.47)***	(4.18)***	(4.74)***	(4.28)***	(4.53)***	(4.34)***	(4.63)***
				Announcement of work schedule (November 28, 2002)					
Cond	0.026	0.325	−0.028	0.001	−2.768	−0.002	0.008	0.009	0.041
	(0.98)	(0.97)	(1.75)	(1.96)**	(2.71)***	(0.62)	(0.46)	(0.14)	(0.43)
TA	−0.001	−0.001	−0.002	−0.003	−0.001	−0.002	−0.002	−0.002	−0.002
	(0.84)	(1.06)	(1.95)	(2.17)**	(1.23)	(1.34)	(1.53)	(1.71)	(1.58)
No. of observations	11,680	11,680	11,680	11,680	11,680	11,680	11,680	11,680	11,680
No. of banks	80	80	80	80	80	80	80	80	80

Note: See text for explanation of variables (column heads).

***Significant at the 1 percent level.

**Significant at the 5 percent level.

to stop regulatory-capital arbitrage using deferred tax assets. Third, the market evaluation on the Takenaka Plan varied over time. Among financial conditions, the number of significant coefficients monotonically increases over time, from zero (Release), to two (Work Schedule), further to four (Resona), and finally to five (Ashikaga). Market participants seem to change their expectation gradually on the implementation of the financial reform. Particularly, the credibility to the Takenaka Plan drastically increases in the latter two. The turning point may be the failure of Resona in which the government nationalized Resona by not allowing Resona to overestimate differed tax assets as bank capital. Another applicant may be the monetary policy that played a role of guaranteeing the implementation of the financial reform.

We next turn to the Resona event. There is much controversy on the government's statement for the protection of the existing shareholders following nationalization. Some observers stress this statement as a revival of forbearance. Yamori and Kobayashi (2007) report that in their estimation for the event day of May 21, 2003, the bank size has a significant effect on the stock market return, and conclude that the government's statement for the protection of Resona shareholders seem to have induced market participants to perceive the nationalization as a too-big-to-fail policy.

We estimate equations (2) through (9) using May 21, 2003 as an event day. If market participants perceive the nationalization of Resona as a too-big-to-fail policy, the log of total assets, denoted TA, should have a positive and significant coefficient.

Table 9.5 reports estimation results for equation (3), (4), and (5). The

Table 9.5   **Abnormal returns of surviving banks for the statement for protection of Resona shareholders**

	Day 0	Day +1	[0, +1]
The government announcement to protect shareholders of Resona (May 21, 2003)			
Simple mean	0.011	0.007	0.009
t-statistic	1.43*	1.75**	1.68**
Weighted mean	−0.018	−0.001	−0.010
t-statistic	−2.15**	−0.27	−1.54**
Median	−0.004	0.002	−0.004
Positive	25	45	25
Negative	55	35	55
Sign-test; *z*-statistic	−2.93**	2.24**	−4.37***
$H_0 : \gamma_1 = \ldots = \gamma_{80}$			
F-statistic	1.34**	2.06***	3.41***
χ^2-statistic	107.22**	165.34***	272.77***

***Significant at the 1 percent level.
**Significant at the 5 percent level.
*Significant at the 10 percent level.

first row, denoted "Simple Mean," reports that the average of the individual abnormal returns is positive and significant in any of the three windows. On the contrary, the results on "Weighted Mean" report that the average is negative in any of the three windows and significant for Day0 and the [0, + 1] window. This result may reveal that stock prices of small and regional banks rose, but those of large banks declined. Market participants do not perceive the statement for the protection of existing shareholders as a too-big-to-fail policy.

Table 9.6 reports the estimation results. The variable SUB is positive and significant, while it is insignificant in the estimation of May 19 to 20, 2003 (see table 9.2). Market participants seem to perceive the statement for protection as a revival of a forbearance policy. The variable SH is positive, and the t-values of the coefficient improve relative to the estimation of May 19 to 20, 2003. This result is contrasted with the case of Ashikaga in which SH is negative and significant. The contrasting result between the two will reflect the different attitude of the government toward bank shareholders. The variable TA is insignificant in all of the estimations. We do not find any result to support the too-big-to-fail policy.

Our estimation differs from Yamori and Kobayashi (2007) in three respects. First, as a measure of bank size, they use a dummy variable that takes unity if the total asset of a bank is larger than that of Resona and zero otherwise, while we use the log of total assets. Second, they control for three variables representing the financial condition of banks, CAPITAL, NPL, and DEF in our definition, while we use more variables including SUB and RISKY. Third, we use the variable SH to control for the exposure of a bank to the failed bank through equity holding.

9.7 Conclusion

Using event-study methodology, we study how the stock market evaluates the Japanese financial reform, the Takenaka Plan that started in October 2002. We investigate several financial events that occurred in 2002 and 2003, including the release of the Takenaka Plan, the announcement of the work schedule for implementing that plan, the release of a package of monetary policies, and the failures of Resona Bank and Ashikaga Bank. Market participants came to perceive gradually that the government appropriately implements the Takenaka Plan in an attempt to improve bank governance. The credibility of the reform seems to have increased after the events that occurred in 2003, the failures of Resona and Ashikaga. In these estimations, bank shareholders differentiate individual banks by their financial conditions. This suggests financial supervision seems to have improved to some extent. Monetary policy also played an important role. The turning point may be the failure of Resona, in which the government nationalized Resona by not allowing Resona to overestimate differed tax

Table 9.6   Effects of the government announcement to protect shareholders of Resona for event day or event window $k \in [0,1]$

	NPL	LLR	RISKY	CAPITAL	SUB	DEF	LIQ	STO	GAIN
	The government announcement to protect shareholders of Resona (May 21, 2003)								
Cond	-0.061	-0.016	-0.026	0.084	0.040	-0.004	-0.003	0.163	-0.295
	(1.62)	(1.70)	(1.33)	(1.23)	(2.10)**	(0.62)	(0.12)	(1.52)	(1.31)
TA	0.000	0.000	0.000	-0.001	0.000	0.000	0.000	0.000	0.000
	(0.17)	(0.96)	(0.57)	(1.63)	(1.58)	(0.86)	(0.77)	(1.96)**	(1.22)
SH	0.305	0.278	0.328	0.291	0.277	0.302	0.292	0.294	0.285
	(1.96)	(1.78)	(2.08)**	(1.87)	(1.78)	(1.93)	(1.87)	(1.88)	(1.82)
	Failure of Ashikaga Bank (December 1, 2003)								
Cond	-0.138	-0.038	-0.003	0.338	-0.050	-0.030	0.012	-0.069	-0.100
	(3.32)***	(4.02)***	(0.13)	(4.90)***	(2.55)**	(4.73)***	(0.52)	(0.62)	(0.44)
TA	-0.002	-0.001	-0.001	-0.002	0.000	0.001	-0.001	0.000	-0.001
	(0.89)	(0.74)	(0.46)	(1.29)	(0.21)	(0.31)	(0.35)	(0.13)	(0.42)
SH	-1.932	-2.223	-1.965	-1.902	-1.952	-1.647	-2.077	-1.984	-1.970
	(3.69)***	(4.23)***	(3.75)***	(3.64)***	(3.70)***	(3.13)***	(3.80)***	(3.78)***	(3.77)***
No. of observations	24,560	24,560	24,560	24,560	24,560	24,560	24,560	24,560	24,560
No. of banks	80	80	80	80	80	80	80	80	80

Note: See text for explanation of variables (column heads).

***Significant at the 1 percent level.

**Significant at the 5 percent level.

assets as bank capital. Another applicant may be the monetary policy that played a role of guaranteeing the implementation of the financial reform.

References

Brewer, E., III, and H. Genay, W. C. Hunter, and G. G. Kaufman. 2003. Does the Japanese stock market price bank-risk? Evidence from financial firm failures. *Journal of Money, Credit and Banking* 35 (4): 507–43.
Caballero, R. J., T. Hoshi, and A. K. Kashyap. 2003. Zombie lending and depressed restructuring in Japan. Paper presented at the NBER/CEPR/CIRJE/EIJS Japan Project meeting, Tokyo, Japan.
Fukao, M., and TCER. 2003. *Kennsyo Ginnko Kiki-Suuti ga Simesu Keiei Jittai (Evidence of quantitative effects of the banking crisis)*. Tokyo: Nihon Keizai Shimbun-sha.
Hoshi, T. 2000. *Naze Nihon ha Ryuudousei no Wana kara Nogareraretanoka?* (Why didn't Japan escape from the liquidity trap?). In *Zero Kinri to Nihon Keizai*, ed. M. Fukao and H. Yoshikawa. Tokyo: Nihon Keizai Shimbun-sha.
Hoshi, T., and A. K. Kashyap. 2004. Japan's financial crisis and economic stagnation. *Journal of Economic Perspective* 18 (1): 3–26.
Hosono, K., and M. Sakuragawa. 2002. Soft budget problems in the Japanese credit market. Nagoya City University, Discussion Paper.
Ito, T., and K. Harada. 2004. Credit derivative premium as a new Japan premium. *Journal of Money, Credit and Banking* 36 (5): 965–68.
Ito, T., and Y. N. Sasaki. 2002. Impacts of the Basel capital standard on Japanese banks' behavior. *Journal of the Japanese and International Economies* 16:372–97.
Peek, J., and E. S. Rosengren. 2001. Determinants of the Japan premium: Actions speak louder than words. *Journal of International Economics* 53:283–305.
———. 2005. Unnatural selection: Pervasive incentives and the misallocation of credit in Japan. *American Economic Review* 95:1144–66.
Sakuragawa, M. 2002. *Kinnyu Kiki no Keizai Bunseki (The economic analysis of the financial crisis)*. Tokyo: Daigaku Syuppannkai.
Shrieves, R. E., and D. Dahl. 2003. Discretionary accounting and the behavior of Japanese banks under financial duress. *Journal of Banking and Finance* 27:1219–43.
Skinner, D. J. 2005. The rise of deferred tax assets in Japan: The case of the major Japanese banks. University of Chicago, Graduate School of Business, Working Paper.
Spiegel, M. M., and N. Yamori. 2003. The impact of Japan's financial stabilization laws on bank equity values. *Journal of the Japanese and International Economies* 17:263–82.
———. 2004. The evolution of bank resolution policies in Japan: Evidence from market equity values. *Journal of Financial Research* 27 (1): 115–32.
Yamori, N., and A. Kobayashi. 2007. Wealth effect of public fund injections to ailing banks: Do deferred tax assets and auditing firms matter? *Japanese Economic Review* 58 (4): 466–83.

Comment   Takatoshi Ito

Let me first illustrate what I think the most important aspect of the so-called Takenaka plan. By now, many policymakers and academics share a high praise for the Takenaka plan of October 30, 2002 as the decisive way of ending the decade-long banking crisis of Japan.[1] However, few remember how its reputation has evolved from being too tough to being too compromised, and finally to producing moral hazard by rescuing shareholders of a failing bank. Ironically, appearing too tough made the stock prices decline, and failure, nationalization, and bailing out shareholders of the Resona Bank produced a moral hazard rally in May 2003.

Let me explain the evolution briefly. (See Hoshi and Ito [2004] for a review of the Financial Services Agency from 1998 to 2004.) In the spring to summer of 2002, a hot debate regarding the soundness of the Japanese banking system took place. Minister Yanagisawa, then in charge of Financial Services Agency (FSA), maintained the position that banks have ample capital and basically sound. Critics, including Mr. Takenaka, Minister for State for Economic and Fiscal Policy, argued that much of bank capital consists of deferred tax assets (DTA) that are based on optimistic profit streams in the future. Mr. Takenaka won the debate and the FSA Minister position. When Mr. Takenaka took the position of minister in charge of the FSA, he planned to use discounted cash flow (DCF) for classification of firms, to harmonize classification of large borrowers among commercial banks, to assess rigorously the collateral values, and to disallow banks to count much of DTAs toward Tier 1 capital.

The previous classification of performing and nonperforming loans relied on whether interest and principal payments have been made as scheduled. However, banks were suspected to have assisted firms to continue pay interest by lending more. This was called *ever-greening* (Peek and Rosengren 2001). This concern prompted Mr. Takenaka to propose DCF.

Because banks have reported heavy losses in 2000 to 2001, they could carry over losses toward the future for offset. If they would earn profits in the future, corporate income taxes would be waived in order to offset carried-over losses. This tax rebate in the future was declared as deferred tax assets (DTA). This is part of normal accounting rule for expecting fu-

Takatoshi Ito is a professor at the Graduate School of Economics and the Graduate School of Public Policy at the University of Tokyo, and a research associate of the National Bureau of Economic Research.

1. The so-called Takenaka plan is officially called "Program for Financial Revival—Revival of the Japanese Economy through Resolving Non-Performing Loans Problems of Major Banks" issued on October 30, 2002. The link can be found at http://www.fsa.go.jp/en/news/2002.html#02oct.

ture extra income. What was unusual was that the DTA was allowed to be counted toward Tier 1 capital in the risk-based capital ratio (Basel capital adequacy rule). Moreover, the portion of DTA in Tier 1 capital had become more than half for some banks. What if a bank would not earn profits, but just break even? Then the DTA would disappear, thus depressing the Tier 1 capital instantly. It is not hard capital, but could be a mirage—many critics argued.

The Takenaka plan of adopting DCF and disallowing DTA would reduce greatly the banks' capital. Then the government would be ready to nationalize any banks being undercapitalized for the Basel capital adequacy standard. Minister Takenaka was reported to have said that no bank was too big to fail, which prompted a big decline in the stock prices. The original version of his plan was attacked by bank executives and the bank lobby at the Diet. Bank executives argued that the change in the capital adequacy rule on DTA would be like a change of the rule in the middle of a game: the DTA was introduced to accelerate the write-off of nonperforming loans without worrying too much about undercapitalization by counting future tax rebates as Tier 1 capital. Minister Takenaka, by proposing to disallow part of DTA for Tier 1 capital, was portrayed as being naive for pushing too tough a plan that would make most banks being nationalized.

The stock market reacted negatively to tough talks by Mr. Takanaka right after his assuming the minister position in September 2002. By the time of disclosure of the Takenaka plan at the end of October, threatening words had disappeared. The stock prices, especially those in the banking sector, declined sharply after the plan was announced and the conflict arose between the Minister and the bank executives. Those who regarded that a tough action would be good news for the market were disappointed by the negative reaction of the stock market. The stock prices continued to decline toward the end of the year. The Nikkei 225 went down from 9,619 yen at the end of August to 9,383 yen one month later, to 8,640 yen two months later. Although the stock prices rose in November, it sank again in December, and the Nikkei 225 ended the year at 8,579 yen.

With political opposition being strong, and the stock market being weak, Minister Takenaka had to retreat a little bit. This compromise, or truce, was crafted toward the end of 1997, in that the DTA was allowed to be used as before, but an accounting firm had to evaluate how realistic it would be to have a projection of future profits from which DTA would be derived. Pressure was placed on accounting firms in that if an accounting firm certifies the balance sheet and a bank fails only a few month later, the accounting firm has to be held responsible. In classifying firms into non-performing and performing categories, the discount cash flow (DCF) method was proposed for evaluation of true worth (and solvency) of a firm. Also, a special examination of banks was introduced to make sure that all banks were putting a particular firm in the same category of nonperforming loans.

The stock price continued to decline in the first four months of 1998, and by the end of April, the Nikkei 225 index became 7,831 yen—a 20 percent decline in eight months.[2] In April 1998, the accounting firm of Resona Bank refused to allow full DTA that the banks thought to deserve. The accounting firm argued that the prospect of profit trajectory, which indicated a sharp rise in profits in the next several years, was unrealistic. On May 17, Resona Holdings applied for capital injection by the government. Due to less DTA, Resona Bank became undercapitalized even for a domestic bank (minimum of 4 percent capital ratio). Resona Bank was nationalized although it was still determined as solvent. The Takenaka plan was indeed implemented although it took seven months to crystallize into some concrete result. Despite nationalization, the shareholders of Resona Bank were essentially bailed out, keeping their shares at the remaining values of the bank. The government maintained that the bank was undercapitalized, but solvent, to that shareholders should have claims to the remaining assets, while the government would take over the bank by obtaining newly issued stocks. Shares were diluted, but the existing shareholders were allowed to continue having rights to assets in the bank.

The stock prices of other banks started to soar at the news of Resona Bank nationalization, without hurting the current shareholders. The apparent moral hazard at Resona Bank was good news for shareholders of other large banks—who would surely escape zero valuation even at the nationalization. The stock prices started to rally after the nationalization, and by the end of May, it rose to 8,425 yen, a 9 percent rise from a month earlier. The stock prices continue to increase. The Nikkei 225 index rose to 10,560 yen by the end of October.

On November 29, 2003, Ashikaga Bank was determined to have failed when its accounting firm denied all of the DTA for the Bank. This time, the bank was regarded to be insolvent so that shareholders lost their values. However, this did not stop bank stocks from rising further. Four days earlier, the major banks, except for Resona Bank, reported positive profits for the half year (ending September 2003). The increasing trend of stock prices was not affected.

Now let me turn to my comments to the Sakuragawa and Watanabe paper. The stated objective of Sakuragawa and Watanabe is to evaluate market reactions to the Takenaka reform. They examined the stock price reactions to five events: the announcement of the Takenaka plan (October 30, 2002), the announcement of its work schedule (November 28, 2002), the release of the package of monetary policies (March 25, 2003), the failure of

2. The bottom of Nikkei 225 was on April 28 at 7,607 yen.

Resona Bank (May 17, 2003), and the failure of Ashikaga Bank (November 29, 2003). For each event, the authors examined the stock market return as a whole, whether returns are similar among other banks, and whether price changes reflect individual banks' balance sheets or a contagion.

I have several comments on identifying event dates and expected signs on abnormal returns on each event date. First, the so-called Takenaka plan was announced on October 30, 2002, as mentioned in the Sakuragawa and Watanabe paper. However, this was after one month of tough talks by Mr. Takenaka who assumed the minister position on September 30, 2002. He had been very vocal about how to force the banks to restructure, which caused stock prices to decline. The Nikkei 225 index dropped by 7 percent, from 9,384 yen in September 30, 2002 to 8,756 yen on October 30, 2002. By taking October 30 as an event day, the analysis misses the earlier tough talks that were real shocks to the market (and bank executives). In fact, compared to the specific threat during the first month of Takenaka's term, the announced plan was not that tough, but a compromise. The market was more relieved than shocked. Although the bank stock prices were affected, the negative abnormal returns on the day of plan announcement were not large.

Second, the real difference between the Resona Bank and the Ashikaga Bank was the differential treatment of shareholders of the two banks. Shareholders of the Resona Bank were bailed out, while the shareholders of the Ashikaga Bank, including those firms and municipal governments who subscribed to new share issues by Ashikaga bank, suffered sudden total losses. This difference is not discussed enough in the paper. The temporary nationalization of the Resona bank produced a turning point and a minirally in the stock prices, while the Ashikaga did not. After the Resona failure, the Nikkei 225 rose by 10 percent in less than three weeks. After the Ashikaga failure, no such rally took place. This observation put a question on evaluating only a two-day window. The effect of such a plan may extend for several days because analyzing the plan may take a week.

Third, expected signs of surviving banks' stock prices may not be so straightforward. An event analysis should take only an unexpected part of the "announcement," or a surprise, as a variable. This is a standard procedure in the literature dealing with macroeconomic statistical release, where such an expectation can be measured by consensus forecast. However, for events described in this paper, it is rather difficult to construct such a surprise. Hence, even a failure of a bank could produce a positive reaction among surviving banks, except a few, if it is taken as a sign of taking appropriate actions.

Fourth, a new monetary policy package on March 25 is only one of a series of monetary policy measures in 2003 to 2004 (see Ito and Mishkin [2006] for details). Why March 25 is singled out is not clear, although it may be an event, signaling a new policy by a new governor. Bank of Japan had played significant role in attempts to stabilize the financial system as well as to prevent deflation from becoming a serious deflationary spiral. Providing ample liquidity is one way that would work both to stabilize the financial system and to stop deflation. This was implemented by increasing target amounts of the current account balance (held by financial institutions) at Bank of Japan in 2003 to 2004. The target amount of current account balance had become an instrument of monetary policy when the interest rate became zero in the spring of 2001.

The Nikkei 225 stock prices hit the bottom at 7,607 yen on April 28 and started a recovery. What made that turnaround may be interesting to discuss (in the future work). Whether new monetary policy contributed to this more than the Takenaka plan can be debatable.

The paper highlights the importance of the Takenaka plan, but further investigations in the future would produce a comprehensive assessment of the role of Minister Takenaka's role at the bottom of the financial crisis in Japan.

References

Hoshi, Takeo, and Takatoshi Ito. 2004. Financial regulation in Japan: A sixth year review of the Financial Services Agency. *Journal of Financial Stability* 1 (2): 229–43.
Ito, Takatoshi, and Frederic S. Mishkin. 2006. Two decades of Japanese monetary policy and the deflation problem. In *Monetary policy with very low inflation in the pacific rim,* ed. T. Ito and A. Rose, 131–93. Chicago: University of Chicago Press.
Peek, Joe, and Eric S. Rosengren. 2001. Determinants of the Japan premium: Actions speak louder than words. *Journal of International Economics* 53:283–305.

Comment   Randall Morck

This chapter is a useful addition to our knowledge of bank regulation. Its importance transcends Japan because it is really about how monetary and fiscal authorities should go about providing lender-of-last-resort services. But its importance also transcends macroeconomics because it is ultimately about how strategic thinking needs to guide economic institutions.

The framework the authors use to develop these issues is Japan's prolonged financial malaise around the turn of the twenty-first century. Successive capital investment, stock market, and real estate bubbles left the country's banks severely weakened. These bubbles played out roughly along

Randall Morck is the Stephen A. Jarislowsky Distinguished Professor of Finance and University Professor at the University of Alberta, and a research associate of the National Bureau of Economic Research.

the formula Kindleberger (1976) describes—genuine growth opportunities attract capital, but the attraction persists even after the opportunities are exhausted. Overinvestment and asset price inflation ensue until the dissonance with fundamentals becomes too obvious to ignore, at which point the house of cards collapses and liquidity evaporates. The economy is left without adequate credit for sound investments and a recession persists.

This synopsis, of course, grossly oversimplifies Japan's economic malaise, as it does the scores of other financial crises Kindleberger reviews. But this, like all the others, follows the basic pattern closely enough that same fundamental paradox is the rub.

As Kindleberger explains (1978, 9) "A lender of last resort should exist, but his presence should be doubted." If the economy develops a severe financial crisis, the central bank should step forth to bail out the collapsing financial system. But the owners, managers, and creditors of financial firms must not expect such bailouts, lest they grow lax and permit financial crises to develop. Kindleberger proceeds to write a book about how sustaining this essential time inconsistency is imperative to macroeconomic stability.

One path that sometimes leads through this logical morass is "secrecy": sustain the dead financial institutions on financial respirators, but let the public believe the bank is hale and healthy. Financial history shows this remarkably successful on occasion. For example, virtually all the major Canadian banks were technically bankrupt at the height of the Great Depression, but the government buried the evidence. Even as depositors queued for blocks to withdraw their savings from collapsing American banks, the major Canadian banks stood in quiet serenity. Half a century later, the records were opened and these facts laid out (Kryzanowski and Roberts 1998, 1999). The conventional wisdom that nationwide branch systems geographically diversified the Canadian banks, and thus stabilized them, was overturned. Financial forbearance to zombie banks, not geography, stabilized the Canadian banking system.

This sort of forbearance was precisely the strategy the Japanese authorities tried first. For about ten years, from the bursting of the bubble economy in the late 1980s to 1997, the government studiously avoided the issue—waiving regulations and injecting funds into clinically dead banks. But this meant the banks had to play along by feigning health and not recognizing their past errors. As the authors point out, this was not good for the economy because "The regulatory forbearance in helping undercapitalized banks allowed banks to roll over loans to nearly insolvent firms. . . . The subsidized lending led to credit misallocation from manufacturing firms with high productivity to nonmanufacturing firms with low productivity." Perhaps something similar happened in Canada in the 1930s—certainly the Great Depression there was no less calamitous than in the United States.

A second way through the paradox of the lender of last resort is to bail out innocent bystanders, while leaving banks' decision makers to the consequences of their decisions. This is the next path the Japanese government tried. In 2002, the government "requested" that banks disclose their nonperforming loans more honestly and ended its regulatory forbearance, but simultaneously established a system of deposit insurance to bail out households if their banks failed. This Takenaka Plan confirmed the existence of a lender of last resort—for banks' depositors, but not for their managers, shareholders, customers, or other creditors. There would be no U.S. Great Depression-style bank runs because the Japanese government would guarantee households' bank accounts.

But this worked little better—in part because of the unusually thick ties between Japan's banks and their client firms. Japanese banks, unlike banks in most countries, hold corporate shares as capital. As word spread of the mismanagement of major Japanese businesses, and of their banks' abetting that mismanagement, stock prices tumbled, reducing the banks' capital reserves and rekindling fears of a crisis. The government responded with further liquidity injections into the banking system plus a nontraditional monetary policy—the government purchased banks' shareholdings. This was another bailout, for the government almost certainly paid the banks higher prices than their shareholdings would have fetched had they all been dumped onto the open market.

Finally, the Japanese government adopted a third path—it let a misgoverned bank die quickly and painlessly. This final switch in policy is the focus of this chapter's empirical analysis. I would not have done some of the analysis in quite the same way. In particular, I worry that merging annual report numbers with daily stock returns to construct very large firm-day panels might bias some of the t-ratios in some of the tables. Nonetheless, the findings are useful.

On the news that the government both let a bank fail and offered no bailouts to its shareholders, it is reasonable that other banks' share prices adjusted up or down depending on each bank's financial health or frailty. In other words, watching an ill-run bank die clarifies the importance of a healthy balance sheet in the minds of other banks' shareholders.

The chapter deliberately closes with modest conclusions. This is appropriate because the findings are a preliminary first pass and are presented as such. But they clearly delineate directions for future work.

First, the chapter illustrates the utility of the event study methodology in clarifying directions of causation. These changes in policy—the government's actions in bailing out a bank's depositors but not its shareholders, and so on—clearly and unambiguously "caused" other banks' share prices to change. This is a much cleaner methodology for ascertaining the flow of causation than identification via instrumental variables in multistage regressions and might profitably be more widely used by macroeconomists.

Second, the study provides a concise chronology of the Japanese authorities' responses to their country's prolonged financial malaise. In particular, the problems Kindleberger (1978) highlights arising from an overly fervent belief in a lender of last resort are beautifully sketched out. Economists seeking to understand the panic of 2008 will learn much from the discussion of the political economy beneath these responses and how the expectations induced by each policy affected the next.

References

Kindleberger, Charles. 1978. *Manias, panics, and crashes: A history of financial crises.* 3rd ed. New York: Wiley, 1996.

Kryzanowski, Lawrence, and Gordon S. Roberts. 1998. Capital forbearance: Depression-era experience of life insurance companies. *Canadian Journal of Administrative Sciences* 15 (1): 1–16.

———. 1999. Perspectives on Canadian bank insolvency during the 1930s. *Journal of Money, Credit and Banking* 31 (1): 130–36.

10

Big Business Stability
and Social Welfare

Kathy Fogel, Randall Morck, and Bernard Yeung

Many countries appear to have excessively stable big business sectors, in that higher rates of big business turnover are clearly correlated with faster economy growth. Public policies that stabilize big business sectors are sometimes justified as supportive of social objectives. We find no consistent link between big business stability and public goods provision, egalitarianism, or labor empowerment. While absence of evidence is not evidence of absence, these findings suggest that other explanations, such as

Kathy Fogel is assistant professor of finance at the Sam Walton College of Business, University of Arkansas. Randall Morck is the Stephen A. Jarislowsky Distinguished Professor of Finance and University Professor at the University of Alberta, and a research associate of the National Bureau of Economic Research. Bernard Yeung is Dean and Stephen Riady Distinguished Professor of Finance, National University of Singapore; the Abraham Krasnoff Professor of Global Business and a professor of economics and of management at the Stern School of Business, New York University.

We are grateful for insightful comments and suggestions by Daron Acemoglu, Philippe Aghion, Melsa Ararat, Africa Ariño, Edgar Cabral, Partha Chatterjee, Petra Christmann, Pushan Dutt, Mara Faccio, Joseph Fan, Ray Fisman, Pankaj Ghemawat, Klaus Gugler, Campbell Harvey, Peter Holgfelt, Simon Johnson, Boyan Jovanovic, Andrew Karolyi, Tarun Khanna, E. Han Kim, Jung-Wook Kim, Bent Kromand, Larry Lang, Don Lessard, Ross Levine, Vikas Mehrotra, Joel Mokyr, Emi Nakamura, Andris Nobl, Hakan Orbay, Federica Pazzaglia, Enrico Perotti, Raghuram Rajan, Eric Rasmusen, Rahul Ravi, Joan Enric Ricart, Tom Scott, Andrei Shleifer, Jeremy Stein, Jan Svejnar, Steen Thomsen, Daniel Trefler, Saif Warraich, Marina Whitman, Clas Wihlborg, and Luigi Zingales. We also thank conference participants at the Academy of Management; American Finance Association; Asian Institute for Corporate Governance Conference; Canadian Economics Association; Canadian Institute for Advanced Research; Financial Management Association Doctoral Student Seminar; Instituto de Estudios Superiores de la Empresa, University of Navarra; Harvard Business School First International Workshop on Creating Value through Global Strategy; Multinational Finance Association; National Bureau of Economic Research (NBER) East Asian Seminar on Economics; NBER Summer Institute in Corporate Finance; Swedish Institute of Economic Research; Turkish Corporate Governance Forum; World Bank Global Corporate Governance Forum; as well as seminar participants at the University of Alberta; University special interest politics or behavioral biases favoring the status quo, also be considered.

10.1   Introduction

Schumpeter (1912) describes capitalism as a system in continual flux. Observing carriage makers fall to automakers, traditional steel mills cede markets to the Bessemer process, and cotton mills quake at the advent of rayon, Schumpeter saw capitalism's unique forte as harnessing this turmoil to lift humanity above its millennia-long Malthusian trap. Creative entrepreneurs build innovative upstart firms that destroy staid and established firms in an ongoing turmoil Schumpeter (1942) called *creative destruction*. The new firms are more productive than the old ones they displace, so aggregate wealth rises steadily as individual firms and fortunes rise and fall— often abruptly and unpredictably. A large and rapidly solidifying body of theoretical and empirical work, surveyed in Aghion and Howitt (1998), now confirms the essential validity of Schumpeter's ideas. Given this, rescuing the losers without undermining the process of creative destruction itself becomes a critical public policy challenge.

In a recent study, Fogel, Morck, and Yeung (2008) show that economies whose leading businesses die as new leading firms arise grow faster than economies whose lists of leading firms remain stable. The key variable in that study is "big business stability"—measured as the fraction of a country's largest employers in 1975 that persist to 1996. Persistence is defined variously as remaining in the top ten list, growing no slower than gross domestic product (GDP), retaining in 1996 at least 50 percent, 25 percent, or 10 percent of its 1975 labor force. Using any of these measures, they show that real per capita GDP growth, economy total factor productivity growth, and aggregate capital accumulation are all significantly higher in economies with less stable big business sectors.

This finding suggests that many economies pay for excessively stable big business sectors with depressed growth. One possibility, alluded to by Fogel, Morck, and Yeung (2008), is that some governments may balance other policy goals against economic growth. This is plausible, for "man does not live by bread alone." Indeed, the social objectives of modern societies are often framed, as by the republican idealists of the French Revolution, in terms like "liberty, fraternity, and equality!" A high per capita GDP can help with

of Amsterdam; Baruch College; University of California at Berkeley; Concordia University; Copenhagen Business School; Duke University; Harvard Business School; University of Illinois; Korea University; University of Maryland; New York University; University of Toronto; Washington University at St Louis; and Yale's International Institute of Corporate Governance. Randall Morck gratefully acknowledges financial support from the Social Sciences and Humanities Research Council of Canada. (SSHRC) Bernard Yeung gratefully acknowledges financial support from the Berkeley Center for Entrepreneurial Studies at New York University, Stern School of Business.

these, but the legitimacy of public policy goals other than economy growth must be conceded.

Might a more stable big business sector help a country attain these goals? Toned down creative destruction makes more predictable each firm's future revenue streams, the composition of the big business sector, and the identities of the people in charge. The transactions costs of collecting tax revenues from a smaller number of larger firms, redistributing income via industrial policies, and co-opting business into social pacts may all be lower if big businesses are longer lived players. Big businesses might partake such transactions to maximize long-term profits, or to assuage their controlling shareholders' souls or egos. These arguments, developed at greater length in the following, are admittedly highly tentative, and counterarguments are easy to generate. But we seek reasons why many countries' big business sectors appear excessively stable, so we allocate the benefit of the doubt to these rationalizations—at least for now.

To see if this is so, we correlate big business stability with a variety of social development indicators, controlling for per capita GDP. We find largely insignificant results throughout, though occasionally big business stability correlates with worse social outcomes.

We speculate that the countervailing policy benefits might be either more obscure or tightly focused on narrow interest groups. Alternatively, the well-documented *conservative bias* detected elsewhere in behavioral finance may induce suboptimal policy in some countries.

The article is organized as follows: Section 10.2 provides some background to motivate the assumption that excessive big business stability may indeed be a deliberate public policy goal. Section 10.3 describes the data and section 10.4 the results. Section 10.5 concludes, entertains our speculative explanations, and calls for further work.

10.2   On Stability

Instances of politicians using public funds to rescue tottering corporate giants are not rare. For example, when Philipp Holzmann AG disclosed a DM2.4 billion-mark problem in its books, its banks demanded a comprehensive restructuring. *The Wall Street Journal* (November 25, 1999) describes the subsequent politicking as follows: When the banks rejected Holzmann's DM4.3-billion restructuring proposal as inadequate, a chorus of German politicians vilified the banks' unwillingness to "shield a 150 year old German company and save the jobs of Holzmann's 17,000 domestic workers." German Chancellor Gerhard Schroeder, after buying the banks' acquiescence with a federal guarantee on a DM100 million loan and DM150 million in new capital, exulted "The banks have recognized their economic and social responsibility."

Such respect for corporate stability is not confined to European politicians. *Business Week* (September 11, 1998) quotes an anonymous prominent businessman explaining that the Malaysian prime minister, Mahathir Mohamad "doesn't believe in bankruptcies. He has a moral objection to them." The *Business Week* article added that during the Asian crisis when "the intensity of business collapses and bank collapses was like tenpins falling every day," Mr. Mahathir Mohamad "couldn't stand it. He doesn't believe in bankruptcies."

Politicians can protect the stability of established corporate empires in less direct ways than bailouts. Although Thai Petrochemical Industries was insolvent in 1997, the firm was not officially declared bankrupt until 2000. According to the *Wall Street Journal* (February 12, 2001), the CEO, Prachai Leophairatana, filed thirteen different lawsuits and a criminal embezzlement charge against the creditors. Although the creditors formally fired him, he continued to occupy the CEO's office and run the company. The Thai government seemed unable or unwilling to evict him.

In Africa, too, government policies can tilt the playing field to favor old established firms and undermine upstart innovators. In the mid 1990s, the government of Zimbabwe invested a great deal of effort to save the state telephone utility, PTC, from a cell phone company being organized by Strive Masiyiwa, an entrepreneur. The story, according to the *National Post* (February 26, 2000), is as follows. PTC phone lines served 1.4 percent of Zimbabweans, and the hundreds of thousands of people requesting new lines endured waits of up to four years and were expected to pay large bribes to bureaucrats. When Masiyiwa proposed a joint venture with PTC to provide cell phone service, he recounts that "They looked at me and said: 'We don't see a future in it. We certainly aren't going to waste valuable resources on it.'" When Masiyiwa decided to go it alone, PTC forbade it on the grounds that the state had a monopoly on telecommunications. Masiyiwa hired an American lawyer, challenged PTC's position in court, and won. He then formed a company, Econet, and with foreign partners built base stations across the country. A few days before service was to begin, Zimbabwe's president Robert Mugabe invoked emergency presidential powers and made it illegal for a private business to build a cellular network. Offenders would face two years in jail. Masiyiwa recounts that "Parliament sat through three sittings to turn [the decree] into law in one day." He returned to the courts, and a judge finally ordered that a cell phone license be put up for public tender. A string of politically connected consortia sprung up to bid, and Telecel, a consortium backed by Leo Mugabe, the president's nephew and a member of parliament, won the license. Masiyiwa's salvation was an anonymous civil servant, who leaked documents proving that a corrupt official had docked 20 percent from Econet's score on the tender bid. Strive Masiyiwa should have won in the first place. After more court battles, a cabinet shuffle, and threats of resignation from the late vice president, Econet finally got a license to operate. Within a week of its launch, the company had 10,000 subscribers and rapidly overtook Telecel and the state-run cell phone company, NetOne. As the situation in Zimbabwe further deteriorated in the late 1990s, Masiyawa found it prudent to move his base of operations to South Africa.

Anecdotal evidence is not proof, but the incidents reviewed in the preceding at least justify the hypothesis that stabilizing a country's big business sector might be a commonplace public policy goal, or at least a perceived means to other policy goals, that countervail any slowing of economic growth.

How might a stable big business sector aid in the achievement of laudable policy goals beyond the purely economic ones?

10.2.1   Liberty

A more stable big business sector might ease government's fiscal uncertainty by providing stable and predictable tax inflows. This might be important in funding health care, education, public infrastructure, or other public goods that must be built up slowly over time. Some of the costs of these goods might even be off-loaded to large stable firms. For example, many health care costs are paid by large firms, not government, in the United States and Switzerland. Education costs can also be paid by employers on occasion, as when firms pay for advanced business degrees for their managerial staff or for technical skills upgrading for blue-collar workers.

Public goods are a critical, and often overlooked, aspect of development. Sen (1999) argues that development should be defined as that which expands human freedom. Educated people have more options to choose from than illiterates, so better education is an important component of development. Healthy people have more options than the chronically ill. People living near roads, ports, and airports have more options than those isolated in impenetrable wilderness. All of these considerations lead Sen to conclude that governments need to invest heavily in public goods like education, infrastructure, and health care to provide basic necessary freedoms to their peoples. An overly single minded focus on GDP growth is inadequate.

10.2.2   Equality

The crux of the matter might be egalitarianism. In public pronouncements explaining decisions to support large established firms, politicians often take an instrumental perspective—a stable big businesses sector is not desirable per se, but because it leads to other desirable public policy outcomes, such as high quality public goods, labor rights, or an egalitarian income distribution. Such factors apparently moved the German government's bailout of Philipp Holzmann, which Finance Minister Hans Eichel justified thus: "The government has a responsibility to step in if a major German company is about to collapse and cost thousands of people their jobs."[1] A like motive seems to underlie Chancellor Gerhard Schroeder's pressing German banks to "save the jobs" of the 22,000 employees of the bankrupt engineering firm Babcock Borsig AG with a $700 to $800 million bailout.[2]

If big business stability, by preserving blue-collar jobs, sustains incomes across a wide segment of the population while letting innovative upstarts displace them benefits only a handful of entrepreneurs, egalitarianism might bias government policies against upstarts to protect established large firms. Governments might have to choose a balance between the rapid growth of unfettered creative destruction and the equality attainable by slowing that process.

10.2.3   Fraternity

But public goods might not be the only noneconomic goal at issue. Several of the politicians we cite in the preceding proclaim big business stability desirable because it coheres society. The underlying economics is often obscure, but this linkage may have led the Japanese government to propose a ¥200 billion ($1.90 billion) bailout of Sogo Department Stores, which *Asiaweek* described as part of Japan's long tradition of corporate bailouts designed to minimize "confusion."[3] *Asiaweek* continues that, to the bewilderment of senior politicians, the bailout was derailed when "[t]he public exploded over the use of their tax money to rescue a poorly managed private company."

The long-term stability of large Japanese firms is sometimes stressed as economically advantageous because it promotes implicit labor contracts, workers' firm-specific human capital accumulation, and otherwise reduces labor market transactions costs (Aoki 1988). This logic might apply to Japan, but if it were more generally valid, these economic advantages should be evident in faster economy growth, all else equal.

But a stable big business sector might nonetheless be viewed by some politicians as a useful tool in the art of nation building. For example, *Business Week* reports that Malaysian Prime Minister Mahathir is unapologetic about his government's policy of selecting a handful of wealthy businessmen for privileges and assigning them the role of creating jobs, implementing big projects, and keeping the economy growing. The article quotes Mustapha Mohamed of the Finance Ministry as saying "We view Malaysia as a corporation, and the shareholders in the government are companies"

---

1. See Edmund Andrews, "Navigating the Economy of a Changing Germany," *New York Times,* December 7, 1999.

2. See "Schroeder Seeks Bailout Aid for Bankrupt Firm," *International Herald Tribune,* July 6, 2002, 11.

3. See Jonathan Sprague and Murakami Mutsuko, "Tokyo's Sogo Shocker—A Bailout and a Reversal Show No Policy at All," *Asiaweek,* 26 (29), July 28, 2000.

and that "To the extent you help the bigger guys, the smaller guys benefit."[4] Some mixture of nation building and the promotion of social cohesion seem evident in these remarks.

Such thinking reflects the corporatist tripartite bargaining intrinsic to many European social democracies (Högfeldt 2005). In these countries, representatives of big labor, big government, and big business periodically got together to map out economic strategies for the entire country. Such negotiations are obviously easier if the same big businesses are involved year after year (Roe 2003). Innovative and dynamic upstart big businesses may, quite understandably, fail to adhere to tripartite agreements made by their more sedately run former competitors. Indeed, staid established firms might even be able to use such bargains to drive through labor or social agendas favorable to themselves and detrimental to potential creative upstarts (Rajan and Zingales 2003).

10.3   Data

Our measures of the stability of each country's biggest businesses are from Fogel, Morck, and Yeung (2008). They list the biggest employers in each country in the 1975 and 1996, from *Dun & Bradstreet's Principals of International Business*. These lists include a wide spectrum of businesses: listed and unlisted firms, corporations and other businesses, as well as private-sector and state-controlled enterprises (SCEs).[5] This catholicism evades sample selection problems due to stock markets, and thus listed firms, being more or less common in some economies. Enterprises not usually considered "businesses," such as educational institutions, medical institutions, membership organizations, government agencies, and the like are excluded, though.

La Porta, Lopez-de-Silanes, and Shleifer (1999), Claessens, Djankov, and Lang (2000), Faccio and Lang (2002), and others show that large businesses outside the United States and United Kingdom are often members of business groups, not freestanding firms. Using raw data provided by those researchers, as well as data on controlling shareholders from *Hoover's online, Worldscope, SDC,* Forbes' annual lists of billionaires, newspaper archives, case studies, academic research papers, corporate Web sites, corporate histories, and business family biographies, Fogel, Morck, and Yeung (2008) consolidate group member firms into business groups. They define a firm as controlled if it is so defined in any of these sources, or if 20 percent or more

---

4. See Sheri Prasso, Mark Clifford, and Joyce Barnathan, "Malaysia: The Feud—How Mahathir and Anwar Became Embroiled in a Clash That Threatens to Send Malaysia into Upheaval," *Business Week,* October 28, 1998.
5. We use the term *state-controlled enterprise* (SCE) rather than *state-owned enterprise* (SOE) because the state may hold a control block without owning the firm outright.

of its stock is voted by a wealthy family, government, trust, or bank.[6] The stability of big business is thus gauged by the continued importance of the largest businesses, whether groups or freestanding firms, in each country. This avoids problems due to intragroup asset transfers. However, consolidating firms into groups leaves countries like Sweden and South Africa only a few extremely large businesses. Because even the fifteenth or twentieth biggest business in such countries is quite small, the stability measures define each country's *big business sector* as its ten largest employers (if there are ties in tenth place, all the ties are included).

Gauging the stability of a country's large business sector requires determining whether each leading 1975 business persist to 1996. One obvious approach is to define *persist* as "still in the top ten list in 1996." But a truly vibrant economy might admit new businesses to the top ten, even as the 1975 top ten prosper. A more suitable definition might thus target 1975 top ten businesses that grow no slower than GDP to 1996; though this might be inappropriate for an economy that shrank from 1975 to 1996. Or a firm might *persist* if it employs no less than 50 percent, 25 percent, or 10 percent of its 1975 workforce in 1996.

In the following, we use a combined definition—a top ten 1975 business *persists* if it retains top ten list in 1996 *or* grow at least as fast as its country's GDP from 1975 to 1996. Thus, we define persistence for each 1975 top ten business I as the maximum of δ_i and η_i, with

$$(1) \qquad \delta_i = \begin{cases} 1 \text{ if } i \text{ is in the top ten lists in both 1975 and 1996} \\ 0 \text{ otherwise} \end{cases}$$

and

$$(2) \qquad \eta_i = \begin{cases} 1 \text{ if its employment grew no slower than GDP in both 1975} \\ \text{and 1996} \\ 0 \text{ otherwise} \end{cases}$$

The country's *equal-weighted stability index* is then

$$(3) \qquad \Omega_E = \frac{1}{10} \sum_{i=1}^{10} \max(\delta_i, \eta_i)$$

and its *labor-weighted stability index* is

$$(4) \qquad \Omega_L = \frac{\sum_{i=1}^{10} \max(\delta_i, \eta_i) L_i}{\sum_{i=1}^{10} L_i},$$

6. La Porta, Lopez-de-Silanes, and Shleifer (1999) show that 51 percent is not necessary as a single dominant shareholder can exert effective control when all other shareholders are small. We use voting rights to assign control, for cash flow rights and voting rights diverge substantially in some countries because of dual share classes and control pyramids.

with the L_i the 1975 labor forces of the countries top ten 1975 businesses. Using this procedure, Fogel, Morck, and Yeung (2008) construct various alternative stability measures including or excluding financial firms, multinational subsidiaries, and sometime state-controlled enterprises in all possible combinations. Because they find two of these to be representative of the others, we focus here on *minimally inclusive* indexes $\underline{\Omega}_E$ and $\underline{\Omega}_L$ using the top ten private-sector nonfinancial domestically controlled businesses only, and *maximally inclusive* indexes $\overline{\Omega}_E$ and $\overline{\Omega}_L$ that also include sometime state-controlled enterprises, foreign controlled enterprises, foreign controlled enterprises, and financial firms as well. Table 10.1 presents summary statistics for these four measures.

Our objective is to see if big business stability, shown to correlate with slow growth by Fogel, Morck, and Yeung (2008), might correlate positively with offsetting laudable social outcomes. We, therefore, examine a broad spectrum of measures of such outcomes.

We first consider several measures of public goods provision:

10.3.1   Health

We use three indicators to measure the average level of public health from 1996 to 2000. "Infant mortality" is the number of infants dying before reaching age one, per 1,000 live births. "Child mortality" is the estimated number of infants dying before reaching age five, per 1,000 live births, assuming the current age-specific mortality rates hold. "Life expectancy" is the number of years a newborn baby would live holding the current patterns of mortality constant throughout its life. All three indicators come from the World Development Indicators (WDI) database online, made available by the World Bank.

10.3.2   Education

Measures of public expenditures on education are collected from WDI for the period of 1996 to 2000. "Public spending on education" consists of current and capital public expenditure on education and subsidies to private education as a percentage of total GDP. We also obtain data on "education attainment" from Barro and Lee (2001). This variable indicates the total number of years of schooling in the adult population aged twenty-five or older in 1995.

10.3.3   Infrastructure

We are interested in four aspects of infrastructure essential to social economic development: "electricity" is the net production of electric power by power plants, measured in MWH per capita; "roads" is kilometers of paved roads as a percentage of all roads in the country; "telecommunication" is fixed and mobile phone line subscribers per 1,000 people; and

Table 10.1   **Summary statistics of big business stability measures**

	N	Mean	Standard Deviation	Min.	Max.
Maximally inclusive labor-weighted $\overline{\Omega}_L$	43	0.498	0.225	0.071	0.839
Maximally inclusive equal-weighted $\overline{\Omega}_E$	43	0.385	0.179	0.100	0.727
Minimally inclusive labor-weighted $\underline{\Omega}_L$	43	0.456	0.228	0.064	0.842
Minimally inclusive equal-weighted $\underline{\Omega}_E$	43	0.355	0.168	0.091	0.700

	$\overline{\Omega}_L$	$\overline{\Omega}_E$	$\underline{\Omega}_L$	$\underline{\Omega}_E$
Argentina	0.31173	0.2	0.39277	0.3
Australia	0.66851	0.6	0.73239	0.6
Austria	0.83342	0.5	0.22772	0.2
Belgium	0.40802	0.3	0.53091	0.5
Bolivia	0.74855	0.3	0.27430	0.3
Brazil	0.47057	0.5	0.29455	0.3
Canada	0.40118	0.4	0.57342	0.4
Chile	0.43968	0.4	0.27919	0.3
Colombia	0.28799	0.2	0.60121	0.5
Denmark	0.56300	0.4	0.72525	0.4
Finland	0.78035	0.7	0.57816	0.5
France	0.56400	0.4	0.55802	0.4
Germany	0.76277	0.7	0.73497	0.7
Greece	0.38197	0.3	0.07193	0.1
Hong Kong	0.60582	0.3	0.60582	0.3
India	0.12107	0.1	0.56486	0.4
Indonesia	0.31485	0.3	0.39913	0.3
Ireland	0.45014	0.3	0.39698	0.2
Israel	0.59483	0.6	0.74440	0.4
Italy	0.76126	0.4	0.78853	0.3
Japan	0.72527	0.7	0.59077	0.6
Korea	0.45119	0.5	0.34111	0.4
Malaysia	0.07326	0.1	0.12253	0.1
Mexico	0.76431	0.5	0.62523	0.5
The Netherlands	0.83944	0.6	0.84228	0.6
New Zealand	0.20476	0.2	0.24253	0.3
Norway	0.30084	0.3	0.12190	0.1
Pakistan	0.22827	0.2	0.45168	0.4
Peru	0.45936	0.5	0.26775	0.2
The Philippines	0.25999	0.2	0.07253	0.1
Portugal	0.34266	0.2	0.08388	0.1
Singapore	0.56019	0.4	0.06400	0.1
South Africa	0.57996	0.5	0.66960	0.6
Spain	0.46344	0.3	0.30168	0.3
Sri Lanka	0.07093	0.1	0.24317	0.2
Sweden	0.78482	0.5	0.78337	0.4
Switzerland	0.83344	0.7	0.83344	0.7
Thailand	0.74212	0.6	0.60927	0.5
Turkey	0.20833	0.1	0.38338	0.2
United Kingdom	0.23128	0.2	0.53862	0.4
United States	0.53122	0.5	0.53122	0.5
Uruguay	0.49031	0.3	0.40564	0.2
Venezuela	0.77755	0.5	0.40070	0.4

"Internet" is broadband internet access subscribers per 1,000 people. All four measures are taken from WDI and are averaged from 1996 to 2000.

10.3.4 Pollution

We measure "water pollution" by the number of metric tons of organic water pollutant emissions per day and "air pollution" by the number of metric tons of carbon dioxide emissions per capita. Both measures again come from WDI and take the average values of 1996 to 2000.

10.3.5 Overall Quality of Life

We use the United Nation's Human Development Index (HDI) to measure the overall quality of life. This index is constructed to incorporate three dimension indexes capturing nations' achievements in health, education, and standard of living relative to the best performing country in each dimension. Specifically, the health dimension index is based on life expectancy at birth; the education dimension on adult literacy and the gross enrollment of primary, secondary, and tertiary schools combined; and the standard of living dimension on purchasing power parity adjusted GDP per capita values in U.S. dollars. The technical note of each year's Human Development Report contains further details of the index construction and can be accessed at http://hdr.undp.org. This paper uses the average HDI from 1997 to 2000.

To gauge each economy's concern for inequality, we consider measures of income distribution and abject poverty:

Poverty

We use poverty headcount ratios to measure poverty. Poverty defined using "$1 a day" is the percentage of the population living on less than $1.08 a day at 1993 prices, adjusted for purchasing power parity. Poverty defined using "$2 a day" is similarly defined, with the benchmark set at $2.15 a day. A value of 2 percent is assigned to countries whose poverty rate sits below 2 percent. Data is averaged between 1996 and 2000 wherever possible but is missing for twenty-four countries, twenty-one of which are Organization for Economic Cooperation and Development (OECD) members, plus Hong Kong, Israel, and Singapore. A value of zero is assigned to these countries.

Income Inequality

Gini coefficients, first introduced by the Italian statistician Corrado Gini in 1912, are widely accepted as a measure of income inequality. To ensure robustness of results, we use two versions of Gini coefficients, one published by the WDI database, and the other by the World Income Inequality Database (WIID), detailed in Deininger and Squire (1996). The WDI data is undated, whereas the WIID data is for 1996 or the closest year available.

Finally, we consider measures of the bargaining power of labor.

Unemployment

We use unemployment rate as a percentage of total labor force to account for the share of the total labor force that is currently without work but seeking employment. For robustness, we also use unemployment rates by gender, similarly defined. The data is retrieved from the online WDI database.

Labor Rights

We use three measures of labor rights, all taken from Botero et al. (2004). First, "union density" is the percentage of the total labor force affiliated to labor unions in 1997. Second, "the right to form unions" is a four-value dummy that assumes a maximum value of 1 if the country's constitution expressly grants the right to form labor unions. The dummy is set to 0.67 if labor unions are described as a matter of public policy or public interest, 0.33 if labor unions are otherwise mentioned in the constitution, and 0 otherwise. Third, "minimum wage" is a dummy variable that equals 1 if a mandatory minimum wage is either defined by statute, or established by mandatory collective agreement and made legally binding for most sectors of the economy, and 0 otherwise.

Labor Protection

We measure the protection of labor afforded by social security laws with indexes capturing "old age, disability, and death benefits," "sickness and health benefits," and "unemployment benefits." A higher value of the old-age benefits index means higher postretirement life expectancy, fewer months of contributions or employment required for normal retirement by law, lower deductions in the worker's monthly salary to cover these benefits, and larger proportion of the net preretirement salary covered by the pension. A higher value of the sickness benefits index means fewer months of contributions or employment required to qualify for these benefits by law, lower deductions in the worker's monthly salary to cover these benefits, shorter waiting period, and higher percentage of the net salary covered for a two-month sickness spell. The unemployment benefits index is defined similarly to the sickness benefits index, with a higher value indicating fewer months of contribution, lower deduction, shorter waiting period, and higher percentage of salary covered for a one-year unemployment spell. All three indexes come from Botero et al. (2004).

Each specific variable and its source are described in detail in table 10.2. Their summary statistics are displayed in table 10.3.

10.4   Findings

Section 10.2 outlined three sets of arguments as to why big business stability might be socially desirable even if it retards economic growth

Table 10.2   Descriptions of control and social development variables

GDP control		
GDP per capita	Log of per capita GDP in thousands of 2000 international dollars, purchasing power parity (PPP) adjusted, average of 1996–2000.	Penn World Tables 6.2.

Social development measures		

Public Goods

Health

Infant mortality	Number of infants dying before reaching age one per 1,000 live births, average of 1996–2000.	World Development Indicators (WDI) Online
Child mortality	Probability of infants dying before reaching age five per 1,000 live births assuming the current age-specific mortality rates, average of 1996–2000.	
Life expectancy	Number of years a newborn baby would live holding the current patterns of mortality constant throughout its life, average of 1996–2000.	

Education

Education attainment	Log of the average years of schooling for people aged ≥25 in 1995.	Barro and Lee (2001)
Public spending in education (% of GDP)	Current and capital public expenditure on education and subsidies to private education as a percentage of GDP, average of 1996–2000.	WDI Online

Infrastructure

Electricity	Net production of electric power by power plants (MWH per capita), average of 1996–2000.	WDI Online
Paved roads	Paved roads as a percentage of all roads in the country, average of 1996–2000.	
Telecommunications	Fixed and mobile phone line subscribers per 1,000 people, average of 1996–2000.	
Internet	Broadband Internet access subscribers per 1,000 people, average of 1996–2000.	

Environmental protection

Water pollution	Tons of organic water pollutant emissions per day, average of 1996–2000.	WDI Online
Air pollution	Tons of carbon dioxide emissions per capita, average of 1996–2000.	WDI Online

Quality of life

UN human development index (HDI)	Higher values of HDI indicates longer and healthier life span, better education, and higher standard of living relative to the best performing countries, average of 1997–2000.	http://hdr.undp.org/

Equality

Poverty

Poverty, $1 a day	Percentage of the population living on less than $1.08 a day at 1993 prices, PPP adjusted, average of 1996–2000.	WDI Online
Poverty, $2 a day	Percentage of the population living on less than $2.15 a day at 1993 prices, PPP adjusted, average	

(*continued*)

Table 10.2 (continued)

of 1996–2000.

Income inequality

Gini, avg. 1996–2000 (WDI)	Index value ranges from 1 to 100, with higher value indicating more income inequality, average of 1996–2000 wherever possible.	WDI Online
Gini, 1996 (WIID)	Gini coefficients based on high quality income or expenditure data for all national population and ranges from 1 to 100, with higher value indicating more income inequality, 1996 or the closest year available.	http://www.wider.unu.ed/wiid/wiid.htm

Labor power

Unemployment

Unemployment in total labor force	Unemployment rate as a percentage of total active labor force, average of 1996–2000.	WDI Online
Unemployment in male labor force	Unemployment rate as a percentage of male active labor force, average of 1996–2000.	
Unemployment in female labor force	Unemployment rate as a percentage of female active labor force, average of 1996–2000.	

Labor rights

Union density	Percentage of the total labor force affiliated to labor unions in 1997.	Botero et al. (2004)
Right to form union	A dummy that assumes 1 if the country's constitution expressly grants the right to form labor unions, 0.67 if labor unions are described as a matter of public policy or public interest, 0.33 if labor unions are otherwise mentioned in the constitution, and 0 otherwise.	
Minimum wage	A dummy that equals 1 if a mandatory minimum wage is either defined by statute, or established by mandatory collective agreement and made legally binding for most sectors of the economy, and 0 otherwise.	

Labor protection

Old age, disability, and death benefits	A higher index value means higher postretirement life expectancy, fewer months of contributions requirement, lower deductions in the worker's monthly salary to cover these benefits, and larger proportion of the net preretirement salary covered by the pension.	Botero et al. (2004)
Health benefits	A higher index value means fewer months of contribution requirement, lower deductions in the worker's monthly salary, shorter waiting period, and higher percentage of the net salary covered for a two-month sickness spell.	
Unemployment benefits	A higher index value indicates fewer months of contribution, lower deduction, shorter waiting period, and higher percentage of salary covered for a one-year unemployment spell.	

Table 10.3   Summary statistics of control and social development measures

	Mean	Standard Deviation	Min.	Max.
Control variable				
GDP per capita, avg. 1996–2000				
(in thousands)	16.1	9.28	2.41	32.3
Public goods quality measures				
Infant mortality	17.0	19.7	3.48	85.0
Child mortality	21.3	25.4	4.30	108
Life expectancy	74.0	6.15	50.3	80.6
Education attainment	2.00	0.355	0.866	2.50
Public spending in education				
(% of GDP)	4.79	1.44	1.36	8.29
Electricity	5.50	5.14	.243	245
Paved roads	64.6	32.5	6.0	100
Telecommunications	578	374	22.0	1201
Internet	3.28	6.01	0.000	23.2
Water pollution	318	480	11.8	2457
Air pollution	6.72	4.68	0.434	20.1
UN human development index (HDI)	0.838	0.107	0.510	0.939
Income equality measures				
Poverty ($1 a day)	4.27	8.04	0.000	41.8
Poverty ($2 a day)	13.5	20.9	0.000	80.4
Gini, avg. 1996–2000 (WDI)	39.0	9.81	24.7	59.6
Gini, 1996 (WIID)	41.0	9.77	23.7	59.0
Labor power measures				
Unemployment in total labor force	7.82	4.43	2.16	23.6
Unemployment in male labor force	6.99	3.63	2.12	20.3
Unemployment in female labor force	9.18	5.99	2.12	27.9
Union density	0.312	0.234	0.012	0.900
Right to form union	0.597	0.475	0.000	1.000
Minimum wage	0.651	0.482	0.000	1.000
Old age, disability, and death benefits	0.625	0.139	0.233	0.846
Health benefits	0.716	0.228	0.000	0.988
Unemployment benefits	0.558	0.360	0.000	0.997

Note: Sample is the forty-three countries listed in table 10.1, with the exception of infant and child mortality rate, for which Hong Kong is missing.

somewhat. First, big business stability might permit sustained investment in public goods. Second, big business stability might permit stronger labor rights. Third, big business stability might level income distributions and contribute to a more egalitarian society.

In the following tables, we first document simple correlation coefficients of the stability variables with a set of social outcomes, and then regress the social outcome measures on stability and per capita GDP. This is because countries with higher *per capita* GDP are likely to exhibit better outcomes across a range of development outcomes—economic and social. We wish to test for big business stability contributing to laudable social outcomes through channels other than economic prosperity.

10.4.1   Public Goods

Table 10.4 considers the possibility that a stable big business sector permits governments to invest more in public goods. We gauge the quality of a country's public goods in a variety of ways. Its health care is reflected in its infant mortality rate, child mortality rate, and overall life expectancy. Table 10.4 shows lower infant and child mortality rates as well as greater life expectancies in countries with more stable maximally inclusive lists, suggesting a possible social offset to laggard economic growth. But these correlations disappear or switch signs after controlling for per capita GDP. If anything, countries at a given level of per capita GDP that opt for big private-sector business stability appear to exhibit both worse health care and slower economic growth.

A very important social goal is education. Measures of the quality of the countries' education—mean education attainment and public spending on education—show no correlation with big business stability after controlling for *per capita* GDP—though the simple correlations with the maximally inclusive stability indexes are significant.

Public infrastructure is also composed of critically important public goods. Electricity provision, the quality of roads, telecommunication infrastructure, and Internet penetration all exhibit intermittently significant positive simple correlation coefficients with the stability indexes, but all fade to insignificance after controlling for per capita GDP.

Another set of high demand public goods pertains to environmental protection, which we gauge by water pollution and air pollution (in terms of CO_2 emissions) statistics. Worse pollution correlates with more stable big business sectors. The correlations between air pollution and big business stability significantly weakens after controlling for *per capita* GDP; however, water pollution is highly significantly and positively associated with private-sector stability even with per capita GDP as a control variable. Finally, the United Nations assesses the overall quality of life in each of its member countries. This can be interpreted as an overall measure of the consumption of private and public goods by the population, for it weights health care and education against purely economic outcomes like a high per capita GDP. Big business stability is positively correlated with the human development index, but this correlation evaporates when we control for per capita GDP.

If big business stability helps governments direct resources toward public goods, others than those in table 10.4 must be the focus. Insignificance cannot prove the absence of a relation, but a tie to the quality of public goods is clearly elusive.

Table 10.4 **Big business stability and the quality of public goods**

	Simple correlations				Regressions controlling for log of per capita GDP averaged over 1996–2000			
	$\overline{\Omega}_L$	$\overline{\Omega}_E$	$\underline{\Omega}_L$	$\underline{\Omega}_E$	$\overline{\Omega}_L$	$\overline{\Omega}_E$	$\underline{\Omega}_L$	$\underline{\Omega}_E$
	A. Public health							
Infant mortality	**−0.279**	**−0.344**	−.0841	−.0296	6.77	6.46	**13.80**	**18.91**
	(.07)	**(.03)**	(.60)	(.85)	(.37)	(.44)	**(.04)**	**(.04)**
Child mortality	**−0.278**	**−0.348**	−.0868	−.0307	8.46	6.98	**17.29**	**24.02**
	(.07)	**(.02)**	(.58)	(.85)	(.42)	(.53)	**(.05)**	**(.05)**
Life expectancy	**0.27**	**0.273**	0.12	0.0171	−1.78	−3.24	−3.08	−5.60
	(.08)	**(.08)**	(.44)	(.91)	(.46)	(.38)	(.31)	(.28)
	B. Education							
Education attainment	**0.322**	**0.425**	0.227	0.214	−0.01	0.18	0.00	0.11
	(.04)	**(.00)**	(.14)	(.17)	(.94)	(.34)	(1.00)	(.62)
Public spending on education	**0.274**	0.239	0.233	0.144	0.43	0.04	0.56	0.30
	(.08)	(.12)	(.13)	(.36)	(.64)	(.97)	(.55)	(.79)
	C. Infrastructure							
Electricity	0.234	**0.348**	0.177	0.149	−1636	1138	−645	32.58
	(.13)	**(.02)**	(.26)	(.34)	(.62)	(.76)	(.86)	(.99)
Roads	**0.265**	0.2	0.209	0.0294	−0.57	−19.99	3.56	−21.44
	(.09)	(.20)	(.18)	(.85)	(.97)	(.41)	(.82)	(.32)
Telecom	**0.403**	**0.413**	**0.32**	0.189	48.05	12.92	102.05	−6.69
	(.01)	**(.01)**	**(.04)**	(.23)	(.66)	(.93)	(.29)	(.95)
Internet	0.165	0.182	0.129	0.113	−0.33	−0.27	0.21	0.91
	(.29)	(.24)	(.41)	(.47)	(.92)	(.95)	(.94)	(.79)
	D. Environmental protection							
Water pollution[a]	−.0234	0.1322	0.2034	**0.3175**	−0.955	0.390	**0.444**	**0.926**
	(.88)	(.40)	(.19)	**(.04)**	(.72)	(.30)	**(.05)**	**(.02)**
Air pollution	**0.309**	**0.438**	**0.257**	**0.309**	−0.07	3.31	0.91	4.39
	(.04)	**(.00)**	**(.10)**	**(.04)**	(.97)	(.15)	(.67)	(.17)
	E. Quality of life							
Human development[b]	**0.393**	**0.421**	0.214	0.146	3.432	3.51	−27.6	−32.9
	(.01)	**(.00)**	(.17)	(.35)	(.86)	(.89)	(.32)	(.37)

Notes: The left panel reports correlation coefficients between big business stability and variables measuring the quality of public goods provision. The right panel presents regressions of the form: public goods = $\beta_0 + \beta_1$ stability + $\beta_2 \ln(y) + \varepsilon$. Only coefficient estimates on stability (β_1) are shown. Numbers in parentheses are probability levels for rejecting the null hypothesis of zero correlation coefficients or regression coefficients. Heteroskedasticity-consistent standard errors are used to calculate *p*-levels in all regressions. Sample includes forty-three countries listed in table 10.1, with the exception of infant mortality and child mortality for which Hong Kong is missing. Boldface indicates rejection of the null hypothesis of a zero point estimate at 10 percent confidence in two-tailed tests.

[a] Regression coefficient to be multiplied by 10^3.

[b] Regression coefficient to be divided by 10^3.

Table 10.5   **Big business stability and poverty and income inequality**

	Simple correlations				Regressions controlling for log of per capita GDP averaged over 1996–2000			
	$\overline{\Omega}_L$	$\overline{\Omega}_E$	$\underline{\Omega}_L$	$\underline{\Omega}_E$	$\overline{\Omega}_L$	$\overline{\Omega}_E$	$\underline{\Omega}_L$	$\underline{\Omega}_E$
A. Poverty								
Poverty ($1 per day)	**−0.252**	**−0.313**	−0.111	−0.0453	3.1	2.02	4.35	5.92
	(.10)	(.04)	(.48)	(.77)	(.44)	(.65)	(.23)	(.12)
Poverty ($2 per day)	**−0.343**	**−0.345**	−0.142	−0.0645	3.48	8.47	**11.73**	**16.19**
	(.02)	(.02)	(.36)	(.68)	(.54)	(.24)	(.05)	(.03)
B. Income inequality								
GINI coefficient (WDI)	−0.1365	−0.2173	−0.2397	−0.1466	3.55	0.19	−4.58	−2.64
	(.38)	(.16)	(.12)	(.35)	(.53)	(.98)	(.41)	(.72)
GINI, 1996 (WIID)	−0.116	−0.165	−0.132	−0.132	4.22	3.20	0.25	−1.97
	(.46)	(.29)	(.40)	(.40)	(.39)	(.67)	(.96)	(.78)

Notes: The left panel reports correlation coefficients between big business stability and variables measuring the degree of poverty and income inequality. The right panel presents regressions of the form: poverty or inequality = β_0 + β_1 stability + β_2 ln(y) + ε. Only coefficient estimates on stability (β_1) are shown. Numbers in parentheses are probability levels for rejecting the null hypothesis of zero correlation coefficients or regression coefficients. Heteroskedasticity-consistent standard errors are used to calculate *p*-levels in all regressions. Sample is the forty-three countries listed in table 10.1. Boldface indicates rejection of the null hypothesis of a zero point estimate at 10 percent confidence in two-tailed tests.

10.4.2   Income Equality

If stable big businesses provide employment to those who would otherwise be marginalized, this may be a public policy outcome worthy for which a few points of GDP growth might well be sacrificed. Table 10.5 measures egalitarianism by each country's Gini coefficient and by the fraction of the population condemned to live on less than one or two dollars per day.

More stable big business sectors are actually correlated with worse inequality in the simple correlation coefficients. If inequality is measured by the fraction of people living on less than two U.S. dollars per day, the table actually shows worse inequality where big business is more stable even after controlling for per capita GDP.

If big business stability seeks to promote egalitarian outcomes, it is remarkably unsuccessful.

10.4.3   Labor Power

Table 10.6 correlates big business stability to the status of labor in the economy. Unemployment—total, male, and female—is utterly uncorrelated with big business stability. So are labor rights, for unions are neither more common nor easier to form where big businesses are more stable.

Table 10.6   **Big business stability and the voice of labor**

	Simple correlations				Regressions controlling for log per capita GDP averaged over 1996–2000			
	$\bar{\Omega}_L$	$\bar{\Omega}_E$	$\underline{\Omega}_L$	$\underline{\Omega}_E$	$\bar{\Omega}_L$	$\bar{\Omega}_E$	$\underline{\Omega}_L$	$\underline{\Omega}_E$
A. Unemployment								
Total labor force	−0.0513	−0.0643	0.0906	0.102	−0.44	−0.89	2.39	3.25
unemployment	(.74)	(.68)	(.56)	(.52)	(.89)	(.84)	(.46)	(.51)
Male labor force	−0.0359	−0.0227	0.137	0.147	−0.47	−0.25	2.52	3.46
unemployment	(.82)	(.89)	(.38)	(.35)	(.87)	(.95)	(.34)	(.41)
Female labor force	−0.101	−0.136	0.0323	0.0504	−0.93	−2.42	2.34	3.22
unemployment	(.52)	(.39)	(.84)	(.75)	(.83)	(.67)	(.59)	(.60)
B. Labor rights								
Union density	**0.265**	0.164	0.113	−0.0055	0.143	.00336	.00963	−0.119
	(.09)	(.29)	(.47)	(.97)	(.44)	(.99)	(.95)	(.48)
Rights to form	0.0858	0.0112	−0.178	−0.152	0.404	0.298	−0.287	−0.339
union	(.58)	(.94)	(.25)	(.33)	(.23)	(.50)	(.42)	(.46)
Minimum wage	**−0.291**	−0.235	−0.235	−0.0786	−0.217	−0.043	−0.211	0.077
	(.06)	(.13)	(.13)	(.62)	(.52)	(.92)	(.52)	(.86)
C. Labor protection								
Old age, disability,	0.1154	0.1558	0.2307	0.0663	−0.083	−0.085	0.049	−0.042
and death benefits	(.46)	(.32)	(.14)	(.67)	(.39)	(.41)	(.52)	(.67)
Sickness and health	**0.3749**	0.2046	0.1665	0.063	**0.349**	0.174	0.115	0.026
benefits[a]	**(.01)**	(.19)	(.29)	(.69)	**(.07)**	(.46)	(.45)	(.90)
Unemployment	**0.3193**	**0.353**	**0.3594**	**0.3251**	0.052	0.096	0.269	0.397
benefits	**(.04)**	**(.02)**	**(.02)**	**(.03)**	(.79)	(.69)	(.25)	(.18)

Notes: The left panel reports correlation coefficients between big business stability and variables measuring the voice of labor. The right panel presents regressions of the form: labor rights = $\beta_0 + \beta_1$ stability + $\beta_2 \ln(y) + \varepsilon$. Only coefficient estimates on stability (β_1) are shown. Numbers in parentheses are probability levels for rejecting the null hypothesis of zero correlation coefficients or regression coefficients. Heteroskedasticity-consistent standard errors are used to calculate *p*-levels in all regressions. Sample includes forty-three countries listed in table 10.1. Boldface indicates rejection of the null hypothesis of a zero point estimate at 10 percent confidence in two-tailed tests.
[a] Significance disappears if Indonesia, Malaysia, and Sri Lanka are dropped.

Minimum wages are also not more likely to be mandatory by law, and various benefits for old age, disability, and death or for illness are no more generous. (Health benefits are higher where big businesses are more stable if the visibly extreme observations of Indonesia, Malaysia, and Sri Lanka are retained.) Unemployment benefits appear positively correlated with big business stability in simple correlations, but these are rendered insignificant when per capita GDP controls are added.

If big business stability permits a greater voice for organized labor, we cannot detect it.

10.4.4   Robustness Checks

We conduct residual analysis and robustness checks to ensure that our results are not driven by outliers or other statistical anomalies.

Generalized White tests suggest the presence of heteroskedasticity in regressions involving public health measures, electricity, education attainment, inequality, and labor rights. We follow White (1980) to deal with this problem by reporting heteroskedasticity-consistent standard errors (HCSEs) for all regressions in the tables, although using ordinary least squared standard errors does not qualitatively change the results. A close inspection of the data indicates wide tails, particularly the right ones, in the social outcome variables' distributions. Substituting versions of these variables winsorized at 10 percent eliminates this problem, leaving White's generalized tests indicating no heteroskedasticity, and generates qualitatively similar results to those shown.

Our control variable is the average of the logarithm of per capita GDP from 1996 to 2000. Our results do not change if we replace the control by the log of 1990 per capita GDP. Using the latter avoids possible distortions of GDP figures by the late 1990s economic and financial crisis in the Asian countries.

Wherever possible, we also substitute closely related variables for our variables to confirm robustness. For example, using "government spending on education as a percentage of government expenditure" yields qualitatively identical results to those using "government spending on education as a percentage of GDP." Similarly, using the inverse of "labor participation rates" instead of unemployment rates results in qualitatively similar predictions.

Finally, we produce residual diagnostics such as Cook's D and student residual and an "added-variable (AV)" plot (also referred to as a "partial regression plot") for each regression to identify unusual or influential observations. The AV plot essentially lets us plot the residuals from the dependent variable, given the control, against the residuals from the independent variable of interest (in this paper, the stability indexes), given the control. If any observation seems influential, we rerun the regression without it and check for changes in the signs and significance of the regression coefficients. For example, South Africa appears to be an outlier in the "public health" regressions. However, removing it does not change the results qualitatively. The only place where outliers are evident is in the "sickness and health benefits" regression, and its results with and without the outliers are discussed in the text accordingly.

10.5 Conclusions

We undertook this exercise hoping to find evidence that big business stability might correlate with laudable social outcomes—liberty, equality, and fraternity in the words of the French revolutionaries. Such noneconomic goals are legitimate policy objectives, and if stability in the large corporate sector contributed to them in any important way, no matter how indirectly, policies designed to stabilize that sector might be justifiable even if they impede growth by slowing the process of creative destruction.

Absence of evidence is not evidence of absence. This is a first pass analysis only, and much more work is needed to conclude that no such contribution exists. But if one does exist, it must be subtle or well hidden. General equilibrium interconnections, more complicated statistical interactions, or any number of complications might be in play. But our inability to find clear evidence of big business stability contributing to laudable noneconomic policy goals suggests that we might entertain other reasons politicians might value big business stability.

One possibility is political rent-seeking (Krueger 1974, 1993). Big businesses might be well positioned to invest in political favors they can call in when needed.[7] If so, big business stability might well be a wholly undesirable condition—inimical to rapid growth and primarily a result of special interests manipulating the political system. Enhancing the stability of the big business sector might thus bestow substantial benefits, but on a narrow special interest group—the insiders of those businesses—not on the economy as a whole.

Another possibility is that policies aimed at saving or stabilizing large established businesses reflect behavioral finance influencing public policy (Shleifer 2000). Kahneman and Tversky (1979) demonstrate that people are *loss averse*—a loss of a given magnitude has negative welfare effects that far outweigh the positive effects of an equal sized gain. This gives rise to a so-called conservative bias in human behavior. If voters irrationally fear losing a current set of jobs, even though better ones are likely to come along, politicians intent on winning elections should represent such concerns in public policy decisions—even if this slows growth.

We wholeheartedly concede the tentative nature of these musings and welcome further research that might clarify matters. In particular, the role of cognitive biases in explaining seemingly unjustifiable economic policies merits consideration.

References

Aghion, Philippe, and Peter W. Howitt. 1998. *Endogenous growth theory.* Cambridge, MA: MIT Press.
Aoki, Masahiko. 1988. *Information, incentives, and bargaining in the Japanese economy.* Cambridge, UK: Cambridge University Press.

7. A growing empirical literature documents the first-order importance of rent-seeking relationships between politicians and the business sector in low-income economies. See, for example, Fisman and Svennson (2007) and Fisman (2001), as well as developed economies, see, for example, Fisman and Di Tella (2004).

Barro, Robert I, and Jong-Wha Lee. 2001. International data on educational attainment: Updates and implications. *Oxford Economic Papers* 53 (3): 541–63.

Botero, Juan, Simeon Djankov, Rafael La Porta, and Florencio Lopez-de-Silanes. 2004. The regulation of labor. *Quarterly Journal of Economics* 119 (4): 1339–82.

Claessens, Stijn, Simeon Djankov, and Larry H. P. Lang. 2000. The separation of ownership and control in East Asian corporations. *Journal of Financial Economics* 58 (1–2): 81–112.

Deininger, Klaus, and Lyn Squire. 1996. A new dataset measuring income inequality. *World Bank Economic Review* 10 (3): 565–91.

Faccio, Mara, and Larry Lang. 2002. The ultimate ownership in Western European corporations. *Journal of Financial Economics* 65 (3): 365–95.

Fisman, Raymond. 2001. Estimating the value of political connections. *American Economic Review* 91 (4): 1095–1102.

Fisman, Raymond, and Rafael Di Tella. 2004. Are politicians really paid like bureaucrats? *Journal of Law and Economics* 47 (2): 477–514.

Fisman, Raymond, and Jakob Svensson. 2007. Are corruption and taxation really harmful to growth? Firm-level evidence. *Journal of Development Economics* 83 (1): 63–75.

Fogel, Kathy, Randall Morck, and Bernard Yeung. 2008. Big business stability and economic growth: Is what's good for General Motors good for America? *Journal of Financial Economics,* 89 (1): 83–108.

Högfeldt, Peter. 2005. The history and politics of corporate ownership in Sweden. In *A history of corporate governance around the world,* ed. R. Morck, 517–79. Chicago: University of Chicago Press.

Kahneman, Daniel, and Amos Tversky. 1979. Prospect theory: An analysis of decision under risk. *Econometrica* 47:263–91.

Krueger, Anne. 1974. The political economy of the rent-seeking society. *American Economic Review* 64 (3): 291–303.

———. 1993. Virtuous and vicious circles in economic development. *American Economic Review* 83 (2): 351–55.

La Porta, Rafael, Florencio Lopez-de-Silanes, and Andrei Shleifer. 1999. Corporate ownership around the world. *Journal of Finance* 54 (2): 471–517.

Rajan, Raghuram, and Luigi Zingales. 2003. The great reversals: The politics of financial development in the twentieth century. *Journal of Financial Economics* 69 (1): 5–50.

Roe, Mark. 2003. *Political determinants of corporate governance.* New York: Oxford University Press.

Schumpeter, Joseph. 1912. *Theorie der wirtschaftlichen entwichlung (The theory of economic development).* Trans. R. Opie. Cambridge, MA: Harvard University Press.

———. 1942. *Capitalism, socialism and democracy.* 3rd ed. New York: Harper & Brothers.

Sen, Amartya. 1999. *Development as freedom.* New York: Alfred Knopf.

Shleifer, Andrei. 2000. *Inefficient markets: An introduction to behavioral finance.* New York: Oxford University Press.

White, Halbert. 1980. A heteroscedasticity-consistent covariance matrix estimator and a direct test for heteroscedasticity. *Econometrica* 48:817–38.

Comment   Partha Chatterjee

Is it in a country's best interest to have a stable big business sector? Fogel, Morck, and Yeung investigate that question from the perspective of innovation and growth. They find that countries with more stable big businesses grow at a slower pace. They show that countries with less stable big business sector not only benefit in terms of growth rates of gross domestic product (GDP) per capita, but also in terms of growth rates of total factor productivity (TFP) and capital accumulation. So should governments spend any public money to ensure stability of big businesses? The answer is yes if big businesses helped the government achieve some or any of its social objectives. And this is what the authors investigate here—does a country with a more stable big business sector outperform other countries in terms of achieving certain social goals?

The authors identify these social goals and categorize them under *liberty*: health care, education, public infrastructure, environmental protection, overall quality of life; *equality*: income distribution, poverty; and *fraternity*: unemployment, labor rights, labor protection. They find measures for each of those, sometimes several, and find correlations between those measures and big business stability. They also develop several measures of big business stability. Further, they also regress between big business stability and each of the previously mentioned indicators, controlling for per capita GDP.

The range of variables that they use in the paper is quite large and varied. For a large number of cases, the authors fail to find any correlation between the variables and big business stability. In some cases, even if there seems to be a raw correlation between a variable and big business stability, it disappears when controlled for GDP per capita. Thus, overall the authors find almost no evidence of a link between big business stability and better performance of the social sector in a country.

The absence of a connection between big business and better performance in the social sector is quite clear. However, do countries actually choose to have big businesses? The authors provide quite a few anecdotal evidences from incidents and events, as reported by the news media, from both developing and developed countries. I think it would add much value to the paper if this section is further developed. The authors need to investigate if there is a systematic bias toward big businesses in policy making, both in legislations and in public spending.

Once it is conclusively established that presence of big business is just

Partha Chatterjee is an assistant professor of economics at the National University of Singapore Business School.

not incidental or some historical accident, but rather a product of policy making, the authors can draw stronger conclusions regarding the motives of the political system (like political rent-seeking, or influencing public opinion to win elections) in its dealings with big businesses.

Further, this research can be extended to examine if the bias toward big business stability varies across countries—is there a difference between rich and poor countries? Or maybe democratic and nondemocratic countries? Perhaps the role played by big businesses in a more democratic country is different than the role played in a less democratic country. I think it might be worthwhile to explore some of these questions.

Overall, this paper is a step forward in closely examining the contribution of the big businesses to the society. This paper also brings forth some important open questions that need to be examined in the future.

Comment   Pushan Dutt

Schumpeter first advanced the notion of "Creative Destruction" in his book *Theory of Economic Development* (1912). It was here that he made a clear distinction between innovation and invention. Schumpeter argued that while anyone can come up with an invention, it takes an entrepreneur to see its economic viability and to exploit its potential. The entrepreneur was seen by Schumpeter as an indispensable "hero" and the driving force in a capitalist economy.

The world that Schumpeter invoked was dynamic, messy, intrinsically uncertain, and far from the neoclassical world of equilibriums, steady states, and smooth trajectories. In such a turbulent world, businesses, individuals, and institutions based on earlier innovations are constantly undermined and swept away by new technological and organizational innovations. Growth in capitalist economies is not a smooth process but one of creative destruction. The Schumpeterian notion of creative destruction is much cited, even modeled (Aghion and Howitt 1992; Grossman and Helpman 1991) but has been rarely put directly to an empirical test. This is where this paper makes a very important contribution—by constructing an index of business stability, it shows that countries characterized by big business stability exhibit lower rates of economic growth.

A forthcoming version of the paper in the *Journal of Financial Economics* starts off by asking the question "Is What's Good for General Motors Good for America?" Surprisingly, unlike the Schumpeter of 1912, the later Schumpeter of 1942 would probably answer this question in the affirma-

Pushan Dutt is an assistant professor of economics and political science at INSEAD.

tive. Schumpeter in *Capitalism, Socialism, and Democracy* (1942) no longer looked upon the entrepreneur as the sole agent of innovation. He believed that much of innovation was, in fact, performed by teams of people within existing large corporations, with the innovation financed by retained corporate earnings. This allows us to cast this paper as an interesting test of who was right—the early Schumpeter of 1912 who emphasized creative destruction or the later Schumpeter of 1942 who saw a bigger role for stable and large firms. As an aside, the existing literature on innovation has also attempted to tackle this question directly. One of their consistent findings has been that large firms have no advantages in research and development (R&D) and that R&D productivity declines with size (Scherer 1991; Cohen and Klepper 1996).

The paper in this volume starts off by carefully, diligently, and cleverly constructing a variety of big business stability indexes. The alternate methodologies used in the construction of the stability index allow the authors to tease out a variety of interesting results. First, they vary the kinds of businesses (private sector versus public sector, foreign owned versus domestic; financial versus nonfinancial firms) to include in their various lists. Second, they vary the definition of what constitutes survival by checking whether employment in the firms grew at least as fast as gross domestic product (GDP) or whether it managed to retain 10, 25, or 50 percent of their labor force. This allows them to show that the death of old firms (rather than old firms being overtaken by rise of new ones) is the key driver of economic growth. Therefore, the earlier Schumpeter is proved right. The authors are also able to evaluate the relative importance of financial, state-controlled, and foreign-controlled firms in the growth process. While causality remains a concern, as in much of this literature, the authors find that good instruments are difficult to come by. However, by careful choice of time windows, by varying the definitions of stability and through a series of controls for latent effects, they make a convincing case for the creative destruction story. One caveat is in order: the study analyzes growth over the period 1990 to 2000. Given that Schumpeter had longer time horizons in mind when he wrote about creative destruction, and given that we know that it is sustained growth rates that matter, it would be interesting to examine if the results hold over longer time frames.

One concern with these results is that the authors base their stability indexes on an indicator (η_i) that takes the value 1 if the labor force in company *i* grows as fast as the country's GDP over the period 1975 to 1996. However, the proportion in which firms combine factors and substitute for labor is a choice variable for firms. For instance, we know that firms become more capital intensive or skill intensive as countries grow. So high growth countries are more likely to have $\eta_i = 0$, which again raises questions of causality.

A second set of results in the paper examines the drivers of business stability—these results have fewer problems with respect to endogeneity and measurement error. The authors show that banking system size, red tape, and civil law (for labor-weighted indexes) increase big business stability and that trade and foreign direct investment (FDI) openness (once we exclude financial and state controlled firms) lower it. The authors also argue that big businesses may capture government and preserve their dominance. However, they do not examine how various political institution variables affect big business stability, which seems an interesting area to pursue. Table 10C.1 shows a regression of their labor-weighted and equal-weighted stability index on four political variables: political instability that captures fluctuations in the degree of democracy (see Dutt and Mitra 2008); leadership turnover in a country without a change in underlying political institutions; a dummy variable for Majoritarian systems; and a dummy variable for presidential systems.

The results show that higher levels of political instability in a country lower the stability of business. Leadership turnover does not seem to play a role nor does whether a country has a Presidential form of government. There is some evidence that countries with majoritarian systems, who are likely to experience more pronounced electoral cycles, (Persson 2002) also exhibit lower levels of business stability. Because political instability has been shown to affect economic growth (Alesina and Perotti 1996), perhaps the authors should also include it as a control in their growth regressions.

Finally, it would be interesting to examine the relationship between per capita GDP (rather than *growth* of per capita GDP) and big business stability. If we plot this relationship (for per capita GDP in the year 2000) and

Table 10C.1   Effect of political variables on big business stability

	Labor weighted	Equal weighted
Political instability	−0.052**	−0.044**
	(0.027)	(0.022)
Leadership turnover	−0.006	−0.007
	(0.023)	(0.018)
Majoritarian system	−0.154**	−0.071
	(0.076)	(0.061)
Presidential system	0.053	0.024
	(0.109)	(0.088)
Constant	0.488***	0.368***
	(0.122)	(0.098)
No. of observations	38	38
R^2	0.22	0.19

Note: Standard errors are in parentheses.
***Significant at the 1 percent level.
**Significant at the 5 percent level.

regress per capita GDP on business stability (as shown in fig. 10C.1), there seems to be a positive and significant relationship between the two.

However, a closer look at the scatter hints at a nonlinear relationship between per capita GDP and big business stability. Regressing per capita GDP on stability and stability-squared in fact leads to a better fit (see fig. 10C.2).

These results seem to suggest that perhaps there is an optimal level of business stability (equal to 0.66 from the preceding baseline regression),

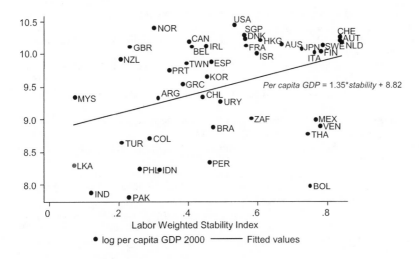

Fig. 10C.1   Per capita GDP and business stability index

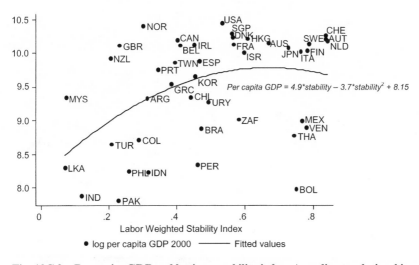

Fig. 10C.2   Per capita GDP and business stability index: A nonlinear relationship

which is approximately equal to that of Australia. A little bit of business stability is good for the level of development, while too much stability may be detrimental.

Overall, this is a very original and interesting piece of work. In addition, there seem to be many interesting questions that remain for the authors to explore in the future.

References

Aghion, P., and P. W. Howitt. 1992. A model of growth through creative destruction. *Econometrica* 60 (2): 323–51.
Alesina, A., and R. Perotti. 1996. Income distribution, political instability, and investment. *European Economic Review* 40 (6): 1203–28.
Cohen, W. M., and S. Klepper. 1996. A reprise of size and R & D. *Economic Journal* 106 (437): 925–51.
Dutt, P., and D. Mitra. 2008. Inequality and the instability of polity and policy. *Economic Journal,* 118 (531): 1285–1314.
Grossman, G. M., and E. Helpman. 1991. Quality ladders and product cycles. *Quarterly Journal of Economics* 106 (2): 557–86.
Persson, T. 2002. Do political institutions shape economic policy. *Econometrica* 70 (3): 883–905.
Scherer, F. M. 1991. Changing perspectives on the firm size problem. In *Innovation and technological change: An international comparison,* ed. Z. J. Acs and D. B. Audretsch, New York: Harvester Wheatsheaf.
Schumpeter, J. 1912. *Theorie der wirtschaftlichen entwichlung (The Theory of Economic Development).* Trans. R. Opie. Cambridge, MA: Harvard University Press.
———. 1942. *Capitalism, Socialism and Democracy.* 3rd ed. New York: Harper & Brothers.

Contributors

Eric Chan
Representative Office for Asia and the
   Pacific
Bank for International Settlements
78th floor, Two International Finance
   Centre
8 Finance Street, Central
Hong Kong

Partha Chatterjee
Department of Business Policy
NUS Business School
National University of Singapore
BIZ 1 Building, 04-16
1 Business Link
Singapore 117592

Menzie Chinn
Department of Economics
University of Wisconsin
1180 Observatory Drive
Madison, WI 53706

David Cook
Department of Economics
Hong Kong University of Science and
   Technology
Clearwater Bay, Kowloon
Hong Kong SAR China

Michael Davies
Institutional Markets Section
Domestic Markets Department
Reserve Bank of Australia
GPO Box 3947
Sydney NSW 2001 Australia

Pushan Dutt
INSEAD
1 Ayer Rajah Avenue
Singapore, 138676

Kathy Fogel
Department of Finance
Sam M. Walton College of Business
University of Arkansas
Fayetteville, AR 72701

Richard Green
USC Lusk Center for Real Estate
University of Southern California
Los Angeles, CA 90089

Yasushi Hamao
Marshall School of Business
University of Southern California
3670 Trousdale Parkway, Bridge Hall 308
Los Angeles, CA 90089-0804

Takeo Hoshi
School of International Relations and
    Pacific Studies
University of California, San Diego
9500 Gilman Drive
La Jolla, CA 92093-0519

Kaoru Hosono
Faculty of Economics
Gakushuin University
Mejiro 1-5-1, Toshima-ku
Tokyo 171-8588, Japan

Hiro Ito
Department of Economics
Portland State University
1721 SW Broadway
Portland, OR 97201

Takatoshi Ito
Graduate School of Economics
University of Tokyo
7-3-1 Hongo, Bunkyo-ku
Tokyo 113-0033, Japan

Winston T.H. Koh
School of Economics
Singapore Management University
90 Stamford Road
Singapore 178903

Peter Nicholas Kriz
School of Economics
Singapore Management University
90 Stamford Road
Singapore 178903

Edwin Lai
Research Department
Federal Reserve Bank of Dallas
P.O. Box 655906
Dallas, TX 75265-5906

Mario B. Lamberte
Asian Development Bank Institute
Kasumigaseki Building 8F
3-2-5, Kasumigaseki, Chiyoda-ku
Tokyo 100-6008, Japan

Liew Yin Sze
Monetary Authority of Singapore
10 Shenton Way MAS Building
Singapore 079117

Youngjae Lim
Korea Development Institute
PO Box 113
Choengnyang, Seoul 130-D12, Korea

Mei-Rong Lin
Department of Money and Banking
National Chengchi University
No. 64, Zhi-nan Road Section 2
Wen-shan District, Taipei, Taiwan
    (R.O.C.)

Roberto S. Mariano
School of Economics
Singapore Management University
90 Stamford Road
Singapore 178903

Robert N. McCauley
Bank for International Settlements
Centralbahnplatz 2
CH-4002 Basel, Switzerland

Randall Morck
Faculty of Business
University of Alberta
Edmonton, T6G 2R6 Alberta, Canada

Tetsuji Okazaki
Faculty of Economics
The University of Tokyo
7-3-1 Hongo, Bunkyo-ku
Tokyo 113-0033, Japan

Chang-Gyun Park
College of Business Administration
Chung-Ang University
221 Heukseok-dong, Dongjak-gu
Seoul 156-756, Korea

Andrey Pavlov
Faculty of Business Administration
Simon Fraser University
8888 University Drive
Burnaby, BC V5A 1S6 Canada

Edward Robinson
Monetary Authority of Singapore
10 Shenton Way MAS Building
Singapore 079117

Andrew K. Rose
Haas School of Business
   Administration
University of California
Berkeley, CA 94720-1900

Koji Sakai
Japan Society for the Promotion of
   Science
2-1 Naka, Kunitachi
Tokyo 186-8601, Japan

Masaya Sakuragawa
Faculty of Economics
Keio University
2-15-45 Mita, Minato-ku
Tokyo 108-8345, Japan

Wimboh Santoso
Bank Indonesia
J1. MH. Thamrin 2
Jakarta 10350, Indonesia

Chung-Hua Shen
Department of Finance
National Taiwan University
No. 1, Sec. 4, Roosevelt Road
Taipei, 10617 Taiwan (R.O.C.)

Kotaro Tsuru
Research Institute of Economy, Trade,
   and Industry (RIETI)
11th floor, Annex, Ministry of
   Economy, Trade and Industry
   (METI)
1-3-1, Kasumigaseki Chiyoda-ku
Tokyo 100-8901, Japan

Susan Wachter
Real Estate Department
The Wharton School
University of Pennsylvania
Philadelphia, PA 19104-6302

Yoshitsugu Watanabe
Global Security Research Institute
Keio University
2-15-45 Mita, Minato-ku
Tokyo 108-8345, Japan

Barry Williams
Faculty of Business, Technology, and
   Sustainable Development
Bond University QLD 4229
Australia

Julian Wright
Department of Economics
Faculty of Arts and Social Sciences
National University of Singapore
AS2 Level 6, 1 Arts Link
Singapore 117570

Ho-Mou Wu
China Center for Economic Research
Peking University
Beijing 100871 China

Bernard Yeung
National University of Singapore, and
   Stern School of Business
New York University
44 W. 4th Street, KMC 7-87
New York, NY 10012

Author Index

Subject Index

Page references followed by t or f refer to tables and figures, respectively.